European Yearbook of International Economic Law

Special Issue

The European Yearbook of International Economic Law (EYIEL) is an annual publication in International Economic Law, a field increasingly emancipating itself from Public International Law scholarship and evolving into a fully-fledged academic discipline in its own right. With the yearbook, the editors and publisher intend to make a significant contribution to the development of this "new" discipline and provide an international reference source of the highest possible quality. The EYIEL covers all areas of IEL, in particular WTO Law, External Trade Law for major trading countries, important Regional Economic Integration agreements, International Competition Law, International Investment Regulation, International Monetary Law, International Intellectual Property Protection and International Tax Law. In addition to the regular annual volumes, EYIEL Special Issues routinely address specific current topics in International Economic Law.

Tapiwa Victor Warikandwa
Howard Chitimira • Patrick C. Osode
Editors

Law and Policy of the African Continental Free Trade Area (AfCFTA)

Prospects and Challenges for Trade and Investment in Africa

Springer

Editors
Tapiwa Victor Warikandwa
Mercantile and Private Law Departments, School of Law
University of Venda
Limpopo, South Africa

Howard Chitimira
Faculty of Law
North-West University
Potchefstroom, South Africa

Patrick C. Osode
Department of Mercantile Law, Faculty of Law
University of Fort Hare
East London, South Africa

ISSN 2364-8392 ISSN 2364-8406 (electronic)
European Yearbook of International Economic Law
ISSN 2510-6880 ISSN 2510-6899 (electronic)
Special Issue
ISBN 978-3-032-01121-3 ISBN 978-3-032-01122-0 (eBook)
https://doi.org/10.1007/978-3-032-01122-0

This Springer imprint is published by the registered company Springer Nature Switzerland AG
The registered company address is: Gewerbestrasse 11, 6330 Cham, Switzerland

Preface

The African Continental Free Trade Area (AfCFTA) represents a significant opportunity for international corporations looking to expand their presence in Africa. The AfCFTA also offers opportunities for realising Africa's Agenda 2063 goals as well as Sustainable Development Goals. Further, the AfCFTA provides a platform for the growth of intra-African trade. In principle, the AfCFTA offers an opportunity for market access and growth, investment and partnerships, cost savings and efficiency gains, and sustainable development as well as corporate social responsibility initiatives aimed at benefiting local needs. However, the AfCFTA involves a complex legal framework with multiple agreements, protocols, and annexes that govern trade and investment across the continent. Understanding and navigating this legal landscape is crucial to ensure compliance and take advantage of the AfCFTA's opportunities. AfCFTA member states have their own legal and regulatory requirements, which may vary significantly from one another. Understanding and complying with each participating country's specific laws and regulations will reduce the risk of legal disputes and penalties and increase the benefits from trade and investment. Therefore, contributors in this book point out that whilst the AfCFTA offers notable significant opportunities, there are also potential challenges it will encounter. Such challenges, as the different contributors reveal, centre on the existence of different regulatory environments in African countries, political instability, technical and technological shortcomings, infrastructure limitations, policy inadequacies, lack of finances, and businesses' failure to access credit from banks, amongst other challenges. There is thus a need for solutions to be advanced in order to address the challenges identified by contributors in this book. It is clear that the AfCFTA offers the opportunity to expand intra-African trade and grow foreign investments, yet there is an undeniable need to address the challenges identified. There is a need to adopt appropriate regulatory and policy frameworks which are harmonised to enable intra-African trade, foreign direct investment, and the ease of doing business on the continent. Therefore, as the contributors argue in this book, the success of the AfCFTA is largely dependent on the ability of African governments to exploit available opportunities and address or mitigate the effects of the challenges identified. The contributors also provide recommendations which African governments and policymakers could do well to consider. The success of the AfCFTA will require strategic planning, risk management, and a deep understanding of the diverse African markets.

This edited book also celebrates the contributions of Professor Patrick Osode to the academia and the discipline of international trade. Professor Patrick Osode has been an academic luminary who has shared his immense knowledge in mercantile law to many students, policymakers, and intellectuals on the African continent and beyond. The co-editors of this book, Tapiwa Victor Warikandwa and Howard Chitimira, are Professor Osode's protégés. There is no better way of celebrating Professor Patrick C. Osode's glittering career and contributions than to grace his efforts with a book project of this magnitude, on a subject that he has been passionate about throughout his career. With academic luminaries such as Professor Patrick C. Osode, there is room to obtain solutions aimed at unlocking Africa's trade potential and realise the key objectives of the AfCFTA.

Limpopo, South Africa — Tapiwa Victor Warikandwa
Potchefstroom, South Africa — Howard Chitimira
East London, South Africa — Patrick C. Osode

Contents

Contributors

Victor T. Amadi Centre for Comparative Law in Africa, Cape Town, South Africa

Howard Chitimira Faculty of Law, North-West University, Potchefstroom, South Africa

Jérôme Duperrut Economic Analysis and International Institutions, SICPA, Lausanne, Switzerland

Lulama Edith Gomomo University of Fort Hare, East London, South Africa

Pie Habimana School of Law, University of Rwanda, Kigali, Rwanda

Tamanda Kamwendo Department of Private Law, University of the Free State, Bloemfontein, South Africa

Shelton Tapiwa Mota Makore Department of Mercantile Law, University of the Free State, Bloemfontein, South Africa

Sharon Munedzi Faculty of Law, North-West University, Mahikeng, South Africa

Chidochashe Nicolette Ncube Faculty of Law, University of Western Cape, Cape Town, South Africa

Bella Morufa Ngobeni University of Limpopo, Mankweng, South Africa

Gerda Van Niekerk University of Limpopo, Haenertsburg, South Africa

Rhodah N. K. Nyamongo Institute for Austrian and International Tax Law, Vienna University of Economics and Business, Vienna, Austria

Ignatious Nzero Faculty of Law-Zimbabwe Open University, Zimbabwe and Competition Law and Policy, Mergers and Acquisitions Consultant, Harare, Zimbabwe

Patrick C. Osode University of Fort Hare, East London, South Africa

Jeffrey Owens OECD Centre for Tax Policy and Administration, and Vienna University Global Policy Center, Institute for Austrian and International Tax Law, Vienna University of Economics and Business, Vienna, Austria

Chebo Nfor Tamajong Centre for Comparative Law in Africa, Cape Town, South Africa

Elfas Torerai Faculty of Law, North-West University, Potchefstroom, South Africa

Ruth Wamuyu Institute for Austrian and International Tax Law, Vienna University of Economics and Business, Vienna, Austria

Tapiwa Victor Warikandwa Mercantile and Private Law Departments, School of Law, University of Venda, Limpopo, South Africa

Dunia Prince Zongwe School of Law, University of Namibia, Windhoek, Namibia

Department of Legal Studies, Walter Sisulu University, Windhoek, South Africa

Increasing Trade and Investment in Africa Through the AfCFTA and the WTO: An Introduction

Tapiwa Victor Warikandwa, Howard Chitimira, and Patrick C. Osode

Abstract International trade and investment informed by the World Trade Organisation's multilateral trade rules are essential for promoting economic growth and prosperity in today's interconnected world. With a shared objective to make trade and investment more sustainable, efficient and attractive, the African Continental Free Trade Area (AfCFTA) adopted the Protocol on Investment in 2023. The AfCFTA's Protocol on Investment has emerged on the global stage promising to reshape how nations engage in investment activities. The AfCFTA Investment Protocol may appear complex but, if efficiently implemented, its potential to foster economic development, encourage sustainable foreign investment and create new opportunities for the African continent can transform the international trade and investment landscape. The AfCFTA Investment Protocol aims at promoting, facilitating and protecting intra-African trade and investments. This is in line with its objective to create a single market through intra-African progressive trade liberalisation and, in turn, improve the business environment for Africa. This chapter introduces the AfCFTA and its significance to growing world trade as well as investment in Africa and the rest of the world. It points to the potential that the AfCFTA has in promoting inclusive growth in Africa and the rest of the world.

T. V. Warikandwa (✉)
Mercantile and Private Law Departments, School of Law, University of Venda, Limpopo, South Africa
e-mail: Warikandwat@ub.ac.bw; Tapiwa.Warikandwa@univen.ac.za

H. Chitimira
Faculty of Law, North-West University, Potchefstroom, South Africa
e-mail: Howard.Chitimira@nwu.ac.za

P. C. Osode
Department of Mercantile Law, Faculty of Law, University of Fort Hare, East London, South Africa
e-mail: POsode@ufh.ac.za

T. V. Warikandwa et al. (eds.), *Law and Policy of the African Continental Free Trade Area (AfCFTA)*, European Yearbook of International Economic Law,
https://doi.org/10.1007/978-3-032-01122-0_1

1 Introduction

The African Continental Free Trade Area (AfCFTA) was adopted in Kigali, Rwanda, in 2018 after what appeared to be an eternity of negotiations. The AfCFTA is the product of negotiations by African countries aimed at broadening the continent's intra-Africa trade ratio[1] as well as using trade as a vehicle for poverty reduction and realising Sustainable Development Goals (SDGs) on the continent.[2] Premised on yesteryear deliberations of African luminaries such as Julius Nyerere and Kwame Nkrumah, the AfCFTA offers hope to a continent that has solely relied on trade with Europe,[3] United States of America, and Asia with the greater share of the proceeds going to the developed trade partners and not circulating in the continent.[4] The net effect of this trade pattern is that there has been little trade amongst African countries themselves a development which has contributed to incidences of chronic poverty on the continent.

There have often been cries that whilst trade is a vital cog for development and contributes to global efficiency,[5] multilateral trade driven by the World Trade Organisation (WTO) does not leave African countries on an equal footing with their developed counterparts.[6] This development has left some to question if there is anything to gain for African countries in the WTO driven multilateral trade system. It is not contestable that African countries have to trade on regional, continental and multilateral levels. When countries open up to trade, capital and labour shifts towards industries a development which translates to increased revenue and enhancing societies' ability to realise a significant level of socio-economic welfare.[7] This implies that trade is a significant driver of sustainable economic development in the world. With regional and continental trade being viewed as mechanisms for increasing developing countries' benefits from trade,[8] the AfCFTA and its subsequent agreement have been adopted with much anticipation from all Africans, including those conducting informal businesses on the continent. With the WTO being perceived as a platform for superpowers and global elites, with little to no room for developmental agendas but free market policies,[9] there is anticipation that the AfCFTA will usher in a new era of a sustainable development centred trade agenda on the African continent.

---

[1] TRALAC (2024). See also Yaw et al. (2024), pp. 1–20, TRALAC (2025), pp. 1–16, and Páez (2024).

[2] World Bank (2022). See also United Nations Economic Commission for Africa (2023), pp. 1–69.

[3] The European Union trades significantly with Africa. In 2019 alone, the European Union received 28% of the total African exports. See The European Commission (2020), pp. 1–3.

[4] Ndori (2023).

[5] WTO (n.d.).

[6] Chemutai and Low (2016). See also Warikandwa and Osode (2017), p. 180.

[7] Zahoor et al. (2023), p. 823.

[8] Ndukwe (2004).

[9] Warikandwa and Osode (2014), p. 41. See also Drabek (2024), pp. 1–19.

The AfCFTA is anticipated to offer to Africa what the WTO might not have been able to offer, in the absence of a developmental agenda in the multilateral trade system.[10] It is arguably understandable that the WTO may not be the appropriate vehicle for driving trade for sustainable development on the African continent. Perhaps it is not the objective of the WTO to drive a trade agenda that is tailored for inclusive growth but one that is focused on removing barriers to trade and promoting free trade. Considering that trade is not an accidental occurrence but a designed initiative, the AfCFTA is expected to harness the power of trade as an engine for sustainable development on the African continent.[11] The AfCFTA thus offers an opportunity for African countries to build on from the WTO set foundation and legacy, to a new trade dispensation in which Africans reap more benefits from their governments' trade policies.[12] Further, the AfCFTA is expected to leverage African economies through solid trade policies and practices which enable African countries to integrate into the New World Order premised global economy on a stronger footing. The AfCFTA brings hope for the reduction of economic vulnerabilities and points to the building of resilience in African economies.[13]

If effectively managed and implemented appropriately, the AfCFTA is expected to advance development on the African continent.[14] However, the most critical question to ask is whether or not the AfCFTA will lead to the ideal trade strategies and policies to produce results in a polarised African continent which is still grappling with challenges posed by neo-colonial and neoliberal agendas teeming on the continent. There is greater anticipation that the AfCFTA will promote and protect intra-Africa trade and investment in a more defined manner compared to the WTO multilateral trade framework.[15] The argument is not that the AfCFTA will act independent of the WTO multilateral trade framework but that the AfCFTA should provide the opportunity to advance trade from within and without the continent.[16] How the AfCFTA achieves this crucial objective, which sounds good on paper but complex in practice, depends on the AfCFTA commitments and legal instruments that will be implemented overtime to realise the key objectives of the continental free trade system, as set out in articles 3 and 4 of the AfCFTA agreement.

This book, through contributions from authors from different contexts, disciplines, countries and continents on the world will assess the prospects of success of the AfCFTA and its potential pitfalls. The overall expectation from the implementation of the AfCFTA, from the contributors (and perhaps the rest of Africa and the world) is that African countries must increase the share of intra-African trade whilst

[10] Mlambo et al. (2022), pp. 1–32.

[11] See the Preamble and Art 3(2)(b) of the AfCFTA Agreement.

[12] Tayo and Alaamer (2023).

[13] See the Preamble of the AfCFTA Protocol on Trade in Services 2019.

[14] Art 3(2)(a), (b), and (d) of the AfCFTA Protocol on Trade in Services 2019. See also Erasmus (2023) How is the AfCFTA's industrial development agenda shaping up? TRALAC 18 October 2023.

[15] See Arts 3 and 4 of the AfCFTA Agreement.

[16] Zhang (2022).

promoting investments and the attraction of foreign investors to invest in capital intensive sectors such as mining and the financial sectors. This can only materialise if income per capita increases, economies grow and clear and predictable policies are adopted to drive trade and investment. The AfCFTA must therefore be seen to address non-tariff barriers to trade,[17] integrate markets and economies on the continent and beyond,[18] reduce and eliminate tariffs,[19] amongst other issues.

It is also anticipated that the AfCFTA through clear and concise investment policies, will promote women empowerment, address youth unemployment, harness skills development, and drive industrialisation and infrastructure development. Should the AfCFTA promote investment in the envisaged manner, industries will grow and Africa will emerge as a beneficiation, value addition, and production oriented continental economy as opposed to a consumptive economy. Further, in an Artificial Intelligence driven fourth and fifth industrial revolution eras, the AfCFTA is expected to foster the adoption of policy initiatives which attract investments aimed at connecting Africa to the world markets through innovation and competitiveness. African countries must be deliberate about adopting fourth and fifth industrial revolution sensitive investment strategies which are coherent, well coordinated, systematic, and synergised to drive industrial growth. African countries, as informed by the AfCFTA, must focus on strategic growth sectors and value addition in order to stimulate industrialisation and sustainable development on the continent.[20]

2 The AfCFTA and Africa's Developmental Aspirations

The African Heads of State, by adopting the AfCFTA Agreement[21] set the basis for the adoption of trade inclusive, liberal domestic and foreign investment policies aimed at harmonising institutional and regulatory frameworks to strengthen investment for sustainable development. Emphasis was also placed on including the traditional marginalised groups, the youth, the unemployed and women into the trade matrix of Africa. Further, emphasis was placed on eradicating barriers to trade, improving investment governance on the continent and adopting a clear, concise and transparent investment legal framework aimed at attracting foreign investors

[17] Art 12 of the AfCFTA Agreement.

[18] See the Preamble of the AfCFTA, Arts 3(a) & (h), 19(2), 18(1) and 28(1) of the AfCFTA Protocol on Trade in Services.

[19] Art 4(a) of the AfCFTA Agreement.

[20] The sectors that are likely to qualify as strategic growth sectors include the following: (1) extractive natural resources; (2) agriculture; (3) blue economy; (4) digital and banking; (5) education; (6) services; and (7) clothing and textile. More emphasis should also be placed on harnessing Indigenous Knowledge Systems for development in areas such as medicine, tourism, theatre, intellectual property amongst other strategic areas.

[21] The AfCFTA entered into force on the 30th of March 2019. It had been adopted and opened for signature on the 21st of March 2018 in Kigali, Rwanda.

and promoting intra-Africa trade on the continent. Equally, there was emphasis placed on addressing the time and cost for investment entry into the continent and between borders, within the continent. A digital platform for handling data[22] was also proposed as well as calls for financial inclusion aimed at ensuring that informal traders access lines of credit to finance their trade activities. This is attributed to the fact that informal trade constitutes a significant portion of Africa's trade. Further, Africa still has fragmented investment regulatory frameworks which need to be consolidated to ensure investment cooperation and coordination on the African continent.

The success of an investment system must be accompanied by an effective dispute settlement system, fair competition rules, and an effective E-commerce system to facilitate trade in the twenty-first Century Africa. The adoption of protocols such as the Protocol on Investment[23] which was adopted on the backdrop of lessons learnt from formulating policies such as the Pan-African Investment Code[24] and Regional Economic Communities[25] investment instruments, amongst other regional and national instruments, ushered in novel principles derived from investment policy frameworks such as the United Nations Conference on Trade and Development.[26]

Africa requires sustainable and improved internal and external investment aimed at reducing poverty, promoting industrialisation and creating the basis for a vibrant private sector that promotes human development and practices investments which are cognisant of human rights. Africa's current challenge has been that some investors come to plunder natural resources on the continent and leave little by way of notable developments.[27] The AfCFTA therefore comes in as an economic vehicle aimed at ushering in a new trade and investment trajectory for Africa which will bring hope to the expectant Africans. Whether this remains to be realised is an issue which contributors in this book will grapple with. There are certainly opportunities to ensure the success of the AfCFTA, only if there is political will and commitment to go with such opportunities. A few of the critical issues pertinent to the success of trade and investment in Africa under the AfCFTA are briefly outlined below. The concerned issues have been dealt with under the WTO and are now expected to be implemented in a manner that serves the best interests of African countries. The outline will start with a brief presentation of the use of domestic laws and regulations for purposes of admitting investors or investments in Africa.

[22] See art 7(3) of the Protocol on Investment (POI) was adopted on the 18/19 February 2023 during the 36th Summit of the African Union in Kigali Rwanda.

[23] POI was adopted to support the objectives of the AfCFTA as set out in arts 3 and 4 of the AfCFTA Agreement.

[24] The Pan-African Investment Code is generally accepted as the first model investment treaty for Africa. See for example Mbengue and Schacherer (2017), p. 414. See also Schacherer (2021).

[25] See in general African Union (n.d.-b) Regional Economic Communities. https://au.int/en/recs.

[26] See UNCTAD (2015), pp. 1–157.

[27] Warikandwa and Osode (2016), p. 102.

3 African Countries Are to Use Domestic Laws and Regulations in Admitting Investors

The central objective of beneficial and effective investments is that host African countries' laws and regulations must be utilized in matters pertaining to investment to avoid complex dispute settlement processes. Article 4 of the Protocol on Investment (POI) to the AfCFTA places significance on the need to ensure that host countries utilize domestic laws concerning the admission of investments in order to promote state sovereignty and realize national development goals. Obviously, emphasis must be placed on ensuring that in the long run, the African countries will formulate uniform standards aimed at ensuring common but differential application of standards in so far as investment is concerned in Africa within the context of the AfCFTA. This will also promote responsible investments and avoid instances of where lowering of standards in investment laws to attract investments will compromise the ultimate objectives of the AfCFTA.[28]

4 Using Intra-African Investments as a Vehicle to Promote Regional Integration

Before the advent of the AfCFTA, one of the notable weaknesses of Africa's trade regime has been the minimal volume of trade taking place amongst Africa countries.[29] Intra-Africa trade does not exceed 18% of the overall trade on the continent.[30] However, there appears to be greater emphasis being placed on growing the share of intra-African trade on the continent for purposes of realizing sustainable development. More significantly, there is emphasis being placed on intra-African trade which is sensitive to human rights.[31]

5 Sustainable Economic Development and the AfCFTA

The AfCFTA has been tailormade to be a critical vehicle for realizing sustainable economic development in Africa. It has been adopted at a time when emphasis is being placed on realizing Sustainable Development Goals[32] and the targets of the

---

[28] See art 1 of the POI to the AfCFTA Agreement.

[29] Zongwe (2024).

[30] See the African Union (n.d.-a) Action Plan for Boosting Intra-African Trade. https://au.int/sites/default/files/newsevents/pressreleases/26498-pr_action_plan_for_boosting -african_trade_f-english.pdf.

[31] See art 5 of the POI to the AfCFTA Agreement.

[32] Art 3(2)(b) of the AfCFTA Protocol on Trade in Services.

African Union's Agenda 2063.[33] The preamble of the AfCFTA Agreement places emphasis on realizing "structural economic transformation". The POI to the AfCFTA Agreement also places emphasis on investment that fosters inclusive growth and sustainable development.[34] There is thus a notable emphasis placed by the appropriate instruments enabling the AfCFTA on inclusivity (financial inclusion),[35] promoting small and medium enterprises,[36] promoting the best interests of the youth and women,[37] marginalized people as well as indigenous communities. It is also critical that there is sensitivity, in the context of the AfCFTA, to common but differential application of standards as informed by the differences in the levels of development of African countries.[38] On paper and in theory, the AfCFTA holds much potential, however, it remains to be seen if in practice there are tangible results and set objectives that will be realized much as to ensure sustainable development on the continent.[39] African countries' Achilles heel has not been policy formulation but implementation.[40] The AfCFTA is one such good policy initiative which might or may not realize its fundamental objectives of ensuring sustainable development on the continent. Only time will tell.

6 Formulating Appropriate Investment Protection Standards

The AfCFTA Agreement sets as one of its primary objectives, the need to promote and encourage investment.[41] In order to achieve this objective, the POI sets out the standards of promoting and protecting investment.[42] What is important about the investment standards set out in the POI is that they place emphasis on public interest. Emphasis is placed on the need to promote reasonable investments[43] and not just the mere notion of absolute investment. Further, greater significance is placed on regulating investment practices in pursuit of public interest and/or narrow and broader sustainable development goals.[44] This is a stark departure from the previous and traditional forms of investment attraction in Africa which placed emphasis on

[33] African Union (2023), pp. 1–116.

[34] See Arts 2 and 3 of the POI to the AfCFTA Agreement.

[35] Art 3(e) of the AfCFTA Agreement.

[36] Art 27(d) of the AfCFTA Agreement.

[37] Art 27(d) of the AfCFTA Agreement. See also art 6(g) of the POI to the AfCFTA Agreement.

[38] Art 24 of the POI to the AfCFTA Agreement. See also Erasmus (2024).

[39] Fofack (2020), pp. 1–36.

[40] Jaoko (2016), pp. 1–24.

[41] Art 3(2)(c) of the AfCFTA Protocol on Trade in Services.

[42] Arts 12 to 23 of the POI to the AfCFTA Agreement.

[43] Art 6 of the POI to the AfCFTA Agreement.

[44] Art 24 of the POI to the AfCFTA Agreement.

investor security only without balancing the same with public interest.[45] Provision has also been made for guaranteeing a level-playing field between domestic and foreign investors.[46] This approach implies that the traditional fair and equitable standard has been done away with, a development that enables African countries to determine their national investment laws and designate the sectors which they deem appropriate for foreign investors to operate in.[47] Equally, African countries can also determine the sectors which they want to reserve for local people and development that will foster locals' participation in the economic mainstream and sustainable economic growth. More importantly, the POI makes provision for fair and equitable arbitration. In particular the POI, with regards to administrative and judicial treatment,[48] provides a credible basis for the legitimate protection of investors and their investments.[49]

However, it is worth noting that whilst there is a notable improvement in setting investment standards and ensuring equitable arbitration standards, there are exclusions from the scope of the POI which may cause potential challenges around dispute settlement. The rights and obligations of the parties as set out in the POI do not extend to matters pertaining to host states' responsibility to pass laws or regulations concerning investment made with capital or assets of illegal origin, government subsidies under national development programmes, taxation and government procurement, amongst other issues.[50] Whilst the passing of laws and regulations in the listed areas has been left to the state, such areas may need to have standards being set at the AfCFTA level to ensure harmonization of standards and laws. This is something the African Union (AU) can look at in the near future.

7 Risks and Sustainable Investments

Africa's ability to resist and adjust to different forms of risk will have a significant impact on the continent's attempts to attract foreign direct investment. In this regard, the POI places significance on states' responsibility to pass laws and/or regulate in pursuit of public interest in order to address or respond to prevailing risks such as health matters (such as those which characterized the COVID-19 pandemic),

---

[45] For challenges associated with absolute investment, see for example *Baleni and Others v Minister of Mineral Resources and Others* (73768/2016) [2018] ZAGPPHC 829; [2019] 1 All SA 358 (GP); 2019(2) SA 453 (GP) (22 November 2018). See also Maphanga et al. (2020), p. 277.

[46] See on national treatment, Art 12 of the POI to the AfCFTA Agreement.

[47] Art 4 of the POI to the AfCFTA Agreement.

[48] Article 17 of the POI to the AfCFTA Agreement.

[49] There is no basis for past arbitration practices which were characterised by discrimination on gender, race religion grounds. Arbitrary practices driven by discrimination on the grounds of nationality, duress, coercion, abusive treatment, and corruption, might now be a thing of the past in terms of the POI.

[50] See art 3 of the POI to the AfCFTA Agreement.

economic shocks, and climate change,[51] amongst other issues.[52] However, contestable issues still remain around the issue of lowering regulatory standards to attract investment. The World Bank Ease of Doing Business Index[53] places emphasis on regulatory flexibility as opposed regulatory rigidity in order to attract investors. The AU through the POI, has taken a bold step to ensure that labour,[54] environmental[55] and consumer standards[56] are not lowered to attract investors. African countries have thus been set a minimum standard for regulating labour, environment and consumer protection matters.[57]

The AfCFTA thus has set the platform for African countries to regulate matters concerning investments, with a view to setting obligations[58] to investors. The idea implicit in this approach is to rebalance rights and obligations in investments.[59] Emphasis is now placed on states' obligations to protect the rights of indigenous people,[60] labour rights, and human rights in investment related matters on the continent. Further, African countries have been given the obligation to regulate in matters related to corruption and money laundering, amongst other issues. The obligations set for investors are thus specific. More significantly, investors have the obligation to adhere to host countries' domestic legislation as well as the applicable international laws. This approach is progressive yet it remains to be seen if it will be practical in a continent teeming with challenges relating to state and judiciary capture.

8 The Way Forward for African Countries

The AfCFTA has set a decent framework for growing investments and sustainable development on the continent. What is now critical is for African countries to turn the letter of laws and policy into practice through implementation. African countries often adopt decent laws and policies yet there is minimal implementation. It is anticipated that the AfCFTA will not suffer the same fate. There is thus need for the AU and its member states to mobilize financial resources aimed at financing capital projects, promoting business development and offering key role players with the necessary technical support in order to facilitate investment. It may also be ideal for a comprehensive dispute settlement system to be adopted to ensure that investment

[51] Art 26 of the POI to the AfCFTA Agreement.
[52] Art 10 of the POI to the AfCFTA Agreement.
[53] World Bank (2020), pp. 77–86.
[54] Art 25 of the POI to the AfCFTA Agreement.
[55] Art 25 of the POI to the AfCFTA Agreement.
[56] Art 25 of the POI to the AfCFTA Agreement.
[57] See Chapter 4 of the POI to the AfCFTA Agreement.
[58] See Chapter 5 of the POI to the AfCFTA Agreement.
[59] Art 24 of the POI to the AfCFTA Agreement.
[60] Art 35 of the POI to the AfCFTA Agreement.

disputes are appropriately handled. The AfCFTA has thus set a premise for implementing a clear, concise and coherent investment vision for the continent. On the basis of the background information set out in this introductory chapter, the next section to this chapter will present an outline of chapters. In the respective chapters, contributors will engage with different issues pertaining to the implementation and potential successes and failures of the AfCFTA. It is anticipated that the discussions advanced in the chapters will inform policy makers, academics, technocrats, students, heads of state amongst others, on the prospects and challenges of the AfCFTA.

9 Outline of Chapters

Tapiwa V. Warikandwa, Howard Chitimira and Patrick C. Osode introduce the central thesis of the book. They point out that in today's interconnected world, international trade and investment can play a pivotal role in driving economic growth and prosperity. The authors point to the role that the AfCFTA can play in advancing what the WTO has managed to date and address the shortcomings emanating from the multilateral trade regime. The authors refer to selected provisions of the AfCFTA Agreement and the POI as a means of showing that on paper, Africa has an ideal regulatory and policy framework to grow investment and realise sustainable development on the content. Warikandwa, Chitimira and Osode point out that whilst the AfCFTA and POI agreements may appear complex they have the potential to foster economic development, if implemented. The same instruments can foster sustainable foreign investment and create new opportunities for the African continent that can transform the international investment landscape. With a shared objective to make investments more sustainable, efficient and attractive, the AfCFTA can create a single market through intra-African progressive trade liberalisation and, in turn, improve the business environment for Africa and significantly reduce poverty on the continent. The AfCFTA and its protocols have been reasonably formulated in order to promote, facilitate and protect intra-African trade and investments. The authors emphasise that the AfCFTA significantly places emphasis on sustainable investment by outlining some obligations on investors towards the host economies. Warikandwa, Chitimira and Osode thus introduce the AfCFTA and its significance to growing trade and investment in Africa and the rest of the world. The authors set the premise upon which chapters in the book will be developed. It is clearly stated by the authors that the AfCFTA has the potential to promote inclusive growth in Africa and the rest of the world. However, the authors also emphasise that what is good on paper may not essentially be realised or materialise in practice. Africa has the notoriety of developing sound and cogent policies which are not implemented effectively.

Howard Chitimira and Sharon Munedzi emphasise that the AfCFTA creates a transformative opportunity for African countries to strengthen economic integration and foster intra-African trade. Regulatory cooperation emerges as an essential aspect to ensure the effectiveness of the AfCFTA. Chitimira and Munedzi explore the significance of regulatory cooperation in promoting market integration and efficient continental free trade. The authors point out that regulatory cooperation entails collaborative regulatory measures among member states to establish and align regulatory frameworks, best practices and international standards to govern the African continental free trade area. Such cooperation is essential for eliminating unnecessary barriers, increased competitiveness, protection of consumer rights, promoting information sharing, reducing trade costs and fostering a conducive environment for business through mutual recognition, harmonization and convergence of regulations. However, Chitimira and Munedzi also acknowledge the challenges associated with implementing regulatory cooperation mechanisms. For example, they submit that differing regulatory philosophies, institutional capacities and political dynamics are a problem when it comes to implementing regulatory standards. Consequently, strategies to address such challenges are explored and measures to circumvent the challenges are proposed. The authors propose collaborated dispute resolution mechanisms and phased regulatory approaches to ensure the implementation of a robust intra-African trade regulatory framework. The authors underscore the importance of proactive collaboration, information sharing and ongoing dialogue to enhance regulatory cooperation within the AfCFTA so as to maximize its benefits for all stakeholders.

Tamanda Kamwendo argues that the existence of Regional Trade Agreements (RTAs) is not a new phenomenon to the African continent. While most RTAs during the post-colonial era were driven by the political vision of establishing the AU, their present existence is founded on an unwavering desire to foster economic growth and sustainable development in Africa through trade growth. Accordingly, the formation of the AfCFTA was aimed at enabling Africa to reach trade liberalisation and ultimately sustainable development. The expectation is that the Tripartite Agreement will be a pivotal step to escape from the constraints of the split-up economies of Africa's past. However, as inspiring as these objectives are, the existing barriers to trade within the multilateral trade system are still a cause for concern. Moreover, the COVID-19 pandemic has had a massive impact on global and regional trade, even on long-standing RTAs. As witnessed, trade under the AfCFTA was expected to commence in 2020, but due to the COVID-19 pandemic, this timeframe was pushed back. COVID-19 has tested the fundamental principle that underpins the AfCFTA -enhanced integrated decision-making as States demonstrated the primacy of national interests at the expense of advancing regional trade. Kamwendo thus discusses whether or not the AfCFTA can indeed be considered a beacon of hope in ensuring market access for Africa as a whole. Kamwendo also analyzes if the impact of the COVID-19 on the inception of AfCFTA could be a compelling reason to remodel and build a more resilient AfCFTA.

Howard Chitimira and Elfas Torerai argue that the use of mobile money has transformed the lives of many poor people across the Southern Africa Development Community (SADC). Millions of individuals who are excluded from the mainstream and formal financial sector are using mobile money to access financial services. In this regard, mobile money plays a huge part in enabling those in the informal sector to use mobile money in furtherance of the African continent's digital and financial inclusion agenda. Financial inclusion is a central enabler of the

AU's growth agenda in line with the United Nations' SDGs such as poverty alleviation, expanding economic opportunities and promoting market access. AfCFTA seeks to establish one of the world's biggest trade and economic markets. While the AfCFTA is shaping up, it is important to note that financial technology (fintech) products such as mobile money can greatly assist in improving cross-border trade especially among the poor and small to medium enterprises. However, several challenges are hampering the sustainable use of mobile money in the SADC. There are regulatory challenges affecting the use of mobile money in many SADC countries owing to the absence of robust regulatory frameworks. Digital illiteracy is also a challenge because policymakers and the general populace lack the requisite know-how to use fintech products optimally. Some governments in the SADC region have not fully embraced mobile money, making it difficult to drive digital financial inclusion for the poor. In this chapter, the authors argue that the AfCFTA can leverage the goal to create a single common market for goods and services on the proven ability of mobile money to ramp up digital financial inclusion and trade in the SADC region. Although the authors' focus is on the SADC region, the analysis in this chapter is reflective of experiences in other regional economic communities across the African continent. Chitimira and Torerai further argue that policymakers should consider improving the regulatory frameworks of fintech products in their respective SADC countries. There should be improved digital and financial literacy for the general public, especially the poor, unbanked and financially excluded persons in the SADC region to enhance their participation in the formal trade and businesses in the financial sector.

Pie Habimana emphasizes that the AfCFTA is at the centre of interest among politicians, economists, lawyers, amongst others, who discuss its plausible outcomes. A successful AfCFTA will greatly change the overall socio-economic situation in Africa through the liberalisation of internal trade. Be that as it may, the AfCFTA can also be viewed from other angles, such as its potential impact on harmful tax competition in Africa. Unlike the European Union, whose success in the single market is due to several factors, including effective regulation of harmful tax competition, this area is still uncharted territory for Africa. There is, therefore, a high risk that a successful AfCFTA will encourage companies to locate in countries with favourable taxation, as businesses will be able to trade across the African continent. As a result, a successful AfCFTA in terms of trade liberalisation will, on the other hand, exacerbate harmful tax practices that erode the sovereigns' tax bases. Habimana shows that a successful AfCFTA carries the risk that multinational companies will shift their profits and relocate in order to minimise the tax payable. To prevent this, Habimana proposes the adoption of an Additional Protocol based on Article 8(3) of the AfCFTA Agreement. The credo of such a protocol should be the promotion of trade liberalisation in Africa, but not at the expense of another country's tax base. To adequately control this, Habimana contends that such protocol should clearly define harmful tax competition, set out the standards and the procedure for detecting harmful tax practices and have a clear sanctioning regime.

Shelton Tapiwa Mota Makore argues that the AfCFTA encapsulates a dynamic liberal regime governing Africa's trade in agriculture. AfCFTA imposes continental-wide commitments for contracting parties to liberalise trade in agriculture through the incremental elimination of tariffs and non-tariff barriers. This liberal regulatory regime promoted under the AfCFTA is recognised as a vehicle for boosting intra-African agricultural trade flows, and lowering of Africa's dependence on food imports for its food security needs, among other loft objectives. Mota Makore also examines the regulation of trade in agriculture under the AfCFTA with a view to determine whether a liberal model adopted under the aforesaid agreement is accommodative of the food security needs of the African countries. The author further argues that the underlying free trade thesis which constitutes the very ideological justification for the AfCFTA agricultural trade has wider cracks and is unsustainable when examined in scope of the international and domestic obligations imposed by the human right to food on contracting parties. Therefore, Mota Makore concludes that there is a need for the AfCFTA liberal rules in agriculture to be recalibrated so that they advance the realisation of the human right to food.

Lulama Edith Gomomo notes that the emergence of digital markets has disrupted the enforcement of competition law and policy. Most jurisdictions are grappling with the unorthodox business models characterised by complex market structures, network effects, zero-pricing, multi-sided markets, and monetisation of data. The AU conceded that anti-competitive practices may hinder trade liberalisation and sustainable development goals. The digital economy can stimulate economic growth, but high concentration of economic power and anti-competitive conduct by few dominant digital undertakings can increase inequality. But there is a lack of enforcement of competition policy at continental level. The AU has recently adopted the Protocol to the establishment of the African Continental Free Trade Area on Competition Policy (AfCFTA Protocol on Competition Policy) including provisions that distinctively regulate the digital markets. Gomomo critically evaluates the AfCFTA Protocol on Competition Policy, whether it incorporates concepts that reflect the realities of the digital markets including, zero-pricing, multi-sided markets, and the small but significant non-transitory decrease in quality in competition analysis. It also explores the novel integration of the gatekeeper's ex-ante obligations and abuse of economic dependence to specifically deal with dominant digital platforms. Finally, Gomomo investigates the interface of competition, consumer welfare, and data protection policies.

Ignatious Nzero and Chidochashe Nicolette Ncube contend that multilateral trade seeks to promote market access and in turn economic growth and improved standards of living of the citizens. This is because they will have access to cheaper and quality goods and services including those produced outside their domestic markets. Similarly, domestic producers and suppliers will be motivated to innovate so as to effectively compete with quality and cheaper imports that will have unrestricted access to domestic markets. However, whereas trade liberalisation through the rules aimed at reducing barriers to trade have had significant impact on national spheres, the same cannot be said of the private spheres. Within the private spheres, private business enterprises through anti-competitive practices have eroded the gains of trade by distorting trade and erecting barriers to trade. Nzero and Ncube further argue that the place of competition enforcement within the trading system has been a subject of debate for some time. The establishment of the AfCTA and the adoption of a competition system within the continental trading system have given impetus to this debate. Nzero and Ncube largely argue that the AfCTA, through its competition agreement, is a welcome development to the African economy for there exists strong mechanism such as capacity building and strengthening of national competition authorities to ensure that they become building blocks for regional and then continental integration.

Tapiwa Victor Warikandwa points out that the AfCFTA Agreement is one of the flagship initiatives of the AU's Agenda 2063's first ten-year implementation plan (2014–2023). The implementation of AfCFTA is intended to focus primarily on the elimination of non-tariff and tariff barriers, trade facilitation, and investment promotion, among other relevant variables that might boost Africa's competitiveness in the global economic environment. The full implementation of AfCFTA is equivalent to the establishment of a continental market, which would need concerted measures to decrease all trade costs and restrictions. For Warikandwa, the significance of banks in the successful development of the African economy, and hence in the expansion of the African economy, cannot be overstated. One of the most important functions of banks in Africa and other African economies is to provide the necessary capital to facilitate the establishment of businesses of all sizes—small, medium, and large—in order to stimulate the economy's development and growth. In this chapter, Warikandwa robustly argues that banks will play a significant role in key industries such as manufacturing, health, agriculture, oil and gas, education, energy, telecommunications, and infrastructure, to name a few. The AfCFTA sees financial institutions, especially banks, as underpinning its trade finance policy execution. There is considerable evidence to demonstrate that banks offer the necessary financial assistance to promote intra-economic activity such as the manufacturing of commodities and the supply of critical consumer services. Banks actively engage in and offer the required financial support to enterprises to promote inter-country or intra-continental trade promotion. To maintain consistency and effectiveness, banks have taken proactive initiatives to address critical operational weaknesses in order to provide significant value to their financial intermediation function. For example, flaws in supervisory rules in critical areas such as limits on insider activities and capital standards; inadequate credit risk management; and bad credit choices have improved in recent years. However, Warikandwa emphasises that it is important to note that the latter inadequacies are frequently caused by governments and political influence on loan allocations.

Dunia Prince Zongwe dives into the newly launched, first-ever continent-wide online payment system. Formally launched by the African Export-Import Bank (Afreximbank), the Pan-African Payment and Settlement System (PAPSS) aims to make it easier for individuals and businesses to buy goods and services online in local currencies. Afreximbank set up the PAPSS as one of the five instruments specially designed to implement the AfCFTA Agreement. Zongwe contends that despite widespread attention garnered by PAPSS, scholars have not yet probed the law and economics behind this digital platform, nor has anyone examined how the system will interact with the electronic transactions laws and payment-and-settlement systems of the municipal laws of the AU. Yet understanding this legal and policy framework, if any, can prevent major disputes from arising a few months or years down the line. Today, cross-border payments require third currency, usually a hard currency, such as the United States (US) dollar or the Euro, which takes time, increases transaction costs, and poses risks that parties will disagree over exchange rates. Furthermore, unless Afreximbank or the PAPSS provides the monetary infrastructure necessitated by deeper levels of regional economic integration, they will doom the PAPSS to fail. To uncover the key legal and economic aspects of PAPSS in general and in relation to domestic laws of AU member states, the author organized this chapter in five parts. Following the introduction, the first section gives the background to the adoption of the PAPSS and the currency conundrum that has plagued the PAPSS since its inception. Second, the chapter describes the legal framework for the PAPSS and how it interfaces with the laws on electronic transactions and the PSSs of AU member states. Then, the chapter relies on the 'publicness' or public values of global administrative law to assess that framework (in the third section) and on perspectives from economics to tackle the questions whether this digital payment system has managed to make traders trust it and whether it enables traders to credibly commit (in the fourth section). Lastly, the chapter puts forward suggestions as to how Afreximbank or the AU could bridge the gaps as well as the (f)law that the chapter canvassed. Overall, the author argues that the biggest flaw of the PAPSS is that it lacks a proper law. This (f)law renders the PASS unnecessarily cloudy and complex, while inducing traders to stay away from the PAPSS and weakening public confidence in this payment platform. Nevertheless, the PAPSS holds great promise for intra-African trade after the AfCFTA Agreement came into force on May 30th, 2019. Experts estimate that the PAPSS will help AU member states save about 5 billion US dollars in payment transaction costs every year. All the same, if the experts do not bring out and assess the law and the economics behind the PAPSS, cross-border intra-African payments will not only confront high transaction costs; they will incur huge litigation costs too.

Bella Morufa Ngobeni points out that customs play a significant role in trade. They ensure that domestic trade laws are complied with and implement controls that secure revenue. Nonetheless, many African countries are notoriously known to have bad customs environments. Their borders are gridlocked with manual customs operations which consequently induce time delays at borders, customs offices charging excessive customs fees, goods being in transit for long durations, and unscrupulous payments received by people tasked with regulating customs operations and measures at border crossings. As a result, Africa is considered one of the most expensive continents to trade in and with. The excessive administration at borders, police roadblocks, and checkpoints are considerable barriers that make it difficult to trade within and outside the African continent. The effectiveness and coherence of customs measures have a significant influence on the growth of trade in the continent, and the advancement of the African marketplace. Ngobeni thus investigates the effects of the continent's poor customs efficiency on the realisation of the AfCFTA Agreement and surfaces the need to digitalise customs procedures and ensure better enforcement of customs laws, as means of improving the custom inefficiencies in Africa.

Gerda Van Niekerk points out that as outlined in Agenda 2063, the AU believes that a successful monetary union on the African continent is an essential prerequisite for the full implementation of the AfCFTA. The challenges of forming a monetary union and the convergence criteria to create such must be investigated to determine whether an African Monetary Union is feasible. Challenges include the formulation of a shared monetary policy and the establishment of a common central bank as well as a single currency for Africa. Achieving a small deficit in the current account and a common interest rate for all African countries may also be problematic. Van Niekerk thus argues that an African customs union is more achievable than an African monetary union, and the focus in Africa should preferably be on the former. This would be in harmony with the AfCFTA agreement that determines in Article 3(d) that one of the general objectives of the AfCFTA is to lay the foundation for establishing a Continental Customs Union.

Jeffrey Owens, Ruth Wamuyu and Rhodah NK Nyamongo argue that despite having similar underlying principles, that is the elimination or reduction of barriers to trade, international tax and trade law have traditionally evolved separately. Even so, these disciplines are intrinsically linked. First, while multinationals consider an array of factors when selecting an investment location, tax benefits and incentives, all factors remaining constant, influence the attractiveness of a location. Therefore, offering more attractive tax incentives based on the location or origin of investors would have a distortive effect on international trade. In addition, double taxation of investment income would impede the free movement of capital. In this way, tax would constitute a barrier to trade. Though tax measures may in some instances contradict fundamental trade principles, the interaction between trade and tax law is often difficult as it requires balancing the sovereign right to tax and trade liberalisation obligations. However, in the recent years, it has become increasingly clear that tax measures can be used to further protectionist policies. Unsurprisingly, this has led to an increase in tax related cases at the WTO dispute settlement body, which confirms that despite protests from tax policymakers and exemptions under trade laws, tax laws may be subject to WTO rules. In respect to the AfCFTA, the question arises on how African countries should react to the inevitable interaction between the two disciplines. In this regard, the authors evaluate the potential tax implications of the AfCFTA, consider the treatment of tax under WTO and specifically analyse the arguments raised in tax-related cases at the WTO dispute settlement body. The authors consider the lessons from the WTO cases and propose a regional response to the interaction between tax and trade.

Jérôme Duperrut points out that African countries plan to increase domestic revenue mobilisation to strengthen macro-economic stability, lessen their debt burden, and finance much needed public expenditure. According to Duperrut, while the AfCFTA will lower trade barriers and expand trade opportunities, it is expected to reduce revenue collection from import duties, which are significant in many African countries. A key mitigating strategy in the context of the AfCFTA is to strengthen the potential of excise duty as part of the domestic revenue mobilisation strategy.

African countries could aim at collecting 2 percent of GDP from excise duty, in line with current best performers. Excise duty is non-discriminatory as it applies similarly to domestic and imported products. It is commonly used to address negative externalities (health, environment, inequality) and in Africa is typically levied on a range of products (tobacco, alcoholic and sweetened beverages, cosmetics, cement, fuels, telecommunications). The tax compliance gap on excise duty is often significant, due to tax evasion, smuggling, and other illicit trade schemes. Revenue mobilisation from excise duty is maximised when optimally combining tax policy and tax administration measures. Duperrut is of the view that the AfCFTA might constrain excise tax policy at national level, as it might lead to a harmonisation of the list of excisable goods and of the applicable tax rates. The author concludes that the implementation of stronger tax administration measures—such as digital excise tax stamps management systems already successfully in place in several African countries—will enhance the capacity of tax authorities through digitalisation and contribute to maximising revenue mobilisation.

In the last chapter of the book, Chebo Nfor Tamajong and Victor T Amadi note that within international trade discourse, extant literature highlights the developmental impact of trade. However, in the context of law and development, for sustained economic progress, the nature of a country's law can impact how such a country receives or actualises such economic growth. A wide range of restrictive practices, like customs and administrative entry procedures, make trade difficult, which can stifle the development agenda. Research shows that most African countries face the challenge of burdensome customs procedures underpinned by complex and poor customs administration and inefficient control of border processes. In the chapter, Tamajong and Amadi undertake a comparative analysis of the legal frameworks and policies enabling customs reforms and facilitating cross-border trade in Nigeria, Liberia, Rwanda, and Mauritius. These countries demonstrate the diverse developmental status of most African countries as either developing (Nigeria and Mauritius) or least developed (Liberia and Rwanda) countries. Further, Rwanda emphasises the landlocked qualities shared by sixteen African countries. As a small island State and developing nation, Mauritius also emphasises the geographical traits shared by five other African countries. This discussion aims to provide recommendations that, if considered or applied in other developing or least developed countries, could result in reforming legal policies and frameworks to facilitate cross-border trade. As a background, the chapter will examine the legal frameworks influencing trade facilitation under the AfCFTA and selected Regional Economic Communities, which, if adopted and implemented domestically, would aid domestic reforms and bring about a positive role in facilitating trade in Africa.

10 Conclusion

The effective implementation of the AfCFTA will provide the African continent with a reasonable basis of establishing a unitary, modern continental investment framework which is coherent. The AfCFTA offers an opportunity for Africa to replace the fragmented and dated patchwork of intra-African investment rules that appear to be susceptible to broad and ineffective interpretations. There is need for Africa to have sustainable and efficient investment facilitation and promotion measures. The AfCFTA offers the opportunity to foster economic growth and development on the continent through intra-African trade. It is anticipated that the discussions undertaken in various chapters in this book will provide the relevant stakeholders with the much needed impetus to accelerate Africa's quest for trade expansion and sustainable development. It is also anticipated that the book will prompt robust discussions on the AfCFTA with a view to surfacing its strengths and weaknesses in order to formulate viable and lasting solutions aimed at ensuring that Africa realizes its SDGs and Agenda 2063 goals. It is anticipated that the book will have a positive contribution on advancing initiatives aimed at realizing sustainable economic development on the African continent.

References

African Continental Free Trade Area Agreement 2019

African Continental Free Trade Area Agreement Protocol on Trade in Services 2019

African Union (2023) Africa Sustainable Development Report: Accelerating the recovery from the coronavirus disease (COVID-19) and the full implementation of the 2030 Agenda for Sustainable Development and the African Union Agenda at all levels, pp 1–116

African Union (n.d.-a) Action Plan for Boosting Intra-African Trade. https://au.int/sites/default/files/newsevents/pressreleases/26498-pr_action_plan_for_boosting-african_trade_f--english.pdf

African Union (n.d.-b) Regional Economic Communities. https://au.int/en/recs

Baleni and Others v Minister of Mineral Resources and Others (73768/2016) [2018] ZAGPPHC 829; [2019] 1 All SA 358 (GP); 2019(2) SA 453 (GP) (22 November 2018)

Chemutai V, Low P (2016) African perspectives on trade and the WTO. Great Insights Magazine 5(6). https://ecdpm.org/work/shifts-in-trade-development-volume-5-issue-6-december-2016-january-2017/african-perspectives-on-trade-and-the-wto

Drabek Z (2024) Is the WTO terminally ill? Threats Int Trading Syst 4:1–19

Erasmus G (2023) How is the AfCFTA's industrial development agenda shaping up? TRALAC 18 October 2023

Erasmus G (2024) What does the AfCFTA Agreement provide for in respect of climate change? TRALAC 10 January 2024

Fofack H (2020) Making the AfCFTA work for 'The Africa we Want' Africa Growth Initiative at Brookings Working Paper, December 2020, pp 1–36

Jaoko I (2016) Implementation remains the Achilles Heel of the African Union: a study of the African Peer-Review Mechanism (APRM). Strathmore Law Rev January: 1–24

Maphanga T, Shale K, Gqomfa B, Zungu VM (2020) The state of public participation in the EIA process and its role in South Africa: a case of Xolobeni. South Afr Geograph J 105(3):277–305

Mbengue MM, Schacherer S (2017) The Africanisation of international investment law: the Pan-African investment code and the reform of the international investment regime. J World Invest Trade 18(3):414–448
Mlambo VH, Thusi X, Zubane SP, Mlambo DN (2022) The African continental free trade area: challenges and possible successes. Latin Am J Trade Policy 12:1–32
Ndori O (2023) AfCFTA to Spur intra-Africa trade. ZBC News, 17 May 2023
Ndukwe FO (2004) Promoting Trade: Regional Integration and the Global Economy. https://www.elibrary.imf.org/display/book/9781589062627/ch06.xml
Páez L (2024) The African continental free trade area: making the most of free trade and investment in global markets. Palgrave Macmillan
Protocol on Investment 2023
Schacherer S (2021) The AfCFTA investment protocol: an opportunity to converge and propel the Pan African Investment Code (PAIC) insights from the negotiations of the PAIC. African Arbitration Association, 4 May 2021
Tayo T, Alaamer K (2023) How the AfCFTA and the WTO can work towards sustainable investment in Africa. World Economic Forum, 1 December 2023
The European Commission (2020) The European Union and Africa: Partners in Trade, pp 1–3
TRALAC (2024) The African Continental Free Trade Area: A TRALAC Guide 12th (ed) May 2024
TRALAC (2025) Frequently Asked Questions: African Continental Free Trade Area (AfCFTA). Updated May 2025 available at https://www.tralac.org/documents/resources/faqs/5889-afcfta-frequently-asked-questions-updated-may-2025/file.html
UNCTAD (2015) Investment Policy Framework for Sustainable Development, pp 1–157
United Nations Economic Commission for Africa (2023) Leveraging the African Continental Free Trade Area for the Reduction of Poverty and Inequality in Southern Africa. Draft Report, Southern Africa Office, pp 1–69
Warikandwa TV, Osode PC (2014) Legal theoretical perspectives and their potential ramifications for proposals to incorporate a social clause into the legal framework of the World Trade Organisation. Speculum Juris 28(2):41
Warikandwa TV, Osode PC (2016) Chinese companies' trade practices and core labour standards: a South African, Zambian and Zimbabwean Perspective. Afr Nazarene Univ Law J (JUTA) 4(1):102
Warikandwa TV, Osode PC (2017) Trade liberalization, developing countries and the discipline of trade-impacting measures related to environmental conservation: an appraisal of United States-measures concerning importation, marketing and sale of Tuna Products. Speculum Juris 31(2):180
World Bank (2020) Ease of doing business score and ease of doing business ranking doing business. pp 77–86
World Bank (2022) Free Trade Deal Boosts Africa's Economic Development. World Bank Group, 30 June 2022
WTO (n.d.) Mainstreaming trade to attain the Sustainable Development Goals. https://www.wto.org/english/res_e/booksp_e/sdg_e.pdf
Yaw AD, Olabade OE, Olan F, Nyuur RB (2024) The African Continental Free Trade Area (AfCFTA): Taking stock and looking ahead for. Int Bus Reach 30(2):1–20
Zahoor N, Wu J, Khan H, Khan Z (2023) De-globalisation, international trade protectionism, and the reconfigurations of global value chains. Manage Int Rev 63:823–859
Zhang DDG (2022) Both AfCFTA and WTO are important to support Africa's growth and prosperity. World Trade Organisation 7 September 2022
Zongwe DP (2024) The African Continental Free Trade Area (AfCFTA): the law, the economics, and the research. GlobaLex January/February 2024

Evaluating the Prospects and Related Challenges of Regulatory Cooperation to Enhance Market Integration in the AfCFTA

Sharon Munedzi and Howard Chitimira

Abstract The African Continental Free Trade Area (AfCFTA) creates a transformative opportunity for African countries to strengthen economic integration and foster intra-African trade. Regulatory cooperation emerges as an essential aspect to ensure the effectiveness of the AfCFTA. This chapter explores the importance of regulatory cooperation in promoting market integration and efficient continental free trade. In light of this chapter, regulatory cooperation entails collaborative regulatory measures among member states to establish and align regulatory frameworks, best practices and international standards to govern the African continental trade area. Such cooperation is essential for eliminating unnecessary barriers, increased competitiveness, protection of consumer rights, promoting information sharing, reducing trade costs and fostering a conducive environment for business through mutual recognition, harmonization and convergence of regulations. However, the chapter also acknowledges the challenges associated with implementing regulatory cooperation mechanisms. For example, differing regulatory philosophies, institutional capacities and political dynamics. The authors propose collaborated dispute resolution mechanisms and phased regulatory approaches to ensure the implementation of a robust intra-African trade regulatory framework. The chapter underscores the importance of proactive collaboration, information sharing and ongoing dialogue to enhance regulatory cooperation within the AfCFTA so as to maximize its benefits for all stakeholders.

S. Munedzi
Faculty of Law, North-West University, Mahikeng, South Africa

H. Chitimira (✉)
Faculty of Law, North-West University, Potchefstroom, South Africa
e-mail: Howard.Chitimira@nwu.ac.za

T. V. Warikandwa et al. (eds.), *Law and Policy of the African Continental Free Trade Area (AfCFTA)*, European Yearbook of International Economic Law,
https://doi.org/10.1007/978-3-032-01122-0_2

1 Introduction

Regulatory cooperation entails the establishment of common regulations and standards that are employed by governments, regulators and other relevant stakeholders to harmonise regulations, collaborate and share relevant information in order to curb regulatory flaws, duplication and unnecessary differences. The establishment of the African Continental Free Trade Area (AfCFTA) presents a break from a past of fragmented markets in Africa to foster economic growth and development in the continent. The AfCFTA comes as an opportunity to boost intra-African trade and promote the integration of African financial markets.[1] It also addresses major trade barriers that have been a considerable constraint in the growth and development of the African economy and its contribution to the global economy.[2] The AfCFTA emerges as the world's largest continental free trade area, constituting 55 member states, which creates a single market goods and services to approximately 1.2 billion people.[3] The general objectives of the AfCFTA include creating an integrated market for goods and services in the African region, enhance the competitiveness of member states in continental trade, laying a foundation for the advent of African intra-trade customs and promoting a liberalized market through constant collaboration and information sharing arrangements.[4] However, there are several challenges that may hinder the successful implementation of the AfCFTA, for example, the lack of adequate infrastructure, economic disparities among member states and differing regulatory philosophies.[5] To adequately achieve the objectives of the AfCFTA, this chapter provides an overview of the importance of regulatory cooperation to enhance the integration of financial markets and harmonized continental free trade in Africa. This chapter inclines that regulatory cooperation is essential for establishing aligned standards to govern and align regulatory frameworks of the different member states. The authors propose collaborated dispute resolution mechanisms and phased regulatory approaches to ensure the implementation of a robust intra-African trade regulatory framework. The chapter underscores the importance of proactive collaboration, information sharing and ongoing dialogue to enhance regulatory cooperation within the AfCFTA so as to maximize its benefits for all stakeholders.

[1] African Union (2018), and Africa Bulletin (2025).

[2] Mupangavanhu (2018), p. 17, Samunderu (2024), p. 641, and Baier and Bergstrand (2007), p. 78.

[3] Adebola (2020), p. 234; Baier and Bergstrand (2007) p. 81.

[4] Fofack and Mold (2021), p. 2.

[5] Oyeniyi (2025), and Dlagnekova (2009), p. 5.

2 Overview Framework and the Rationale for Market Intergration

The AfCFTA was established to enhance market integration and economic cooperation in its member states.[6] The establishment of the AfCFTA wasinfluenced by the Lagos Plan of Action 1980 and the Abuja Treaty of 1991that were aimed at establishing a Pan-African economic community by 2025.[7] The need for integrated African markets arose as early as 1991 following the trading blocs of the post-Cold War era. This follows the realization that integrated markets and a larger trade area was imperative for boosting the African economy and grant access to other trading units such as the European Union (EU) and the North American Free Trade Agreement (NAFTA).[8] Accordingly, a single market for goods and services in Africa would promote intra-African trade, foster economic growth and eliminate trade barriers that hindered development.

The narrative of many African states is characterized by slavery, colonization and apartheid, all of which did not empower African communities and their economy.[9] Consequently, Africa remained a marginalised continent with high poverty levels. As such, the establishment of an integrated market and economic cooperation had the potential to foster development as evidenced by its success in other parts of the world.[10] For example, in Asia trade integration resulted in the rapid expansion of Regional Value Chains (RVC) and accelerated notable economic growth and income convergence.[11] However, the differences in economic development levels amongst African countries, the influence of other global trade markets, the lack of a common currency and regulations, continental debts and post-colonial effects were significant barriers to the free cross-border movement of goods and services in Africa. Nonetheless, the continuous decline in Africa's share of world trade since 1970, from about 4.5% to approximately 3% in 2018, a significant fall considering Africa's share of world population, exacerbated the need for an integrated trade area to boost intra-African trade and mitigate the effects of global shocks. Subsequently, the AfCFTA was established, to enhance market efficiency, competitiveness and foster development in Africa. The AfCFTA is to date the largest free trade area globally, covering a market of about 1.2 billion people and a Gross Domestic Product (GDP) of USD 3.4 trillion.[12]

---

[6] Fofack and Mold (2021), p. 2.

[7] Magliveras and Gino (2003), p. 225; Danso (1995), p. 35; and Nshimbi (2019), p. 190.

[8] Magliveras and Gino (2003), p. 225; Danso (1995), p. 35; and Nshimbi (2019), p. 190.

[9] Zidouemba and Mustapha (2021), p. 327 and Fofack and Mold (2021), p. 2.

[10] Bengoa et al. (2021), p. 38; Oyelami (2022), p. 5.

[11] Fofack and Mold (2021), p. 4.

[12] See also United Nations Economic Commission for Africa. African Continental Free Trade Area. https://au.int/sites/default/files/documents/33984-doc-qa_cfta_en_rev15march.pdf.

3 Regulatory Cooperation and its Significance in the AfCFTA

In the context of international trade and regional economic integration, regulatory cooperation refers to the coordinated efforts and processes undertaken by multiple countries or regions to align and harmonize their regulatory frameworks, standards, policies, and procedures.[13] The primary goal of regulatory cooperation is to facilitate the smooth flow of goods, services, investments and people across borders while minimizing unnecessary barriers, duplications, and inefficiencies caused by differing regulatory requirements.[14] In relation to the AfCFTA, regulatory cooperation is essential for aligning market standards considering the diverse nature of regulatory frameworks across its member states. As such, the establishment of aligned regulations in the AfCFTA has the potential to curb trade barriers, attract more investment, and promote economic development across the region by reducing the effects of differing interpretation of laws and implementation strategies.[15] The key aspects of regulatory cooperation include the harmonization of regulatory standards in the region. This entails that member states actively cooperate with one another to develop and adopt common regulatory standards, customs and practices in relation to the quality expectations of products and services.[16] The advantage of establishing harmonized regulatory standards in the AfCFTA is rooted in the need to minimise the confusion that may emanate from multiple sets of standards, costs associated with testing procedures and safeguarding product safety and quality.[17]

One major concern in regional integration is the diverse nature of regulatory landscapes across member states.[18] To address this challenge, regulatory cooperation should be harnessed as a measure to streamline diverse regulatory standards and requirements. The streamlining of regulatory standards and processes in this regard minimizes complexity and redundancy emanating from diverse regulatory structures. This means that aligning regulations through an establishment of standardized procedures and requirements in the AfCFTA trade area eliminates barriers such as differing quality standards, licensing requirements and inequalities. The AfCFTA Protocol on Trade in Services expressly provides for the improvement of the export capacity of formal and informal service providers, particularly micro, small and medium-sized suppliers and women and youth service suppliers.[19] This entails that the AfCFTA seeks to promote development and economic growth by

---

[13] Cai (2010), p. 95; Fafock (2017), p. 82.

[14] Ravenhill (2002), pp. 228–30.

[15] Zidouemba and Mustapha (2021), p. 11; Saygili et al. (2018), p. 5; and Saggi and Yildiz (2010), p. 30.

[16] Zidouemba and Mustapha (2021), p. 11; Saygili et al. (2018), p. 5; and Saggi and Yildiz (2010), p. 30.

[17] Cai (2010), p. 11; Nubong (2021), p. 126; and Ncube (2022), p. 112.

[18] Ncube (2022), p. 17.

[19] Woolfrey and Byiers (2020), p. 7; and Simo (2020), p. 71.

including women and informal traders into intra-African trade.[20] However, there are differing regulatory standards in many African countries in this regard. In many African countries, regulatory oversight has been cited as a major barrier that hinders active participation in the formal trade and financial services.[21] This means that there exists stringent regulatory requirements, such as licensing regulations, which hinder the participation of, specifically, micro, small and medium-sized suppliers who fail to meet the requirements thereof.[22] Accordingly, the relevant authorities should consider introducing adequate regulations that promote the active participation of marginalised informal traders across the AfCFTA member states. In this regard, regulatory cooperation will eradicate stringent requirements that hinder the participation of informal traders in the formal trade sector and harmonise differing laws and regulations in the AfCFTA.

Over the years, several barriers have hindered the participation of women and the youth in economic development initiatives, especially in the SADC region.[23] This could be attributed to discriminatory cultural practices, low education levels and high unemployment rates in some African societies.[24] Nonetheless, the creation of the AfCFTA aims at creating opportunities for better services trade to benefit women and youth through their active participation and breaking existing barriers.[25] The authors argue that this requires member states to adopt an inclusive approach that does not unnecessarily exclude women and the youth from participating in the intra-African trade. This entails giving serious consideration to the establishment of gender-sensitive regulatory and policy frameworks which will enable women and the youth to participate in the increased continental market access.[26] In this regard, regulatory cooperation could provide a coherent and strategic approach towards the implementation of gender-sensitive policies to ensure the active participation of marginalised groups.[27] The AfCFTA member states should develop national and domestic strategies on gender mainstreaming in the AfCFTA to show their commitment to the objectives of the AfCFTA. However, past analysis shows that commitment to implementing regional trade policies and agreements depends on whether the policies are in-line with the political economic dynamics of the country.[28] As such, it is important to ensure that the agreement of gender mainstreaming in the AfCFTA is binding on the member states and are incorporated into national laws as a tenet to achieving regulatory cooperation. The COVID-19 pandemic shifted the focus from AfCFTA issues and affected commitment and engagement of some

---

[20] Woolfrey and Byiers (2020), p. 7.

[21] Svotwa et al. (2023), p. 465.

[22] Barugahara (2021), p. 265.

[23] Sykes et al. (2016), p.4.

[24] Sykes et al. (2016), p.4.

[25] Ravenhill (2002), p.16; and Saygili et al. (2018), p. 17, Warikandwa (2023), p. 207.

[26] Woolfrey and Byiers (2020), p. 10.

[27] Anyanwu (2014), p. 293.

[28] De Melo and Twun (2021), p. 54.

African states and this has affected progress in the implementation of the trade agreement. Nonetheless, the post-pandemic era presents new opportunities to enhance women and youth participation in continental trade in the AfCFTA.

Electronic commerce presents significant opportunities towards economic growth and development in the intra-African trade area.[29] The flow of data from one jurisdiction to the other in the AfCFTA is inevitable. This follows that the scope and nature of trade is rapidly evolving with most transactions being conducted virtually.[30] Contemporary business and trade largely relies on the internet and this raises significant complexities and/or challenges relating to data sovereignty. The interconnection between e-commerce and data sovereignty raises important considerations regarding data management, privacy and regulatory control of the flow of data across borders.[31] Data sovereignty can be simplified as the concept that data is governed by the laws and regulations of the country in which it is located.[32] Cross border data flows refer to the transfer of data from one jurisdiction to another electronically for the purpose of concluding transactions or other trade related business.[33] E-commerce largely depends on the flawless flow of data from one country to another in the AfCFTA. This involves personal data connected to transactions, payment information and shipping details. Consequently, data sovereignty conflicts arise when data generated in one country is stored or processed in another country. Conflicts may arise when determining the laws applicable when processing such data. In the AfCFTA, where cross border data flows are essential for trade and economic integration, regulatory cooperation should be employed to address potential conflicts such as conflicting laws, data localization requirements and enforcement mechanisms that may hinder e-commerce, information sharing and data flow. [34] Data sovereignty issues have serious implications on digital trade and e-commerce, particularly cross-border data flows, regulatory compliance, and consumer trust and if left unaddressed these my affect the reliance on e-commerce to enhance regional trade in Africa.

.[35] This creates conflicts considering that e-commerce platforms involve international transactions which will have to be subjected to several data localization principles.[36] The authors argue that most African states are under resourced to navigate the complexities of data localization requirements. This may hinder their participation in cross-border e-commerce. In this regard, regulatory cooperation could alleviate the challenges caused by data sovereignty issues in e-commerce by fostering

[29] Banga et al. (2020), p. 15; and Clement (2021), p. 165.

[30] Banga et al. (2020), p. 15; and Clement (2021), p. 166.

[31] Cho and Sagynov (2015), p. 25; and Howe (2015), p. 15.

[32] Banga et al. (2020), p. 19.

[33] Ajambo and Chukuwebuka (2021), p. 18.

[34] Banga et al. (2020), p. 21; Wu (2017), p. 22.

[35] Gregory (2011), p. 235.

[36] Tavengerwei et al. (2022), p. 13.

dialogue and collaboration among member state.[37] Regulatory cooperation entails the establishment of common regulations and standards that govern data processing and storage to balance national sovereignty and the need to participate in e-commerce.

The first objective of the AfCFTA is to "create a single market for goods, services, facilitated by movement of persons in order to deepen the economic integration of the African continent and in accordance with the Pan African Vision of 'An integrated, prosperous and peaceful Africa' enshrined in Agenda 2063". This entails establishment of a regional market with relaxed movement restrictions to harness its full potential and opportunities. The AfCFTA represents a break from a past where the movement of people was a major constraint to growth and economic development.[38] The AfCFTA offers an opportunity to enhance intra-African trade and boost the continent's economy through the integration of financial markets. Free movement of people to conduct business around the continent should be considered as an essential measure to increase participation and movement in the trade area.[39] Free movement of people enables Africa's people, such as consumers, entrepreneurs, workers and other business professionals, to travel across the continent and trade in goods and services. In this regard, regulatory cooperation is essential for the establishment of regulations that grant access to markets and other African countries on terms as favorable as domestic markets.[40] This entails that member states should enact laws and regulations that authorize businesses and service providers to move across other countries to supply services. This also requires changes to national legislations to grant access to markets and reduce current restrictions on the movement of people in the African region. AfCFTA member states should also enact laws that grant migrants access to their domestic labour markets across the region. However, challenges often arise when balancing the rights of migrant workers and the nationals.[41] Accordingly, the authors submit that regulatory cooperation is an essential measure to harmonise labour laws across member states and ensure that nationals are granted the same rights, equal opportunities and access to services.

The AfCFTA is a central pillar to the recovery of the African economy after the COVID-19 crisis.[42] It is imperative to bring into perspective the implications of the COVID-19 to inform regulatory considerations to manage crisis and unforeseen circumstances. The COVID-19 pandemic emerged at a time when the implementation of the AfCFTA agreement was at a critical phase. Due to the travel restrictions and border closures, the expectations and aims of intra-African trade were hampered. The pandemic drove the global markets and economy in general into a recession which consequently resulted in a significant decline in demand for African

---

[37] Obiora (2022), p. 12; and Mishra (2016), p. 10.

[38] See also a related discussion by Jordaan (2014), p. 521.

[39] Woolfrey and Byiers (2020), p. 11; and Habiyaremye (2015), p. 415.

[40] Asiedu (2021), p. 34; and Ndonga et al. (2020), p. 781.

[41] Nshimbi and Fioramonti (2014), p. 58; and Nwankwo and Ajibo (2020), p. 304.

[42] Hamadou (2020), p. 339; and Asiedu(c) (2021), p. 15.

commodities.[43] For example, agricultural products (namely barley, palm oil, sugar, cocoa bean and cotton), energy (such as coal and oil), industrial metal (such as copper, iron ore, aluminum and zinc) and precious metals (such as gold).[44] This affected the African economy as supply chains were disrupted as well as the demand for trade and services.[45] The authors argue that, despite the disruptions caused by the pandemic and the effects thereof, it creates an opportunity for AfCFTA member states to cooperate and collaborate with each other to establish regulations to manage a crisis, in case of a future pandemic.[46] This means that, there is need to develop a regulatory framework that sets standards and practices that may be implemented to manage crisis and protect market integrity.[47] For example, instead of closing entry points, countries could develop regulations that enable trade and services across borders to continue amidst crisis. This includes regulations to control and minimize the movement of people for trade purposes, rather than putting regional trade to a halt. Such regulations should be uniformly implemented and enforced in all member states.

Effective regulatory cooperation is an important mechanism to prevent and address disputes arising from differing regulatory standards, interpretation of regulations and/or non-compliance with established regulations.[48] The AfCFTA Protocol on Dispute Settlement (Dispute Protocol) is a measure by the AfCFTA to settle market integration related trade disputes amongst member states.[49] The Dispute Protocol establishes rules and procedures for dispute resolution in the AfCFTA. The Dispute Protocol is an integration of dispute resolution mechanisms provided by other regional judicial bodies, namely, the Southern African Community Development Community (SADC) and the Tripartite Free Trade Area Agreement (TFTA) that are adopted from the World Trade Organization (WTO).[50] Dispute Settlement Mechanisms (DSM) is utilised to curb disputes in the AfCFTA. The Dispute Protocol establishes transparent, predictable and ascertainable provisions on dispute resolution to promote market integration. The same efforts should be replicated in all aspects of the AfCFTA agreement to promote the harmonised approach to address any matters relating to trade and market integration among member states.

---

[43] Banga et al. (2020), p. 21; Pasara (2020), p. 5; and Adam et al. (2020), p. 342.

[44] Banga et al. (2020), p. 21; Pasara (2020), and p. 5; Adam et al. (2020), p. 342.

[45] Nkamleu (2020), p. 304.

[46] Olaniyan (2021), p. 5.

[47] Yaya et al. (2020), p. 4.

[48] Akinkugbe (2020), p. 142; and Nanjira (2022), p. 69.

[49] Akinkugbe (2020).

[50] Akinkugbe (2020), p. 143.

4 Challenges Affecting Regulatory Cooperation in the AfCFTA

For the purposes of regional economic integration agreements like the AfCFTA, regulatory cooperation is crucial due to the diversity of regulatory frameworks across participating countries. Countries may reduce trade barriers, attract more investments and promote economic growth and development across the AfCFTA region by aligning regulations. However, achieving successful regulatory cooperation often requires political will, institutional capacity, technical expertise, and ongoing dialogue among participating member countries in the AfCFTA. The effectiveness of regulatory cooperation largely relies on ratification, domestication, implementation and compliance with established policies.[51] It also largely rely on the member states' willingness to participate and put into effect regulatory measures to foster compliance in the AfCFTA. Moreover, the establishment of regulatory cooperation in the African region is not without challenges.[52] Several key challenges such as regulatory divergence, limited resources, political factors and the absence of institutional mechanisms may hinder the realisation of regulatory cooperation in the AfCFTA. Understanding these challenges is imperative to establishing measures to circumvent the challenges and comprehending their potential risk on market integration.

The AfCFTA member states have varying regulatory frameworks and standards which pose harmonization challenges.[53] Differences in customs procedures, product standards and technical regulations may create trade barriers for businesses and individuals trading across borders of AfCFTA member states.[54] An integrated market that facilitates regional trade requires the harmonisation of economic policies of all member states. There is a common challenge of the lack of consideration for foreign traders and investors who conclude trading agreements governed by national laws of particular countries, which they may not be aware of or are not suited to govern inter-state trade.[55] Accordingly, the establishment of uniform cross-border trade policies for all member states will circumvent the barriers caused by regulatory divergence and uncertainty in the AfCFTA. AfCFTA member states should be conferred with a duty to take all necessary measures to harmonise and enact uniform trade laws.[56] Failure of which should be accompanied by a fine or sanctions on the absconding member state. This is essential to foster compliance and enforcement of regulatory cooperation measures.

Past experiences in African regional trade show that political factors and dynamics at domestic level significantly influence the manner in which member states

[51] Woolfrey and Byiers (2020), p. 11.

[52] Udombana (2003), p. 64.

[53] Woolfrey and Byiers (2020), p. 11.

[54] Dlagnekova (2009), p. 6; Forje (2004), pp. 16–17.

[55] Dlagnekova (2009), p. 2; and Ndulo (1993), p. 105.

[56] Art. 5(3) of the AEC Treaty; Ndulo (1993), p. 105; and Dlagnekova (2009), p. 3.

implement and comply with regional trade agreements in Africa. Some AfCFTA member countries are more likely to implement regional trade agreements that are commensurate with their political interests and incentives of business elites.[57] Political challenges are also magnified by political wrangling amongst the AfCFTA member states. This is evidenced by the difficulties experienced in collectively agreeing on uniform rules of origin for the AfCFTA agreement. The originating status clause is the core of the trade agreement and determines African RVCs. Some countries argued for stringent rules of origin to ensure that preference accrues only to members and is not deflected to non-members, whilst the least developed countries with weaker productive capacities preferred flexible rules that would enable them to acquire inputs from the cheapest and most competitive locations. Accordingly, any political differences among member countries could hinder the establishment and promotion of regulatory cooperation in the AfCFTA.

The data protection regulatory measures across African states is disintegrated, each country either has a unique data protection framework or still lags behind in regulating data protection. Consequently, the lack of a uniform continental regulatory framework could hinder digital trade in the AfCFTA. This follows that compliance with distinct data protection laws may be demanding and inhibit free trade, the same challenge that the AfCFTA seeks to circumvent. Accordingly, uniform standards and flexible enforcement requirements should be established to circumvent barriers caused by distinct regulatory standards.

Another challenge that may hinder regulatory cooperation in the AfCFTA is the lack of adequate resources to implement established provisions.[58] For example, less developed countries could lack resources to implement data localization as a measure to manage issues and concerns of data sovereignty. Many African states encounter capacity constraints to effectively implement and enforce common regulatory standards.[59] This could be attributed to the huge continental debts and colonisation ties that characterise most African countries and delayed economic development and sustainability in Africa. In some instances, the availability of relevant personnel and expertise required to engage in the development of effective regulatory cooperation is also another challenge.[60] A lack of clear, robust structures for regulatory cooperation can hinder progress. To circumvent these challenges, the relevant persons should consider the establishment of an AfCFTA regulatory body that represents all member states. This body should be tasked with enforcement of established trade regulations and developing a coordinated regulatory approach in the AfCFTA. The members of the proposed AfCFTA regulatory body should be appointed by member states through unanimous votes and elected members may serve for a prescribed period. This will promote the active participation of all member states in contributing to the establishment of laws and regulations to govern the

[57] Baier and Bergstrand (2007) p. 81; and Nyirabu (2004), p. 26.

[58] Salami (2022), p. 282.

[59] Nwankwo and Ajibo (2020), p. 310; and Sommer and MacLeod (2019), p. 75.

[60] Aniche (2020), p. 7.

AfCFTA. Accordingly, the AfCFTA Secretariat should collaborate with international partners to provide capacity-building programs enhance the capacity of regulatory institutions and facilitate compliance with established regulations. Lessons can be drawn from the World Trade Organisation (WTO) on how the proposed regulatory body can be funded to ensure its optimum operation. For instance, member states of the WTO make membership contributions to sustain the regulatory operational needs of the WTO.[61] Moreover, the WTO also charges its member states fees for dispute resolution processes and such fees are used to cover costs related to the functioning of the organisation.[62] Regulatory divergence can also result in unbalanced conditions for companies participating in the AfCFTA. Thus, companies conducting business in countries with less stringent regulations could acquire an upper hand over businesses operating in countries with stringent and more robust standards. This could hinder efforts by benefitting AfCFTA member states to participate in the development of uniform rules and policies that foster competition in the AfCFTA. Thus, the establishment of a regulatory body that is tasked with clear mandates and appropriate accountability measures to oversee all matters relating to regulatory cooperation should be considered in the AfCFTA.

5 Conclusion

Several measures should be considered to ensure the effectiveness and robustness of regulatory cooperation in the AfCFTA and combat the gaps and flaws highlighted in this chapter. Accordingly, it is submitted that the relevant authorities should strengthen information sharing arrangements in the AfCFTA. This will enhance and promote proactive information sharing among AfCFTA member states. The relevant authorities should further establish a centralised platform for AfCFTA members to share trade regulatory matters. Effective dispute resolution mechanisms specifically designed to address regulatory disputes should also be employed to help member states to resolve regulatory matters without resorting to lengthy and costly litigation processes. It is also essential for AfCFTA member states to align their domestic policies to regional and international regulatory goals for consistency. This will ensure that AfCFTA member states are equipped to implement and enforce regional and international regulations. It is also imperative that AfCFTA member states consider the implications of each regulatory approach to ensure that they are equipped with adequate resources for implementation. Given that the AfCFTA member states have distinct regulatory approaches and policies, careful consideration should be made to effectively achieve regulatory cooperation in the AfCFTA.

[61] Andrea (2018), p. 33.

[62] Ogunyemi (2017), p. 34.

References

Adam C, Henstridge M, Lee S (2020) After the lockdown: Macroeconomic adjustment to the COVID-19 pandemic in Sub-Saharan Africa. Oxf Rev Econ Policy 36(1):338–358

Adebola T (2020) 'Mapping Africa's Complex Regimes: Towards an African Centered AfCFTA Intellectual Property Protocol.' 1 African Journal of International Economic Law 233–290

Africa Bulletin (2025) The African Continental Free Trade Area (AfCFTA): An update. 26 February 2025 available at https://africabulletin.com/introduction-to-the-african-continental-free-trade-area-afcfta/

African Union (2018) Agreement establishing the African Continental Free Trade Area. https://au.int/sites/default/files/treaties/36437-treaty-consolidated_text_on_cfta_-_en.pdf

Ajambo E, Chukuwebuka E (2021) The African Continental Free Trade Area (AfCFTA): maximising benefits for the continent. Harv Afr Policy Jurnal 13:15–27

Akinkugbe OD (2020) Dispute settlement under the African Continental Free Trade Area Agreement: a preliminary assessment. Afr J Int Comp Law 28(1):138–158

Andrea C (2018) African Continental Free Trade Area: opportunities and challenges. De Gruyter: The Federalist Debate 3:32–35

Aniche ET (2020) African Continental Free Trade Area and African Union Agenda 2063: the roads to Addis Ababa and Kigali. J Contemp Afr Stud 1–16

Anyanwu JC (2014) Does Intra-African Trade reduce youth unemployment in Africa? Afr Dev Rev 26(2):286–309

Baier LS, Bergstrand JH (2007) Do Free Trade Agreements actually increase members. International Trade? J Int Econ 71(1):72–95

Banga K et al (2020) Africa Trade and COVID-19: the supply chain dimension. ODI Working Paper 586:1–52

Barugahara S (2021) Financial inclusion in Zimbabwe: determinants, challenges and opportunities. Int J Financ Res 12:254–270

Bengoa M, Mathur S, Narayanan B, Norberg HC (2021) Environmental effects of the African Continental Free Trade Agreement: a computable general equilibrium model approach. J Afr Trade 8(2):36–48

Cai KG (2010) The politics of economic regionalism: explaining regional economic integration in East Asia. Palgrave, Basingstoke

Cho YC, Sagynov E (2015) Exploring factors that affect usefulness, ease of use, trust, and purchase intention in the online environment. Int J Manag Inf Syst 19(1):21–36

Clement AD et al (2021) Live-streaming consumer experience: the future of E-Commerce and digital marketing in Africa: evidence from China. Int J Inf Manage Sci 32(2):157–176

Danso K (1995) The African economic community: problems and prospects. Afr Today 118(808):31–55

De Melo J, Twun A (2021) Prospects and challenges for supply chain trade under the Africa Continental Free Trade Area. J Afr Trade 8(2):42–54

Dlagnekova P (2009) The need to harmonise trade-related laws within countries of the African-Union: an introduction to the problems posed by legal divergences. Fundamina 15(1):1–37

Fafock H (2017) The globalisation of corporate governance and implications for African corporates in a changing regulatory landscape. World Econ 18:75–114

Fofack H, Mold A (2021) The AfCFTA and African Trade - an introduction to the special issue. J Afr Trade 8:1–11

Forje JW (2004) Facing the challenges of globalization and regional integration: problems and prospects for Africa at the dawn of the new millennium. J Mod Afr Ident 5:12–23

Gregory A (2011) Data governance—protecting and unleashing the value of your customer data assets. J Direct Data Digit Mark Pract 12(1):230–248

Habiyaremye A (2015) Enhancing productive capabilities through intra-regional trade and cross-border investments in Southern Africa. Dev South Afr 36(4):409–425

Hamadou A (2020) Free movement of persons in West Africa under the strain of COVID-19. Am J Int Law 114(1):337–341

Howe J (2015) Trade impact for good international E-Commerce in Africa: the way forward. Int Trade Centre Work Pap 12:1–45

Jordaan AC (2014) Regional integration in Africa versus higher levels of Intra-Africa trade. Dev South Afr 31(3):515–534

Magliveras KD, Gino JN (2003) The Pan-African parliament of the African Union: an overview. Afr Human Rights Law J 3(2):222–234

Mishra N (2016) Data localization laws in a digital world: data protection or data protectionism? Public Sphere 19(5):1–18

Mupangavanhu Y (2018) The protection of intellectual property rights within the Continental Free Trade Area in Africa: is a balance between innovation and trade possible? Int J Bus Econ Law 15(4):14–22

Nanjira A (2022) Two sides of the same coin? Analysing the efficacy of the African Continental Free Trade Area and WTO's dispute settlement mechanisms in resolving trade disputes between African States in J Baumler et al. Eur Yearb Int Econ Law 12:61–85

Ncube CB (2022) Intellectual property and the African Continental Free Trade Area: lessons and recommendations for the IP protocol. J Int Trade Law Policy 21(2):105–121

Ndonga D, Laryea E, Chaponda M (2020) Assessing the potential impact of the African Continental Free Trade Area on least developed countries: a case study of Malawi. J South Afr Stud 46(4):773–792

Ndulo M (1993) Harmonisation of trade laws in the African economic community. Int Comp Law Q 42:101–108

Nkamleu GB (2020) African agriculture in the context of COVID-19: finding salvation in the Devil. Afr J Agricult Resour Econ 15:302–310

Nshimbi CC (2019) Pan-African aspirations drive a new Free Trade Pact. Curr Hist 108:188–193

Nshimbi CC, Fioramonti L (2014) The will to integrate: South Africa's responses to regional migration from the SADC region? Afr Dev Rev 26(1):52–63

Nubong G (2021) Developmental regionalism and the success prospects of Africa's Continental Free Trade Area (CFTA): lessons from Africa's early integration experience. Afr Rev 13(1):1–10

Nwankwo CM, Ajibo CC (2020) Liberalizing regional trade regimes through AfCFTA: challenges and opportunities. J Afr Law 64(3):297–318

Nyirabu M (2004) Appraising regional integration in Southern Africa. Afr Secur Rev 13(1):21–32

Obiora C, Osegbue C, Osuji A (2022) Export trade diversification and the African Continental Free Trade Area (AfCFTA): implications on improved intra-regional trade performances in Africa. J Public Policy Dev Stud 1(1):1–23

Ogunyemi I (2017) African Continental Free Trade Area: challenges and opportunities for small and medium scale enterprises in Nigeria. Am J Bus Econ Manage 5:30–37

Olaniyan O (2021) The African Continental Free Trade Area (AFCFTA) in the Post COVID-19 Era. Nigerian J Econ Soc Stud 63(3):1–15

Oyelami L (2022) Revenue, Welfare and Trade Effects of African Continental Free Trade Agreement (AFCFTA) on Nigerian economy. J Public Aff 22(4):1–10

Oyeniyi A (2025) Key challenges facing Africa's Free Trade Agreement: examining the obstacles to the successful implementation of AfCFTA. 30 January 2025 available at https://spectator.africa/2025/01/30/key-challenges-facing-africas-free-trade-agreement/

Pasara MT (2020) COVID-19: challenges and opportunities for Africa. Afr Growth Agenda 17:4–8

Ravenhill J (2002) Institutional evolution at the trans-regional level: APEC and the promotion of liberalisation. In: Beeson M (ed) Reconfiguring East Asia: regional institutions and organisations after the crisis. Routledge, London, pp 225–240

Saggi K, Yildiz H (2010) Bilateralism, multilateralism and the quest for global free trade. J Int Econ 81(1):26–37

Salami E (2022) Implementing the AfCFTA agreement: a case for the harmonization of data protection law in Africa. J Afr Law 66(2):281–291

Samunderu E (2024) Liberalisation of trade regime under AfCFTA: a perspective analysis on Africa's single market. In: The economic effects of air transport market liberalisation. Advances in African economic, social and political development. Springer, Cham

Saygili M, Peters R, Knebel C (2018) African Continental Free Trade Area: challenges and opportunities of tariff reductions. UNCTAD Blue Ser Pap 82(1):1–15

Simo RY (2020) Trade in services in the African Continental Free Trade Area: prospects, challenges and WTO compatibility. J Int Econ Law 23(1):65–95

Sommer L, MacLeod J (2019) How important is special and differential treatment for an inclusive AfCFTA? In: David L, MacLeod J (eds) Inclusive trade in Africa: the African Continental Free Trade Area in comparative perspective. Routledge, London, pp 69–86

Svotwa TD, Wealth E, Mkanyeza C (2023) Policy and regulatory frameworks for financial inclusion in South Africa, Botswana, Namibia and Zimbabwe. In: Chitimira H, Warikandwa T (eds) Promoting and prioritising financial inclusion in Southern Africa: a contemporary law and economics perspective. Springer, Germany, pp 459–491

Sykes J, Elder S, Gurbuzer Y, Principi Y, Principi M (2016) Exploring the linkages between youth financial inclusion and job creation. Evidence from the ILO school-to-work transition surveys. Int Lab Org 4:1–45

Tavengerwei R, Mumbo V, Kira B (2022) What to consider ahead of the AfCTFA Phase II negotiations: focus on digital trade policy issues in four Sub-Saharan African countries. Oxford Pap Ser 16:1–44

Udombana NJ (2003) The unfinished business: conflicts, the African Union and the new partnership for Africa's development. George Wash In Law Rev 35(1):58–72

Warikandwa T (2023) Financial inclusion, Intra-African Trade and the AfCFTA: a law and economics perspective. In: Chitimira H, Warikandwa TV (eds) Financial inclusion and digital transformation regulatory practices in selected SADC countries. Springer, Germany, pp 207–228

Woolfrey S, Byiers B (2020) The promise of the African Continental Free Trade Area (AfCFTA) political economy dynamics of regional organisations in Africa. Eur Centre Dev Policy Manage 287:1–15

Yaya S, Akaninyene O, Labonté R (2020) Globalisation in the time of COVID-19: repositioning Africa to meet the immediate and remote challenges. Glob Health 16(1):1–7

Zidouemba PR, Mustapha SJ (2021) The African Continental Free Trade Area and the trade facilitation agreement: some regional macroeconomic impacts. Int J Trade Glob Mark 14(3):325–337

COVID-19 Pandemic and the African Continental Free Trade Agreement

Fostering a More Robust Regional Trade Integration?

Tamanda Kamwendo

Abstract The existence of Regional Trade Agreements (RTAs) is not a new phenomenon to the African continent. RTAs are founded on an unwavering desire to foster economic growth and sustainable development in Africa through trade enhancement. Accordingly, the formation of the African Continental Free Trade Agreement (AfCFTA) was aimed at enabling Africa to reach trade liberalisation and ultimately sustainable development. The expectation is that the Tripartite Agreement will be a pivotal step to escape from the constraints of the split-up economies of Africa's past. However, as inspiring as these objectives are, the existing barriers to trade within the multilateral trade system are still of concern. Trade under the AfCFTA was expected to commence in 2020, but due to the COVID-19 pandemic, this timeframe was pushed back. COVID-19 has tested the fundamental principle that underpins the AfCFTA—enhanced integrated decision-making as States demonstrated the primacy of national interests at the expense of advancing regional trade. This chapter aims to examine whether the AfCFTA can indeed be considered a beacon of hope in ensuring market access for the African region. The chapter also analyzes if the impact of the global pandemic on the inception of AfCFTA trade could be a compelling reason to remodel and build a more resilient AfCFTA.

T. Kamwendo (✉)
Department of Private Law, University of the Free State, Bloemfontein, South Africa
e-mail: Kamwendot@ufs.ac.za

T. V. Warikandwa et al. (eds.), *Law and Policy of the African Continental Free Trade Area (AfCFTA)*, European Yearbook of International Economic Law,
https://doi.org/10.1007/978-3-032-01122-0_3

1 Introduction

An essential goal of African leaders has been to unite all African states in order to pursue and improve socioeconomic growth and development. This goal is demonstrated by the emergence of multiple Regional Trade Agreements (RTAs) in Africa.[1] African leaders' efforts to establish RTAs to unite African States clearly demonstrates that African nations recognized that isolation and inadequate connections among African governments could be contributing factors to Africa's delayed economic development. As a result, encouraging integration could be an appropriate starting point for pursuing Africa's prosperity, integration, and social cohesion.[2] Accordingly, without dismissing the simple reality that some regional organizations in the Global South have not always been bastion of economic development, trade considerations are frequently considered crucial in providing the political foundation for regionalism and inspiring internal stakeholders within member states to support or oppose regional integration in any regionalist project.[3]

Despite decades of pan-African integration, some researchers have emphasized that significant impediments persist, making sustainable economic integration in Africa problematic. The main objective of this chapter therefore is to situate the establishment of the African Continental Free Trade (AfCFTA) Agreement in the quest to attain intra Africa trade liberalization. The chapter therefore evaluates the extent to which African states have been able to achieve their goal of regional integration in the African continent over the years. Thereafter, the chapter focuses on the AfCFTA, outlining the agreement's achievements, challenges and missed opportunities in the midst of the COVID-19 pandemic. Finally, the chapter analyses a post COVID setting based on the chapter finds. An analysis is undertaken in order to determine whether the AfCFTA has acquired resistance as a result of the COVID-19 pandemic to withstand future pandemics or whether the challenges encountered are a compelling reason to remodel the initiative.

2 An Overview of Regionalism in Africa

Regionalism may be defined as 'actions by governments to liberalise or facilitate trade on a regional basis, sometimes through free-trade areas or customs unions.'[4] Lorenz also defines regionalism as 'the formal regional integration using preferential or free trade agreements or the formation of customs or economic unions.'[5] Regionalism is therefore the consequence of regions' efforts to respond to various

[1] Odeku and Rikhotso (2023), p. 112.
[2] Odeku and Rikhotso (2023), p. 114.
[3] Junior & Luciano l. (2020), p. 1499.
[4] Hirakawa (2005), p. 200.
[5] Lorenz (1991), pp. 3–10.

push and pull elements, particularly historical, social, and political contexts, by establishing collaboration with various regional framework settings. Regionalism helps to achieve a variety of goals, including more rapid and equitable improvements in administrative efficiency, economic development, enhancing democracy and representation, promoting cultural identity, and stimulating innovation.[6] The terms regionalism and regionalisation are often used interchangeably yet scholars have argued that they have differing connotations and that regionalism brings about regionalisation. It is argued that regionalism is a political process characterized by cooperation and policy coordination, whereas regionalisation is an economic process in which trade and investment within the region take precedence over trade and investment with the rest of the world.[7] Consequently, the concept of regionalism implies that regions undergo reform at the politico economic level in order to facilitate collaboration and interconnectedness.[8] This is then followed by regionalisation, which is characterised by regional concentration of economic activities.[9] Given that distance can be a barrier to trade, regionalisation is more likely to occur when trade flows occur within a certain geographic region.[10] Therefore, regionalisation revolves around harnessing economic activities or processes in order to further national and regional economic goals. It is through regionalisation that countries improve their economic standing in the global trading market.[11]

Africa has a long history of regional cooperation, thus having one of the oldest trade and monetary integration systems in the developing world.[12] As such, the presence of RTAs on the African continent is not a new phenomenon. The African Union acknowledged that globalization and international agreements were not providing substantial benefits to the region's governments.[13] As such, the Organization of African Unity (OAU) adopted the Abuja Treaty, which established a step-by-step strategy to regional integration in Africa by establishing Regional Economic Communities (RECs) and charting an agenda towards the establishment of an African Economic Community by 2028.[14] Hence, the establishment of Free Trade Agreements (FTAs) was the first step along this path. The African Union recognizes eight African Regional Economic Communities (RECs). These are the Arab Maghreb Union (AMU), the Common Market for Eastern and Southern *Africa* (COMESA), the Community of Sahel–Saharan States (CEN-SAD), the East *African* Community (EAC), the Economic Community of Central *African* States (ECCAS), the Economic Community of West *African* States (ECOWAS), the Intergovernmental

---

[6] Takele (2019), p. 4.

[7] Oladejo (2022), p. 3.

[8] Teunissen (1996), p. 11.

[9] Lorenz (1991), pp. 3–9.

[10] Gaulier (2004), pp. 14–15.

[11] Borrman and Koopmann (1994), p. 163.

[12] Aniche (2020), p. 70.

[13] Takele (2019), p. 3.

[14] Ismail (2017), p. 138.

Authority on Development (IGAD), and the Southern *Africa* Development Community (SADC).[15] Their existence demonstrates a real desire among African countries to seek regional integration in order to enhance economic growth.[16] However, by the early 2000s, Africa's RECs began to overlap, resulting in a "Spaghetti Bowl" of overlapping regional arrangements since several nations were members of more than one REC and had pledged to join more than one Customs Union.[17]

Accordingly, RTAs in Africa highlight the critical question of why regional integration is attempted in Africa. The most compelling argument, however, is to accelerate economic growth and promote long-term development in Africa through trade expansion. During the post-colonial era, however, most RTAs were motivated by a political vision of encouraging African unity rather than economic gains.[18] The classical African regionalism, as founded in Pan-Africanism, was premised on continental unity strategy on issues of decolonization, anti-colonial and neocolonial struggles. On the other hand, modern African regionalism entails integration efforts with the means of establishing continental unity, ensuring collective self-reliance as well as economic transformation by implementing strategies for addressing Africa's developmental issues.[19] Notably, one characteristic that appears to be shared by all of these recent integration arrangements is a core idea of collective action through cooperation and/or integration to achieve certain development goals. As expressed in 1963 by Kwame Nkrumah during the creation of the Organization of African Unity (OAU), "We must unite now or perish". Thabo Mbeki expressed comparable sentiments in an article commemorating the OAU's 50th anniversary, headlined "Africa Must Unite!".[20] The desire for African unification is therefore not something new and these sentiments encapsulate Africa's long-standing aspirations for a united Africa. Among the various motivations for a unified Africa is the need to lessen conflict and to foster the creation of a culture of peace-building via greater interdependence and cooperation. Economically, this also translates into increased global bargaining strength for Africa. Odeku and Rikhotso argue that although issues of integration and social cohesion are often used interchangeably in debates concerning regional integration, they both aim at creating a climate conducive for economic opportunity and prosperity, from which all African governments can benefit substantially.[21] In 2013, the OAU celebrated its golden jubilee since its inception. Dr. Nkosazana Dlamini-Zuma, as Chairperson of the AU Commission, reiterated Nkrumah's gripping words made at the establishment of the OAU. She said, "Never

[15] Vhumbunu et al. (2023), p. 44.

[16] UNCTAD (2015), p. 5.

[17] Kritzinger-van Niekerk (2023).

[18] Kritzinger-van Niekerk (2023).

[19] Aniche (2020), p. 70.

[20] Moloi, (2019), p. 1.

[21] Odeku and Rikhotso. (2023), p. 115.

before has unity of action been more desirable and urgent; never before have nations faced such a challenging and splendid opportunity for concerted action".[22]

All of these variables play an important role in African governments' ambition to elevate their ranking in the global economy. Renato Ruggiero avers that the rapid advancement of global economic integration means that, while regional initiatives remain important, they are insufficient to manage international trade ties. Similarly, as regional agreements became increasingly common, the former WTO Director-General Mike Moore expressed concern about the survival of the global trading system. His concerns were expressed in his remarks when he asked:

> Is there a risk that regionalism is becoming a stumbling –block, more than a building block, for the new WTO, draining energy from multilateral negotiations, fragmenting internal trade, and creating a new international dis-order characterised by growing rivalries and marginalisation and the possibility of hostile blocks?[23]

Renato Ruggiero and Mike Moore did not question the benefits of RTAs; however, they were concerned that the spread of RTAs could jeopardize the global trading system's future.[24] I suggest however that regionalism must be viewed as an important instrument for facilitating the integration of smaller economies into the global economy. As a result, regionalism might develop a common approach to trade discourse or negotiations.

As RTAs are promoted as strategies to assure equal chances and unbiased competition for minority countries, Bhagwati believes regionalism affects the multilateral system's predominance and shares reservations about the detrimental consequences of regionalism.[25] He argues that regionalism is diverting attention away from multilateral trade. Bhagwati believes that regionalism should not be an alternative to the multilateral economic system, but rather a supplement to it.[26] Winter, on the other hand, believes that regionalism, due to its coercive nature, serves as a means of assembling trade partners for the multilateral negotiation table.[27] Tiziana asserts that regionalism allows both the developing and developed countries to handle issues that would otherwise be impossible to overcome in a broader multilateral framework. She contends that because the majority of the main trading countries are members of more than one RTA, the most favored nation premise will most likely be the exception rather than the norm in this situation.[28] According to Bhala, the development of an RTA entails granting preferential treatment to suppliers in the Member States, hence encouraging commercial activity

---

[22] Moloi, (2019), p. 1.2.

[23] Donald, (2002), p. 53.

[24] Lunani, (2011), p. 23.

[25] Bhagwati, (1992), p. 540.

[26] Bhagwati (1992), p. 543.

[27] Winters (1996).

[28] Tiziana (2023).

among suppliers.[29] He goes on to assert that when countries join RTAs, consumers benefit from a wider selection of goods at lower rates.[30]

The WTO agreements recognize that regional agreements and closer economic integration can benefit countries, particularly developing countries. It also recognizes that regional trade agreements might be harmful to the trade interests of other countries in some cases. Nonetheless, the GATT allows for the establishment of Regional Trade Agreements as long as certain conditions are followed. That is, these agreements must enable the free flow of trade among group members while not imposing trade barriers with the rest of the international community. In other words, regional integration should complement rather than compete with the multilateral economic system. In this respect, Art XXIV: 4 of the GATT[31] provides that, "a customs union, free trade area or an interim agreement should aim to facilitate trade between the constituent territories and not to raise barriers to the trade of third parties."

Thus, Art XXIV allows WTO members to deviate from the Most Favored Nation principle[32] by offering preferential treatment to trading partners under a Customs Union or FTA. Furthermore, Art XXIV stipulates that when a RTA or customs union is established, duties and other trade barriers in all trade sectors within the community should be reduced or removed. However, non-Members should not find trading with the region any more difficult than it was before the region was formed. Other clauses in the WTO agreements allow developing countries to enter into regional or worldwide agreements aimed at decreasing or eliminating tariffs and non-tariff trade barriers among themselves. However, it should be underlined that Art XXIV must function within the framework of WTO principles.

It is apparent that the African continent has seen an upsurge in the number of RTAs. Each RTA was founded with distinct purposes in mind, and as a result, most African countries have overlapping participation in the RTAs. To put it another way, most nations in the region are members of more than one RTA. However, such membership overlap can be interpreted to suggest that these RTAs are not effectively suited to deal with the trade impediments faced by most African countries.[33] As a result, countries find it more effective to participate in more than one RTA in order to overcome the different trade barriers they encounter. Even though these RTAs are targeted at regional economic integration and promotion, there was still need for an agreement that would unite all African governments, and the AfCFTA agreement was developed as a result. Beinga RTA, the AfCFTA may depart from the guiding principles of the WTO because it is preferential in nature. Hence, the establishment of the AfCFTA might be a crucial step towards the establishment of a pan-

[29] Bhala (2006), p. 36.

[30] Bhala (2006), p. 36.

[31] Art. XXIV(4) of the GATT 1994.

[32] The MFN principle entails treating all trading partners equally. Countries cannot typically discriminate between their trading partners under WTO agreements.

[33] Krist (2021).

continental trading system. Accordingly, the next section will discuss the establishment of the AfCFTA agreement.

3 Understanding the African Continental Free Trade Area (AfCFTA)

The AfCFTA is one of the flagship projects of the African Union (AU)'s Agenda 2063's First Ten-Year Implementation Plan (2014–2023), which has been regarded as critical in driving economic growth and development in Africa.[34] This is one of the milestones agreed to by AU member states in the Abuja Treaty of 1991, which entered into force in June 1994.[35] The AfCFTA agreement was signed and launched during the AU's Assembly on 21 March 2018 in Kigali, with the agreement entering into force on 30 May 2019. The AfCFTA is an amalgamation of three African Regional Agreements: SADC, COMESA, and EAC. According to UNECA, the expectation is that the AfCFTA will increase intra-African trade by up to US$35 billion while decreasing imports by up to US$10 billion by 2022.[36] This would transform the continent into a US$3 trillion economic bloc of 1.2 billion people. However, trading under the AfCFTA only begun on first January 2021although it would have begun 6 months earlier, albeit not for the COVID-19 epidemic. Although the COVID-19 pandemic has had an enormous impact on global and regional trade, even on long-standing RTAs, it remarkably took less than a year for the negotiation to implementation of the AfCFTA. Till date, 47 out of 55 nations have ratified the AfCFTA agreement, 46 have ratified and deposited their instruments of ratification, seven have signed but have yet to ratify, and only one has yet to sign.

Since the AfCFTA includes close to the total number of African nations,—at least 47 countries—the economic impact for such countries are theoretically immense.[37] Based on the 2020 market exchange rates, the AfCFTA region has an overall population of 1.3 billion people as well as a cumulative GDP of 3.4 trillion USD.[38] Consequently, the establishment and the commencement of trade under the AfCFTA in early 2021 positions the bloc as the world's 14th biggest economy.

The primary goal of this agreement is to build a unified African continental market for products and services, with free movement of business people and investments, paving the way for the Customs Union to be established more quickly. In achieving the aforementioned goal, the AfCFTA aims to gradually eliminate tariffs and non-tariff barriers to trade in goods; liberalize trade in services; cooperate on all

---

[34] Vhumbunu (2022), p. 12.

[35] Vhumbunu (2022), p. 12.

[36] Louw-Vaudran et al. (2019), p. 10.

[37] Mold and Mukwaya (2016), p. 2.

[38] Louw-Vaudran et al. (2019), p. 10.

trade-related issues and on customs matters as well as implement trade facilitation measures.

The AfCFTA agenda therefore aims at strengthening intra-African trade and this was necessitated due to the low amount of intra-African trade prior to its formation. The expectation is that the CFTA will result in significant economic gains in the African region. This stems from its key objective of increasing trade among the countries involved, which will benefit consumers by providing them with access to cheaper and higher-quality products. As a result, the CFTA might be viewed as a vital step in breaking free from the restrictions of Africa's prior split-up economies.[39]

4 A chronology of Africa's Continental Relations Before the AfCFTA

To understand the impact of the COVID-19 pandemic on the AfCFTA and trade volumes, it is necessary to first highlight the situation of trade with and within Africa before to the AfCFTA's implementation. The initial post-colonial era in Africa is dominated by the wave of attaining independence, with the bulk of African governments gaining independence at nearly the same time. Konadu-Agyemang argues that the inadequate growth of trade in Africa is not caused by a failure of economic ties, but by hurdles that serve as modern-day instruments of the Africa's past colonial masters.[40] European countries have always had the most engagement with Africa in contrast to other countries on other continents since pre-colonial Africa. These Europe-Africa exchanges have been channeled towards trade and economic development. Although Economic Partnership Agreements have resulted from the commercial and economic development relations between Africa and Europe, African leaders have expressed concern that these agreements are structured in a way that benefits the EU's ulterior goals rather than aiding the realization of Africa's interests.[41] This trade was centered on the exportation of raw goods such as agricultural products, minerals, and, to a considerable degree, human resources. In exchange, African states imported from European countries and paid a higher price for processed or value-added commodities created from the same raw materials exported from Africa.[42]

As highlighted earlier, there were relatively low levels of intra Africa trade before the establishment of the AfCFTA. The post-colonial African states' trade and economic development relations are said to have not improved much and as a result, the African continent is classified as the world's poorest continent.[43] The impact of

[39] Mold and Mukwaya (2016), p. 3.

[40] Konadu-Agyemang, (2002), p. 474.

[41] Engelbert and Dunn (2013).

[42] Bhaca (2021), p. 55.

[43] Bhaca (2021), p. 47.

colonial rule in Africa has resulted in the continent's and its inhabitants' impoverishment while the continent's natural richness has been exploited to the profit of foreign companies and markets. At the same time, the low level of Africa's participation of global trade is seen as one of the most important contributors to its impoverishment.[44] Bilal argues that there may be other intra-continental trade barriers that are impoverishing the continent from within.[45] One of the factors classified as the barriers to intra-Africa trade is poor infrastructure development on the continent. Poor infrastructure hampers trade between African governments which then makes it less expensive to purchase commodities from foreign markets than it is to import from an African state. The history of this unfavourable infrastructure is rooted in colonial rule, when vital transportation lines, such as railways, were developed and built with an international export-oriented mindset to enable a more systematic exploitation of Africa's natural wealth.[46]

The nature of commodities among African states also appears to be another factor discouraging intra-Africa trade. Africa is well-known for its exporting raw materials therefore if African states were to trade with one another, they would trade the same or similar commodities, thus defeating the aspect of trading—exchanging what you have in plentiful amounts for what you lack. Hence, the element of variety of commodities in intra Africa trade is compromised since most African states rely on trade with raw commodities as compared to manufactured commodities.[47]

Socio-political turmoil sometimes coupled with violent conflicts in certain parts and regions of the continent contributes significantly to the discouragement of intra-Africa commerce and economic development.[48] Unfortunately, there is a high level of illicit trade companies that thrive in those zones at the expense of the lives of African people. The magnitude of illicit trade in Africa is claimed to have a disastrous influence on the continent's overall growth and development. In the licit economy, the trade of minerals and precious stones is recognized as the primary contributor to a state's GDP growth. The devastating repercussions of illicit trade on the political, humanitarian and economic elements of the African continent are catastrophic for all. Politically, minerals are known to have financed armed conflicts, some of which were even directed towards legitimate governments. On the economic side, illicit trading has been disastrous on the states by causing widespread unemployment and a low standard of living.[49] The humanitarian consequences of illicit mineral trade involve child labour in these mines as well as committing crimes against humanity in pursuance of the illicit mineral trade. The most noteworthy humanitarian disaster is that of the Democratic Republic of the Congo, Sierra Leone

[44] Bhaca (2021), p. 61.

[45] Bilal (2013), p. 34.

[46] Oppong (2010), pp. 92–103.

[47] Oppong (2010), pp. 93–95.

[48] Bhaca (2021), p. 47.

[49] Bhaca (2021), p. 102.

and the Central African Republic where wars over minerals have caused harm to the entire nation at large.[50]

5 Challenges and Opportunities of the African Continental Free Trade Area

The AfCFTA is intended to develop a large market by establishing a single economic space. Most African countries will have more market opportunities to trade manufactured goods and services within the AfCFTA as a result of this.[51] Prior to the AfCFTA, slow progress has been made towards African economic integration because a few African nations[52] dominate intra-African commerce. Africa has a lot of undiscovered resources that companies would be interested in investing in. Accordingly, the very existence of the AfCFTA serves as an economic driver for investment in the region, attracting new investors. Unlike other regional RTAs, the AfCFTA aims to lower border thickness across the continent in order to encourage inter-regional trade and endless economic growth across the continent while also taking into account Africa's unequal economies.[53] The AfCFTA recognizes that more prominent regional economies are more likely to dominate a given industry and therefore protection should be given to infant industries.[54] This is because other Member States have already established themselves in these areas, as opposed to infant manufacturers attempting to enter these markets.

The AfCFTA therefore aspires to provide chances to infant industries who have faced difficulties participating in intracontinental trade due to import and export obstacles. This is made possible by the Agreement's proposal to reduce and/or eliminate import taxes, allowing these emerging businesses to import raw materials at a lower cost.[55] It was estimated that eliminating tariffs on goods alone by the AfCFTA would enhance intra-African trade by 40 to 50 per cent by 2040.[56] According to Moyo, the AfCFTA will have victors and losers. The winners being the continent's more advanced and industrialised countries, which have the capacity to produce and export intermediate and manufactured goods; the losers will be low-income, less industrialised economies, which have limited capacity to produce and export on a large scale.[57]

---

[50] Bhaca (2021), p. 102.

[51] Mold and Mukwaya (2016), p. 2.

[52] Such as South Africa, Kenya, Nigeria, Egypt and Côte d'Ivoire.

[53] de Melo (2023).

[54] An infant industry is defined as a national strategic interest that has been in existence for less than 5 years and has been tainted by high start-up costs that make it difficult to compete with equivalent imports.

[55] Schoeman (2023).

[56] Moyo (2020), p. 2.

[57] Moyo (2020), p. 2.

In order to secure maximum market penetration, the infant industries must therefore strive to generate low-cost, high-quality goods retailed at competitive prices of which consumers in Africa will profit from increasing competition as the price of goods falls.[58] However, instead of closing the gap between countries, the AfCFTA may worsen disparities unless mechanisms are put in place to ensure that all countries benefit from the agreement. It may also amplify existing inequities based on gender, generation, and geography.[59] Odeku and Rikhotso further argue that the possibility of AfCFTA to improve intra-continental trade among African communities is undeniable. However, the AfCFTA has its drawbacks, particularly for small-scale enterprises who it is erroneously believed that their only problem in participating in intra-continental trade is overcoming import and export constraints without considering what requirements, skills, and resources will be expected of them.[60]

The AfCFTA's objective of integrating African states and promoting intra-continental commerce appears to be practicable for any African state to follow, implement, and achieve. However, the diverse levels of economic development and size, as well as the fragmented nature of African economies, present both an opportunity and a threat to the AfCFTA's viability.[61] This is because each African state has unique trade barriers, they may have different perspectives on the agreement and face different challenges in achieving the agreement's objectives.[62] Vhumbunu argues that the differing sizes of African economies may contribute to protectionism in both the larger economies (which compete for markets) and the smaller economies (which compete against the larger economies).[63] For example, countries such as Djibouti, Ethiopia, Madagascar, Malawi, Sudan, Zambia, and Zimbabwe have expressed concern about liberalisation because they worry it will destroy their fragile establishments.[64] On the other hand nations such as Nigeria, Egypt, South Africa, and Kenya enjoy market dominance in their respective regions due to their market size and economic strength, which may perpetuate hegemonic tendencies thus endangering the AfCFTA's success.[65] It may therefore be envisaged that the nations' varying sizes and degrees of development may limit their ability to reap the benefits of the AfCFTA as the less developed countries may be reluctant to fully commit to the AfCFTA since they believe their benefits under the AfCFTA will be less or non-existent as compared to the more established nations. Additionally, if its implementation is hampered by greed and a desire for power, the AfCFTA may simply be a weapon of devastation for Africa, giving birth to a new type of colonialism.

[58] Pasara (2019), p. 20.

[59] Moyo (2020), p. 2.

[60] Odeku and Rikhotso (2023), p. 116.

[61] Vhumbunu (2020), p. 134.

[62] Odeku and Rikhotso (2023), p. 118.

[63] Vhumbunu (2020), p. 134.

[64] Moyo (2020), p. 2.

[65] Vhumbunu (2020), p. 134.

More so, even though the CFTA appears to be the key to liberalizing trade in Africa and hence boosting economic growth, the principal beneficiaries are expected to be multinational firms based in major African cities but originating outside of Africa.[66] This is because the majority of Africa's largest firms originate outside of the continent. It is envisaged that increased commerce under the AfCFTA would have a multiplier effect on African economies, raising export receipts, increasing government income, and enhancing GDP growth.[67] This will increase economies' ability to invest in enhancing their inhabitants' quality of life. The reality is that GDPs of most African countries are driven by a variety of enterprises, the majority of which are non-African corporations. This would imply that the expected integration of African states may be less than expected, given that these major corporations may not participate in the Free Trade Area for a variety of reasons, including a lack of interest in the vision of Africa's integration.[68]

Furthermore, prior to the agreement, majority of African enterprises cited customs and trade rules as a barrier to commerce. The AfCFTA may appear to be a dream comes true for enterprises that wanted to participate in intra-continental commerce but were hampered by high tariffs and customs costs. This is strengthened further by Art 15 of the Agreement, which requires Member States to facilitate the transfer of goods in transit to the other Member States. Art 15 of the Agreement specifies transit commerce regulations by stating that 'Member States should grant other Members all transit traffic freedom to traverse through their territories and not to impose any import or export duties on transit traffic.'[69] This however raises the possible loss of revenue for governments, as customs duties are a substantial source of revenue for governments. This revenue loss will occur when import tariffs are cut or eliminated as a way of fostering inter-regional trade, resulting in a loss of customs income received on imported goods.[70] According to Makochekanwa, most countries acquire up to 50% or more of their government revenue via customs duties.[71] As a result, lowering import duties will dramatically reduce government revenue. Additionally, the potential depletion of revenue could have an impact on the delivery of critical public services in the countries. This will drive already-disadvantaged countries to implement fiscal changes in order to avoid customs revenue losses. This could involve raising the Value-Added-Tax (VAT) in order to generate revenue. Makochekanwa goes on to suggest that only a few nations, such as Angola and South Africa, will benefit from the TFTA's trade liberalisation because barely 5% of their customs taxes account for all government revenue.[72]

---

[66] Miller (2004), p. 178.

[67] Moyo (2020), p. 2.

[68] Odeku and Rikhotso (2023), p. 121.

[69] Arts 1 & 2 of the Annex on Transit Trade and Transit Facilities (Annex 5).

[70] Pasara (2019), pp. 2–3.

[71] Makochekanwa (2014), p. 185.

[72] Makochekanwa (2014), p. 185.

Gumede also highlights that the political interactions between African governments are critical to accomplishing the AfCFTA's objectives. He argues that implementing the AfCFTA's aims will be easier and more practicable if Africa forms a political federation.[73] It is practical to claim that the AfCFTA is more of a commercial and economic union than a political bloc. However, the opportunities for the political challenges, on the other hand, must not be underestimated. As Gumede avers, the challenges posed by the political environment could jeopardize the efficient execution of the AfCFTA. However, there are currently regions that are unstable due to violence, such as the Sahel, sections of West and East Africa, and (to a lesser extent) Southern Africa.[74] This is worrisome as governance, peace, and security challenges have hampered the effective implementation of other continental projects, which may be good reason to be sceptical of the AfCFTA's success.[75] This is not to say some African RTAs have not been helpful in taking a collaborative approach to tackling regional difficulties stemming from the political environment. For example, the establishment of the SADCC was a regional approach of the then independent states of the southern region of Africa to defend their fragile states and economies against the then apartheid South Africa.[76] Nevertheless, it is hoped that the effective implementation of the AfCFTA will lead to a more politically connected Africa, given that the AfCFTA will be a common goal for African governments thus creating and maintaining a peaceful and secure African continent.

Additionally, it is crucial to emphasize that the necessity to achieve industrialisation through the AfCFTA will necessitate the attraction of FDI (Foreign Direct Investment). A stable political system that is anti-corrupt is one of the desirable attributes for FDI. As such, the leaders of AfCFTA member countries will be required to ensure that the political environment is attractive for FDI inflows in order to achieve the economic progress and prosperity that it seeks to achieve. AfCFTA's successful implementation will therefore generate the necessary economic outcomes while also improving the political environment of the continent as a whole.

6 COVID-19 and the African Continental Free Trade Area

While the AfCFTA seeks to promote opening up borders in order to stimulate free movement of goods across borders, Covid-19 required countries to impose restrictions on cross-border movements of goods and people in order to contain the spread of the virus, which went against the very purpose of intra Africa trade liberalisation.[77] Border closures and lockdowns across Africa were a direct consequence of

[73] Gumede (2020).

[74] Moyo (2020), p. 2.

[75] Vhumbunu (2020), p. 138.

[76] Söderbaum (2004), p. 420.

[77] Pasara (2021), p. 8.

the Covid-19 pandemic which then resulted in a large temporary fall in intraAfrica trade volumes. South Africa, for instance, went into a level 5 strict lockdown from March 2020 to contain the corona virus. Boarders were closed for human trafficking and almost most of the businesses in South Africa had temporarily halted operations. It was only when numbers of Covid-19 cases were manageable that borders begun to progressively reopen.

At the time of the Covid-19 pandemic, the AfCFTA was in its critical phase of implementation and as such the imposition of travel bans and boarder closures had a direct impact intra-Africa trade and mobility. Negotiation of major components of the agreement, such as the Rule of Origin and Tariff Schedules Concession halted due to the pandemic, as some aspects of the agreement required physical contacts in order to be fully operationalized. In terms of bringing the AfCFTA into operation, this meant that negotiating parties of the AfCFTA were unable to travel hence stagnating negotiations. Because of the pandemic, the implementation of the AfCFTA agreement, which was set to start on July 1, 2020, was pushed forward to January 1, 2021. However, one outstanding achievement of the CFTA was the capacity to commence trading within a year after the pandemic was declared and before all lockdown measures were completely eased. Even though it began 6 months later than the intended date, it demonstrated African governments' determination to encourage intra-Africa trade.

Furthermore, although the COVID-19 pandemic led to disruptions in the global supply chain, the pace of digitalization accelerated.[78] According to Devarajan and as highlighted earlier, one of the most severe obstacles that continue to keep Africa the world's least integrated continent is infrastructure integration.[79] There is need therefore, to expand efforts to accelerate infrastructure integration so that African countries can realize the benefits of higher economic productivity, improved physical connection. The COVID pandemic was therefore an opportune time for the AfCFTA to take advantage of better internet access on the African continent to accelerate e-commerce, the digital economy, and the Fourth Industrial Revolution. Companies in the telecommunications sector reported significant revenue growth. Companies like ZOOM and Skype, as well as social media platforms saw their share values skyrocket as individuals and organizations chose for virtual meetings and conferences over traditional face-to-face ones.[80] Pasara argues that this introduced new ways and opportunities for African traders to conduct business virtually using different communication technologies instead of physically travelling great distances via underdeveloped road networks and infrastructure, thus drastically cutting operational expenses in both time and money.[81] This is a benefit that could have had both immediate and long-term benefits.

[78] Pasara (2021), p. 9.
[79] Devarajan (2017).
[80] Pasara (2021), p. 9.
[81] Pasara (2021), p.

7 Establishing Regional Value Chains

Due to limited mobility, COVID-19 promoted a shift away from global supply chains and towards more regionalized and localized supply chains in order to procure commodities to combat the pandemic. African countries are increasingly linked to the global economy, yet they tend to operate at the bottom of the ladder. They primarily supply raw materials and low-value produced goods. This was a missed opportunity by the CFTA to strengthen African regional value chains and African industrialization.COVID-19 altered the manufacturing industry's reliance away from global manufacturing hubs and towards regional and local production. In terms of pharmaceuticals, for example, Africa spends a lot of money importing drugs from Europe and Asia, both of which witnessed major interruptions in their supply chains. African nations having pharmaceutical production capacity such as South Africa could have been assisted under the AfCFTA umbrella to boost inter-regional pharmaceutical commerce for reciprocal intra-African economic gains. The COVID pandemic therefore provided a chance for African countries to shift their reliance away from faraway suppliers and towards more local providers by developing value chains in medical devices, pharmaceuticals, and Personal Protective Equipment (PPEs). With many epidemics affecting Africa such as Tuberculosis and HIV/AIDS, a localized production of various types of pharmaceuticals could assist Africa to emolliate most of the epidemics Africa is battling with as well as increase intra-African supply chains to better deal with any future pandemics. Accordingly, this would have had a number of beneficial implications such as accelerating industrialization in the African region.

This benefit is not only limited to medical supplies, but it also gives the African continent and the AfCFTA the opportunity to explore and offset new methods of engaging, new markets, new products. For example, COVID-19 exacerbated food insecurity due to limited trade and mobility. With a number of African nations being net food exporters and many others importing food from Europe and Asia, the pandemic gave a chance for the AfCFTA to develop food value chains whereby food can be easily conveyed from nations with food surpluses to those with food shortfalls.

Although this chapter has highlighted that the majority of Africa's established manufacturing hubs originate outside of the continent, local production would have still altered economies and assisted African countries to obtain a more equitable share of the value obtained from African goods and labour thus enhancing the lives of African people. The burden of unemployment on the African continent is shared by all African countries; however, the youth of Africa are especially vulnerable to this challenge because Africa's population is made up of more than 60% youth. According to the Mo Ibrahim Report, the root of Africa's high level of unemployment and under-employment is a lack of economic opportunity, which ultimately leads to an increase in poverty.[82] Since demographic projections in Africa indicate a

[82] Bhaca, (2021), p. 110.

continent dominated by youth, youth involvement in the AfCFTA agenda therefore makes a meaningful contribution to the long-term success of the AfCFTA. At the same time, Africa's youth are also a possible risk to regional undertakings such as the AfCFTA if challenges such as unemployment and poor involvement in entrepreneurship initiatives are not addressed.[83] Accordingly, the AfCFTA's economic development efforts should have a significant effort in combatting concerns of forced migration caused by a lack of economic opportunities on the continent or in respective African governments. If properly executed, the AfCFTA is therefore anticipated to generate employment opportunities for the African continent.

However, trade under the AfCFTA only begun a year after its implementation in September 2022, with Kenya and Rwanda exporting their first commodities to Ghana. Madingwaneng and Motswaledi further suggest that the AFCFTA agreement must include a policy prohibiting any African country from trading beyond the borders of the African continent. It must first search for the particular product within the continent's borders, since doing so will not only secure economic progress but will also stimulate collaboration and close Africa into a single economic body.[84] They further argue that failure by the AFCFTA committees to prioritize compulsory intra-African trade may result in African countries importing commodities outside of the continent that are abundant on the continent due to corruption and political connections, and thus failing to realize the vision of AFCFTA.[85]

8 Conclusion

The AfCFTA was established to liberalize borders and address the small and fragmented markets that characterize most African nations, thereby encouraging intra-African trade and economic growth. Without any uncertainty, the AfCFTA is an outstanding success for Africa in the twenty-first century. Hence, the AfCFTA might be a game changer for the continent, since it could bring about economic growth, which has been a determining factor in the continent's progress. Accordingly, this chapter investigated the negative effects of the COVID-19 pandemic on the AfCFTA's implementation, focusing on the repercussions on the attempts to promote intra-Africa trade. The chapter also discussed squandered chances that African countries may have seized even in the midst of the pandemic. The AfCFTA's overall goal was to be a feasible tool for promoting economic development by breaking down trade barriers and uniting African governments to form a single African market, thereby increasing Africa's economic growth and development. Thus, if executed successfully, the AfCFTA might achieve a balance between the advanced and

[83] Mimbale and Mbutamuntu (2021), p. 4.

[84] Madingwaneng and Motswaledi (2023), p. 144.

[85] Madingwanengand Motswaledi (2023), p. 144.

emerging economies, leading to the realisation of post-colonial era goals and objectives envisioned by leaders of independent African governments at the time.

COVID-19, on the other hand, threatened to disrupt the progress made toward its operationalization. To contain the spread of the coronavirus, an opposite approach by closing borders and restricting migration was adopted. One significant achievement of the AfCFTA was to prevent the decision to postpone the commencement of trade in perpetuity because of COVID-19, which would have signalled that the agreement would equally be vulnerable to future crises. Resilience during a pandemic is key in justifying the push that the AfCFTA provides in strengthening cohesion through regional integration. That is, while the pandemic has had an impact on commerce and mobility, it has also emphasized the importance of improving value chains in general and intra-African trade structures in order to better position Africa to deal with any future pandemic. AfCFTA's resilience against COVID-19 therefore demonstrates AfCFTA's possible resistance against future disasters. Going forward, it is hoped that the complete operationalization of AFCFTA will transform the regional market and assure growth in trade outputs and services. As the African economy continues to recover from the COVID-19 pandemic, African partnership through AFCFTA may provide the African economy with the opportunity it needs to remain solid in the global market.[86]

However, the AfCFTA is challenged with other overlapping historical and deep-rooted challenges of the continent. It is critical that issues such as illicit training be rectified as it will most certainly act against the AfCFTA's original mandate and lead to unintended consequences. This is so because the illicit trade economy is made up of international and intra-continental networks and thus addressing such a crisis will necessitate more than the intervention of African governments. Further, there is also need to address the potential that the region's economic hegemons may further exploit smaller economies if the laissez-faire phenomenon is not adequately addressed in the agreement.

References

Aniche ET (2020) From pan-Africanism to African regionalism: a chronicle. Afr Stud 79(1):1–12

Bhaca SP (2021) The challenges and opportunities of intra-continental trade: prospects of the African continental free trade area (AfCFTA). Master's degree, University of Johannesburg, South Africa

Bhagwati J (1992) Regionalism versus multilateralism. World Econ 15(5):535–556

Bhala R (2006) International trade law: interdisciplinary theory and practice, 2nd edn. LexisNexis, Cape Town

Bilal S (2013) External influences on regional integration in West Africa: the role of third parties. In: Sohn R, Oppong AK (eds) Regional trade and monetary integration in West Africa and Europe. WAI-ZEI. Paper 6,, Bonn, pp 33–55

[86] Oladejo (2022), p. 15.

Borrman A, Koopmann G (1994) Regionalisation and regionalism in world trade. Intereconomics 29(4):163–170
De Melo J (2023) The Tripartite Free Trade Africa: Is It the Way to Deepen Integration in Africa?. https://www.brookings.edu/blog/africa-in-focus/2014/11/04/the-tripartite-free-trade-africa-is-it-the-way-to-deepen-integration-in-africa/
Devarajan S (2017) Why is regional integration so elusive?. Brookings, 2017. https://www.brookings.edu/articles/why-is-regional-integration-so-elusive/
Donald A (2002) Calvert how the multilateral trade system under the World Trade Organization is attempting to reconcile the contradiction & hurdles Posed by regional trade agreements, An analysis of the article XXIV of the general agreement on tariffs & trade. Unpublished Master's thesis, George Mason University
Engelbert P, Dunn K (2013) Inside African politics. University of Cape Town Press, Cape Town
Gaulier Guillaume & Jean Sébastien & Ünal-Kesenci,Deniz. 2004. Regionalism and the Regionalisation ofInternational Trade, Working Papers 2004-16, CEPII research center.
Gumede, V (2020) Examining the African Continental Free Trade Area in the Context of a Political Federation for Africa – Towards a United African States. https://www.parliament.gov.za/storage/app/media/Pages/2021/may/24-05-2021_Africa_Day_Lecture/docs/UNISA_Press_Working_Paper_AfCFTA_and_UAS.pdf
Hirakawa H (2005) East Asia and the development of regionalism. In: Lapavistas C, Noguchi M (eds) Beyond market- driven development: drawing on the experience of Asia and Latin America. Routledge, New London and New York, pp 117–135
Ismail FA (2017) Advancing regional integration in Africa through the continental free trade area (CFTA). Law Dev Rev 10(1):1–28
Júnior HR, Luciano BT (2020) Regionalism in the global south: mercosur and ECOWAS in trade and democracy protection. Third World Q 41(9):1498–1517
Kola, Odeku Teron, Rikhotso (2023) (2023) NO ACCESS African Continental Free Trade Area (AfCFTA): An Impetus for Intra-African Trade Integration Journal of African Foreign Affairs 10(1) 111-131 10.31920/AA_JoAFA 10.31920/AA_10_1_April 10.31920/2056-5658/2023/v10n1a6
Konadu-Agyemang K (2002) The best of times and the worst of times: structural adjustment programmes and uneven development in Africa: the case of Ghana. Prof Geogr 52:469–483
Krist W (2021) Trade Agreements and Economic Theory. https://www.wilsoncenter.org/chapter-3-trade-agreements-and-economic-theory
Kritzinger-van Niekerk L (2023) Regional integration: concepts, advantages, disadvantages and lessons of experience. https://sarpn.org/documents/d0001249/P1416-RI-concepts_May2005.pdf
Lorenz D (1991) Regionalisation versus regionalism- problems of change in the world economy. Intereconomics 26(1):3–10
Louw-Vaudran L, Mohamed Diatta M, Attah-Asamoah A, Woldemichael S (2019) Africa's free trade initiative could bolster continental peace. ISS Peace Secur Council Rep 119:1–20
Lunani SM (2011) Understanding regionalisation and preferential relations in world trade law and policy: a perspective from the East African Community (EAC). Unpublished LLM thesis, University of Western Cape, 2011
Makochekanwa A (2014) Welfare implications of COMESA-EAC-SADC tripartite free trade area. Afr Dev Rev 26(1):186–202
Mimbale J, Mbutamuntu J (2021) FRICAN YOUTH: stimulus and brake to the effective implementation of the African continental free trade area. Academia Letters, Art 3802
Mold A, Mukwaya R (2016) Modelling the economic impact of the tripartite free trade area: its implications for the economic geography of southern, eastern and northern Africa. J Afr Trade 3(1–2):57–84
Moloi SL (2019) Debating the African Unity debate: interrogating six decades of converging and diverging dynamics towards continental unification. Master's, University of Johannesburg, South Africa
Moyo T (2020) The African continental free trade agreement (AfCFTA). A political economy analysis of opportunities, challenges and prospects. Africa Insight 50(1):2

Madingwaneng MJ, Motswaledi TR (2023) The impact of AfCFTA on African economy and the reconfiguration to integrate sustainably competitive on world free trade: a critical review. J Afr Foreign Aff 10(1):133–149
Odeku K, Rikhotso T, (2023) African Continental Free Trade Area (AfCFTA): An Impetus for Intra-African TradeIntegration Journal of African Foreign Affairs 10(1):111–131
Oladejo AO (2022) Regionalisation and economic resilience in a pandemic: making a case for the African continental free trade area (AfCFTA). J Law Soc Dev 9:21
Oppong R (2010) The African union, African economic community and Africa's regional economic communities. Untangling a complex web. Afr J Int Comp Law 18:92–103
Pasara MT (2021) The dual effects of COVID-19 on intra-African trade: a viewpoint of the AfCFTA. Africagrowth Agenda 18(4):8–11
Pasara MT (2019) The welfare effects of economic integration in the tripartite free trade area. Doctor of Philosophy in Economics, North-West University, South Africa
Schoeman M (2023) What does the TFTA really mean for regional integration in Africa?. South African Institute of International Africa (SAIIA). http://www.saiia.org.za/opinion-analysis/what-does-the-tfta-really-mean-for-regional-integration-in-africa
Söderbaum F (2004) Modes of regional governance in Africa: neoliberalism, sovereignty-boosting and shadow networks. Glob Gov Rev Multilater Int Org 10(4):419–436
Takele TB (2019) The relevance of coordinated regional trade logistics for the implementation of regional free trade area of Africa. J Transp Supply Chain Manage 13(0):a417
Teunissen JJ (1996) Regionalism and the global economy: the case of Africa. FONDAD, The Hague
Tiziana, B 'Multilateralism and Regionalism: Enhancing Integration of Developing Countries into the MultilateralTrading system through Regionalism.' A paper prepared by Ms Tiziana Bonapace, Economic Affairs officer, TradePolicy Section, International Trade and industry Division, ESCAP (undated). available http://www.unescap.org/tid/publication/chap1-2161.pdf, accessed 1 April 2019.
UNCTAD 'Building the African Continental Free Trade Area: Some Suggestions on the Way Forward' (2015)United Nations 5.
Vhumbunu CH (2022) Promoting gender equality and women empowerment in the African continental free trade area: lessons from SADC. Alternation 29(2):121–141
Vhumbunu CH (2020) The African continental free trade area. A new era for African integration or another grandiose razzmatazz? Africa Insight 50(1):134
Vhumbunu CH, Rudigi JR, Mawire C (2023) Assessing infrastructure integration in African regional economic communities (RECs): progress, challenges, and opportunities. J Afr Union Stud 12(1):44
Winters, LA (1996) 'Regionalism versus Multilateralism Policy', Research Working Paper, The World BankInternational Economics Department International Trade Division, at 26.

A SADC Perspective on the Selected Challenges Affecting the Use of Mobile Money to Promote Digital Financial Inclusion and Trade in the AfCFTA

Elfas Torerai and Howard Chitimira

Abstract The use of mobile money has transformed the lives of many poor people across the Southern Africa Development Community (SADC). Millions of individuals who are excluded from the mainstream and formal financial sector are using mobile money to access financial services. In this regard, mobile money plays a huge part in enabling those in the informal sector to use mobile money in furtherance of the African continent's digital and financial inclusion agenda. Financial inclusion is a central enabler of the African Union (AU)'s growth agenda in line with the United Nations (UN)'s Sustainable Development Goals (SDGs) such as poverty alleviation, expanding economic opportunities and promoting market access. The African Continental Free Trade Area (AfCFTA) seeks to establish one of the world's biggest trade and economic markets. While the AfCFTA is shaping up, it is important to note that financial technology (fintech) products such as mobile money can greatly assist in improving cross-border trade especially among the poor and small to medium enterprises (SMEs). However, several challenges are hampering the sustainable use of mobile money in the SADC. There are regulatory challenges affecting the use of mobile money in many SADC countries owing to the absence of robust regulatory frameworks. Digital illiteracy is also a challenge because policymakers and the general populace lack the requisite know-how to use fintech products optimally. Some governments in the SADC region have not fully embraced mobile money, making it difficult to drive digital financial inclusion for the poor. In this chapter, the authors argue that the AfCFTA can leverage the goal to create a single common market for goods and services on the proven ability of mobile money to ramp up digital financial inclusion and trade in the SADC region. Although our focus is on the SADC region, the analysis in this chapter is reflective of experiences in other regional economic communities (REC) across the African

E. Torerai
Faculty of Law, North-West University, Mmabatho, South Africa

H. Chitimira (✉)
Faculty of Law, North-West University, Potchefstroom, South Africa
e-mail: Howard.Chitimira@nwu.ac.za

T. V. Warikandwa et al. (eds.), *Law and Policy of the African Continental Free Trade Area (AfCFTA)*, European Yearbook of International Economic Law,
https://doi.org/10.1007/978-3-032-01122-0_4

continent. We further argue that policymakers should consider improving the regulatory frameworks of fintech products in their respective SADC countries. There should be improved digital and financial literacy for the general public, especially the poor, unbanked and financially excluded persons in the SADC region to enhance their participation in the formal trade and businesses in the financial sector.

1 Introduction

The use of financial technology (fintech) products such as mobile money have profoundly influenced and enhanced global trade. Mobile money allows faster payments, ease of access to financial resources, and broader connection between businesses and consumers.[1] In this regard, mobile money can play a significant role in enhancing the participation of the poor in trade across the Southern Africa Development Community (SADC) in line with the ideals of the Agreement establishing the African Continental Free Trade Area (AfCFTA). The Agreement establishing AfCFTA seeks to, *inter alia*, establish an unrestricted single continental market for trade and investment in goods, services, and facilitate the movement of persons in order to promote economic integration of the African continent in line with Agenda 2063.[2] It is envisaged that the AfCFTA will be the biggest economic market in the world having in excess of 1.3 billion people and a combined gross domestic product (GDP) of about US$3.4 trillion.[3] The establishment of the AfCFTA came at a time when global trade is increasingly going electronic. We argue that the success of trade depends largely on the extent of digital financial inclusion of all people, including the poor. In this regard, the success of the AfCFTA objectives is contingent, partly, on the ability of residents to participate fully in the continent's financial and trade markets. Nonetheless, financial inclusion is still a major hindrance to AfCFTA goals given that the majority of the adult population in the SADC is still unbanked.[4] The use of digital financial services (DFS) such as mobile money, has significantly contributed to the financial inclusion of the poor and previously unbanked persons in SADC and Sub-Saharan Africa (SSA).[5] This owes to the exponential adoption of cellular phones in developing countries, especially those in the SADC region.[6] Mobile money has ameliorated many challenges and bottlenecks that previously made it difficult for the poor, unbanked and low-income earners to

[1] López González and Ferencz (2018), pp. 8–9, and Osabutey and Jackson (2024), pp. 1–13.

[2] See Art 3 of the Agreement Establishing the African Continental Free Trade Area which was adopted on 21 March 2018.

[3] The World Bank 'The African Continental Free Trade Area' https://www.worldbank.org/en/topic/trade/publication/the-african-continental-free-trade-area.

[4] Warikandwa (2023b), p. 211.

[5] Nyagilo et al. (2017), pp. 554–561; Apeti and Edoh (2023), p. 2; Bille et al. (2018), pp. 22–23.

[6] Chitimira and Torerai (2021), p. 2; Wealth et al. (2023), pp. 78–79.

access formal financial services in the SADC region.[7] It has also transformed the financial services landscape and made it possible for financially excluded persons to participate in the mainstream financial markets in the SADC region and the other developing regions of the world.[8] The Financial Stability Board (FSB) defines fintech as technology-enabled innovation within the financial services sector that brings about new business models, applications, processes or products that can materially affect the provision of financial services.[9] Mobile money fits this definition. In this regard, people without bank accounts are able to transact, make and receive payments, borrow money, save in their mobile money accounts, pay for utility bills and school fees using their mobile phones.[10] It is envisaged that the AfCFTA can leverage the attainment of the world's single biggest continental trade market through the use of mobile money to promote digital financial inclusion. Thus, policymakers should strive to adopt laws and policies that advance and enhance financial inclusion of the poor, low-income earners and unbanked persons to increase their participation in the AfCFTA and SADC formal trade platforms.

This chapter seeks to discuss some of the challenges affecting the use of mobile money in promoting digital financial inclusion and the participation of the poor, low-income earners and unbanked persons in trade across the SADC region. It also defines key terms and provides the background to the development of mobile money. Moreover, the chapter discusses the use of mobile money services to promote financial inclusion and trade in the SADC region. The chapter further examines selected challenges affecting the regulation and use of mobile money services to promote financial inclusion and trade for the poor, low-income earners and unbanked persons in the SADC region. Thereafter, conclusion and recommendations are provided.

2 Definition of Key Terms

There is no single standard definition for mobile money. However, for the purposes of this chapter, mobile money refers to digital or electronic financial services that are delivered through mobile phones or any other hand-held electronic devices that connect to a mobile telephone network through a subscriber identification module (SIM) card, without the need for bank accounts.[11] In this regard, mobile money differs from mobile banking in that the latter refers to the use of electronic gadgets to access banking account services through applications that allow an account

---

[7] Winn and De Koker (2013), p. 156.

[8] Winn (2013), p. 200. See also Apeti and Edoh (2023), p. 2.

[9] Financial Stability Board (FSB) (2017), p. 7. The FSB is an international body that monitors and makes recommendations about the global financial system.

[10] Lumsden (2018), p. 7. See also Wealth et al. (2023), p. 78.

[11] Chitimira and Torerai (2022), p. 372.

holder to transact or check balances without visiting a bank in person.[12] Thus, mobile money occurs when financial transactions are carried through mobile devices such as mobile phones while mobile banking refers to the use of certain bank applications on mobile devices to access and utilise banking services.[13] Mobile money is an alternative platform to the traditional banking services and it is more beneficial to the poor and financially excluded persons, particularly in the SADC region and other African regions.

Financial inclusion is another term with varied definitions. Malladi, Soni and Srinivasan submit that financial inclusion refers to the delivery of basic financial services to the marginalised and excluded members of society.[14] They further argue that financial inclusion is the opening up of lines of credit towards the poor at a reasonable cost.[15] Financial inclusion also promotes a culture of savings, especially among the previously unbanked and informal businesses, thus, potentially driving economic growth. While the above attributes of financial inclusion are sound, this chapter defines financial inclusion as the provision of access to affordable, convenient, useful and sustainable financial services to all people in a safe and well-regulated manner.[16]

In this regard, digital financial inclusion means accessing the said financial services through electronic devices such as mobile phones. Thus, financial inclusion equips the poor and marginalised people to access financial services and products using digital technologies. The antithesis of financial inclusion is financial exclusion. For its part, financial exclusion goes along with social exclusion which breeds a fertile ground for financial crimes and social ills such as intergenerational poverty, food insecurity, and civil unrest.[17]

The term 'digital trade' refers to the use of electronically enabled transactions of goods and services that may be digitally or physically delivered.[18]

There is no standard definition of the term 'poor people'. However, for the purposes of this chapter, this term refers to economically marginalised individuals who may be unemployed, do not have reliable source of income or earn below the prescribed minimum wage in their respective countries.[19]

---

[12] Kabala et al. (2021), pp. 57–58.

[13] Kabala et al. (2021), p. 57.

[14] Malladi et al. (2021), pp. 128–129.

[15] Malladi et al. (2021), pp. 128–129.

[16] Chitimira and Torerai (2023a), p. 390.

[17] See related comments by De Koker (2013), pp. 182–185; Yawe et al. (2022), pp. 4–5.

[18] See López González and Ferencz (2018), p. 9.

[19] Chitimira and Torerai (2023a), p. 390; See related comments by Mhlanga (2020), pp. 169–170.

3 Overview Background on the Use of Mobile Money and Digital Trade in SADC and Other Jurisdictions

3.1 The Development of Mobile Money and Digital Trade

Notably, mobile payments were first introduced in the Philippines in 2001.[20] However, mobile money became more prominent through the success story of M-Pesa, a flagship mobile money platform launched in 2007 in Kenya.[21] Measures similar to M-Pesa have been adopted in other countries in Africa and elsewhere. Various other mobile money platforms and/or products were later launched in many countries across the SADC region and other parts of the developing world. Examples include platforms such as Orange Money in Botswana, Mobile Telephone Network (MTN) Mobile Money (MoMo) in South Africa, Ecocash in Zimbabwe and Airtel Money in Zambia. People can open and manage mobile money wallets on their cell phones just like banking applications.[22] The Global System for Mobile Communications Association (GSMA)'s 2023 report stipulates that there are about 1.6 billion mobile money wallets or accounts globally.[23] In 2017, the number of mobile money accounts was around 700 million.[24] While it took about 16 years to reach the 700 million mark, the five years from 2017 to 2022 saw the biggest increase in the number of mobile money wallets globally.[25] This sharp increase in the use of mobile money could be attributed to the use of digital financial services since the outbreak of the coronavirus (COVID-19) pandemic in late 2019.[26] In this regard, mobile money has significantly contributed to digital trade in Africa. The SSA region accounts for about two-thirds of the growth in mobile accounts during the last five years.[27] The number of mobile money accounts surpasses that of bank accounts in countries such as the Democratic Republic of Congo (DRC), Madagascar, Zimbabwe, Zambia, Cameroon, Gabon, Kenya, Uganda and Tanzania.[28] More African countries are joining this growing list.

Mobile money transactions have also surpassed the value of US$1 trillion annually.[29] Since 2020, mobile money became an unexpected palliative remedy to the outbreak of the COVID-19 pandemic and related challenges that mostly affected the

[20] Clifford (2020), pp. 8–9.

[21] Buku and Meredith (2013), p. 379; Nyagilo et al. (2017), pp. 560–561.

[22] Chitimira and Torerai (2023b), p. 244; and Lumsden (2018), p. 21.

[23] Global System for Mobile Communications Association (GSMA) (2023), p. 13.

[24] GSMA (2023), p. 13.

[25] GSMA (2023), p. 13.

[26] Chitimira and Torerai (2023b), pp. 242–243.

[27] GSMA (2023), pp. 13–14.

[28] Chipa and Mwanza (2021), pp. 178–179.

[29] GSMA (2023), pp. 5–8.

poor and unbanked persons in across Africa, especially in the SADC.[30] While production and revenue from many other sectors took a dip due to COVID-19, the GSMA report that the value of mobile money transactions soared from US$27.5 billion to US$495 billion in 2020 alone.[31] In this regard, mobile money provided resilience for the poor, low-income earners and unbanked persons to withstand the COVID-19 pandemic challenges.[32] In addition, mobile money provided a reprieve to financial markets in Africa, that were affected by COVID-19 induced lockdowns, company closures and declining revenue from taxes, exports and tourism activities.[33] Thus, mobile money has contributed to the struggle against a possible COVID-19 induced humanitarian crisis in Africa. Governments and relevant authorities should leverage the potential of mobile money to drive digital trade and digital financial inclusion in the SADC.

3.2 The Adoption and Use of Mobile Money in Africa

It appears that Africa has become the leader in the use of mobile money. Africa should use this peculiar advantage to set the trend for international best practices of mobile money. This owes to the fact that there is more mobile money-induced digital financial inclusion in Africa than any other part of the world.[34] Africa can be divided into five distinct economic regions. In terms of mobile money adoption and use, the East Africa region leads with 390 million mobile money accounts followed by West Africa at 290 million.[35] The Central Africa region comes third with 65 million mobile money accounts.[36] North Africa and the SADC are tied up at 18 million accounts each although the latter accounts for more in terms of transaction value.[37] In East Africa, countries such as Kenya, Tanzania, Rwanda, Uganda and Ethiopia account for the huge usage of mobile money services. West Africa countries such as Cote d'Ivoire, Burkina Faso, Benin, Mali, Niger and Senegal which also utilise mobile money. North Africa has countries such as Egypt, Tunisia, Algeria and Morocco that utilise mobile money while in SADC, there is extensive use of mobile money in countries such as Zimbabwe, South Africa, Botswana, and Zambia.

In the SADC region, mobile money is used to process payment services ranging from peer-to-peer (P2P), business-to-business (B2B), business-to-person (B2P) to

30 Mpofu (2022), pp. 2–3.

31 Mpofu (2022), p. 2. See also GSMA (2020).

32 Chitimira and Ncube (2023), p. 237; Chitimira and Torerai (2023b), pp. 242–243.

33 Chitimira and Torerai (2023b), p. 237.

34 Goncalves (2013), pp. 32–33.

35 GSMA (2023), p. 10.

36 GSMA (2023), p. 10.

37 GSMA (2023), p. 10.

government-to-person (G2P).[38] This highlights the extent to which mobile money is used to improve financial inclusion for the poor and low-income earners in Africa. Achieving financial inclusion for the poor and low-income earners opens the gateway to the attainment of the United Nations (UN)'s 2030 Sustainable Development Goals (SDGs) such as poverty reduction, economic growth and reduced inequalities.[39] The Agreement establishing the AfCFTA and the African Union (AU)'s Agenda 2063 do not have express provisions promoting the use of mobile money to improve financial inclusion for the poor and low-income earners.[40] Nonetheless, mobile money should also play a significant role in the attainment of the AfCFTA objectives and Agenda 2063's socio-economic goals that are in line with the UN's SDGs. These goals include eradicating poverty, promoting social and economic equality, and achieving an integrated single economic market for all people on the continent.[41]

3.3 Fintech Developments and the Use of Mobile Money to Enhance Digital Financial Inclusion and Digital Trade in the SADC Region

The SADC region is an economic community comprising 16 member states. It has a significant mobile money footprint which enables the poor and economically marginalised persons to curb financial exclusion challenges. In this section, the authors discuss the evolution of mobile money in general, before narrowing the focus to related challenges in the SADC region.

Mobile money empowers people to process both small and huge transactions cheaply unlike exorbitant service costs charged at banks.[42] In addition, keeping mobile money accounts active does not attract service charges as is the case with bank accounts. Thus, unlike with banks, individuals' mobile money accounts are usually not closed for any failure to pay service charges. Owing to this, mobile money enables digital financial inclusion not only for the poor, unbanked and financially underserved persons, but it has also become a financial service of choice to many people who have lost their savings and investments due to hyperinflation or bank failures in countries such as Zimbabwe.[43] Millions of people may open mobile money wallets on their cell phones in order to save, deposit and transfer funds, more or less similar to what a person using an online banking application or internet banking would do. While Internet banking requires smartphones, mobile money

[38] Fonte (2017), pp. 556–557. See related comments by Chitimira and Torerai (2021), p. 8.

[39] Wealth et al. (2023), pp. 81–82.

[40] African Union (AU) (2015).

[41] AU (2018).

[42] See related comments by Buckley et al. (2015), pp. 436–437; Mashiri et al. (2017), pp. 95–97.

[43] See related comments by Hamadziripi and Munedzi (2023), p. 115.

services can be accessed using a basic cellphone as long as the said phone has an activated SIM card.[44] Mobile money leverages on mobile network infrastructure which generates Unstructured Supplementary Service Data (USSD) codes that act as prompts or guiding short message services (SMS) that a mobile money sender or receiver uses in transacting.[45] Accordingly, any cell phone that can receive SMS is compatible with mobile money operations. Therefore, any person with a basic mobile phone can also trade on mobile money platforms.

In addition to accessibility and affordability factors, mobile money also provides convenience and flexibility to users and this enables people to process transactions at any time of the day and from any location where there is mobile network connection.[46] A significant number of families in SADC countries depend on remittances from relatives and friends working in far-away cities or other countries in the diaspora. In this regard, such people depend on mobile money to access and receive the funds and/or remittances.[47] For instance, South Africa hosts possibly the highest number of economic migrants from countries within the SADC region. Mobile money provides a cheaper alternative to remittances sent through banks or other bank-linked money transfer platforms such as Western Union, MoneyGram and Wise.[48] The traditional money transfer platforms also require remittance recipients to travel long distances to cities where they can access the offices for cash-out services whereas mobile money is direct to a recipient's cell phone. Therefore, it is cost-effective for people to use mobile money for remittances compared to banks or other traditional money transfer platforms. Small and medium enterprises (SMEs) and other informal businesses have also found an economic lifeline in mobile money services where they are not charged prohibitive amounts in processing their transactions.[49] Mobile money can foster economic development, alleviate poverty and address income inequality in Africa by enabling access to financial services for marginalised persons.[50] Notably, some African cities such as Johannesburg, Harare, Gaborone, Maputo, Kampala have a leading influence on the use of fintech products, particularly mobile money.

Nonetheless, apart from the immense potential that mobile money has in promoting digital financial inclusion, several challenges affect its full adoption and use in many SADC countries. Some of these factors include insufficient regulation, policy misalignment, fintech-averse communities, digital illiteracy, trust deficit in the financial services sector, lack of infrastructure, poor network effects leading to unavailability of mobile money in deep rural areas, criminal abuse of the platforms

[44] Chitimira and Ncube (2023), pp. 125–140.

[45] Robb et al. (2017), p. 215.

[46] Chitimira and Torerai (2023b), pp. 219–220; Baganzi and Lau (2017), pp. 1–3; Chitimira and Torerai (2021), p. 2.

[47] Soutter et al. (2019), p. 42; and Baganzi and Lau (2017), p. 2.

[48] Fonte (2017), pp. 556–557.

[49] See related comments by Wealth (2023), p. 87.

[50] Chitimira and Torerai (2023c), pp. 241–243; see related comments by Robb and Vilakazi (2016), p. 10; Shrier (2016), p. 3.

such as overcharging consumers, high costs of running mobile money services and weak regulatory frameworks.[51] Additionally, there are risks such as money laundering, terrorism financing and scams that also come with the use of mobile money in the SADC region.[52] In this regard, it is important to explore in detail some of the highlighted impediments in order to expose the barriers that hinder mobile money from reaching its full potential in promoting financial inclusion for the poor, low-income earners and marginalised persons in SADC. This could assist policymakers to come up with measures that provide a conducive environment for mobile money to thrive in promoting financial inclusion for the poor, low-income earners, unbanked and underbanked persons across the SADC region.

In light of the above, this chapter discusses selected challenges that hinder full adoption and use of mobile money by the poor, low-income earners, unbanked and underbanked persons in SADC. These challenges curtail the expansion of financial inclusion and digital trade in the SADC. We argue that policy makers should deal with the highlighted challenges in order to reduce financial exclusion of the poor, low-income earners and financially excluded persons in the SADC region.

4 The Use of Mobile Money Services to Promote Financial Inclusion and Trade in the SADC Region

Technological advancements have caused a shift from traditional mechanical devices to digital technologies globally. Mobile network telecommunications have replaced fixed-line telephones and this development has had far-reaching implications for many economic sectors in the SADC region, especially in the financial services.[53] As mobile network operators (MNOs) installed network infrastructure goes beyond the cities and towns into rural areas, the demand for mobile phones has increased.[54] Thus, the wide reach of MNOs caused an unprecedented use of mobile phones in SADC and across Africa. MNOs and other non-banking institutions have ventured into the provision of Internet connectivity and mobile money services in SADC and across Africa. Countries that have hugely benefitted from mobile money services include Botswana, Zambia, South Africa, Mozambique, Malawi, Zimbabwe, Kenya, Nigeria, Tanzania, Uganda and Egypt.[55] Mobile money has benefited people in rural areas where banks have failed to service for many years. A significant number of people in rural areas own mobile phones and this connects them to relatives and friends not only for communication purposes but also for

[51] Financial Stability Board (FSB) (2017), pp. 13–15; see related comments by Wealth (2023), pp. 87–88.

[52] Chitimira and Torerai (2023a), p. 386.

[53] See related comments by Chitimira and Torerai (2023c), pp. 242–243.

[54] See related comments by Chitimira and Torerai (2023a), p. 391.

[55] See related comments by Wealth (2023), pp. 82–83.

access to digital financial services.[56] We argue that mobile money is a socially and economically important fintech product in SADC and entire Africa. The ever-increasing innovation in the Information Communication Technologies (ICTs) sector is likely to further improve the quality and reach of mobile money services in SADC and the SSA.

In 2007, Safaricom, an MNO in Kenya started M-Pesa, a mobile money platform that stands as the beacon of digital financial services in Africa.[57] Since then, mobile money has grown exponentially across the SSA region.[58] Mobile money has changed many people's lives and it is a very powerful digital financial inclusion avenue for the poor, low-income earners, unbanked and financially excluded in SADC.[59] To date, mobile money continues to provide opportunities for the poor and unbanked persons who are financially excluded from accessing financial services due to, inter alia, cumbersome and costly banking services. Some of the reasons for financial exclusion in SADC could be attributed to onerous customer due diligence (CDD) and the know your customer (KYC) requirements when opening bank accounts, the cost of financial services, the distance to financial service outlets, a lack of trust in formal financial services and negative perceptions on aspects such as dress etiquette and language use at banks.[60] Although traditional financial institutions may not have written rules on language and dress for their clients, there is pressure on consumers to speak in non-native language to access financial services and trade in most countries. Consumers may also feel obliged to dress in a particular way when going to a banking hall. For many poor and unbanked persons, the language and the perceived dress code barriers contribute to financial exclusion. Mobile money is free from all these impediments hence it is considerably popular with the poor and other economically marginalised people in the SADC region. People can easily access mobile money services through mobile money agents who have stalls at local shops and garages where there are little or no formalities and the need to travel long distances.[61] Moreover, mobile money agents usually converse with mobile money users in commonly used local languages, making it easier even for the illiterate to understand and participate on the mobile money platforms.[62]

Generally, there has been an increase in the adoption and use of new mobile money technologies in the SADC region. In countries where early mobile money initiatives failed to ignite such as South Africa, there have been relaunches or the emergence of new mobile money products.[63] Mobile money has facilitated easy

---

[56] Hamadziripi and Munedzi (2023), pp. 118–119.

[57] The 'M' in M-Pesa stands for 'mobile' while 'Pesa' is the Swahili word for 'money'. Thus, M-Pesa is short for 'mobile money'; Buku and Meredith (2013), p. 378; see related comments by Lumsden (2018), p. 27.

[58] GSMA (2023), p. 10.

[59] Chitimira and Torerai (2023a), p. 385.

[60] Chitimira and Torerai (2023b), pp. 218–219.

[61] Gibson et al. (2017), p. 2.

[62] Buckley et al. (2015), p. 451.

[63] Chitimira and Torerai (2023a), p. 391.

disbursement of G2P social assistance programmes due to its affordability and ease of access in hard-to-reach remote rural areas in SADC.[64] The outbreak of the COVID-19 pandemic added impetus to the use of mobile money services and statistics show that mobile money has become a vital cog in driving financial inclusion in SADC.[65] To a greater extent, mobile money was instrumental in ameliorating disruptions in trade that were caused by the COVID-19 pandemic restrictions and regulations.[66] Thus, mobile money enabled the flow of money, P2P transfers, G2P relief disbursements, credit, deposits, salaries, and investments even during the COVID-19 pandemic.[67] In this regard, the SSA region has become a reference point for mobile money operations to enhance the financial inclusion of the poor, unbanked and low-income earners.

5 Selected Challenges Affecting the Adoption and Use of Mobile Money to Promote Digital Financial Inclusion and Trade in SADC

Mobile money has arguably emerged as the leading fintech product in the SADC region. The Bali Fintech Agenda provides that fintech products such as mobile money offer wide-ranging possibilities in enhancing efficiencies in the financial services sector to broaden access to such services for underserved people to promote financial inclusion.[68] However, mobile money is yet to reach full scale owing to several challenges in the SADC region as highlighted above.[69] Some of the notable challenges include, *inter alia*, the absence of robust regulation comparable to that of banking services that are offered in the formal financial sector and inadequate education on mobile money services.[70] Consumer protection challenges are also rife due to weak consumer protection measures and general poor adherence to the rule of law in some SADC countries.[71] The absence of educational programmes to promote the use and benefits of mobile money gave rise to apathy and jitters among its potential end-users. Consequently, there is general distrust and skepticism that hamper full adoption and use of mobile money services in SADC. In the absence of sufficient awareness, many people still consider it a risk to transact and/or trade on mobile money platforms. Lack of adequate technology, poor infrastructure, insufficient power supplies and harsh taxation policies add to the list of hin-

---

[64] Chitimira and Torerai (2023b), p. 223.

[65] GSMA (2023), p. 10.

[66] Warikandwa (2023a), p. 405.

[67] Chitimira and Torerai (2023a), p. 391; and Warikandwa (2023a), pp. 405–406.

[68] International Monetary Fund (IMF) (2018).

[69] See paragraph 3.3 above.

[70] See related comments by Wealth et al. (2023), pp. 87–90.

[71] Chitimira and Torerai (2022), pp. 377–379; and Wealth et al. (2023), pp. 90–91.

drances curtailing the use of mobile money to trade, especially by the poor who reside mostly in rural areas in SADC and AfCFTA.

Additionally, mobile money lies outside the regulatory ambit of the current financial regulatory frameworks in SADC's 16 member states.[72] This poses significant risks to the growth, adoption and smooth operation of mobile money services. Accordingly, some of the challenges affecting the adoption and use of mobile money in the SADC region are discussed below.

5.1 *The Regulatory Conundrum*

Mobile money, like other fintech products, has created what we call a regulatory conundrum in that governments in the SADC region were ill-prepared and/or reluctant to regulate mobile money.[73] The challenge may not necessarily be pinned down to the mobile money service but perhaps to service providers such as the MNOs. It is possible that authorities had not anticipated that MNOs could venture into financial services and rival banks. Some of the MNOs offering mobile money services had also struggled to get registered as telecommunications service providers. This follows the fact that many governments held a monopoly in the provision of telecommunication services and they were reluctant to open space for other role-players in this sector. For example, in South Africa, Telkom used to be the only telecommunications service provider while in Zimbabwe TelOne used to enjoy the same status. Accordingly, some governments had to be dragged to the courts before they could open up the telecommunications space for MNOs. For instance, Econet Wireless's owner, Strive Masiyiwa struggled to get a license from the Zimbabwean government for five years before he was allowed to operate.[74] Some MNOs had to fight in order to get licenses and they also faced resistance to their mobile money services, especially in Zimbabwe.

Through innovation, MNOs such as Econet Wireless, Safaricom, MTN and others introduced mobile money services to, inter alia, promote trade and financial inclusion. Mobile money disrupts the monopoly of mainstream banking institutions that had support from African governments, not only in the provision of financial services but through financial inclusion of the poor, low-income earners, unbanked and financially underserved communities in SADC and entire Africa. This has created regulatory challenges. Firstly, the SADC governments are slow to provide regulatory measures that are commensurate to the speed of innovation that drives mobile money. The longer policymakers delay in coming up with adequate laws, the more difficult it becomes to catch up with the pace and reach of technology. The proper regulation of mobile money services has remained a challenge in

[72] Wealth et al. (2023), pp. 88–89.

[73] See related comments by Wealth et al. (2023), pp. 87–88.

[74] Wealth et al. (2023), p. 88.

SADC. Secondly, mobile money services have opened up financial inclusion opportunities for the poor, low-income earners, unbanked persons and underserved communities in SADC. Most of the poor, low-income earners and unbanked persons are usually considered too risky for the viability of financial institutions such as banks.[75] The fact that such people are now part of the mainstream financial markets requires adequate regulatory safeguards to combat risks such as money laundering, terrorism financing and fraud.[76] So far, there has not been adequate regulation of mobile money in many SADC countries, heightening threats to financial markets' integrity, stability and trade in the AfCFTA.

There have been attempts to use the extant financial regulatory frameworks to regulate mobile money services in SADC.[77] However, it has proved very difficult to balance the need for effective regulation and the pace of innovation in mobile money. Whereas the traditional financial regulatory frameworks in SADC require consumers to provide proof of income, residential addresses, income and employment, mobile money wallet opening requires only an identity document and a working cell phone.[78] In addition, the traditional financial regulatory frameworks in SADC have made trade and financial services not so effective by using the same frameworks to regulate mobile money services. Mobile money services are more affordable, convenient and faster.[79] The ever-evolving nature of mobile money makes it difficult for traditional financial regulatory frameworks to be effective in the regulation of mobile money in SADC to promote trade and financial inclusion. Therefore, this has created a legal conundrum that possibly slows down the adoption and safe use of mobile money to promote financial inclusion and lawful trade for the poor, unbanked and financially underserved people in SADC and the AfCFTA. In this regard, regulatory authorities in SADC and AfCFTA should consider adopting regulatory technology (regtech) and supervisory technology (suptech) measures that are technology-driven.

The Institute of International Finance (IIF) defines regtech as the use of new technologies to address regulatory and compliance requirements more effectively and efficiently.[80] Suptech refers to the use of artificial intelligence (AI) and machine learning (ML) by public regulators and supervisors.[81] AI and machine learning refers to a catalogue of computer systems, methods and technologies that display human-like intelligent behaviour, ability to analyse their environment and take appropriate action toward specified outcomes, with a fair degree of autonomy and

---

[75] Wealth et al. (2023), pp. 87–88.

[76] See related comments by Chitimira and Torerai (2023a), pp. 391–392.

[77] Chitimira and Torerai (2023a), p. 386.

[78] Chitimira and Torerai (2023a), p. 386.

[79] See Chitimira and Torerai (2023a), pp. 385–386.

[80] Institute of International Finance (IIF) (2016), pp. 23–24; also see Zeranski et al. (2020), pp. 314–316.

[81] FSB (2017), pp. 3–8; See related comments by Zeranski and Sancak (2020), pp. 317–319.

accuracy.[82] Regtech and Suptech solutions can strengthen compliance and support the monitoring of mobile money operations in accordance with the relevant laws and regulatory mechanisms.[83] Using extant financial regulatory frameworks without adapting them to the complexities of mobile money[84] will not give rise to adequate regulation.

5.2 *Absence of a Coherent Regulatory Model*

Since the advent of mobile money in the SSA region through M-Pesa in Kenya around 2007, there has been no universally agreed licensing and regulatory model for mobile money. There are predominantly two mobile money models, namely, the telco-led model and the bank-led model.[85] In Kenya, the telco-led model has largely been preferred where MNOs such as Safaricom and Airtel Kenya Networks (AKN) lead in running mobile money services.[86] However, there was a shift in 2022 when the GSMA reported that AKN decided to split its mobile money business into a distinct entity that the Central Bank of Kenya (CBK) regulates separately.[87] This move is historic in that Kenya's parliament was involved in driving this separation of AKN's network service and mobile money business entities. Once the viability of this move is clear, other jurisdictions with the telco-led model may follow suit.

SADC countries such as Botswana, South Africa, Zambia and Zimbabwe utilises the telco-led mobile money model.[88] Nonetheless, there are no clear regulatory guidelines for mobile money operations and the promotion of trade and financial inclusion in the SADC region and the AfCFTA. This contrasts with the situation in Ethiopia and Nigeria where MNOs and other non-bank service providers are required to set up separate legal entities in order to obtain mobile money licenses.[89] According to the GSMA, the newly introduced regulatory framework in Uganda changed MTN and Airtel's telco-led to bank-led models.[90] Meanwhile, in the Central African Economic and Monetary Community (CEMAC) region, payment services such as mobile money are provided by payment institutions licensed by the Bank of Central African States (BEAC).[91] In light of this, the SSA region does not speak in one voice on the best mobile money model to follow. The lack of best practices

[82] Biallas and O'Neill (2020), p. 1.

[83] FSB (2017), pp. 3–8; see also the IMF Bali Fintech Agenda.

[84] FSB (2017), p. 19.

[85] Gibson et al. (2017), pp. 26–45; See related comments by Chitimira and Torerai (2023b), p. 244.

[86] GSMA (2023), pp. 40–41.

[87] See GSMA (2023), p. 41.

[88] See related comments by Chitimira and Torerai (2023b), p. 244.

[89] GSMA (2023), p. 41.

[90] See GSMA (2023), p. 41.

[91] GSMA (2023), p. 41.

leads to policy variations on the regulation of mobile money and this potentially impedes the uptake and use of this fintech product by more people in Africa. Given that the SSA region leads in the usage of mobile money services, policy makers can leverage this to develop standards that the rest of the world can follow.

5.3 Fintech-phobia

Fintech-phobia connotes the fear directed at fintech products and services. Although mobile money adoption stands at almost 50% of the population in most African countries,[92] there are still some pockets of resistance towards full adoption and use of mobile money in SADC. The GSMA records that Ethiopia and Nigeria registered considerable growth in the use of mobile money and other fintech products in 2022.[93] Ethiopia and Nigeria have recently managed to overcome fintech-phobia and introduced regulations licensing the operation of mobile money.[94] However, the use of mobile money remains relatively low in SADC. For instance, mobile money is considerably low in South Africa although the MTN's MoMo service was launched in 2020.[95] However, stakeholders such as banks, other traditional financial institutions and governments have not fully embraced the use of mobile money to conclude financial transactions and/or trade in SADC and AfCFTA. Those inclined to the traditional banking model remonstrate that mobile money operations are given a free pass in terms of regulation while banks and other traditional financial institutions are saddled with over-regulation.[96] In this regard, there is a failure to realise that mobile money and related fintech products require specific, new and adequate regulatory mechanisms tailormade for them.

Moreover, mobile money services are sometimes perceived to be upsetting power dynamics in the financial services sector and this may be the reason why there is fintech-phobia in SADC. The power and control of mobile money services resides in the hands of fintech companies or MNOs. These are basically considered outliers in financial services circles and many governments who have exerted their control on banks and other traditional financial institutions.[97] Some of the MNOs could be stoking the fintech-phobia flames by shunning interoperability overtures where they refuse to share their platforms with other stakeholders in the financial services sector.[98] There could be a sense of loss to those who have used their political muscles

---

[92] GSMA (2020).

[93] GSMA (2023), pp. 20–22.

[94] GSMA (2023), p. 21.

[95] GSMA (2023), p. 21.

[96] See related comments by Mashiri et al. (2017), p. 97.

[97] See comments by Malady et al. (2018), p. 4.

[98] See related comments by Mawejje and Lakuma (2017), p. 7. In Zimbabwe, Ecocash spurned attempts by banks to share its platform owing to the absence of sufficient regulatory measures.

to exert control and influence on traditional financial services such as banks. This breeds fintech-phobia and retards the pace at which mobile money could have been adopted in SADC. To overcome this challenge, there should be adequate interoperability guidelines that enable MNOs to share their platforms without ceding power to their competitors. The Bali Fintech Agenda provides that policy makers should address, *inter alia*, the risks of market concentration and foster standardisation, interoperability, and fair and transparent access to key infrastructure.[99] This should be carefully done in order to allay fears that interoperability may be abused by the relevant authorities to force MNOs to accommodate banks and other traditional financial institutions on their platforms.

5.4 *'Cash is King' Mentality*

Despite the general drift towards digital payments and a cashless society that mobile money is primed for, there is a deep-seated perception that 'cash is king' in the SADC region.[100] Put differently, many people still prefer to use cash than mobile money. This perception inhibits the adoption and use of mobile money services and digital financial inclusion in SADC. Many economies in the SADC are still cash-based. This owes to the fact that a bigger percentage of the population is informally employed in the informal sector. For example, in Zimbabwe, there is barely formal employment and there are more P2P transactions done in hard cash as opposed to B2P, B2B and G2P transactions. On the other hand, South Africa has a thriving informal sector that is cash-based and it is also a leading SADC country in terms of formal financial services.

However, there is a trend among the banked population in South Africa to shun cash and opt for tap-and-go and other forms of digital transactions.[101] As a result, there has been a marked decline in the use of cash as consumers either swipe their credit or bank cards or transact online in South Africa.[102] While it is noteworthy that financial consumers in South Africa are turning towards digital transactions, these are mainly bank-driven as opposed to mobile money services. Therefore, the dependence on cash, especially among the poor, low-income earners, the unbanked and financially underserved people is still very high. In this regard, the reliance on cash impedes the adoption and use of mobile money services by the poor, low-income earners and the unbanked persons across the SADC region and in the AfCFTA. It is submitted that mobile money service providers should do more to educate people on the benefits of mobile money wallet/account. Additionally, governments in SADC

[99] IMF (2018).

[100] See related comments by Chitimira and Ncube (2020), pp. 337–351; Nyanhete (2017), p. 257; and Mugarura (2019), p. 312.

[101] Kruger (2023).

[102] Kruger (2023).

should also start preparing people for the impending time when fiat currency or cash will no longer be used. It is crucial to educate people on the dangers that come with cash such as theft, robbery and huge temptations to squander the money.[103]

5.5 *Market Disruption Factors*

There are perceived risks associated with mobile money and these breed scepticism, suspicion and outright distrust in this fintech product. It is submitted that an innovative fintech product such as mobile money is considered disruptive owing to it challenging well-established financial services providers and the general management of finances.[104] Moreover, financial regulators should adequately respond to the opportunities and risks of fintech products and embrace regtech and suptech mechanisms in order to deal with unforeseen risks that come with these products.[105]

Mobile money poses the biggest competition and threat to the existence of banks in SADC. Banks have been in operation for a very long time but they have failed to reach some customers that are now being serviced by mobile money in SADC and AfCFTA. In light of this, mobile money has somewhat disrupted dominant players such as banks. This has affected the growth and use of mobile money services in SADC. Some of the banks have gone into overdrive, launching digital banking platforms and other services that allow customers and non-customers to process money transactions using their platforms.[106] A good example is the real-time financial services offered by the major banks in South Africa. The First National Bank (FNB), Standard Bank, and the Amalgamated Banks of South Africa (Absa), to name but a few, have 'e-wallet', 'instant money', and 'cash send' facilities, respectively. These services allow a bank account holder to send money to the mobile phone of any other person in South Africa. The recipient may not necessarily have a bank account. An SMS confirming the transaction and the details to use in cashing out the money is sent to the recipient's mobile phone. Cashing out can be done at an automated teller machine (ATM) of the sender's bank or at the till point at participating supermarkets or retail stores in South Africa. These services make it difficult for mobile money to gain traction in South Africa. This could explain why there has been limited use of mobile money in South Africa unlike other countries in the SADC region. The competition with banks retards the adoption and use of mobile money in some SADC countries.

[103] Kruger (2023).

[104] De Koker et al. (2019), p. 91.

[105] De Koker et al. (2019), p. 91.

[106] See related comments by Alam et al. (2021), pp. 1146–1147.

5.6 Perceived Mobile Money Risks

Perceived risks affecting mobile money services include money laundering, terrorism financing, Internet scams and fraud.[107] In part, the risks owe to the rapidity and pseudonymous nature of transactions which make it difficult for regulatory authorities and law enforcement agencies to apprehend criminals.[108] In early 2023, Kenyan authorities detected eight suspects who were running a major mobile money fraud scheme.[109] This mobile money fraud scheme defrauded mobile money users of money over 500 million shillings. Its *modus operandi* involved the use of about 123,000 mobile SIM cards that were disguised as if they belonged to M-Pesa agents.[110] Up to a certain point, the SIM cards would be used to divert money from mobile money users' wallets to accounts of fraudsters before they were discarded.[111]

In SADC, South Africa experienced breaches of its counter-terrorist financing (CTF) measures after about R400 million was reported to have been illegally channeled out of the country between 2020 and 2021 through mobile money platforms.[112] It is further alleged that the money was used to fund several suspected terrorist attacks that killed 11 people and left 39 others wounded in Uganda in 2021.[113] The transactions are said to have been done using many SIM cards registered in different names. The said breaches could also have contributed to the grey-listing of South Africa by the Financial Action Task Force (FATF). This also affected the use of mobile money by South African participants to trade in the AfCFTA.

Zimbabwe has also had its fair share of mobile money-induced risks. In 2020, the Reserve Bank of Zimbabwe (RBZ) banned some mobile money aspects on the grounds that mobile money agents had become conduits of illegal transactions bordering on money laundering and the creation of phantom or fictitious money.[114] Many people had their money frozen after the RBZ froze the accounts of mobile money agents during criminal investigations. As a result, users and potential users became skeptical about using mobile money platforms in Zimbabwe and AfCFTA. These and many other factors pose challenges to mobile money operations and impede the digital financial inclusion of many people in the SADC region.

---

[107] Winn and De Koker (2013), p. 156.

[108] Chitimira and Torerai (2023a), p. 392.

[109] Matinde (2023).

[110] Matinde (2023).

[111] Matinde (2023).

[112] Hyman et al. (2023).

[113] Hyman et al. (2023).

[114] Reserve Bank of Zimbabwe (RBZ) '2020'; also see Chitimira and Torerai (2023c), pp. 253–254.

5.7 Digital Illiteracy

Another challenge affecting the use of mobile money is the high levels of digital illiteracy among the poor in SADC.[115] Although many people possess mobile phones, some cannot use the gadgets for any other functions other than just receiving calls. This is particularly true for most poor people who live in rural areas and informal settlements across the SADC region. Such people usually have low-level education or are illiterate.[116] Such individuals cannot return missed calls, read or let alone write SMSes or any other text that comes to their mobile phones. It is nearly impossible for illiterate people to operate digital devices in order to benefit from many other services available to them such as mobile money. Perhaps this explains why there is a huge deficit between the number of mobile phones in a particular jurisdiction and the number of mobile money accounts.

Moreover, without adequate digital literacy, consumers can contribute to the susceptibility of mobile money to money laundering, terrorism financing and fraud.[117] Unscrupulous people can prey on the personal data of illiterate persons for nefarious acts of criminality.[118] Without sufficient digital literacy, it is dangerous for people to participate on digital platforms. For as long as digital illiteracy is high, many people remain financially excluded in SADC. Therefore, there is a need to improve literacy levels among the poor and marginalised so that more people can read and write in SADC and AfCFTA.

5.8 Consumer Protection Concerns

Consumer protection has become precarious and a point of concern during this technological and digital era. Financial products such as loans, credit and insurance are now easily available heightening the risk of over-indebtedness among the poor in SADC.[119] Fintech products such as mobile money have opened up the sluice gates that used to limit and filter access to some of the financial services to the extent that unregulated access to finance is creating new challenges. In addition, there is data harvesting of consumers' personal information in what has become a scramble for data control by big corporates.[120] Mobile money users are exposed to unsolicited

115 Hamadziripi and Munedzi (2023), pp. 117–120.

116 See related comments by Makanyeza et al. (2023), pp. 165–177.

117 See related comments by Chitimira and Torerai (2022), pp. 373–375.

118 Chitimira and Torerai (2022), pp. 378–379.

119 See related comments by Makanyeza et al. (2023), pp. 165–177; Chitimira and Torerai (2022), pp. 373–375.

120 Da Vega et al. (2019), pp. 399–400.

marketing emails, calls, SMS, invasion of their privacy, fraudulent schemes and identity theft owing to poor consumer protection measures in some of the digital platforms.[121]

There have been numerous data breaches too, where computer servers of corporates are hacked leading to situations where consumers' personal data end up in wrong hands.[122] It appears that mobile money and other fintech products have outpaced traditional consumer protection measures and regulatory mechanisms to the extent that there is a sense of despair from both regulatory authorities and consumers. These are some of the pitfalls that have come with digital financial services and they deter a considerable number of people from utilising fintech products such as mobile money to trade in the SADC region and AfCFTA. Therefore, the threats of irresponsible product offering, unsolicited marketing, cybercrime and data breaches without due and speedy recourse are some of the factors that dissuade people from mobile money-driven digital financial inclusion in SADC and AfCFTA.

6 Conclusion

The AfCFTA objective of a single market for goods and services should be enhanced through digital financial inclusion, especially of the poor, low-income earners and unbanked persons. The use of mobile money has played a crucial role in promoting financial inclusion in SADC and AfCFTA. However, the full adoption and use of mobile money faces has not been very successful in facilitating effective trade in SADC and AfCFTA. Although the chapter focused on the SADC region, arguments advanced herein can be transposed to other regions in Africa. Notably, although banks, micro-financial institutions and other deposit-taking institutions have been around for over a century in the SADC region, they are out of reach for the poor, low-income earners and unbanked persons. Most of these financial institutions are concentrated in towns and cities which makes it difficult for the people who reside in rural areas and informal settlements to access them. In addition, formal financial services are very expensive for the poor and low-income earners giving rise to their financial exclusion. Consequently, banks and other financial institutions have not established branches outside metropolitan areas across the SADC since they consider it not profitable to do so. As a result, the SADC and other African regions have poor financial inclusion of the poor and low-income earners which also negatively affects the promotion of effective trade in the AfCFTA.

---

[121] See related comments by the Organisation for Economic Cooperation and Development (OECD) (2020), p. 5.

[122] Chitimira and Torerai (2022), pp. 378–379.

Mobile money provides convenient, affordable and useful financial services to the poor, unbanked, low-income earners and economically marginalised people in SADC and other developing regions of Africa. This perhaps explains why the SSA region tops the charts on the adoption and use of mobile money services. Nonetheless, there are still several challenges that curtail the full adoption and use of mobile money in SADC and AfCFTA. These barriers include poor regulatory frameworks, perceived risks, fintech-phobia, extensive reliance on cash, poor consumer protection and inadequate knowledge in the use of mobile money services.

In this regard, it is recommended that there should be adequate development of regtech and suptech solutions to regulate mobile money in SADC. The governments in SADC should make use of regulatory sandboxes where mobile money operations are monitored and regulated in a specific environment. This enables mobile money services to operate within the relevant laws and regulations in order to reduce systemic risks in SADC and AfCFTA.

Moreover, the governments in SADC should consider deploying AI and machine learning techniques to supervise mobile money activities. Fintech products, including mobile money require a systematic approach to sufficiently supervise and regulate them. In this regard, AI and machine learning techniques should be used to monitor mobile money transactions to detect potential criminal activities. The speed and pseudonymous nature of mobile money transactions requires AI to be coded in a way that detects suspicious transactions in SADC and AfCFTA. Such a move can enhance the chances of combating money laundering, terrorism financing and related crimes involving mobile money transactions.

SADC governments should provide adequate mobile money awareness programmes to promote financial inclusion and trade activities in SADC and AfCFTA. The duty to educate people on the use and benefits of mobile money has largely been left to mobile money agents. Therefore, more needs to be done to improve consumer education on mobile money and enhance digital financial inclusion and trade in the SADC and AfCFTA, especially for the poor and low-income earners.

SADC countries should consider shifting towards digital forms of money. This follows the fact that the fourth industrial revolution (4IR) is in full swing and digital technology appears to be taking over every aspect of human life, including finance.[123] Unlike cash, digital money offers many advantages to people. For instance, keeping one's money in the phone is safer compared to cash that can attract thieves and robbers. In countries where cash heists and counterfeiting are a challenge such as South Africa, digital money can significantly combat financial crimes. Moreover, the use digital money and mobile could enhance trade and digital financial inclusion for the poor and low-income earner in SADC and AfCFTA.

---

[123] See Mhlanga (2020), pp. 1–2.

References

Alam MM, Awawdeh AE, Muhamad AIB (2021) Using E-wallet for business process development: challenges and prospects in Malaysia. Bus Process Manag J 27(4):1142–1162

Apeti AE, Edoh ED (2023) Tax revenue and mobile money in developing countries. J Dev Econ 161:1–24

African Union (AU) Agenda 2063: The Africa We Want (AU Addis Ababa 2015), accessed on 30 June 2021, https://au.int/sites/default/files/documents/36204agenda2063_popular_version_en.pdf

African Union (AU) The African Continental Free Trade Area Agreement (AU Addis Ababa 2018), accessed on 15 August 2023, https://au.int/sites/default/files/treaties/36437-treaty-consolidated_text_on_cfta_-_en.pdf

Baganzi R, Lau AK (2017) Examining trust and risk in mobile money acceptance in Uganda. Sustainability 9(12):1–22

Biallas M, O'Neill F (2020) Artificial intelligence innovation in financial services. International Financial Corporation, World Bank Group

Bille FS, Buri S, Crenn TA (2018) Digital access: the future of financial inclusion in Africa. World Bank Group, Washington DC

Buckley R, Greenacre J, Malady L (2015) The regulation of mobile money in Malawi. Wash Univ Global Stud Law Rev 14(3):435–498

Buku MW, Meredith MW (2013) Safaricom and M-Pesa in Kenya: financial inclusion and financial integrity. Wash J Law Technol Arts 8(3):375–400

Chipa N, Mwanza BG (2021) Factors impeding mobile money expansion in Zambia. Int J Eng Manag Res 11(1):178–186

Chitimira H, Ncube M (2020) Legislative and other selected challenges affecting financial inclusion of the poor and low-income earners in South Africa. J Afr Law:337–355

Chitimira H, Ncube M (2023) The Prospects and Challenges for Mobile Regulation and the Promotion of Financial Inclusion in Zimbabwe (Springer, Cham) pp 125–140

Chitimira H, Torerai E (2021) The nexus between mobile money regulation, innovative technology and the promotion of financial inclusion in Zimbabwe. Potchefstroom Electron Law J 24(1):1–33

Chitimira H, Torerai E (2022) The role of financial education in the promotion of protection for poor consumers of digital financial services in Zimbabwe. Speculum Juris 36:371–386

Chitimira H, Torerai E (2023a) A regulatory analysis of digital financial services and the adoption of Central Bank Digital Currencies in Zimbabwe and South Africa. Tribune Juridica 13(3):384–407

Chitimira H, Torerai E (2023b) A regulatory analysis of mobile money to promote financial inclusion for the poor in Zimbabwe during the COVID-19 pandemic. In: Chitimira HT, Warikandwa TV (eds) Promoting and prioritising financial inclusion in Southern Africa: a contemporary law and economics perspective. Juta, Claremont, pp 213–244

Chitimira H, Torerai E (2023c) Policy implications and mobile money regulatory approaches to promote financial inclusion of the poor in Zimbabwe after the COVID-19 pandemic. De Jure Law J 56(1):241–258

Clifford K (2020) The causes and consequences of mobile money taxation an examination of mobile money transaction taxes in Sub-Saharan Africa. GSMA June, Bill & Melinda Gates Foundation, pp 1–52

Chitimira H, Torerai E (2023) A Regulatory Analysis of Digital financial Services and the Adoption of Central Bank Digital Currencies in Zimbabwe and South Africa. Tribune Juridica 384-407

De Koker L (2013) The 2012 Revised FATF recommendations: assessing and mitigating mobile money integrity risks within the new standards framework. Wash J Law Technol Arts 8(3):165–196

De Koker L, Morris N, Jaffer S (2019) Regulating financial services in an era of technological disruption. Law Context: Socio-Legal J 36(2):90–112
Da Veiga A, Vorster R, Li F, Clarke N, Furnell SM (2019) Comparing the protection and use of online personal information in South Africa and the United Kingdom in line with data protection requirements. Information and Computer Security 399–422
Financial Stability Board (FSB) (2017) Financial stability implications from FinTech: supervisory and regulatory issues that merit authorities' attention. Financial Stability Board, Basel
Fonte E (2017) US regulatory overview of mobile wallets and mobile payments. Wake Forest J Bus Intellect Prop Law 17(4):549–608
FSB (2017) The use of supervisory and regulatory technology by authorities and regulated institutions: market development and financial stability implications. Financial Stability Board Basel, Basel
Gibson E, Lupo-Pasini F, Buckley R (2017) Regulating digital financial services agents in developing countries to promote financial inclusion. Univ New South Wales Law Res Ser 27:1–19 (initially published in (2015) in the Singapore Journal of Legal Studies, pp 26–45)
Goncalves DER (2013) Financial inclusion in Peru: lessons from Kenya's regulatory approach to E-Money. Univ Miami Int Comp Law Rev 21(1):31–51
Global System for Mobile Communications Association (GSMA) The Causes and Consequences of Mobile Money Taxation. An Examinination of Mobile Money Taxation in Sub-Saharan Africa (GSMA London 2020). https://www.gsma.com/mobilefordevelopment/resources/the-causes-and-consequences-of-mobilemoney-taxation-an-examination-of-mobile-money-transaction-taxes-in-sub-saharan-africa/
Global System for Mobile Communications Association (GSMA) The State of the Industry Report on Mobile Money 2023 (GSMA London 2023). https://www.gsma.com/sotir/#download
Hamadziripi F, Munedzi S (2023) An overview analysis of selected digital financial services and the promotion of financial inclusion in Zimbabwe. In: Chitimira HT, Warikandwa TV (eds) Promoting and prioritising financial inclusion in Southern Africa: a contemporary law and economics perspective. Juta, Claremont, pp 107–128
Hyman A, Hosken G, Makhetha T (2023) How millions in terror funding flowed through SA. The Sunday Times. https://news.knowledia.com/ZA/en/articles/how-millions-in-terror-funding-flowed-throughsa1b8fd7478e2544e797fc27958668851fbd5778d47
Institute of International Finance (IIF) (2016) Regtech in financial services: solutions for compliance and reporting. Institute of International Finance, Washington DC
International Monetary Fund (IMF) The Bali Fintech Agenda: A Blueprint for Successfully Harnessing Fintech's Opportunities (IMF Washington DC 2018). https://www.imf.org/en/News/Articles/2018/10/11/pr18388-the-bali-fintech-agenda
Kabala E, Mapoma R, Nalutongwe C, Muyani D, Lungu J (2021) An ethnological analysis of the influence of mobile money on financial inclusion: the case of Urban Zambia. Zambia Soc Sci J 7(1):53–76
Kruger A (2023) Cash is King No More: The Trend towards Lighter Pockets. Banks Confirm a Steady March towards a Cashless Society as More Customers Adopt Digital Payment Methods. https://www.moneyweb.co.za/news/companies-and-deals/people-want-less-cash-in-their-hands/
Lumsden E (2018) The future is mobile: financial inclusion and technological innovation in the emerging world. Stanford J Law Bus Finance 23(1):1–44
López González J, Ferencz J (2018) Digital Trade and Market Openness, OECD Trade Policy Papers, No. 217 (Paris, OECD Publishing 2018)
Makanyeza C, Svotwa TD, Wealth E (2023) Consumer protection and financial literacy: insights from Botswana, Namibia, South Africa and Zimbabwe. In: Chitimira HT, Warikandwa TV (eds) Promoting and prioritising financial inclusion in Southern Africa: a contemporary law and economics perspective. Juta, Claremont, pp 153–183
Malady L, Buckley RP, Didenko A, Tsang CY (2018) A regulatory diagnostic toolkit for digital financial services in emerging markets. University of New South Wales Research Series, pp 1–30

Malladi CM, Soni RK, Srinivasan S (2021) Digital financial inclusion: next frontiers - challenges and opportunities. CSI Trans ICT 9:127–134
Mashiri E, Dzingirai C, Nyamwanza L (2017) Micro-determinants of customer level interoperability: a feasibility study between traditional banks and mobile network operators in Zimbabwe. J Appl Finance Bank 7(4):93–113
Mawejje J, Lakuma PCE (2017) Macroeconomic effects of mobile money in Uganda. Economic Policy Research Centre, pp 1–27
Mhlanga D (2020) Industry 4.0 in Finance: the impact of Artificial Intelligence (AI) on digital financial inclusion. Int J Financ Stud 8(3):1–14
Mhlanga D, Dunga SH, Moloi T (2020) Financial inclusion and poverty alleviation among smallholder farmers in Zimbabwe. Eurasian J Econ Finance 8(3):168–182
Mpofu FY (2022) Industry 4.0 in financial services: mobile money taxes, revenue mobilisation, financial inclusion and the realisation of Sustainable Development Goals (SDGs) in Africa. Sustainability 14:1–24
Mugarura N (2019) The use of mobile phones in changing the banking regulatory landscape in Africa. Afr J Int Comp Law 14(14):308–331
Matinde V (2023) Kenyan Authorities Uncover Major Mobile Money Fraud. ICT and Governance. https://itweb.africa/content/8OKdWMDXnxYMbznQ
Nyagilo VO, Sakwa MM, Namusonge GS (2017) Efficiency of mobile led financial services and its effect on financial inclusion in Kenya. Int J Bus Manag Finance 7(3):554–576
Nyanhete A (2017) The role of international mobile remittances in promoting financial inclusion and development. Eur J Sustain Dev 6(2):256–266
Osabutey ELC, Jackson T (2024) Mobile money and financial inclusion in Africa: emerging themes, challenges and policy implications. Technol Forecasting Soc Change 202:1–13
Organisation for Economic Cooperation and Development (OECD) 2020 Personal Data Use in Financial Services and the Role of Financial Education: A Consumer-Centric Analysis. http://www.oecd.org/daf/fin/financial-education/Personal-Data-Use-in-Financial-Services-and-the-Role-of- Financial-Education.pdf
Robb G, Vilakazi T (2016) Mobile payments markets in Kenya, Tanzania and Zimbabwe: a comparative study of competitive dynamics and outcomes. Afr J Inf Commun 17:9–37
Robb G, Tausha I, Vilakazi T (2017) Competition and regulation in Zimbabwe's emerging mobile payments markets. In: Klaaren J, Roberts A, Vilakazi T (eds) Competition law and economic regulation in Southern Africa CCRED Working Paper Series, pp 215–233
Reserve Bank of Zimbabwe (RBZ) Monetary Policy Statement 2020. 2020. https://www.rbz.co.zw/documents/mps/Monetary-Policy-Statement-17-February-2020.pdf
Shrier D, Canal G, Pentland A (2016) Mobile money and payments. Massachusetts Institute of Technology, pp 1–26
Soutter L, Ferguson K, Neubert M (2019) Digital payments: impact factors and mass adoption in Sub-Sahara Africa. Technol Innov Manag Rev 9(7):41–55
The World Bank. The African Continental Free Trade Area. https://www.worldbank.org/en/topic/trade/publication/the-african-continental-free-trade-area
Warikandwa TV (2023a) Digital financial inclusion and Covid-19 in SADC: a comparative socio-legal study of Namibia and South Africa. In: Chitimira HT, Warikandwa TV (eds) Promoting and prioritising financial inclusion in Southern Africa: a contemporary law and economics perspective. Juta, Claremont, pp 403–441
Warikandwa TV (2023b) Financial inclusion, Intra-African Trade and the AfCFTA: a law and economics perspective. In: Chitimira H, Warikandwa TV (eds) Financial inclusion and digital transformation regulatory practices in selected SADC countries: South Africa, Namibia, Botswana and Zimbabwe. Springer, Switzerland, pp 207–228

Wealth E, Makanyeza C, Svotwa TD (2023) Challenges and prospects of mobile money in promoting financial inclusion in Botswana, Namibia, South Africa and Zimbabwe. In: Chitimira HT, Warikandwa TV (eds) Promoting and prioritising financial inclusion in Southern Africa: a contemporary law and economics perspective. Juta, Claremont, pp 77–105

Winn JK (2013) Governance of global mobile money networks: the role of technical standards. Wash J Law Technol Arts 8(3):197–244

Winn JK, De Koker L (2013) Introduction to mobile money in developing countries: financial inclusion and integrity conference special issue. Wash J Law Technol Arts 8(3):155–163

Yawe BL, Ddumba-Ssentamu J, Nnyanzi JB, Mukisa I (2022) Role of mobile money and digital payments in financial inclusion for sustainable development goals in Africa. In: Mori M (ed) Globalization and sustainability: recent advances, new perspectives and emerging issues. IntechOpen, pp 1–12

Zeranski S, Sancak IE (2020) Digitalisation of financial supervision with Supervisory Technology (SupTech). J Int Bank Law Regul 8:309–329

Can AfCFTA Balance and Reconcile the Impossible Trinity

Promoting Trade Liberalisation, Avoiding Tax Base Erosion and Curtailing Harmful Tax Practices in Africa?

Pie Habimana

Abstract Today, the AfCFTA is at the centre of interest among politicians, economists, lawyers, etc., who discuss its plausible outcomes. A successful AfCFTA will greatly change the overall socio-economic situation in Africa through the liberalisation of internal trade. Be that as it may, the AfCFTA can also be viewed from other angles, such as its potential impact on harmful tax competition in Africa. Unlike the European Union, whose success in the single market is due to several factors, including effective regulation of harmful tax competition, this area is still uncharted territory for Africa. There is, therefore, a high risk that a successful AfCFTA will encourage companies to locate in countries with favourable taxation, as businesses will be able to trade across the African continent. As a result, a successful AfCFTA in terms of trade liberalisation risks, on the other hand, to exacerbate harmful tax practices that erode the sovereigns' tax bases. This chapter shows that a successful AfCFTA carries the risk that multinational companies will shift their profits and relocate in order to minimise the tax payable. To prevent this, this chapter proposes the adoption of an Additional Protocol based on Article 8(3) of the AfCFTA Agreement.

1 Introduction

The African Continental Free Trade Area (AfCFTA) is a hot topic in various forums today. Politicians, economists, lawyers, etc. are all interested in its possible outcomes, the success of which will transform the overall socio-economic situation in Africa. The economic objectives of the AfCFTA have been well identified, but

P. Habimana (✉)
School of Law, University of Rwanda, Kigali, Rwanda
e-mail: p.habimana1@ur.ac.rw

T. V. Warikandwa et al. (eds.), *Law and Policy of the African Continental Free Trade Area (AfCFTA)*, European Yearbook of International Economic Law,
https://doi.org/10.1007/978-3-032-01122-0_5

effective law and dispute settlement mechanisms remain essential to achieve such objectives. Not only that, but research shows that free trade, if not properly managed, risks exacerbating regional inequalities and amplifying uneven development.[1] Indeed, well-designed, and well-implemented laws are essential to the future success of the AfCFTA.

While exploring the momentum of active tax competition regulation, there is ample room to examine the potential impact of the AfCFTA on harmful tax competition in Africa. Realistically, this area is still uncharted territory in all eight regional integrations recognised by the African Union,[2] as the regulation of harmful tax competition has received so far very little attention.

This is in contrast to other comparable communities such as the European Union (EU), whose success in the single market can be attributed to several factors, including effective regulation of harmful tax competition through the EU Code of Conduct on Business Taxation and the Code of Conduct Group reports. EU also relies on the projects of the Organisation for Economic Cooperation and Development (OECD) in relation to harmful tax competition. Examples include the OECD's Report of 1998 on harmful tax competition, the OECD's project on base erosion and profit shifting (BEPS) of 2013, and the OECD's Global Anti-Base Erosion (GloBE) project of 2019, to name a few.

In the absence of a comparable legal regime, a number of questions arise with regard to the plausible success of the AfCFTA: What will a successful AfCFTA look like? What impact will the AfCFTA have on the business location? How can free riders be avoided without jeopardising the objectives of the AfCFTA? These and other related questions are the focus of this chapter. These questions assume that a successful AfCFTA, as in a common market, will encourage the location of businesses in a jurisdiction with favourable taxation, as businesses will be able to trade across the African continent, hence, creating a leeway for harmful tax competition.

The agreement establishing the AfCFTA was signed on 21 March 2018 to come into force on 30 May 2019, following the deposit of instruments of ratification by 24 member states in accordance with Art 23 of the Agreement which makes entry into force conditional on the deposit of the twenty-second (22nd) instrument of ratification.[3] The AfCFTA was launched on 07 July 2019 during the 12th Extraordinary Session of the African Union (AU) Assembly of Heads of State and Government in Niamey, Niger, while trading under the AfCFTA began on 01 January 2021. As of August 2023, the AfCFTA counts 54 African Union (AU) member states that have signed the Agreement and 46 state parties.[4]

---

[1] Africa Policy Research Institute (2023), p. 28, and Patnaik (2025), pp. 14–25.

[2] These are the Arab Maghreb Union (UMA), the East African Community (EAC), the Economic Community of West African States (ECOWAS), the Southern African Development Community (SADC), the Common Market for Eastern and Southern Africa (COMESA), the Community of Sahel-Saharan States (CEN-SAD), the Economic Community of Central African States (ECCAS), and the Intergovernmental Authority on Development (IGAD).

[3] AfCFTA Agreement, arts 23(1) and (2).

[4] About AfCFTA, available at *https://au-afcfta.org*, accessed on 29 August 2023.

The research in this chapter used a qualitative methodology, largely based on the doctrinal approach. The use of the doctrinal approach is based on the recognition that it is considered the most commonly used research method in legal research.[5] Thus, the doctrinal approach used here consisted of a comprehensive review, examination and analysis of the literature relevant to the topic of this chapter. In this way, both primary and secondary materials were consulted. Primary materials consulted include the Agreement establishing the AfCFTA, the EU Code of Conduct on Business Taxation, etc. Secondary materials consulted include scholarly publications, reports, as well as other reliable available documented information. The data were collected through desk research.

This chapter is divided into six sections, including the introduction and conclusion. The first section, the current one, has an introductory function. The second section deals with the phenomenon of harmful tax competition. This section briefly discusses how this phenomenon began as a problem between developed countries, justifying active engagement by the OECD and the EU. The third section examines how the problem of harmful tax competition as a war between titans has been exported to non-titans, namely developing countries. Here the focus is on African countries to link to the theme of this chapter. In the fourth section, the focus switches to the AfCFTA to discuss its genesis and current status. This paves the way to relate the AfCFTA to harmful tax competition in the fifth section, which argues that a successful AfCFTA risks to fuel harmful tax competition. The discussion is done in three interconnected subsections: one on the plausible effects that a successful AfCFTA may have on business location, two on the escalation of business location into harmful tax competition, and three on the possible mitigations to that risk. The sixth section draws a conclusion.

2 Harmful Tax Competition: The War of the Titans

The fight against tax competition began as a war between developed countries. It began three decades ago and continues to this day, with no idea when it will end. In this context, the battles against harmful tax competition are herein labeled as the war of the titans in a figurative sense. Developed countries were concerned that their peers could unfairly erode their tax base by using sophisticated tax schemes that lead multinational companies to pay taxes in a country other than the one where the economic activities take place.

The problem of harmful tax competition began in the 1980s. At that time, the OECD published a report on measures to prevent the abuse of tax havens.[6] Although this report touched on the issue of tax havens, it was not linked to the question of harmful tax competition, which was only taken up in concrete measures on harmful

[5] Hutchinson (2015), p. 131.

[6] Morriss and Moberg (2012), p. 33; Webb (2004), p. 798.

tax competition in the late 1990s. It was only when the OECD produced a report on harmful tax competition in 1998 and the EU adopted a Code of Conduct on Business Taxation in 1997 that the issue of harmful tax competition became known.

Starting with the OECD Report, the project to study harmful tax competition started in May 1996 and was completed in January 1998 while the OECD Council endorsed it in April 1998.[7] The main objective of the project was to develop a better global understanding of harmful tax practices.[8] There was concern about the emergence of harmful tax competition between countries that use tax schemes to attract financial and mobile activities. This could lead to distortion of trade and investment and erosion of national tax bases; thus posing a threat to tax revenues, tax sovereignty, and tax fairness.[9] In this regard, the goal of the project was:

> To develop a better understanding of how tax havens and harmful preferential tax regimes affect the location of financial and other service activities, erode the tax base of other countries, distort trade and investment patterns, and undermine the fairness, neutrality, and broad social acceptance of tax systems in general.[10]

Given the high risk associated with harmful tax competition and, in particular, the erosion of countries' tax bases, the rationale for the project was motivated as follows:

> Governments cannot stand idly by while their tax bases are eroded by the actions of countries that provide opportunities for taxpayers to exploit tax havens and preferential regimes to reduce the tax they would otherwise have to pay.[11]

At the conclusion of the project, the OECD published a report in 1998. According to this report, harmful tax competition causes problems that are summarised in six groups:

> (1) distorting financial and, indirectly, real investment flows; (2) undermining the integrity and fairness of tax structures; (3) discouraging compliance by all taxpayers; (4) altering the desired level and composition of taxes and public expenditure; (5) undesirably shifting the tax burden to less mobile tax bases such as labour, property, and consumption; and (6) increasing administrative costs and compliance burdens for tax authorities and taxpayers.[12]

Furthermore, the 1998 OECD report divides harmful tax competition into two components, namely tax havens and harmful preferential tax regimes. On the one hand, according to this report, tax havens are characterised by the following four factors:

> (a) no or only nominal taxes either in general or in special circumstances for non-residents, (b) laws and/or administrative rules and/or practices that prevent the effective exchange of relevant information with other governments about taxpayers benefiting from the low or no

[7] Littlewood (2004), p. 417.

[8] Salinas (2003), p. 539.

[9] Communiqué issued by G7 Heads of State at their 1996 Lyon Summit, in OECD (1998), p. 7.

[10] OECD (1998), p. 8.

[11] OECD (1998), p. 37.

[12] OECD (1998), p. 16.

> tax jurisdictions, (c) lack of transparency, and (d) the absence of any requirement for substantial activity.[13]

On the other hand, harmful preferential tax regimes are characterised by factors that fall into two categories. The first category consists of four factors, which the OECD calls 'key factors'. These are:

> (a) low or zero effective tax rate on specified kinds of income such as movable sources of income, (b) ring-fencing from the domestic economy, (c) lack of transparency, and (d) no effective exchange of information with other governments.[14]

The second category consists of eight factors, which the OECD calls other factors. These factors play a supporting role to the key factors, and are:

> (a) an artificial definition of the tax base, (b) non-compliance with international transfer pricing principles, (c) exemption of foreign source income from residence-country taxation, (d) negotiable tax rates or tax bases, (e) the existence of secrecy provisions, (f) access to a wide network of tax treaties, (g) promotion of the system as a tax minimisation tool, and (h) promotion by the regime of purely tax-motivated transactions or arrangements.[15]

Of these characteristics of the two components that constitute harmful tax competition, it is important to note that there are two characteristics that are common to both components of harmful tax competition. These are a lack of transparency and a lack of effective exchange of information. These factors are key not only in determining whether a tax practice is harmful, but also in combating harmful tax practices.[16]

It is also important to note that while both components make up harmful tax competition, tax havens are more dangerous because they affect the entire tax system than harmful preferential tax regimes. Indeed, in a harmful preferential tax regime, it is not the entire system itself that is problematic, but rather it contains one or more problematic regime. In this context, tax havens can be distinguished from harmful preferential tax regimes as follows:

> Tax havens have no interest in preventing the race to the bottom, they actively contribute to eroding the tax base of other countries, and they are unlikely to cooperate in curbing harmful tax competition, whereas countries with harmful preferential regimes may have substantial revenues that are at risk and therefore have an interest in eliminating harmful tax competition in a concerted effort.[17]

Several measures have been proposed to address harmful tax competition, including the establishment of the Global Forum on Harmful Tax Practices. This Forum was established following Recommendation No. 15 of the 1998 OECD Report.[18] The Global Forum was established with the initial mandate to monitor and review juris-

[13] OECD (1998), p. 22.

[14] OECD (1998), pp. 26–30.

[15] OECD (1998), pp. 30–34; Liebman et al. (2016), pp. 102–103.

[16] Seeruthun-Kowalczyk (2011), p. 196; Calich (2011), p. 68; and Repyeuski (2008), p. 149.

[17] OECD (1998), p. 43; Van Raad (2013), pp. 1314–1315; (2019), p. 12; Genschel and Schwarz (2011), p. 174; Arnold and McIntyre (2002), pp. 139 and 141; Nikolakakis (2006), p. 59.

[18] OECD (1998), p. 53.

dictions with preferential tax regimes.[19] In 2009, it was renamed to its current name, Global Forum on Transparency and Exchange of Information for Tax Purposes.[20] Its mandate also changed to insuring the implementation of the international standards of international cooperation in tax matters, namely the standards of transparency and exchange of information.[21] Since its inception, the Forum has so far published several reports on harmful tax practices. Following these reports, political pressure has been exerted on certain countries to eliminate harmful tax practices.

In parallel to the OECD, the Economic and Financial Affairs Council (ECOFIN) of the European Union adopted a Code of Conduct on Business Taxation on 1 December 1997. This Code was adopted as part of a package of measures to combat harmful tax competition. The package consisted of three components: the Code of Conduct for Business Taxation, the measures to eliminate distortions in the taxation of capital income, and the measures to eliminate withholding tax on cross-border interest and royalty payments between companies. The Code of Conduct, which directly addresses harmful tax competition, has three objectives: reducing market distortions, preventing excessive tax revenue losses and making tax structures more employment-friendly.[22] The Code of conduct elaborated on five criteria to determine harmful tax competition, namely:

> (1) whether advantages are granted only to non-residents or in relation to transactions with non-residents; or (2) whether advantages are ring-fenced from the domestic market so that they do not affect the national tax base; or (3) whether advantages are granted without any real economic activity or substantial economic presence; or (4) whether the rules for determining the profits of activities within a multinational group of companies deviate from internationally accepted principles, in particular those agreed within the framework of the OECD; or (5) whether the tax measures lack transparency, including cases where legislation is relaxed at administrative level in a non-transparent way.[23]

The above factors can be summarised as follows: lower level of taxation, ring-fencing, lack of substantial activity, lack of arm's length dealing, and lack of transparency.[24] Thus, according to the EU, a tax measure is harmful if it provides for a significantly lower level of taxation and is ring-fenced, does not respect the arm's length principle, lacks substantial activity or lacks transparency.

With these efforts in the 1990s, however, the case of harmful tax competition was not closed. In 2013, the OECD and the G20 embarked on another project called Base Erosion and Profit Shifting (BEPS). This project was homologous to, but more comprehensive than, the 1998 report on harmful tax competition. The main motive

---

[19] OECD (2017), p. 11.

[20] OECD (2009); Englisch and Yevgenyeva (2013), p. 627; Christians and van Apeldoorn (2018), p. 9.

[21] Boulogne (2019), p. 11; Mello (2012), p. 44; Ault (2019), p. 6.

[22] EU Code of Conduct (1997).

[23] EU Code of Conduct (1997), C 2/3; Seeruthun-Kowalczyk (2011), p. 172.

[24] Terra and Wattel (2008), p. 112.

of BEPS was the need to align the location of taxable profits with the location of economic activity and value creation.[25]

The BEPS report was published on 5 October 2015 with a plan of fifteen actions, namely Action 1 to address the tax challenges of the digital economy; Action 2 to neutralise the effects of hybrid mismatch arrangements; Action 3 to strengthen the rules for controlled foreign corporations (CFCs); Action 4 to limit the erosion of the tax base through interest deductions and other financial payments; Action 5 to combat harmful tax practices more effectively, taking into account transparency and substance; Action 6 to prevent treaty abuse; Action 7 to prevent artificial avoidance of permanent establishment status (PE); Action 8 to align transfer pricing with value creation with regard to intangibles; Action 9 to align transfer pricing outcomes with value creation with regard to risks and capital; Action 10 to align transfer pricing outcomes with value creation with regard to other high-risk transactions; Action 11 to measure and monitoring BEPS; Action 12 to require taxpayers to disclose their aggressive tax planning arrangements; Action 13 to review transfer pricing documentation, i.e. country-by-country reporting; Action 14 on improving the effectiveness of dispute resolution mechanisms; and Action 15 on developing a multilateral instrument.

Action five of the fifteen actions is about combating harmful tax practices more effectively. Its intent was stated as follows:

> To counter harmful tax practices with respect to geographically mobile activities such as financial and other service activities, including the provision of intangibles... that unfairly erode the tax bases of other countries and potentially distort the location of capital and services.[26]

Of these 15 actions, the OECD/G20 have recognised that some need to be taken urgently. This urgency goes hand in hand with viewing harmful tax competition as a global phenomenon, whose necessary fight against also requires global efforts. This led the OECD/G20 to select four actions that are referred to as minimum standards. These are Actions 5, 6, 13, and 14. The OECD then invited all countries, especially those outside the OECD, to join these four minimum standards, creating what the OECD calls the Inclusive Framework (IF). Joining the Inclusive Framework was and still is open to any country that commits to the four minimum standards. This is one aspect of exporting the war of the titans to non-titans as elaborated on in section three of this chapter.

From the above, it is clear that after almost four decades, developed countries cannot celebrate themselves as winners of the war. Having failed to win, the titans realised that they are failing because they are not supported by all countries. The question here is who was left out on the battlefield? OECD members and EU members were all engaged. Some countries could double the commitment because they belong to two organisations. The EU currently counts 27 member states, while the OECD has 36. A combination of the OECD and EU members together gives a total

[25] OECD (2015), p. 3; UNECA (2018), p. VI; Oguttu (2018), p. 298; Panayi (2018), p. 1.

[26] OECD (2015), pp. 11 and 13.

membership of 40 because of the overlap, plus dependent and associated territories, so the number is even larger. Given that the concern is taxation here, it is not the number of member states but their taxation situation that is most important. To understand their taxation situation, it is essential to look at their trade and macroeconomic situation.

OECD countries and key partners account for 80% of world trade and investment.[27] As far as the EU is concerned, its percentage of the lion share is not significantly different from that of the OECD. In international trade, the EU alone accounted for 34% of world trade in 2017.[28] These figures show how large the OECD's and the EU's share of international taxation is. Given these figures, it is understandable that a tax system that endangers the global tax system would also put the OECD and EU members in a dangerous position.

Hence, despite all their efforts to fight against harmful tax competition, the titans have realised that they are not winning the war because not all countries in the world are joining in. But who has not got involved? It is mostly developing countries that play a very small role in world trade. These are the countries whose tax systems could pose a challenge to the titans' tax systems! These are the countries that are mainly in Africa. These are the countries that are barely three to four decades from colonisation by the West. These are the countries whose tax systems were largely imported from Europe and only slightly adapted. These are the countries whose budgets were more than 50% financed by loans and aids from the West. These are the countries whose systems were an obstacle for the developed countries to achieve their goals against harmful tax competition. Nevertheless, it was time to export the war of the titans.

3 Exportation of the War of the Titans to Non-Titans

As explained above, tax competition began as a war of the titans between developed countries. It is after a while that developed countries realised that developing countries could also engage in unfair tax competition practices. As a result, developed countries expanded the geographical scope of measures against harmful tax competition. This how the geographical scope of the 1998 OECD report is worldwide with regard to tax havens and OECD members with regard to harmful preferential tax regimes.[29] As for the EU Code of Conduct, it applies geographically to EU Member States, their dependencies and associated territories.[30] Nevertheless, the Code made

[27] OECD (2015).

[28] WTO (2018).

[29] Calich (2011), p. 64; Englisch and Yevgenyeva (2013), p. 626.

[30] EU Code of Conduct (1997), C 2/5; EU Commission (2009), p. 8.

a call to promote its principles in third countries,[31] and this call has been met through blacklisting as a strategy to compel third countries to comply with European standards of good governance in the tax area, including issues of harmful tax competition.

Through this unfair export in the name of fighting harmful tax competition at the global level, countries that should not be concerned by this war in the name of tax sovereignty got involved and ordered the measures to be taken. In this way, some African countries have been pointed out to have harmful tax regimes. In other words, some African countries have been put onto questions as the countries that harmfully compete with developed countries, i.e. countries that erode the tax base of developed countries through harmful tax competition mechanisms. Examples include but are not limited to Mauritius' and South Africa's headquarters company regimes, Botswana's intermediary holding company regime, and Liberia's shipping regime,[32] Morocco,[33] Eswatini, Namibia, South Africa, Tunisia, among others. Some scholars qualified that attack on poor African countries as unreasonable. For instance, S. A. Dean and A. Waris using Liberia as an example, described the OECD's strategy of blacklisting as targeting black and brown, for instance by targeting Liberia over Switzerland, when in fact the less wealthy tropical tax havens posed only a limited threat to wealthy states.[34]

Another example of exporting the war of the titans being applied to non-titans is the OECD's creation of the Inclusive Framework. After finding that the 1998 report and subsequent regulatory assessments had not worked as expected, the OECD feared that BEPS would lead to similar results. Out of this fear, the OECD established the four minimum standards from the BEPS actions that were to be adopted even by non-OECD members under the umbrella of the Inclusive Framework. This extension was justified by the fact that harmful tax competition is a global phenomenon that must also be combated with global measures. The OECD assumes that not including all countries would lead to the fight not being effective.

As of August 2023, 143 countries have joined the Inclusive Framework, including quite a number from Africa. Although this number is interesting, several criticisms have been raised questioning the genuine will of developing countries to join the Inclusive Framework. Indeed, several developing countries joined the Inclusive Framework not because they are genuinely enthusiastic to do so but for reasons such as the fear of the EU blacklist or the need to benefit from EU technical assistance.[35] In contrast, developing countries face several challenges that prevent them from effectively participating in the activities of the Inclusive Framework: fast decision-making processes, complex and highly technical intensive discussions, limited tech-

[31] EU Code of Conduct (1997), C 2/5; EU Com. Communication on good governance in tax matters Ibid.

[32] Oguttu op cit note 25 at 299–302.

[33] EU Commission *Outcome of proceedings on COCG assessment of Morocco's Offshore holding companies regime (MA005)* 7549/19 FISC 195, 15/03/2019.

[34] Dean and Waris (2021), p. 1661.

[35] Christensen et al. (2020), p. 3.

nical capacity of developing countries, lack of financial resources, lack of organised caucuses to negotiate common positions, disjuncture between technical and political aspects, over-representation of developed countries versus limited representation of developing countries,[36] etc.

In general, the exportation of the war between the titans being unjustified led to a slow acceptance by African countries. Indeed, African countries have been reluctant to embrace the global engagements against harmful tax competition. Nonetheless, forced to take measures against harmful tax competition, including changing their domestic tax systems, a few initiatives have been taken in Africa, mainly in the context of regional blocs. But still, given that the war of titans was imported from the West, very few efforts were put in by African countries in such commenced but not concluded initiatives.

In this context, the EAC drafted a code of conduct against harmful tax competition in 2011.[37] SADC member states also signed a Memorandum of Understanding (MoU) in 2002 with a clause against harmful tax competition.[38] However, the question arises as to what is in these documents and where they are now.

Starting with the EAC, the EAC drafted the code of conduct against harmful tax competition with the support of the Deutsche Gesellschaft fuer Internationale Zusammenarbeit (GIZ). Although this draft has been available since 2011, no further action has been taken to date. The draft was neither adopted nor approved and remains a draft that is not legally binding, let alone any political influence. The very fact that a draft has been around for 12 years (2011–2023) without any further action shows that the issue of harmful tax competition is not really taken seriously in the EAC as a regional community. In addition, the draft code itself is full of loopholes that further complicate the optimistic regulation of harmful tax competition in the EAC. For example, the preamble to the draft Code states that it is a political commitment that does not affect the rights and obligations of the Partner States as set out in the EAC Treaty. However, this character is at odds with the mentions towards the end of the same draft, establishing the Code as an agreement to be signed by the representatives of the Parter States, thereby making it more or less binding.

Unlike the 1998 OECD Report and the EU Code of Conduct, the draft EAC Code defines harmful tax competition in art 1(d),[39] harmful tax effects in art 1(e),[40] and

[36] Christensen et al. (2020), p. 7; Mason (2021), p. 383.

[37] For details see Habimana (2023), chapter 5.

[38] SADC, Memorandum of Understanding on Cooperation in Taxation and related matters, 08/08/2002, art 4(3)(a); Robinson (2002), p. 267; van Wijk (2012), p. 67.

[39] The draft Code defines harmful tax competition as "The competition created within an economic block as a result of preferential tax regimes that offer tax advantages to particular entities at the detriment of other entities operating within the same country or other countries thereby putting the other entities in a less competitive position".

[40] The draft Code defines harmful tax effects as "negative spill over to other countries that arise from the harmful preferential tax regimes".

harmful tax practices in art 1(f).[41] Unfortunately, the definition of tax competition in the draft code is not about competition between states, but between companies. This follows from what is called the effect of harmful tax competition. According to this definition, the effect of harmful tax competition is that favoured companies are placed in a privileged position, while other companies are placed in a less competitive position. So this looks like a definition of something else, much closer to state aid or subsidies, but not harmful tax competition. The definition of harmful tax effects in the draft Code is also problematic as it confuses harmful preferential tax regimes with harmful tax practices. The definition of harmful tax practices in the draft Code is also open to criticism: it is not specific that the preferential tax regimes must be harmful; it does not encompass all elements of harmful tax practices as it does not mention some key elements that characterise harmful tax practices, such as ring-fencing, lack of transparency, lack of exchange of information and absence of the requirement of substantial activity; etc.

Apart from the definitions, the scope of the draft Code is also problematic. According to the draft Code, it would apply to 'each tax of every description' collected by the tax authorities of each partner state.[42] This description is too broad, as some taxes have nothing to do with harmful tax practices while others may have *de minimis* impact. In addition, the draft Code contains a provision on state aid and subsidies.[43] This provision is out of place, as matters related to state aid and subsidies are governed by other EAC instruments, such as the Common Market Protocol, the Competition Act, the Customs Union Protocol and the Customs Union Regulations.[44] Art 13 of the draft Code also lists several models and harmonisations that need to be made to ensure effective tax rates such as VAT, income tax and excise duties. Most of the items on this long list are usually not substantially related to harmful tax competition.

In the context of SADC, member states signed a Memorandum of Understanding (MoU) in 2002 that included a clause on tax cooperation to avoid harmful tax competition.[45] While this signalled awareness of the existence of harmful tax competition in SADC, no further progress was made such as the adoption of a code of conduct similar to the EU's. The situation in the EAC and SADC is largely no different from the rest of Africa.

---

[41] The draft Code defines harmful tax practices as "Tax measures by tax havens and/or preferential tax regimes that affect the location of financial and other service activities, erode the tax base of other countries, distort trade and investment patterns and undermine the fairness, neutrality and the broad social acceptance of systems".

[42] EAC Draft Code, art 2(1).

[43] EAC Draft Code, art 12.

[44] EAC, Protocol on the Establishment of the East African Community Common Market, art 34(1) and (2); EAC, the East African Community Competition Act, 2006, secs 14, 15, 16, 17, 22, 24, 37, 42(1), 44, and 46; EAC, the Protocol on the establishment of the East African Community Customs Union 2004, art. 1; EAC, the East African Community Customs Union (Subsidies and countervailing measures) Regulations, 2006, Regulation 7(1).

[45] SADC, Memorandum of Understanding on Cooperation in Taxation and related matters, 08/08/2002, art 4(3)(a); Robinson (2002), p. 267; van Wijk (2012), p. 67.

There may be several reasons that have contributed to the failure of African countries to take action against harmful tax competition. Since this is beyond the scope of this chapter, it should be noted that one reason is that measures against harmful tax competition were exported to African countries that were forced to take such measures without any real valid reason, apart from the fear of sanctions and the deterioration of political-economic relations between the two. So it could not work. In contrast, African countries were looking for solutions that could work internally through the creation of regional communities and trade blocs.

4 There Comes AfCFTA

While the titans were about to celebrate a successful export of the war against tax competition, African countries, aware of the resources and wealth that exist in Africa, but which unfortunately are not maximally utilised and from which the West intentionally or unintentionally benefits, came up with the idea of extending trade liberalisation from the blocs to a single bloc. This is the idea behind the AfCFTA, which is to remove trade barriers and boost intra-trade in Africa. At the same time, it aims to promote industrialisation, job creation and investment, thus improving Africa's competitiveness in international trade.

The Agreement establishing the AfCFTA entered into force on 30 May 2019 after 24 Member States deposited their instruments of ratification in accordance with Art 23 of the Agreement, which makes entry into force conditional on the deposit of the twenty-second (22nd) instrument of ratification.[46] The deposit of the instruments of ratification is governed by Art 24, while Art 8 states that the Protocols and the Annexes and Appendices thereto, once adopted, form an integral part of the Agreement. In this context, several protocols are envisaged, such as a Protocol on Trade in Goods, Trade in Services, Investment, Intellectual Property Rights, Competition Policy, Rules and Procedures for the Settlement of Disputes; and any other protocols deemed necessary to further the objectives of the AfCFTA.

The AfCFTA was launched on 07 July 2019 during the 12th Extraordinary Session of the AU Assembly of Heads of State and Government in Niamey, Niger, while trade under the AfCFTA began on 01 January 2021. As of August 2023, the AfCFTA counts 54 AU member states that have signed the Agreement, and 46 state parties.[47] The AfCFTA aims to boost intra-African trade by eliminating 97% of tariff lines on trade in goods and services, which is a pathway to African industrialisation and prosperity.[48] The AfCFTA is planned to be implemented in two phases of negotiations.[49] Phase one covers trade in goods, trade in services, dispute settlement

[46] AfCFTA Agreement, art 23(1) and (2).

[47] About AfCFTA, available at https://au-afcfta.org.

[48] Africa Policy Research Institute (2023), p. 10.

[49] AfCFTA Agreement, art 7.

mechanisms, customs and trade facilitation; while phase two covers intellectual property rights, investment, competition policy, digital trade, and women and youth in trade. General objectives of the AfCFTA are set out in art 3 and are:

> (a) To create a single market for goods, and services, that facilitates the movement of people; (b) Creating a liberalised market for goods and services; (c) Contributing to the movement of capital and natural persons and to facilitate investment, building on initiatives and developments in States Parties and Regional Economic Communities (RECs); (d) Laying the foundations for the establishment of a continental customs union at a later stage; (e) Promoting and achieving sustainable and inclusive socio-economic development, gender equality and structural transformation in the States Parties; (f) Enhancing the competitiveness of the economies of the States Parties in the continental and global markets; (g) Promoting industrial development through diversification and development of regional value chains, agricultural development and food security; and (h) Addressing the challenges posed by multiple memberships and overlaps and accelerating regional and continental integration processes.

The specific objectives are listed in art 4 and serve to fulfil and achieve the general objectives. The specific objectives are:

> (a) the progressive elimination of tariffs and non-tariff barriers to trade in goods; (b) the progressive liberalisation of trade in services; (c) cooperation in the fields of investment, intellectual property rights and competition policy; (d) cooperation in all trade-related areas; (e) cooperation in customs matters and the implementation of trade facilitation measures; (f) the establishment of a dispute settlement mechanism for rights and obligations; and (g) the establishment and maintenance of an institutional framework for the implementation and administration of the AfCFTA.

To achieve these objectives, nine principles have been identified, namely: (a) driven by AU member states; (b) REC's Free Trade Areas (FTAs) as building blocs for the AfCFTA; (c) variable geometry; (d) flexibility and special and differential treatment; (e) transparency and disclosure of information; (f) preservation of the acquis; (g) most-favoured-nation (MFN) treatment; (h) national treatment; and (i) reciprocity.[50]

It is too early to judge the AfCFTA's likelihood of success. Nevertheless, it is more or less known what a successful AfCFTA will look like. As preached by the AfCFTA itself, it is the largest free trade area in the world with 55 countries that are members of the African Union AU and eight regional economic communities. If successfully implemented, the AfCFTA will create a single continental market with a population of about 1.3 billion and a combined GDP of about $3.4 trillion; 30 million people will potentially be lifted out of extreme poverty; and income in Africa will increase by $450 billion by 2035.[51] Optimistically, these are the expectations that will one day be celebrated. Nevertheless, the question is whether this expected success, summed up in the creation of a liberalised single market for goods and services, coupled with the free movement of persons and capital envisaged in article

[50] AfCFTA Agreement, art 5.

[51] AfCFTA, 'Brief Overview' available at https://au-afcfta.org/about/.

3 of the AfCFTA agreement, will be risk-free, especially in terms of harmful tax competition.

5 A Successful AfCFTA Risks Fuelling Harmful Tax Competition

From the above provisions setting out the objectives and intentions of the AfCFTA, coupled with the European experience, there is a high risk that a successful AfCFTA will attract harmful tax competition. The extent to which this risk exists, how great it is and what remedies are available are discussed below.

5.1 The Plausible Impact of the AfCFTA on Business Location

If the AfCFTA is successfully implemented, Africa's internal trade borders will disappear and Africa will become one single liberalised market. In this way, it will be possible for a producer and/or manufacturer to trade in any member country as if he/she is trading in his/her country of production. Yet, applicable tax, especially corporate tax (CIT), will be paid in the country where the producer is resident. In other words, residence will be relevant as a connecting factor, while source will lose importance. This will encourage companies to seek residence where they will be paying low CIT. In other words, companies will concentrate in low-tax jurisdictions while high-tax jurisdictions will run a risk losing residences.

The extent to which the business location is a serious risk for Africa in the context of the AfCFTA would be answered in the lens of influencing the business location in the context of the EU. The EU is used here as an example of a regional economic community that has liberalised trade in goods and services as well as the free movement of goods, services, and capital among member states. The EU is also used as an example of a regional economic community that has been more or less successful in tackling harmful tax competition in member states.

The extent to which influencing business locations is a serious concern in terms of harmful tax competition is explicated in the Code of Conduct on Business Taxation. Paragraph A of the Code identifies business location and derogation as tests for determining the likelihood of harmful tax competition. According to the Code of Conduct, the concerned measures are those that significantly affect, or may affect, the location of business activities.[52] This implies that tax measures that cannot affect the business location are not concerned by the Code of Conduct. Business

[52] EU Code of Conduct (1997), C2/3; Englisch and Yevgenyeva (2013), p. 636; Ambrosanio and Caroppo (2005), p. 691; Moutarlier (2016), p. 78; EU Commission (2019), p. 6; Boria (2017), p. 169; Wattel (2016), p. 63.

location as a key element for assessing the potential for harmful tax competition has been further developed in the Code of Conduct Group (COCG) Agreed Guidance[53] and in several of its assessments, such as assessment of the Belgian notional interest deduction (NID) regime (BE018);[54] Portugal's NID regime assessment;[55] Poland's 15% CIT rate for small and start-up taxpayers;[56] etc. The same seriousness with regard to the relationship between influence on business location and harmful tax competition should be considered with regard to the AfCFTA. But how is business location related to harmful tax competition?

5.2 *Escalation of Business Location into Harmful Tax Competition*

Business location in itself is not and should not be a problem in the sense of trade liberalisation theories. Nevertheless, there is a strong link between business location and harmful tax practices. This link is so strong that a practice that does not influence the business location can hardly be considered harmful tax competition or lead to it. The link between business location and harmful tax competition occurs in a sequence involving various steps, such as the race to the bottom, erosion of the tax base and profit shifting, then engaging in harmful tax competition *per se*.

In fact, it all starts as normal and ordinary tax competition. This consists of states designing their tax systems to be as attractive and competitive as possible by reducing the internal tax burden through lowering tax rates or the tax bases.[57] This is done by attracting investment, business, economic activity, capital and profits.[58] In this context, ordinary tax competition refers to '*strategic practices by states to lower the internal tax burden in order to gain a larger share of the international tax base by attracting business*'.[59]

Then, from ordinary tax competition, countries end up being engaged in a race to the bottom, and this race to the bottom leads to a business attraction phenomenon. This happens as a result of lowering the tax rate or narrowing the tax base.

---

[53] EU Commission *Agreed Guidance by the Code of Conduct Group (business taxation): 1998-2018* FISC 44 ECOFIN 75, 5814/4/18 REV 4, 20/12/2018, p. 16.

[54] EU Commission *Report on COCG assessment of Belgium's NID regime (BE018)* 14364/18 ADD 1, FISC 481 ECOFIN 1059, 20/11/2018, p. 39.

[55] EU Commission *Report on COCG assessment of Portugal's NID regime (PT018)* 14364/18 ADD 8, FISC 481 ECOFIN 1059, 20/11/2018, p. 16.

[56] EU Commission *Report on COCG assessment of Poland's 15% CIT rate for small taxpayers (PL006)* 14364/18 ADD 7, FISC 481 ECOFIN 1059, 20/11/2018, pp. 2–4.

[57] Pinto (1998), p. 386; Ring (2009), pp. 561–562; Sobotková (2012), p. 344; Wróblewska (2016), p. 15.

[58] Sobotková (2012), p. 344; Pinto (1998), p. 386; Wróblewska (2016), p. 15; Englisch and Yevgenyeva (2013), p. 621; Ring (2008), p. 21.

[59] Habimana (2023), p. 64.

Companies, especially multinationals, then find a space to locate their business in a jurisdiction that offers the possibility of minimising the taxes payable. The motivation for companies to locate in a low-tax jurisdiction lies in the fact that the company will be able to trade in a wide area that offers trade liberalisation. In this way, a multinational company will be based in a low-tax jurisdiction, i.e. having residence there but trades beyond that residence, i.e. having source from other jurisdictions, basically high-tax jurisdictions.

In this scenario, other problems emerge, namely issues of tax base erosion and profit shifting, which then trigger jurisdictions to engage in harmful tax competition. This refers to the practices of countries to poach the tax bases of other countries. This is made possible by '*exploiting the interaction of tax systems by enacting special tax rules that fundamentally erode the tax bases of other countries*'.[60] Put otherwise, harmful tax competition arises from tax rules that erode other countries' tax bases, but not their own tax bases, which remain intact.[61] This becomes possible in particular through ring-fencing mechanisms.

In the context of the AfCFTA, given that the relevance of source will be decreasing, high-tax jurisdictions will run a risk of losing tax revenues as they will not be able to collect revenue on the basis of source nor residence. To increase revenues using the source basis will be difficult and it would mean an explicit exit from the AfCFTA. The remaining option will be therefore to work on the residence. To work on the residence, jurisdictions will need to attract companies through favourable tax measures. In this way, high-tax jurisdictions will be forced to find ways of changing the taxation patterns to become low-tax jurisdictions. This will involve the usual means of attracting companies through lowering the tax burden, i.e. lowering the tax rate or narrowing the tax base.

Given that quite a number of AfCFTA members are in the same predicament, this will certainly trigger a race to tax competition, which will likely to lead to harmful tax competition. Indeed, the jurisdictions members of the AfCFTA that will resort to lowering the tax burden to become competitive, the motive will be to host multinational companies that are resident in that jurisdiction but trade throughout Africa, i.e. that have their sources throughout Africa but do not pay taxes in source jurisdiction rather in residence jurisdiction. In such a scenario, the situation will contribute to the development of free riders as the multinational enterprises will be trading in jurisdictions but pay taxes in others. In other words, they will be trading in source jurisdictions but pay taxes in residence jurisdictions, i.e. free riding the source jurisdictions. This will obviously constitute a case of erosion of the tax base in the source jurisdictions.

At this level, the case will no longer be a case of tax competition, but a clear case of harmful tax competition. In other words, a successful AfCFTA will create a single market that will encourage the location of businesses to jurisdictions with favourable taxation, as businesses will be able to trade throughout the African

[60] Pinto (1998), p. 340.

[61] Habimana (2023), p. 34.

continent, hence, creating an open leeway for harmful tax competition. In this regard, when talking about harmful tax competition here, reference is made to the OECD and EU standards, given the lack of standards for harmful tax competition in Africa. Such qualification will therefore be based on the key OECD and EU standards for determining harmful tax competition, which are further elaborated on in section two.

The extent to which this risk of fuelling harmful tax competition will materialise is a matter of probability. The same applies to the extent of this risk. In fact, the magnitude is high because if the first countries engage in such practices, the rest will tend to do the same, either in retaliation or to learn from best practices, which is common for countries to learn from each other. Since it is common for developing countries to copy and paste other countries' practices for a variety of reasons, such as a lack of technical and financial resources to develop first-hand means or solutions, the risk of copying and pasting from the first countries that will engage in harmful tax competition is likely to happen. If this happens, all African countries that are members of the AfCFTA will end up engaging in harmful tax competition.

5.3 *The Risks Mitigants*

Given the above mentioned risks, mitigation would be to develop measures to counteract potentially harmful tax competition. Such measures should be designed targeting the measures that can be used for harmful tax practices. Since the risk of harmful tax competition will develop in parallel with a successful implementation of the AfCFTA, African countries should start developing such measures as early as possible. To be pragmatic, the starting point would be to design a framework of measures to address harmful tax competition.

Normally, measures to combat harmful tax competition work well when they are designed in the context of regional integration. In this way, regional economic communities in Africa would be advised to develop measures to combat harmful tax competition. However, there is a risk in this approach that the rules may be mismatching or overlapping. Therefore, it would be best if the measures to combat harmful tax competition were adopted in close relationship to AfCFTA. This would happen if they were adopted as an Additional Protocol to the AfCFTA. Such an Additional Protocol would have its origin in article 8(3) of the AfCFTA Agreement, which provides the possibility of adopting additional instruments under the AfCFTA Agreement to further the objectives of the Agreement.

In this regard, the African model will be necessary to regulate harmful tax competition. In the context of this chapter, such a model should be annexed to the AfCFTA Agreement. To be successful, it is imperative that the model defines the context and needs to which it responds and should respond. In this regard, the model should in no way conflict with the objectives of the AfCFTA Agreement. In other words, it should rather promote the objectives of the AfCFTA Agreement while containing the potentially harmful tax competition that would arise from the

AfCFTA Agreement—contrary to its original intention. In this regard, the model should appropriately focus on promoting trade liberalisation in Africa, but not at the expense of another country's tax base. The model should adequately protect the tax base of AfCFTA member countries by controlling any attempt to erode the tax base from a high tax jurisdiction by a low tax jurisdiction.

It is important to note some key elements that should be considered in such an additional protocol. One, the protocol should clearly define the concept of harmful tax competition to distinguish it from acceptable tax competition. This definition is important considering that there are a variety of confusing definitions, to an extent that harmful tax competition has been described as multi-faceted.[62] Not only that, the relevance of such a definition is that not all tax competitions are harmful. It is therefore important to determine which tax competition is good and beneficial and which tax competition is bad and harmful. Such a definition would also help to make a clear distinction line between tax competition and harmful tax competition.[63]

The protocol should establish a clear procedure for detecting and investigating harmful tax practices. The clear procedure concerns both the procedure to be followed and the competent body to deal with harmful tax practices. As far as the procedure is concerned, it should be clearly established who can report a suspected harmful tax practice, how the complaint can be filed, to whom it can be addressed, etc. Then it should be specified which body is responsible for deciding on the complaints filed and whether there can be appeal procedures. It is also important to explain the enforcement mechanisms to prevent such decisions from remaining dead letters.

The protocol should also clearly set out the sanctioning regime. In the experience of the EU and the OECD, member states that engage in harmful tax competition tend to resist measures to curb harmful tax competition. Such resistance can also be expected in the case of the AfCFTA, probably even more. This fear is based on the fact that African regional integration communities have so far shown very low political will to engage in initiatives against harmful tax competition. The model should therefore clarify that any tax measure that constitutes harmful tax competition should be terminated within a certain timeframe in order to eliminate harmful tax competition.

The model should also clearly spell out the standards for harmful tax competition. In other words, it should establish clear criteria for assessing harmful tax practices. Following the OECD and the EU, no or low tax rates should be entry criteria, while other key criteria would be ring-fencing and the absence of substantial economic activity or presence.

---

[62] Pastukhov (2010), p. 163.

[63] For details on the question of boundaries between harmless tax competition versus harmful tax competition, see Habimana (2023), pp. 57–65.

6 Conclusion

The objective of this chapter was to examine the establishment of the AfCFTA in the context of harmful tax competition. As the AfCFTA is less than five years old, it is still very early to assess its potential outcomes, how successful it will be, and what impact it will have on existing structures. The AfCFTA in its current form is also the subject of various analyses, most of which are of course anticipative in nature. One of these topics is the plausible impact of a successful AfCFTA on harmful tax practices by African states.

This has been the focus of this chapter, which assumes that AfCFTA will be successful soon or later. A successful AfCFTA will create a single market on the African continent that will allow African residents to produce in a given African jurisdiction and trade on the rest of African jurisdictions. In this way, the main taxation patterns, namely residence and source as key tax connecting factors, will naturally be more relevant than before. A multinational company resident in Africa will also have a room to arrange its business in a way that minimises the taxes payable. But not only that, countries will also be tempted to minimise the taxes payable by either reducing the effective tax rate or narrowing down the tax base in order to encourage multinationals to locate there. Such mechanisms will potentially result into companies locating their businesses in a jurisdiction with a favourable tax regime. While companies will be tempted to shift their profits from high-tax jurisdictions to low-tax jurisdictions, one way or another, such mechanisms will lead to African states being locked into a race to the bottom. At this level, the potentiality of engaging in harmful tax competition will be obvious and attempts to poach the tax base of other countries will become evident.

This was the preoccupation of this chapter, which began with an explanation of harmful tax competition. This phenomenon was in this chapter called the war of the titans because it was initially a problem between developed countries. Then the extension of the war between titans to non-titans was discussed. Here the focus was on African countries. That preceded a focus on the emergence of the AfCFTA. After that, the concern was about establishing a link between AfCFTA and harmful tax competition. The conclusion of this chapter is that a successful AfCFTA carries a high risk of fuelling harmful tax competition in Africa. This is because a successful AfCFTA will end up with creating a single market that will allow African companies to trade across the continent. Companies will therefore likely seek to establish their residence in low-tax jurisdictions while enjoying the possibility to trade across the continent, including in high-tax jurisdictions. If successfully manipulated, companies will be able to set up structures that allow them to pay taxes in low-tax jurisdictions while trading in all jurisdictions, including high-tax jurisdictions, thereby creating a free-rider situation. This is likely to be enabled by African countries, which will be tempted to set up tax systems that can be used to erode the tax base of other countries. Measures against this likelihood of harmful tax competition are therefore urgently needed. To this end, a Protocol to the AfCFTA should be added in accordance with Article 8(3) of the AfCFTA Agreement.

References

Africa Policy Research Institute (2023) The road to Africa's single market: progress so far and challenges for the future, Trade Policy Brief 13 March 2023
Ambrosanio MF, Caroppo MS (2005) Eliminating harmful tax practices in tax havens: defensive measures by major EU countries and tax haven reforms. Can Tax J 53:685–719
Arnold BJ, McIntyre MJ (2002) International tax primer, 2nd edn. Kluwer Law International, The Hague
Ault HJ (2019) Tax competition and tax cooperation: a survey and reassessment. In: Monsenego J, Bjuvberg J (eds) International taxation in a changing landscape. Wolters Kluwer
Boria P (2017) Taxation in European Union, 2nd edn. Springer
Boulogne F (2019) Reviewing the OECD's and the EU's assessment of Singapore's development and expansion incentive. SMU School of Accountancy Research Paper 7(1):1–64
Calich I (2011) The impact of globalization on the position of developing countries in the international tax system. Doctoral thesis, LSE
Christensen RC, Hearson M, Randriamanalina T (2020) At the table, off the menu? Assessing the participation of lower-income countries in global tax negotiations. ICTD Working Paper 115
Christians A, van Apeldoorn L (2018) The OECD inclusive framework. Bulletin for International Taxation, pp 1–17
Dean SA, Waris A (2021) Ten truths about tax havens: inclusion and the Liberia problem. Emory Law J 70:1661–1684
Englisch J, Yevgenyeva A (2013) The upgraded strategy against harmful tax practices under the BEPS action plan. Br Law Rev 5:620–637
EU Code of Conduct Conclusions of the ECOFIN Council meeting of 1/12/1997 concerning taxation policy (1997) DOC 98/C2/01, OJEC, 6 Jan. 1998
EU Commission Communication from the Commission to the Council, The European Parliament and the European Economic and Social Committee on Promoting Good Governance in Tax Matters COM (2009) 201, 28/04/2009
EU Commission Agreed Guidance by the Code of Conduct Group (business taxation): 1998-2018 FISC 44 ECOFIN 75, 5814/4/18 REV 4, 20/12/2018
EU Commission Outcome of proceedings on COCG assessment of Morocco's Offshore holding companies regime (MA005) 7549/19 FISC 195, 15/03/2019
EU Commission Report on COCG assessment of Belgium's NID regime (BE018) 14364/18 ADD 1, FISC 481 ECOFIN 1059, 20/11/2018
EU Commission Report on COCG assessment of Poland's 15% CIT rate for small taxpayers (PL006) 14364/18 ADD 7, FISC 481 ECOFIN 1059, 20/11/2018
EU Commission Report on COCG assessment of Portugal's NID regime (PT018) 14364/18 ADD 8, FISC 481 ECOFIN 1059, 20/11/2018
Genschel P, Schwarz P (2011) Tax competition: a literature review. Socio-Econ Rev 9(2):339–370
Habimana P (2023) Harmful tax competition in the East African Community: the case of Rwanda with reference to EU and OECD approaches, IBFD
Hutchinson T (2015) The doctrinal method: incorporating interdisciplinary methods in reforming the law. Eur Law Rev 3:130–138
Liebman HM, Heyvaert W, Oyen V (2016) Countering harmful tax practices: BEPS Action 5 and EU initiatives – past progress, current status and prospects, Euro.Tax
Littlewood M (2004) Tax competition: harmful to whom? Mich J Int Law 26(1):411–487
Mason R (2021) The 2021 Compromise. Tax Notes Federal 172:569
Mello LA (2012) Tax competition and the case of bank secrecy rules: new trends in international tax law. SJD Thesis, University of Michigan
Morriss AP, Moberg L (2012) Cartelizing taxes: understanding the OECD's campaign against harmful tax competition. CJTL 4(1):1–64
Moutarlier V (2016) Reforming the code of conduct for business taxation in the new tax competition environment. In: Richelle I, Schön W, Traversa E (eds) State aid law and business taxation, pp 75–84

Nikolakakis N (2006) The International Legal Ramifications of the OECD's Harmful Tax Competition Crusade. LLM Thesis, McGill University
OECD (1998) Harmful Tax Competition: An Emerging Global Issue, United States, OECD
OECD (2009) Council Decision Establishing the Global Forum on Transparency and Exchange of Information for Tax Purposes C (2009)122/Final of 25/09/2009
OECD (2015) Countering Harmful Tax Practices More Effectively Taking into Account Transparency and Substance: – Action 5: 2015 Final Report (2015)
OECD (2017) Harmful Tax Practices – 2017 Progress Report on Preferential Regimes: Inclusive Framework on BEPS Action 5
Oguttu AW (2018) International tax competition, harmful tax practices and the 'Race to the bottom': a special focus on unstrategic tax incentives in Africa. CILJSA 51(3):219–293
Panayi C (2018) The Globalization of Tax Good Governance. SMU School of Accountancy Research Paper 6(1) at 1 available at http://doi.org/10.2139/ssrn.3104977, accessed on 01 June 2023
Pastukhov O (2010) Counteracting harmful tax competition in the European Union. Southwest J Int Law 16:159–180
Patnaik P (2025) The free trade argument and development strategy. Agrarian South: J Polit Econ 14(1):14–25
Pinto C (1998) EU and OECD to fight harmful tax competition: has the right path been undertaken? Intertax 26(12):323–331
Repyeuski P (2008) Free zones in the commonwealth of independent states: a proposed regulatory model. Doctoral thesis, Manchester University
Ring DM (2008) What's at stake in the sovereignty debate: international tax and the nation-state. Va J Int Law 49(1):1–58
Ring DM (2009) Democracy, sovereignty and tax competition: the role of tax sovereignty in shaping tax cooperation. Florida Tax Rev 9(5):1–41
Robinson ZC (2002) Tax competition and its implications for Southern Africa. Ph.D Thesis, University of Cape Town
Salinas JG (2003) The OECD tax competition initiative: a critique of its merits in the global marketplace. Houston J Int Law 25(3):550
Seeruthun-Kowalczyk M (2011) Hard law and soft law interactions in EU corporate tax regulation: exploration and lessons for the future. Doctoral thesis, Edinburgh University
Sobotková V (2012) Revisiting the debate on harmful tax competition in the European Union. Acta Universitatis Agriculturae et Silviculturae Mendelianae Brunensis 60(4):343–350
Terra BJM, Wattel PJ (2008) European tax law, 5th edn. Kluwer, Deventer
UNECA (2018) Base erosion and profit shifting in Africa: reforms to facilitate improved taxation of multinational enterprises. Ethiopia, Economic Commission for Africa
van Raad K (2013) Materials on international & EU tax law, 13th edn. International Tax Centre, Leiden
van Wijk AJ (2012) Whether tax incentives to stimulate foreign direct investment for manufacturing in the SADC region is an indicator of harmful tax competition. Master Thesis, University of Cape Town
Wattel PJ (2016) Comparing criteria: state aid, free movement, harmful tax competition and market distorting disparities. In: Richelle I, Schön W, Traversa E (eds) State aid law and business taxation. Wolters Kluwer, Deventer
Webb MC (2004) Defining the boundaries of legitimate state practice: norms, transnational actors and the OECD's project on harmful tax competition. Unpublished
Wróblewska M (2016) Harmful tax competition in a globalized world: does the world trade organization deal with this issue? Studia Iuridica 4(1):13–23
WTO (2018) World Trade Statistical Review. available at https://www.wto-ilibrary.org/content/books/9789287046246#chapters 26–39, accessed on 01 June 2023

Recalibrating the Regulation of Trade in Agriculture Under the African Continental Free Trade Agreement to Realise the Human Right to Food

Shelton Tapiwa Mota Makore

Abstract The African Continental Free Trade Agreement (AfCFTA) encapsulates a dynamic liberal regime governing Africa's trade in agriculture. AfCFTA imposes continental-wide commitments for contracting parties to liberalise trade in agriculture through the incremental elimination of tariffs and non-tariff barriers. This liberal regulatory regime promoted under the AfCFTA is recognised as a vehicle for boosting intra-African agricultural trade flows, and lowering of Africa's dependence on food imports for its food security needs, among other loft objectives. This chapter examines the regulation of trade in agriculture under the AfCFTA with a view to determine whether a liberal model adopted under the aforesaid agreement is accommodative of the food security needs of the African countries. The chapter argues that the underlying free trade thesis which constitutes the very ideological justification for the AfCFTA agricultural trade has wider cracks and is unsustainable when examined in scope of the international and domestic obligations imposed by the human right to food on contracting parties. Therefore, this chapter argues that there is a need for the AfCFTA liberal rules in agriculture to be re-calibrated so that they advance the realisation of the human right to food.

1 Introduction

The African Continental Free Trade Agreement (AfCFTA) entered into force on the 30th of May 2019 constitutes a comprehensive continental-wide free trade agreement covering, *inter alia*, trade in goods, services, investments, intellectual property

S. T. M. Makore (✉)
Department of Mercantile Law, University of the Free State, Bloemfontein, South Africa
e-mail: MotaMakoreST@ufs.ac.za

T. V. Warikandwa et al. (eds.), *Law and Policy of the African Continental Free Trade Area (AfCFTA)*, European Yearbook of International Economic Law,
https://doi.org/10.1007/978-3-032-01122-0_6

rights, and competition policy.[1] It encapsulates a liberal regime governing Africa's trade in agriculture.[2] AfCFTA imposes continental-wide commitments for contracting parties to liberalise trade in agriculture through the incremental elimination of tariffs and non-tariff barriers.[3] This liberal regulatory regime promoted under the AfCFTA is recognised as a vehicle for boosting intra-African agricultural trade flows, and lowering of Africa's dependence on food imports for its food security needs, among other, loft objectives.[4] For many African countries whose food insecurity condition has been exacerbated by the COVID-19 and the Russia-Ukraine War which disrupted the production and export processes of about 30 million tons of grain, the AfCFTA is posited as an instrument that can potentially improve the availability, affordability and accessibility of food across the continent.[5] However, in an era of globalisation, free trade as propagated by the AfCFTA has increasingly come under intense criticism for its perceived potential negative act on people's livelihoods across the continent. The basic argument is that the current AfCFTA liberal paradigm in agriculture is not amicable to the realisation of the human right to food in Africa.[6]

The AfCFTA imposes obligations to liberalise trade in agriculture that can potentially stand in opposite to African States's obligations to realise the human right to food as provided under international and regional and domestic human rights instruments. At an international level, the Universal Declaration of Human Rights (UDHR), which has become part of customary international law, obliges states to respect, promote, fulfil and realise the human right to food as a constituent of the right to "adequate standard of living." Another source of legal protection for the human right to food at the international level is the International Covenant on Economic, Social and Cultural Rights (ICESCR).[7] This instrument imposes binding legal obligations on African states requiring them to guarantee the effective enforcement of the human right to food within the domestic realm.[8]At the regional level, the African Charter on Human and Peoples 'Rights (ACHPR)[9] protects and promotes the human right to food through Article 22 which encapsulates everyone's right to

[1] The consolidated text of the AfCFTA was adopted and signed at the 10th Extraordinary Summit of the African Union (AU) Assembly in Kigali, Rwanda on March 21, 2018, by forty-four African Heads of State Government and entered into force on May 30, 2019, following ratification by twenty-four countries. As of publication, 54 of the 55 African countries have ratified the AfCFTA. African Union (2018); Fofack and Mold (2021), p. 3; TRALAC (2025).

[2] Seti and Daw (2022), p. 2; Aniche (2020), p. 4.

[3] South African Department of Trade, Industry and Competition (2023).

[4] Food and Agricultural Organisation (2020).

[5] Food and Agricultural Organisation (2023).

[6] A Dall (2020); Chisaira (2018), p. 83.

[7] Chirwa (n.d.).

[8] Elkins et al. (2013), p. 64.

[9] *African Charter on Human and Peoples' Rights* (Banjul Charter) adopted June 27, 1981, OAU Doc. CAB/LEG/67/3 rev. 5, 21 I.L.M. 58 (1982).

economic, social and cultural development.[10] Further, the human right to food is indirectly protected by Articles 4, 5 and 14 of ACHPR which guarantee the human right to health, right to life and the right not to be treated in a cruel, inhuman or degrading manner.[11] There are other regional human rights instruments which protect the human right to food in Africa which includes African Charter on the Rights and Welfare of the Child (ACRWC),[12] and the Protocol to the African Charter on Human and Peoples' Rights on the Rights of Women in Africa. The Protocol to the African Charter on Human and Peoples' Rights on the Rights of Women in Africa requires States Parties to ensure that women's food security needs are prioritised, respected, and promoted.[13]

This chapter examines the regulation of trade in agriculture under the AfCFTA to determine whether a liberal model adopted under the aforesaid agreement is accommodative of the food security needs of the African countries. The substantive part of the chapter commences by providing a critical discussion of the trade law theories underlying the regulatory framework introduced by the AfCFTA. A scholarly reflection on the doctoral foundations of the AfCFTA is necessary to unravel the strengths and weakness of the liberal ideology informing the continental rules applicable to agriculture especially those concerning the elimination of tariffs and non-tariff barriers. In fact, from a legal stand point, the legitimacy and justification of AfCFTA rules and norms is not only rooted in the contractual principle of *pact sunt servanda,* and Pan-Africanism, but rather on the economic theories advanced to support intra-African trade in agriculture.[14] There are three theories deployed to support liberal rules in agriculture under the AfCFTA namely: (a) the theory of comparative advantage: (b) the need to distribute food from surplus regions to deficit regions in Africa through international trade and(c) the food security risk associated with restricting trade in food.[15]

[10] Art 22 of the ACHPR.

[11] Arts 4, 5 and 14 of ACHPR.

[12] The ACRWC was adopted by the Organisation of African Unity (OAU) in 2001. The OAU legally became the African Union (AU) in 1999. See African Charter on the Rights and Welfare of the Child OAU Doc. CAB/LEG/24.9/49 (1990), entered into force Nov. 29, 1999.

[13] Art 14 of the Protocol to the ACHPR on the Rights of Women in Africa. See Resolution AHG/Res.240 (XXXI) of the OAU Assembly of Heads of State and Government, adopted at its 31st Ordinary Session held in Addis Ababa, Ethiopia, in July 1995.

[14] Nshimbi (2019), p. 189; Hauter (2007), p. 1070; McGee (1995), p. 140; Gumede (2021); African Continental Free Trade Area Agreement, adopted 21 March 2018, signed 05 February 2021, entered into force 30 May 2019; Dall (2020); and TRALAC (2019).

[15] Chidebe et al. (2020), p. 300.

2 Defining Trade in Agriculture

Any discourse that seeks to provide a critical assessment of the regulation of trade in agriculture under the AfCFTA is incomplete without defining the elements of trade in agriculture and what it entails.[16] In ordinary parlance, trade in agriculture refers to trade involving the buying and selling of agricultural products and services between natural or juristic persons including States or other socio-economic and political formations often in exchange for something of economic value especially in the form of money.[17] However, this definition of trade in agriculture lacks specificity and does not properly explain trade in agriculture both as an outcome determined by the allocation of power, systems, rights and duties.[18] In a more technical nascent sense, trade in agriculture can be construed as referring to systems of agricultural trade governance that define and determine the supply and distribution of agricultural trade products such as grains, Agro-based seeds, animals, confectionaries, amongst other food products.[19] Given the foregoing definition, a deduction can be made that trade in agriculture, if properly governed can be instrumental to the achievement of the United Nations, Sustainable Development Goals (SDGs) such as poverty alleviation, and tackling hunger in Africa and beyond.[20]

3 Problematising the Theorical Underpinning Informing the Regulation of Trade in Agriculture Under the AfCFTA

As foreshadowed, this part commences with a discussion which problematise the theories underpinning the liberal rules governing trade in agriculture under the AfCFTA. Such liberal theories are in prodigious abundance, and it is only necessary to explore the most relevant to this chapter.[21] Liberal rules constitutes the very ideological foundation for most of the existing multilateral trade agreement governing agriculture concluded under the WTO architecture and, concomitantly, regional and continental free trade agreements across the globe, including the AfCFTA.[22] Liberal rules in agriculture seek to dismantle tariffs and non-tariff barriers that limit the free flow of agricultural products and services across national boundaries.[23] Liberal rules are implemented at multilateral, continental, and regional levels including the AfCFTA through the deployment of various trade instruments which advances agri-

[16] FAO (2007).

[17] Josling et al. (2010), p. 424.

[18] Sen (1981), p. 45.

[19] De Schutter (2009), p. 4.

[20] UN (2022).

[21] Sen (2010); and African Union (n.d.).

[22] Chen (2014), p. 815.

[23] Clapp (2015), p. 105.

cultural trade liberalisation.[24] The primary goal behind agricultural trade liberalisation is to reduce the role played by the state in the distribution of agricultural products and the creation of an environment that is beneficial and favourable for importation and exportation of agricultural products.[25]

The core elements of liberal rules in agriculture is to expand access to agricultural markets by changing the tariffication process, formalising and reducing the regime for tariff rates, reduction of domestic agricultural subsidies considered to be trade distorting and lastly, decreasing the quantity and amount of subsidised food exports.[26] The idea of agricultural trade liberation or liberal rules in agriculture is largely operationalised via various free trade agreement concluded under the WTO giving the semblance that it originates from this institution, and predates the conclusion of the AfCFTA. In reality, liberalism is a product of an ideological push largely steeped in western-centrism introduced by the Bretton Woods institutions, the World Bank (WB), and the International Monetary Fund (IMF).[27] In Africa, these international financial institutions prescribed agricultural trade liberalisation as part of the 1990's structural adjustment programs in response to the economic crisis faced by many countries on the continent.[28] The discussion below will explore the three theories deployed to support liberal rules in agriculture under the AfCFTA namely: theory of comparative advantage, the need to distribute food from surplus regions to deficit regions in Africa through international trade and the food security risk associated with restricting food trade.[29]

3.1 Liberal Thesis Based on Comparative Advantage

The doctrinal foundation of GATT rules, its successor the WTO, and subsequently the newly adopted continental-wide agreement, AfCFTA is the notion that free trade is more desirable than trade protectionism.[30] The ideology of free trade forming the basis of the AfCFTA is the theory of comparative advantage, first spelled out by

---

[24] Fakhri (2021), pp. 212–213; and Baier and Bergstrand (2007), p. 74.

[25] Gammage (2014), p. 780.

[26] United Nations Economic Commission for Africa (2018); Häberli (2016), p. 110; Hathaway and Ingco (1995), pp. 43–45; and Tania and Mapulanga-Hulston (2016), p. 310.

[27] IMF (2023); and IMF (2001).

[28] Chern (1989); IMF (1992).

[29] Johnson et al. (2022), p. 4.

[30] There are other compelling non-economic reasons pushing African States to engage in agricultural trade. For instance, the idea of Pan-Africanism is also pushing them to engage in agricultural trade to strengthen the political relationship among fellow allies. Further, agricultural trade creates a diplomatic bond between parties thereby diminishing the chances of making war and at the same time, increasing the costs of waging a war. This can be an effective deterrence for countries to avoid fighting wars. See Tkara (2012).

Adam Smith and later further developed by David Ricardo in 1817.[31] The theory of comparative advantage posits that efficiency gains from specialised agricultural trade lead to an overall welfare improvement for countries engaged in such trade relationships.[32] The basic logic behind the theory of comparative advantage is that if countries specialise in producing products that they have a competitive edge on and are relatively better at compared to other products, and then engage in trade with one another, they will be better off than they would have been without trade.[33] As Adam Smith asserts:

> What is prudence in the conduct of every private family can scarcely be folly in that of a great kingdom. If a foreign country can supply us with a commodity cheaper than we can make it, better buy it of them with some part of the produce of our own industry employed in a way in which we have some advantage.[34]

The theory of comparative advantage goes deeper to suggest that the gains from trade hold even when a country does not have an absolute advantage in any goods.[35] In other words, efficiency gains will benefit all African countries, when they specialise in the goods which they are relatively better at producing on the continent and then trade with each other.[36] Because each African country faces different opportunity costs in the production of different goods, due to differing endowments such as land, climate, capital, technology, and labour, each contracting state under the AfCFTA has a comparative advantage in at least some goods.[37]

The gains that ought to come from specialisation and trade can be shown arithmetically, which is a large part of the appeal of this theory.[38] It has been modified periodically by economic theorists over the years to consider contemporary conditions, but the basic principle of comparative advantages such as specialisation and trade as a means by which to capture efficiency gains is still at the center of today's international trade theory.[39] There are some mechanisms by which specialisation

---

[31] Fleischacker (2004), p. 4.

[32] Ricardo (1951), p. 1; Gonzalez (2002), pp. 433–433. On the other hand, Smith's contemporary, David Hume in his essay entitled "Of Commerce" recognises agricultural trade as an extension of property rights. His argument is that just as the state should not impair property rights, it should not impair agricultural trade, which is an exercise of contractual autonomy between consenting parties. However, Hume was not a "hard core" free trade advocate either. Instead, he supported the infant industry argument which encourages trade protectionism for the purposes of protecting infant industries or vulnerable economic sectors. See Grose et al. (1812), p. 284.

[33] Tokarick (2008), pp. 199–216. See Baldwin (2004), p. 525; Dollar and Kraay (2002), p. 197. However, some argue that a link between trade and growth is difficult to establish and that trade liberalisation in itself does not guarantee a long-term effect on growth. It has to be combined with other structural policies. See Winters (2002), p. 115.

[34] Smith (1776), p. 478.

[35] WTO (n.d.).

[36] Dollar and Kraay (2002), p. 195; and Carmen (2002), p. 420.

[37] Lamy (2007).

[38] Van den Bossche (2008), p. 2.

[39] Moon and Pino (2016).

and trade should lead to material gains for trading partners.[40] According to the theory, these gains accrue across a variety of trading sectors, including agriculture, and help to bolster a range of policy goals, including the achievement of food security.[41] According to the Food and Agriculture Organisation (FAO), and the World Bank (WB) open trade policies have the potential to enhance food security as well as access to food.[42] The conceptual linkages in these contexts are made more or less along the following lines, and together have formed the underlying basis for pursuit of liberal agricultural trade rules under the AfCFTA as a key ingredient to attain economic growth and development.[43]

Openness to trade at global and continental level fosters competition that leads to specialisation which enhances efficiency.[44] The notion is that certain crops will be produced in those African countries where their production is most efficient and by those that have the natural endowments to enable certain crops to be grown with the scarcest resources using methods that exploit economies of scale.[45] These gains translate into increased production of food on a continental and global scale.[46] The improved ubiquitous food supply will result in the universal accessibility of food across the continent, including by those African countries that now import it rather than produce it themselves.[47] The hypothesis is that since all African countries benefit from trade and thus more food should mean all countries receive a greater share than previously.[48] The implication is that a greater supply of food across the continent should result in lower food prices, as dictated by the forces of supply and demand.[49] Lower food prices should ensure that food becomes more accessible to the poor, hence improving food security.[50] It must be borne in mind that the efficiency gains, including from agricultural trade products, should arithmetically contribute to economic growth, thus creating more employment opportunities under the AfCFTA and lifting the have "knots" from the depths of poverty.[51] The theory further predicts that these notable adjustments within an economy should result in greater incomes, making food more accessible even to those who are not working in the food and agriculture sector.[52] In sum, neoclassical economic trade theory sees specialisation and trade based on the principle of comparative advantage as

[40] Edelman (2014), p. 962.

[41] Van der Mensbrugghe and Beghin (2005).

[42] Chimni (2006), p. 6.

[43] Davis and Neacsu (2001), p. 755.

[44] Ibid para 1 at 734.

[45] Cypher and Dietz (1997), p. 119.

[46] Nkamleu (2020), p. 303; Chimni (2011), p. 263.

[47] Krugman (1994), p. 16.

[48] Trauger (2014), p. 1132.

[49] Fukase and Martin (2020), pp. 1–2.

[50] Van der Mensbrugghe and Beghin (2005), p. 55.

[51] Clapp (2006), p. 563.

[52] Dan and Alan (1993), p. 109.

advantageous for access to food because it enables the harnessing of efficiency and its gains on a global, regional and continental scale resulting in more food, lower prices and better access in Africa.[53]

3.2 Shortcomings of the Liberal Thesis on Comparative Advantage Theory

The theory of comparative advantage has been criticised on various fronts as resting on a flawed thesis. Firstly, the theory is premised on particular assumptions which must be correct if it is to have any convincing intrinsic validity.[54] There has been a heated debate among academic commentators on whether the assumptions are correct in practice.[55] This means that if the assumptions offered by the theory are not credible, then further questions must be asked about the possible effect of agricultural trade liberalisation on the development of agriculture, food security, rural populations, and the realisation of the human right to food in the context of developing countries in Africa.[56] An assessment of studies undertaken by the WB, WTO, FAO and UN reveal a divergence of perspectives in international economic law concerning the value of the theory in realising other polycentric matters such as the human right to food, food security and other social objectives.[57] Whilst the WTO law, WB and AfCFTA approach is pro-liberalisation, FAO has clearly raised questions about the credibility of the assumptions.[58]

Further, the former UN Special Rapporteur on the human right to food in 2011 enjoined countries to minimise their dependence on liberal rules in agriculture as a means to ensure the realisation of the human right to food, a call which sparked an open debate with the WTO Director General at the time.[59] The shortcomings of the theory of comparative advantage become evident when one looks at the plain and implied assumptions propagated by it.[60] Although all economic hypotheses simplify actual conditions to some degree, the question is whether the assumptions are reasonably expressive enough that the predictions of the theory hold, or whether they simplify too much such that the credibility of the theory is heavily diminished.[61] The theory makes a "straight jacket" hypothesis that capital and labour are static between the trading partners: that there is perfect movement of capital and labour within the

[53] Davis and Neacsu (2001), p. 110.
[54] Jarosz (2016), p. 1117; Valensisi (2016), p. 251.
[55] Clem (2015), p. 66.
[56] Schumacher (2013), p. 105.
[57] Birchfield and Corse (2010), p. 693; and Balassa (1965), p. 99.
[58] FAO (n.d.).
[59] Green (2011); Prasch (1996), p. 56.
[60] Fletcher (2010), pp. 95–105.
[61] IISD (2003).

domestic sphere of a country: that markets are perfect with a healthy competition for goods: that there are no externalities; goods are equal: that there are no costs of transportation: that there is full employment; that trade between African countries always balances: that technology, resources and labour productivity are fixed: and that all partners benefit from trade.[62]

Several academic commentators have pointed out that the theory is particularly unrealistic when examined in the context of trade between countries with a relatively better of economies and those who have extremely poor economies.[63] The argument is that if capital and labour were mobile, capital would be drawn to areas where absolute advantage is present and labour would seek out opportunities where wages are highest.[64] The comparative advantage rests on the premise that it is only goods that are mobile across borders, and economies then adjust through various mechanisms. The theory assumes further that all African partners then benefit from low prices and exchange rates as a result of the immobility of capital and labour.[65] This assumption is thus quintessential to the theory. The immobility of capital and labour is the most contested element of the theory of comparative advantage. Critics argue that owing to the globalisation of today's world, capital and labour are very mobile where money and people move across national borders on a daily basis.[66]

A notable fallacy of the theory of comparative advantage is its failure to recognise that in the contemporary era the traffic of capital is very common and it moves to regions of the world including those African countries where there are investor-friendly policies through economic vehicles such as the Transnational Companies (TNCs) and other corporate entities.[67] On the other hand, less mobile than capital, labour can migrate to some extent.[68] Indeed, the assumption underlying comparative advantage which accepts that capital and labour are static becomes problematic. This weakness found in the assumptions has an important effect on food security claims made within the dominant AfCFTA agricultural trade liberalisation discourse.[69] The freely movable capital means that transnational corporates such as TNCs can invest in African countries such as South Africa, Botswana, Rwanda with a conducive economic climate which is relatively better than others with fragile economies to capitalise on absolute advantage that may exist in those locations, perhaps because of their neoliberal economic orientations and currency stability.[70]

62 Chen (2014), p. 10.

63 Gonzalez (2002), p. 433.

64 Gonzalez (2002), p. 433.

65 Gonzalez (2002), p. 434.

66 Murphy (1999), p. 4.

67 Fofack (2017), p. 81; Leary (1996a, b), pp. 177–178.

68 Orford (2015), p. 156; Stiglitz et al. (2012), p. 38.

69 Sykes (1998), p. 82.

70 As Warikandwa and other scholars opine, "there is a growing fear that a "race to the bottom" is occurring in the logic that labour standards are being lowered to attract investors." Indeed, a lot of literature suggests that due to globalisation of international markets, there is a high movement of capital necessitated by the lowering of labour standards specifically in poor countries, thus directly

These TNCs dominate the structure of international agricultural production through financial ownership of farm operations in economically strong African countries.[71] This means that a bigger segment of gains derived from agricultural trade will probably accrue to owners of capital who are (TNC) companies, rather than to the general agricultural workers that supply those firms or work as paid labour on large-scale foreign owned farms.[72]

Following from the above, it can be posited that the mobility of labour across the national boarders has further negative implications for the successful application of comparative advantage theory in the agricultural sector under the AfCFTA.[73] In many African countries, the agricultural sector sources its labour from migrant labour.[74] Farm workers now have the capacity to migrate seasonally, for instance, impoverished farm workers from Zimbabwe, Malawi and Mozambique frequently move to work in relatively better neighbouring economies such as South Africa, Botswana allowing the recipient countries to enhance their own comparative advantage in agriculture while competing with the agricultural production in those countries from which the workers migrated.[75] Such labour migration demographics can result in the decline of the agricultural sector in countries from which the migrants came from and raise pertinent questions about the degree of gains derived from trade for farmers in extremely marginalised countries on the African continent.[76] Moreover, migrant farmworkers usually are denied basic rights to healthcare, decent living conditions and other immunities which diminish the gains emanates from the comparative advantage.[77]

Another critique of the theory of comparative advantage relates to the assumption that the theory makes on the mobility of the factors of production between different activities within an economy which will allow specialisation in some agricultural goods over others.[78] The assumption that labour and capital can easily switch from producing one good to another is essential to the theory as it is what enables countries to specialise, which is required for the efficiency gains to be realised from international agricultural trade.[79] Proponents of agricultural trade liberalisation accept that there may be other adjustment costs emanating from specialisation, but normally assume these costs are minimal and impermanent.[80] In addition,

challenging the assumption that capital is static as propagated by the theory of comparative advantage. Warikandwa (2012), p. 1.

[71] Parpart et al. (2004), p. 53; and Randall (2004), p. 52.

[72] McMahon (2006), p. 15.

[73] McMahon (2006), p. 16.

[74] Anderson et al. (2001), p. 192; and Ismail (2006), p. 133.

[75] Wisborg et al. (2013); Bhorat and Hodge (1999), pp. 155–168.

[76] Brawley and Baerg (2007), p. 602; Nash and Mitchel (2005), pp. 34–37.

[77] Sen (2010), p. 1012.

[78] Mucavele (2000), pp. 1–32.

[79] Margerum (1999), p. 743.

[80] Winters (2002), p. 112.

it is largely assumed that the gains from trade accruing to the country enable governments to cover the adjustment costs and compensate losers.[81] However, it can be argued that the adjustment costs are far more problematic than proponents concede.[82]

It is noteworthy that the mobility of capital has a negative impact not just in terms of the economic costs, but human costs as well.[83] When capital moves, there is no assurance that new employment opportunities created by specialisation will be better or more fulfilling for workers than previous ones.[84] The situation is further exacerbated in instances where the mechanisms to compensate losers are unavailable.[85] Farm workers may be rendered jobless. Indeed, this means that the assumption does not accommodate fully the unique role that agriculture plays in providing rural employment, supporting livelihood and building ultimate safety nets for many vulnerable and potentially destitute peasants across relatively poor economies in Africa.[86] When peasants are pushed out of the farming business, those who are affected are more likely to find it difficult to secure employment in non-farm activities or as agricultural workers.[87] Empirical evidence reveals that compensation for "losers" in the form of social security benefits and schemes such as food assistance programs or in the form of payments to small-scale producers, whose livelihoods are compromised, is beyond the affordability of many economically struggling African countries.[88]

Another critique of the theory is that without perfect competition and a level playing field, efficiency gains emanating from specialisation remain a pipe dream.[89] Academic commentators point out that the assumption of competitive markets is misleading because in reality there are few actual competitive markets in the world.[90] The lack of competitive markets and a level playing field is important for access to food considerations.[91] Reality has shown that market power is concentrated in the hands of a few TNCs who dominate the agricultural sector within few African countries, as well as internationally.[92] In some agricultural food markets, just a minority of corporate entities dominate the market.[93] Competition law experts maintain that in a situation where a firm control forty percent or less of the market share it means

---

[81] De Paula and Pessali (2014), p. 487.

[82] De Paula and Pessali (2014), p. 487.

[83] McGeorge (1992), p. 368.

[84] Gebrehiwot (2019), pp. 85–88.

[85] Trauger (2014), p. 1133.

[86] Einarsson (2001).

[87] Hawkes and Plahe (2012), p. 23.

[88] In some African countries competition law is relatively young and still evolving. It has not been used to eliminate monopolies created by TNC in the area of Agro-food business. See Geldenhuy (2012), p. 15; and Birdi et al. (2002).

[89] Oyelami (2022), p. 2; Valdes (1987), p. 593; and Surya (2006), p. 274.

[90] Zahniser et al. (2015).

[91] Hartzenberg (2006), p. 668.

[92] Valente (2016), pp. 1–8.

[93] WTO (n.d.).

the market is competitive.[94] Ratios higher than that imply some degree of market control, which in economic terms is considered inefficient.[95] When the degrees of anti-competitive practices exceed that percentage, it results in uncompetitive and unfair markets.[96]

According to the statistics published by FAO, about four firms, Monsanto, Bayer, Kraft, Heinz and Dow dominate the global grain market, accounting for more than seventy to eighty percent of the world's grain trade including in Africa.[97] This means that these corporate entities have enough monopoly to manipulate prices in ways that result in devastating results.[98] The situation is worsened by the fact that within countries, certain firms dominate markets.[99] For instance, in the US only four major TNC's account for over eighty percent of the market for processed beef process and only four firms account for fifty percent of the US market for broiler chickens, and forty six percent of the pork market.[100] The same degree of concentration exists for agricultural trade in Africa and other developing countries where just a handful of firms have monopoly over an entire market.[101] Ultimately, it then defies logic for one to argue that there is a natural comparative advantage which develops and results in effective allocation of resources as envisaged by the theory of comparative advantage.[102]

Further, the lack of evenness at the global and continental playing field of the agricultural sectors is more evident when one compares levels of government support for the sector between countries.[103]As it will be seen, some better-off economies in Africa have traditionally given huge levels of subsidies to their own farmers at levels that poorer countries are unable to match for their own farmers often because of obligations to liberalise their economies under programs of structural adjustment.[104] This status quo is also applicable on international level where some larger developing countries, such as India and China have been able to lend support to their farmers in trade liberalisation and food security in recent years; the poorest countries in Africa are typically unable to provide any farmer subsidy support at all. As Khor[105] notes, agricultural production and trade are not determined by comparative advantage at that point, but rather comparative access to subsidies.[106]

[94] FAO (2014).
[95] Calcagno and Walker (2010), p. 892.
[96] Calcagno and Walker (2010), p. 894.
[97] FAO (2015), p. 46.
[98] FAO (2015), p. 46.
[99] Malig (2014), pp. 1–45.
[100] Bloom et al. (2012).
[101] Khor (2010), p. 54.
[102] Pogge (2005), p. 17.
[103] Endean Nierenberg (2011), p. 620.
[104] Chen (2014), p. 8.
[105] Khor (2010), p. 4.
[106] Khor (2010), p. 5.

3.2.1 Liberal Thesis Based on Trade as a Tool for Continental Distribution of Food

Another key argument deployed to support agricultural trade liberalisation under the AfCFTA, which advances the comparative advantage theory, is the necessity of capturing the efficiency gains emanating from specialisation and exchange.[107] The theory maintains that countries have diverse natural endowments some cannot produce all of their own food, while other countries including some in Africa are naturally able to produce more food than they need.[108] This means that trade empowers less endowed African countries to depend on others to provide food through imports when their own production fails to meet the demand.[109] Because world and continental agricultural output is more stable than agricultural production at the national and regional level, due to weather variability and other conditions, reliance on agricultural trade to move food from surplus to deficit regions helps to stabilise food prices.[110]

This means that for proponents of liberal rules under the AfCFTA, there is an ethical obligation to distribute food from the regions of the world including those on the African continent that produce more to where there is a deficit to ensure access to food for the hungry.[111] The preceding logic is substantiated by the fact that since global and continental climate change is threatening food production, it becomes imperative not just on moral grounds, but also on environmental sustainability grounds, to produce food in locations where it is most efficient to do so.[112] Ultimately, this will lead to the efficient use of scarce water and energy resources thereby making food more accessible to the African population.[113]

3.3 *Shortcomings of the Liberal Thesis on the Distribution of Food*

A more forceful indictment mounted against this theory is that despite free trade, food remains unevenly distributed internationally, regionally and nationally.[114] It has become increasingly more accepted within food policy circles that having sufficient food to feed a population within a country's borders, or even internationally, does not bring assurance that everyone will be well fed. According to FAO about

107 FAO (2023), pp. 1–65.

108 Zidouemba and Mustapha (2021), p. 326; and Moon and Pino (2016).

109 De Bres (2010), p. 20; and Esserman (2006), p. 375.

110 Gonzalez (2014), p. 466.

111 Herman (1993), p. 53.

112 WTO (n.d.).

113 Andrea (2018), p. 34; De Schutter (2009), pp. 1–52.

114 Glipo (2003).

811 million people of the world's poorest people are food insecure and of that figure about 140 million Africans are facing hunger and acute food shortages.[115] This is mainly because people's ability to access food is determined by many factors such as the capacity to obtain resources to produce it, buy it or trade personal items for it.[116] Essentially, when African countries lose revenues collected from tariffs in the process liberalisation promoted by the AfCFTA and are typically short of the resources available to compensate the "losers", access to food becomes a pipe dream when such people's source of livelihoods and savings are threatened by adjustments brought into the economy.[117]

Further, some academic commentators argue that agricultural trade liberalisation if not implemented prudently, can yield little results in terms of global and continental distribution of food.[118] They maintain that an overreliance on food imports has left many Least Developed Countries (LDCs), engrossed in a deep food crisis especially when the Russian-Ukraine conflict began.[119] About six African countries, Eritrea, Egypt, Benin, Sudan, Djibouti, and Tanzania imported over 70 percent of their wheat from Ukraine. The African Development Bank observes that this conflict triggered a shortage of about 30 million tons of grains on the African continent, along with a sharp increase in cost.[120] An over dependence on food imports destroys the domestic agricultural sector and exposes marginalised groups to the fluctuations in agricultural commodity often associated with world markets.[121] It encourages imports of cheap food products that often lead to greater market dependence and vulnerability to price shocks in the future.[122] This means that policies designed to protect Africa's poorest are needed to ensure that they are not exposed to high and volatile global food prices. Therefore, the mainstream trade narrative's overemphasis on agricultural trade liberalisation under the AfCFTA can also potentially impede access to food.[123]

---

[115] FAO (2023).

[116] Santos (2005), p. 29.

[117] Gonzalez (2006), p. 67.

[118] Matthews (1988).

[119] Kleen (2008).

[120] African Development Bank (2022).

[121] De Schutter (2009), pp. 1–52.

[122] Nzelibe (2004), pp. 89–90.

[123] FAO (1998).

3.4 *Liberal Thesis Based on Perceived Dangers of Agricultural Protectionism*

A third argument deployed by proponents of agricultural trade liberalisation under the AfCFTA is the heavy economic costs which emanates from continued trade protection in the agricultural sector.[124] In building the case for liberalising agricultural trade in African countries, multinational institutions such as WB contrast the costs of agricultural trade protection with projected gains from liberalisation.[125] They argue that agricultural protectionism including export taxes, export restrictions, tariffs, state-managed marketing boards, and public stockholding are highly inefficient policies and schemes from an economic perspective.[126] These organisations argue that the inefficiencies result in distorted price signals that can result in weaker production levels and higher food prices, both of which harm the poor and exacerbate lack of food globally and continentally.[127] They further point out that protectionist measures can also make agricultural producers in developing nations, including African countries more vulnerable by denying them market opportunities.[128]

Further, trade advocates also argue that the lack of open trading systems for agriculture leads to thin markets.[129] They argue that in situations where only a few suppliers dominate the trade in certain crops in such cases, supply disruptions emanating from just one supplier could result in more volatility and vulnerability to crises for those that rely on imports of that crop.[130] The use of export bans and other export restrictions in this context are seen by trade advocates to be especially problematic, as the erection of sudden barriers to trade can cause price spikes that have direct implications on access to food under the AfCFTA.[131] Thin markets and export restrictions were widely referred to as key contributing factors to the food price spikes which hit the world between 2018 and 2022 periods.[132]

124 Fajgelbaum et al. (2020), p. 4; Wise (2009a), p. 870.
125 Conceiçào-Heldt (2013), p. 432.
126 Watkins (1996), p. 245.
127 Cleveland (2002), p. 132.
128 Jackson (1997), p. 310.
129 Carmen (2002), p. 435.
130 Francioni (2001), pp. 1–392.
131 Simons (2008), pp. 339–340.
132 Powell (2004), p. 220.

3.5 *Shortcoming of the Liberal Thesis on the Danger of Agricultural Protectionism*

The first critique is that trade protectionism is not always detrimental to the agricultural sector.[133] Morrison and Sarris argue that free trade can leave agricultural sectors weak which can impede rather than improve nation's prospects for economic growth, poverty alleviation and food security.[134] In some cases, transnational agrarian movements such as *La Vía Campesina* have maintained that investments in small-scale, diverse farming systems provide meaningful livelihoods, with enormous social benefits, for a significant portion of humanity and government organised food distribution and that social protection programs based on need, rather than market efficiency, are also important to ensure all members of society have access to an adequate diet.[135] If societies are to take access to food seriously, efficiency must not be allowed to trump other less quantifiable objectives to the point that food security is threatened.[136] Careful consideration of multiple social goals is required in the formulation of agricultural and food security policies, including policies guiding agricultural trade.

Opponents of liberal rules in agriculture have argued that it encourages monoculture farming damaging biodiversity and other ecosystem services provided by the agricultural sector, ultimately affecting the long-term sustainability of the food system on which food security relies.[137] They further suggest that there are enormous social costs that result from loss of livelihood for rural people that affect their ability to access sufficient food.[138] In market-oriented agricultural systems that rely on efficiency criteria, purchasing power is a primary determinant of food distribution, rather than need. Some market inefficiencies are important for ensuring food security.[139] Certain short-term inefficiencies introduced through government policies in the agricultural sector can lead to increases in long-term productivity.[140] The ecological resilience of agriculture relies on a measure of redundancy especially in many developing countries on the African continent that can be seen as "inefficient" in economic terms, yet it is vital for the protection of ecosystem services over the long term.[141]

---

133 Meulen (2010), p. 220.

134 Morrison and Sarris (2007); and Wise (2009b).

135 Claeys (2014), p. 30; and Bengoa (2021), p. 37.

136 Madhura (1996), p. 1664.

137 Sen (2010).

138 De Schutter (2009), p. 2.

139 De Schutter (2009), p. 2.

140 Deardorff (2005), p. 1005.

141 Deardorff (2005), p. 1006.

4 Exploring the Assimilation of Liberal Philosophy Through the Substantive Provisions of the AfCFTA

Art 3 of the AfCFTA which provides the general objectives of the continental free trade agreement recognises liberal rules in trade, including those applicable to trade in agriculture as one of the core elements of the agreement. It identifies the objectives of the AfCFTA as to: (i) eliminate tariffs and non-tariff barriers to trade in goods progressively; (ii) liberalise trade in services progressively; (iii) cooperate on investment, intellectual property rights and competition policy; (iv) cooperate on all trade related areas; (v) cooperate on customs matters and the implementation of trade facilitation measures; (vi) establish a mechanism for the settlement of disputes concerning members' rights and obligations and (vii) establish and maintain an institutional framework for the implementation and administration of the agreement. In terms of trade in goods, including agricultural products, the way in which the AfCFTA intend to achieve an increase in intra-African trade is by significantly regulating import and export duties, achieving tariff concessions and removing non-tariff barriers.[142]

Importantly, Art 4 of the AfCFTA makes it clear that the overarching ideology of the agreement is the liberal thesis by obliging contracting parties to fulfilling and realising the objectives set out in Art 3 by (a) progressively eliminate tariffs and non-tariff barriers to trade in goods; (b) progressively liberalise trade in services; (c) cooperate on investment, intellectual property rights and competition policy; (d) cooperate on all trade-related areas; (e) cooperate on customs matters and the implementation of trade facilitation measures; (f) establish a mechanism for the settlement of disputes concerning their rights and obligations; and (g) establish and maintain an institutional framework for the implementation and administration of the AfCFTA.[143] According to art 5 of the AfCFTA, contracting parties should adhere to the following principles driven by Member States of the African Union; recognise Free Trade Areas (FTAs) as building blocks for the AfCFTA (c) variable geometry; (d) flexibility and special and differential treatment; (e) transparency and disclosure of information; (f) preservation of the acquis; (g) Most-Favoured-Nation (MFN) Treatment; (h) National Treatment; (i) reciprocity; 6 (j) substantial liberalisation; (k) consensus in decision-making; and (l) best practices in the RECs, in the State Parties and International Conventions binding the African Union.[144] Given the foregoing liberal rules, currently the pre-eminence of agricultural trade liberalisation as the overarching ideological thesis which guides the regulation of agricultural trade under the AfCFTA is beyond question.

---

[142] Art 3 of the AfCFTA.

[143] Art 4 of the AfCFTA.

[144] Art 5 of the AfCFTA.

5 Reinvisioning Liberal Rules Governing Trade in Agriculture Under the AfCFTA to Realise the Human Right to Food

Considering the above discussion, it is clear that the theoretical justification of liberal rules under the AfCFTA has wider cracks.[145] The efficacy of the liberal ideological basis for AfCFTA rules governing trade in agriculture remains problematic and contestable.[146] Whilst the dominant assumption is that the collective integration of African markets achieved through the adoption of continentally-based liberal rules in agriculture potentially offers an avenue for boosting intra-African agricultural trade, there is a need to re-configure liberal rules in agriculture to off-set the negative bearing of these rules on the realisation of the human right to food.[147] It can be opined that this requires contracting parties under the AfCFTA to strike a new balance between liberalism and illiberalism in pursuit of an effective framework governing trade in agriculture.[148] Further, in an era of illiberalism characterising by trade volatility emanating from the current multiplicity of the geopolitical tensions of the Russian-Ukraine, the Israel-Palestinian conflicts, the ideological cleavages created by the war in Africa's Darfur region, the undemocratic removal of governments in west-Africa, and the hostility between China and United States arising from stiff trade competition and the Taiwan contestations, there is a need to reinvision the AfCFTA rules on agriculture to achieve food sovereign, food self-sufficient and the realisation of the human right to food.[149] The discussion below will examine how liberal rules governing trade in agriculture under the AFCFTA can be re-calibrated in a manner which promotes the food security needs of African countries.

5.1 *Effective Scientific Implementations of Variable Geometry for Trade in Agriculture*

Bearing in mind the potential negative effect that liberal rules have on trade in agriculture including impeding the realisation of the human rights to food and food security, the implementation of the AfCFTA liberal model must be guided by the principle of variable geometry to accommodate food security interest of the less advantaged African countries.[150] As mentioned above, Article 5 (c) of the AfCFTA provides for variable geometry as an important principle which should guide trade

[145] Karingi and Mevel (2013), p. 296; Abbott et al. (2008), p. 353.

[146] Ndonga et al. (2020), p. 4; and Clapp (2015).

[147] Fofack and Mold (2021), p. 5; Daya et al. (2006), p. a99; Bonuedi et al. (2020), pp. 1121–1140.

[148] Sunge et al. (2022), p. 313.

[149] FAO (2022, 2023).

[150] Fusacchia et al. (2022), p. 237.

liberalisation to enable contracting parties to address unique trade-related challenges associated with each of them.[151] The principle of variable geometry was successfully used to guide the EU integration process, as it provided contracting parties with the flexibility to move with different pace towards integration.[152] The concept of variable geometry has its origination under the WTO multilateral trade system and was them utilised to break the impasse of various integration initiatives caused by the breakdown of the Doha development agenda due to lack of consensus between the contracting parties.[153] Variable geometry would protect regulatory sovereignty of contracting parties under the AfCFTA by allowing them to choose the speed of their own integration and to accept or not to accept various commitments which they should honour in the implementation of a particular trade instrument.[154] In the context of trade in agriculture, variable geometry would seek to minimise the cost of liberal rules on agriculture by accommodating the different levels of agricultural development and commitment towards integration of African agricultural markets in pursuit of realising the human right to food and securing food security in member states.[155]

Aside from the above, even though the employment of variable geometry in the context of AfCFTA is desirable as some academic commentators may argue, it makes agricultural trade liberalisation more complex and may slow the initiative toward continental integration.[156] This means more scientifically grounded research on the application of the principle of variable geometry in agriculture should be undertaken under the AfCFTA because the use of the principle should not be the potential cause of the failure of the AfCFTA.[157] Given that the African continent has more than 55 countries, the existence of differences in agricultural development and food security-challenges are beyond question.[158] Nonetheless, the use of variable geometry has its own trade-off including the fact that it is unclear whether allowing many contracting parties not to honour their full agricultural trade liberalisation commitments will in long-term increase intra-African trade in agricultural products or inflow of foreign direct investments.[159] In sum, despite the view that variable geometry will accommodate the food security interests of contracting parties, it can potentially limit the realisation of the goals of AfCFTA.[160] Indeed, the experience that Africa has had with the use of variable geometry in regional integration requires contracting parties to implement it on a contextual and scientific basis rather than

151 Art 5(c) of the AfCFTA.

152 Nissen (2022), p. 123.

153 Cornford (2004), p. 3.

154 Cornford (2004), p. 3.

155 Sucker (2019), p. 758.

156 Sommer and MacLeod (2019), p. 73; and Saurombe and Nkabinde (2013), p. 614.

157 Kuhlmann and Agutu (2020), p. 5.

158 Gumede (2020), pp. 1–39.

159 Weekes et al. (2014), pp. 1–16.

160 United Nations Conference on Trade and Development (n.d.).

taking a blanket wholesale approach which permits all contracting parties under the AfCFTA not to honour their liberal commitments.[161]

5.2 *Towards the Negotiation of a Specialised Agricultural Treaty Under the AfCFTA*

In addition to the implementation of variable geometry alluded above, trade in agriculture should be treated as an exception to the liberal rules applicable to the mainstream ambit of the AfCFTA liberalisation process.[162] The argument is that the overall AfCFTA is not entirely fit to regulate trade in agriculture given that the liberal rules that it imposes have a negative effect on the realisation of the human right to food and other important polycentric issues.[163] This means contracting parties under the continental-wide agreement should adopt a separate legal instrument either in the form of a distinct legally binding agreement or protocol which governs trade in agriculture.[164] This instrument should govern market access, domestic support for agriculture, and subsidies under the AfCFTA.[165] The instrument should operate with some degree of autonomy, separate from the main AfCFTA instruments and Protocol on Trade in Goods which is largely suitable for governing manufactured or industrial products.[166] Whilst a complete clinical isolation of agriculture from other instruments under the AfCFTA would be undesirable because it cause the problem of legal fragmentation, there is a need to achieve a certain level of decoupling and delinking of agricultural trade governance in sync with the current WTO multilateral practices where rules applicable in agriculture exist distinctively from those applicable to industrial products.[167] The proposed agreement can be called, the African Agricultural Trade Agreement (AATA), or the African Protocol Governing Trade in Agricultural Products and Services (APGTAPS) housed under the auspices of the AfCFTA regime.[168] The ideological basis for the proposed agricultural instrument should be the promotion of food sovereignty and self-sufficiency.[169] The liberal ideology should become a secondary subservient ideology.

---

[161] Tangermann (2014), pp. 1–32.

[162] Cardwell and Smith (2013), p. 891.

[163] FAO (2022) 'Update on The World Trade Organisation (WTO) Agricultural Negotiations and Developments In Regional Trade Agreements Related To Agriculture' Seventy-fifth Session, 13–15 July 2022, pp. 1–9.

[164] Kigwiru (2022), pp. 1–36; and Simiyu (2015).

[165] Kigwiru (2022), p. 4.

[166] This idea of a new agreement is largely borrowed from the views tendered by Michael Cardwell and Fiona Smith T in the context of WTO multilateral trade regime. See Cardwell and Smith (2013), p. 867.

[167] Australian Government (2010), p. 5.

[168] Cardwell and Smith (2013), p. 866.

[169] UN (2023), p. 1.

In other words, the proposed instrument should only allow contracting parties under the AfCFTA to implement liberal ideology in agriculture in instances where their food security concerns are adequately accommodated.

6 (De)liberalising, (De)globalising and (De)continentalising AfCFTA Trade in Agriculture

The above discussion has shown that a liberal approach towards the regulation of trade in agriculture under the AfCFTA can potentially negatively impact the realisation of the human right to food in more disadvantaged African economies, whilst largely benefiting relatively economically strong African states.[170] The flooding of cheap food imports into the domestic markets of African states with fragile economies will result in the poor small-scale farmers being unable to compete and taken out of business, a position which opens the door to the creation of monopolistic entities in the food regime, who then charge high prices for their foods because of lack of competition.[171] To mitigate the negative effects of liberal rules on agriculture, there is a need to develop rules which deliberalise and deglobalise trade in agriculture.[172] The AU and the AfCFTA Secretariat should adopt policies that promote food sovereignty and food self-sufficiency in contracting states.[173] By deliberalising trade in agriculture, the AfCFTA would enable contracting parties to have enough policy space to provide domestic policy support for agriculture without violating agriculture rules.[174]

7 Promoting Financial Investment in Agriculture

The aforementioned efforts towards the recalibration of liberal rules in agriculture under the AfCFTA will fail to bear significant results if contracting parties do not have the political will to invest financial resources in agriculture and work towards the higher mechanisation of the sector.[175] Contemporary agricultural practices have become highly mechanised and powered by the application of heavy agricultural equipment, machines, drone technology, and of recently artificial intelligence.[176] The goal to eradicate hunger requires efforts beyond dealing with rules that govern

[170] Karingi and Mevel (2013), p. 296.
[171] Karingi and Mevel (2013), p. 297.
[172] Latin American and Caribbean Parliament (2017).
[173] Trade Justice Movement (2023).
[174] Will (2017).
[175] Reid (1996).
[176] Adriaans and Khan (2020), pp. 1–22.

agricultural trade. Contracting parties under the AfCFTA should pour resources towards agro-based programs tailor-made for subsistence and resettled farmers in peri-urban and remote areas.[177] African countries should build new agricultural infrastructure such as agricultural polytechnical institutions, fast track the equitable distribution of land based on respect for the rule of law and private property rights.[178] The building of new agricultural infrastructure can be achieved through private-public partnerships, leveraging mineral resources and combating the leakage of economic resources through unabated corruption.[179]

8 Conclusion

This chapter has demonstrated that the AfCFTA encapsulates a liberal regime governing Africa's trade in agriculture.[180] It imposes continental-wide commitments which oblige contracting parties to liberalise trade in agriculture through the progressive dismantling of tariffs and non-tariff barriers in agricultural products.[181] This chapter has shown that there are three profound economic arguments deployed to justify the option of liberal rules in the regulation of agricultural trade namely: (a) the theory of comparative advantage; (b) the moral necessity to distribute food from surplus regions of the world to deficit regions through international trade; and (c) lastly the food security risk associated with restricting trade in food.[182] Ever since Adam Smith and David Ricardo systematically articulated the gains from trade, proponents of agricultural trade liberalisation have stressed the higher incomes and productive allocation of resources emanating from improved resource distribution as the main advantages of agricultural trade liberalisation.[183] The chapter has argued that the regulation of trade in agriculture under the auspices of the AfCFTA through the pursuit of a liberal model is not accommodative of the food security needs of the African countries.[184]

It has been argued that AfCFTA rules governing agricultural do not just derive their authority from the contractual principle of *pact sunt servanda*, but rather from the perceived gains which emanate from liberalising trade in agriculture.[185] This chapter has also shown that critics have found mounting evidence which cast doubt on the credibility of the assumptions underlying the dominant economic about the

[177] Simola et al. (2022), pp. 1–10.

[178] FAO (2008), pp. 1–155.

[179] Nash et al. (2013), pp. 1–70.

[180] Simola et al. (2022), pp. 1–10.

[181] Saygili et al. (2018), pp. 1–23; and Apiko et al. (2020), pp. 1–21.

[182] Akullo (2023), pp. 1–187.

[183] Aderemi (2022), pp. 1–6; and Ukwandu (2015), p. 20.

[184] Nwankwo and Ajibo (2020), p. 300.

[185] Berkum and Meijl (2000), p. 541.

regulation of agricultural trade.[186] These antagonists rail against the application of liberal rules in agricultural trade as benefiting corporations, harming small-scale farmers in weak economies, and diminishing the space for poor countries in Africa to pursue policies aimed at achieving food security and food self-sufficiency.[187] The assumption that capital and labour are immobile underpinning agricultural trade liberalisation is deeply flawed.[188] The chapter has posited that, whilst the liberal regulatory regime introduced by the AfCFTA has the potential to be a vehicle for boosting food security, there is a need to temper it with variable geometry in agriculture, the negotiation of a specialised instrument governing African trade in agriculture such as the AATA, or the APGTAPS housed under the AfCFTA regime and further investment in agriculture to offset any negative effect that the agreement may have on the realisation of the human right to food.[189]

References

Abbott P, Bentzen J, Tarp F (2008) Trade and development: lessons from Vietnam's past trade agreements. World Dev 72(2):341–353

Adriaans G, Khan N (2020) Investing for impact in the food and agriculture sector in Africa and South Asia. https://assets.cdcgroup.com/wp-content/uploads/2020/11/18115511/What-is-the-impact-of-investing-in-FA.pdf

African Development Bank (2022) Ukraine war threatens food crisis and political upheaval across Africa, warns top economist. https://www.afdb.org/en/news-and-events/ukraine-war-threatens-food-crisis-and-political-upheaval-across-africa-warns-top-economist-50269

African Union (2018) Agreement establishing the African Continental Free Trade Area. https://au.int/en/treaties/agreement-establishing-african-continental-free-trade-area

African Union (n.d.) The African Union Commission Agenda 2063: the Africa we want. A shared strategic framework for inclusive growth and sustainable development. https://au.int/en/agenda2063/overview

Akullo DO (2023) Food safety and free trade area in East Africa. Walden Dissertations and Doctoral Studies. 11893

Anderson K, Hoekman B, Strutt A (2001) Agriculture and the WTO: next steps. Rev Int Econ, Wiley Blackwell 9(2):192–214

Andrea C (2018) African Continental Free Trade Area: opportunities and challenges. Federalist Debate 31(3):32–35

Aniche ET (2020) African Continental Free Trade Area and African Union Agenda 2063: the roads to Addis Ababa and Kigali. J Contemp Afr Stud 41(3):1–16

---

186 United Nations. Economic Commission for Africa (2017) "United Nations. Economic Commission for Africa (2017-07). Report: the Continental Free Trade Area (CFTA) in a human rights perspective. Addis Ababa pp. 1–167.

187 United Nations Economic Commission for Africa (2017), p. 5.

188 Otenyo (2016), p. 108; Bellace and Haar (2019), p. 48.

189 Food and Agricultural Organisation (2020) The African Continental Free Trade Area Agreement and agricultural development: challenges and prospects. FSN Forum in Africa, Summary of the online discussion No. 15 pp. 1–6.

Apiko P, Woolfrey S, Byiers B (2020) The promise of the African Continental Free Trade Area (AfCFTA). Political Economy Dynamics of Regional Organisations in Africa, Discussion Paper No. 287, pp 1–21
Australian Government (2010) Viability of a critical mass framework for agricultural trade negotiations. https://agrifutures.com.au/wp-content/uploads/publications/10-025.pdf
Baier LS, Bergstrand JH (2007) Do free trade agreements actually increase members' International Trade? J Int Econ 71(1):72–95
Balassa B (1965) Trade liberalisation and revealed comparative advantage. Manchester School 33(2):99–123
Baldwin RE (2004) Openness and growth: what's the empirical relationship? In: Baldwin RE, Winters LA (eds) Challenges to globalisation: analyzing the economics. University of Chicago Press, p 525
Bellace J, Haar B (2019) Perspectives on labour and human rights. In: Bellace J, Haar B (eds) Research handbook on labour, business and human rights law. Routledge
Bengoa M, Mathur S, Narayanan B, Norberg HC (2021) Environmental effects of the African continental Free Trade Agreement: a computable general equilibrium model approach. J Afr Trade 8(2):36–48
Berkum SV, Meijl H (2000) The application of trade and growth theories to agriculture: a survey. Aust J Agric Econ 44(5):505–542
Bhorat H, Hodge J (1999) Decomposing shifts in labour demand in South Africa. South Afr J Econ 67(3):155–168
Birchfield L, Corse J (2010) Between starvation and globalization: realizing the right to food in India. Mich J Int Law 31(4):692–693
Birdi A, Dunne P, Watson D (2002) Labour demand and trade in South Africa: a dynamic panel analysis. http://www.tips.org.za/files/592.pdf
Bloom A et al (2012) Transnational corporations and the right to food. http://chrgj.org/wp-content/uploads/2012/07/TNCsandRTF.pdf
Bonuedi I, Kamasa K, Opoku EEO (2020) Enabling trade across borders and food security in Africa. Food Sec 12:1121–1140
Brawley MR, Baerg N (2007) Structural adjustment, development, and democracy. Int Stud Rev 9(4):601–614
Bres H (2010) Globalising justice: the ethics of poverty, global and international economic law. Cambridge University
Calcagno C, Walker M (2010) Excessive pricing: towards clarity and economic coherence. J Compet Law Econ 6(4):891–910
Cardwell M, Smith FT (2013) Renegotiation of the WTO Agreement on agriculture: accommodating the new big issue. Int Comp Law Q 62(4):865–898
Carmen CG (2002) Institutionalising inequality: the WTO Agreement on agriculture, food security, and developing countries. Columbia J Environ Law 27(2):433–490
Chen Y (2014) Trade, food security, and human rights: the rules in agricultural products and the evolving world food crisis. Ashgate Publishing Company, Burlington, VT
Chern F (1989) The World Bank and structural adjustment in Africa. https://journals.co.za/doi/pdf/10.10520/AJA02562804_662
Chidebe M et al (2020) Liberalizing regional trade regimes through AfCFTA: challenges and opportunities. J Afr Law 64(3):297–318
Chimni BS (2006) Third world approaches to international law: a manifesto. Int Community Law Rev 8(1):1–17
Chisaira LT (2018) The Continental Free Trade Area, neo-liberalism and Africa's resource curses. Young Afr Leaders J Dev 83(2):82–87
Claeys P (2014) Vía Campesina's struggle for the right to food sovereignty: from above or from below. In: Lambek NCS et al (eds) Rethinking food systems structural challenges, new strategies and the law, pp 29–52

Clapp J (2006) WTO agriculture negotiations: implications for the global south. Third World Q 27(4):563–577
Clapp J (2015) Food security and international trade: unpacking disputed narratives: the state of agricultural commodity markets. https://www.fao.org/documents/card/fr/c/63ba0e7a-c737-493a-942e-0a7d81ef87f3/
Clem C (2015) Food security and the World Trade Organisation. In: Ian G, Amir F (eds) Trade policy and world security: improving access to food in developing countries in the wake of high world food prices, pp 65–86
Cleveland SH (2002) Human rights sanctions and international trade: a theory of compatibility. J Int Econ Law 5(1):133–189
Conceiçào-Heldt EC (2013) Emerging powers in WTO negotiations: the domestic sources of trade policy preferences. Int Trade J 27(5):431–449
Cornford A (2004) Variable geometry for the WTO: concept and precedents. UNCTAD Discussion Papers 171, United Nations Conference on Trade and Development
Cypher JM, Dietz JL (1997) The process of economic development. Routledge
Dall A (2020) Exploring the neo-liberal trajectory of the African Continental Free Trade Area: a Pan-African emancipatory approach. https://www.net/publication/341618030_Exploring_the_Neo-liberal_Trajecto
Dan T, Alan N (1993) Equalising exchange: trade liberalisation and income convergence. Q J Econ 44(3):653–679
Davis MH, Neacsu D (2001) Legitimacy, globally: the incoherence of free trade practice, global economics and their governing principles of political economy. UMKC Law Rev 69(3):733–790
Daya Y et al (2006) Intra-Africa agricultural trade: a South African perspective. Indep Res J Manag Sci 6(1):a99
De Paula ND, Pessali H (2014) Agricultural trade negotiations and the challenges for food security. Agrarian South J Polit Econ 33(3):487–496
De Schutter O (2009) International trade in agriculture and the right to food. Dialogue on Globalisation Occassional Papers No. 46, p 4
Deardorff AV (2005) How robust is comparative advantage? Rev Int Econ 1005
Dollar D, Kraay A (2002) Growth is good for the poor. J Econ Growth 7(3):195–197
Edelman M (2014) Food sovereignty: forgotten genealogies and regulatory challenges. J Peasant Stud 41(6):959–979
Einarsson P (2001) 'The Disagreement on Agriculture'. http://www.grain.org/article/entries/309-the-disagreement-on-agriculture
Elkins Z, Ginsburg T, Simmons BA (2013) Getting to rights: treaty ratification, constitutional convergence, and human rights practice. Harv J Int Law 54(1):62–95
Endean Nierenberg LEN (2011) Reconciling the right to food and trade liberalisation: developing country opportunities. Minn J Int Law 22(10):619–647
Esserman S (2006) Just trade under law: do we need a theory of justice for international trade relations. Am Soc Int Law Proc, pp 375–376
Fajgelbaum PD et al (2020) The return to protectionism. Q J Econ 135(1):1–55
Fakhri M (2021) A trade agenda for the right to food. Development 64(3):212–219
FAO (1998) The implications of the Uruguay Round agreement on agriculture for developing countries. http://www.fao.org/docrep/004/w7814e/w7814e00.htm
FAO (2007) Agricultural Trade. Available https://www.fao.org/3/ai115e/ai115e.pdf
FAO (2008) Market-oriented agricultural infrastructure: appraisal of public-private partnerships. Agricultural Management, Marketing and Finance Occasional Paper No. 23, pp 1–155
FAO (2014) International dimensions of the right to adequate food. http://www.fao.org/3/a--i3896e.pdf
FAO (2015) The State of AgriculturalC Markets Trade and Food Security: achieving a better balance between national priorities and the collective good 2015–16. http://www.fao.org/3/a--i5090e.pdf

FAO (2020) The African Continental Free Trade Area Agreement and agricultural development: challenges and prospects. FSN Forum in Africa, Summary of the online discussion No. 15 pp 1–6
FAO (2022a) Impact of the Ukraine-Russia conflict on global food security and related matters under the mandate of the Food and Agriculture Organization of the United Nations. https://www.fao.org/3/nj164en/nj164en.pdf
FAO (2022b) Update on The World Trade Organisation (WTO) agricultural negotiations and developments in regional trade agreements related to agriculture. Seventy-fifth Session, 13–15 July 2022, pp 1–9
FAO (2023a) Global food security challenges and its drivers. https://www.fao.org/3/nn735en/nn735en.pdf
FAO (2023b) Near East and North Africa – regional overview of food security and nutrition: trade as enabler for food security and nutrition 2023. https://doi.org/10.4060/cc4773en
FAO (2023c) The state of food insecurity in the world 2023. https://www.fao.org/documents/card/en/c/cc3017en. Accessed 28 Nov 2023
FAO (2023d) The state of food insecurity in the world, 2023. https://www.fao.org/3/cc3017en/cc3017en.pdf
FAO (n.d.) Symposium on agriculture, trade and food security. http://www.Fao.Org/Docrep/meeting/x3065E.htm
Fleischacker S (2004) On Adam Smith's Wealth of Nations: a philosophical companion. Princeton University Press
Fletcher I (2010) Dubious assumptions of the theory of comparative advantage. Real World Econ Rev 54(2):95–105
Fofack H (2017) The globalisation of corporate governance and implications for African corporates in a changing regulatory landscape. World Econ 18(1):75–81
Fofack H, Mold A (2021) The AfCFTA and African trade - an introduction to the special issue. J Africa Trade 8(2):1–11
Francioni F (ed) (2001) Environment, human rights, and the limits of free trade. Hart Publishing, pp 1–392. https://open.uct.ac.za/server/api/core/bitstreams/bff59ec9-86d0-4e2e-806e-1222d625a259/content
Fukase E, Martin W (2020) Economic growth, convergence, and world food demand and supply. World Dev 132:1–12
Fusacchia I et al (2022) The AfCFTA impact on agricultural and food trade: a value added perspective. Eur Rev Agric Econ 49(1):237–284
Gammage C (2014) Protecting human rights in the context of free trade? The case of the SADC Group Economic Partnership Agreement. Eur Law J 20(6):779–792
Gebrehiwot T (2019) Impact of global food and agriculture laws on Africa's food security. De Jure 51(1):85–101
Geldenhuy M (2012) The effectiveness of competition law as a mechanism for the protection of the right to food in an African context. LLM dissertation submitted at the University of Pretoria 2012
Glipo A (2003) The WTO-AoA: impact on farmers and rural women in Asia. http://www.glow-boell.de/media/de/txt_rubrik_5/sus_arze_ruralwomen.pdf
Gonzalez GG (2002) Institutionalizing inequality: the WTO Agreement on agriculture, food security, and developing countries. Columbia J Environ Law 27(3):432–487
Gonzalez C (2006) Deconstructing the mythology of free trade: critical reflections on comparative advantage. Berkeley La Raza Law J 17(65):65–93
Gonzalez C (2014) The global food crisis: law, policy, and the elusive quest for justice. Yale Hum Rights Dev J 13:462–479
Green D (2011) Food fight at the WTO: de Schutter v Lamy on whether trade leads to food security. https://oxfamblogs.org/fp2p/food-fight-at-the-wto-de-schutter-v-lamy-on-whether-trade-leads-to-food-security/

Grose TH, Green TH, Hume D (eds) (1812) Essays moral, political, and literary. ISN - ETH Zurich, p 284
Gumede V (2020) Examining the African Continental Free Trade Area in the context of a political federation for Africa-towards a United African States. Open Access Working Paper, 1 May 2020, pp 1–39
Gumede V (2021) Examining the African continental free trade area in the context of a political federation for Africa – towards a United African States. https://www.parliament.gov.za/storage/app/media/Pages/2021/may/24052021_Africa_Day_Lecture/docs/UNISA_Press_Working_Paper_AfCFTA_and_UAS.pdf
Habay JG. Investing for impact in the food and agriculture sector in Africa and South Asia. https://assets.cdcgroup.com/wp-content/uploads/2020/11/18115511/What-is-the-impact-of-investing-in-FA.pdf
Häberli C (2016) Agricultural trade: how bad is the WTO for development? Eur Yearb Int Econ Law 7(4):103–117
Hartzenberg T (2006) Competition policy and practice in South Africa: promoting competition for development. Northwest J Int Law Bus 26(3):667–687
Hathaway D, Ingco M (1995) Agricultural liberalisation and the Uruguay Round. In the Uruguay Round and the developing countries. https://bit.ly/3DAw9q
Hauter W (2007) The limits of international human rights law and the role of food sovereignty in protecting people from further trade liberalisation under the Doha Round negotiations. Vanderbilt J Transnatl Law 40(4):1072–1078
Hawkes S, Plahe JK (2012) Worlds apart: the WTO's agreement on agriculture and the right to food in developing countries. Int Polit Sci Rev 34(1):21–38
Herman ED (1993) The perils of free trade. Sci Am 269(5):50–57
IISD (2003) Non-trade concerns in the agricultural negotiations of the World Trade Organization. Available at http://www.iisd.org/pdf/2003/investment_sdc_may_2003_1.pdf
IMF (1992) Structural adjustment and the role of the IMF. https://www.elibrary.imf.org/display/book/9781557753021/ch05.xml
IMF (2001) Global trade liberalisation and the developing countries. https://www.imf.org/external/np/exr/ib/2001/110801.htm
IMF (2021) Structural adjustment and the role of the IMF. https://www.elibrary.imf.org/display/book/9781557753021/ch05.xml
IMF (2023) Trade integration in Africa unleashing the continent's potential in a changing world. https://www.imf.org/en/Publications/Departmental-Papers-Policy-Papers/Issues/2023/05/03/Trade-Integration-in-Africa-Unleashing-the-Continent-s-Potential-in-a-Changing-World-529215
IMF (n.d.) Investing in agriculture. https://www.elibrary.imf.org/view/journals/022/0003/003/article-A007-en.xml
Ismail F (2006) From the Hong Kong WTO ministerial conference to the suspension of the negotiations. World Econ 7(3):133–166
Jackson J (1997) The World Trading System: law and policy of international economic relations. Fordham Int Law J 14(1):309–327
Jarosz L (2016) Defining World Hunger: scale and neoliberal ideology in international food security policy discourse. Food Cult Soc: Int J Multidiscip Res 30(8):1078–1092
John M Leveraging trade agreements to succeed in global markets. https://www.ceintelligence.com/files/documents/Leveraging%20Trade%20Agreements%20to%20Succeed%20in%20Global%20Markets.pdf
Johnson ME, Farris J, Morgan S, Bloem JR, Ajewole K, Beckman J (2022) Africa's agricultural trade: recent trends leading up to the African Continental Free Trade Area. https://www.ers.usda.gov/webdocs/publications/105224/eib-244_summary.pdf?v=3559
Josling T, Anderson K, Schmitz A, Tangermann S (2010) Understanding international trade in agricultural products: one hundred years of contributions by agricultural economist. Am J Agric Econ 92(2):424–446

Karingi S, Mevel S (2013) Towards a Continental Free Trade Area in Africa: a CGE modelling assessment with a focus on agriculture. In: Cheong D, Jansen M, Peters R (eds) Shared harvests: agriculture, trade, and employment, p 296
Khor M (2010) Trade policy implications for Africa's agriculture. http://www.mu.edu.et/eoa/images/AfricaBook_CH04_Martin_trade_web.pdf
Kigwiru VK (2022) Supranational or Confederate? Rethinking the African Continental Free Trade Agreement (AfCFTA) Competition Protocol Institutional Design (March 12, 2022)
Kleen P (2008) So alike and yet so different: a comparison of the Uruguay Round and the Doha Round. http://www.ecipe.org/media/publication_pdfs/so-alike-and-yet-so-different-a-comparison-of-the-uruguay-round-and-the-doha-round.pdf
Krugman P (1994) Rethinking international trade. MIT Press
Kuhlmann K, Agutu AL (2020) The African Continental Free Trade Area: toward a new legal model for trade and development. Georgetown J Int Law 51(4):1–66
Lamy P (2007) Managing global security: the strategic Importance of International Trade. http://www.wto.org/english/news_e/sppl_e/sppl66_e.htm. Accessed 03 Oct 2023
Latin American and Caribbean Parliament (2017) Framework law on the right to food and food sovereignty. https://parlatino.org/wp-content/uploads/2017/09/derecho-alimentacion-soberania-ing.pdf
Leary V (1996a) Workers' rights and international trade: the social clause. In: Bhagwati JN, Hude RE (eds) Fair trade and harmonization. MIT Press
Leary V (1996b) Workers' rights and international trade: the social clause. In: Bhagwati JN, Hude RE (eds) Fair trade and harmonisation, pp 177–230
Madhura S (1996) Structural adjustment, food security, and system of public distribution of food. Econ Polit Wkly 31(26):1633–1681
Malig MLF (2014) Big corporations: the Bali Package and Beyond: deepening TNCs gains from the WTO. http://www.eastasiaforum.org/2014/01/25/indian-food-security-and-the-wtodeal/
Margerum CM (1999) A reappraisal of classical economic nationalism and economic liberalism. Int Stud Q 43(4):733–744
Matthews A (1988) The agricultural negotiations in the Uruguay Round and the developing countries. http://www.trocaire.org/sites/trocaire/files/resources/policy/1988-agriculture-developing-countries-uruguay-round.pdf
McGee RW (1995) The moral Case Free trade. J World Trade 32(4):139–144
McGeorge RE (1992) Accommodating food security concerns in a world of comparative advantage: a challenge for GATT's international trade system. Neb Law Rev 71(2):370–368
McMahon J (2006) The WTO Agreement on agriculture: a commentary. Oxford University Press
Meulen V (2010) The global arena of food law: emerging contours of a meta-framework. Erasmus Law Rev 3(4):217–240
Moon W, Pino G (2016) Comparative advantage, or competitive advantage in explaining agricultural trade? Annual Meeting, February 6–9, 2016, San Antonio, Texas 230031, Southern Agricultural Economics Association
Morrison J, Sarris A (2007) WTO rules for agriculture compatible with development. http://www.fao.org/3/a-a0913e.pdf
Mucavele FG (2000) Analysis of comparative advantage and agricultural trade in Mozambique. SD Publication Series Office of Sustainable Development Bureau for Africa, Technical Paper No. 17 November 2000, pp 1–32
Murphy S (1999) WTO agricultural deregulation and food security. Interhemispheric Resource Center and Institute for Policy Studies 4(34):1–4
Nash J, Mitchel D (2005) How freer trade can help feed the poor. Finance Dev 42(001):34–37
Nash J, Halewood N, Melhem S (2013) 'Unlocking Africa's agricultural potential: an action Agenda for Transformation' Africa region sustainable development series. World Bank Group, Washington DC, pp 1–70
Ndonga D et al (2020) Assessing the potential impact of the African Continental Free Trade Area on least developed countries: a case study of Malawi. J South Afr Stud 46(4):779

Nissen A (2022) Trade with the EU, variable geometry and human rights in the EAC. Milan Law Rev 2(2):103–123
Nkamleu GB (2020) African agriculture in the context of COVID-19: finding salvation in the devil. Afr J Agric Resour Econ 15:302–310
Nshimbi CC (2019) Pan-African aspirations drive a new free trade pact. Curr Hist 118(808):188–193
Nwankwo CM, Ajibo CC (2020) Liberalizing regional trade regimes through AfCFTA: challenges and opportunities. J Afr Law 64(3) October 2020:297–318
Nzelibe JO (2004) Interest groups, power politics and the risks of WTO mission creep. Harv J Law Public Policy 28(1):89–95
Orford A (2015) Law, economics, and the history of free trade: a response. J Int Law Int Relat 11(2):155–180
Otenyo E (2016) Politics and the lack of labour militancy in Kenya: trade unionism after independence. In: Kithinji MM et al (eds) Kenya after 50. Palgrave Macmillan
Oyelami L (2022) Revenue, welfare and trade effects of African Continental Free Trade Agreement (AFCFTA) on Nigerian economy. J Public Aff 22(4):23
Pogge T (2005) Recognized and violated by international law: the human rights of the global poor. Leiden J Int Law 18(4):1–17
Powell SJ (2004) The place of human rights law in World Trade Organization rules. Florida J Int Law 16(1):219–228
Prasch RE (1996) Reassessing the theory of comparative advantage. Rev Polit Econ 8(1):37–56
Reid PA (1996) 'Investing in Agriculture'. https://www.elibrary.imf.org/view/journals/022/0003/003/article-A007-en.xml
Ricardo R (1951) Principles of economics. Springer Publishers
Santos BS (2005) Beyond neoliberal governance: the world social forum as subaltern politics and legality. In: Rodriguez C, Garivito R (eds) Law and globalization from below: towards a cosmopolitan legality, pp 1–38
Saurombe A, Nkabinde HIV (2013) Reforming the multilateral decision-making mechanism of the WTO: what is the role of emerging economies? Potchefstroom Electron Law J 15(5):454–614
Saygili M, Peters R, Knebel C (2018) African Continental Free Trade Area: challenges and opportunities of tariff reductions. United Nations Conference on Trade and Development Research Paper No. 15, UNCTAD/SER.RP/2017/15/Rev.1 pp 1–23
Schumacher R (2013) Deconstructing the theory of comparative advantage. World Econ Rev 16(2):83–105
Schutter OD Human rights and transnational corporations: paving the way for a legally binding instrument. http://www.ohchr.org/Documents/Issues/Food/EcuadorMtgBusinessAndHR.pdf
Sen A (1981) Poverty and famine: an essay on entitlement and deprivation. Clarendon Press, Oxford
Sen S (2010) International trade theory and policy: a review of the literature. https://www.levyinstitute.org/pubs/wp_635.pdf
Seti TM, Daw OD (2022) The implications of the African Continental Free Trade Area on South African agricultural trade: an application of the partial equilibrium mode. South Afr J Econ Manag Sci 24(1):1–11
Simiyu F (2015) Demystifying the quest for developed governance of agriculture in Kenya. https://doi.org/10.2139/ssrn.2692993
Simola A, Boysen O, Ferrari E, Nechifor V, Boulanger P (2022) Economic integration and food security – the case of the AfCFTA. Global Food Secur 35:1–10
Simons P (2008) Binding the hand that feeds them: the agreement on agriculture, transnational corporations and the right to adequate food in developing countries. In: Shan W, Simons P, Singh D (eds) Redefining sovereignty in international economic law, pp 339–429
Sommer L, MacLeod J (2019) How important is special and differential treatment for an inclusive AfCFTA? In: David L, MacLeod J (eds) Inclusive trade in Africa: the African Continental Free Trade Area in comparative perspective, p 69

South African Department of Trade, Industry and Competition (2023) A guide to the African Continental Free Trade Agreement. http://www.thedtic.gov.za/wp-content/uploads/Guide-to-the-ACFTA_2023.pdf
Stiglitz JE et al (2012) Macroeconomic fluctuations, inequality, and human development. J Hum Dev Capabil 13(3):31–58
Surya SP (2006) The notion of free trade and the first ten years of the World Trade Organization: how level is the level playing field. Neth Int Law Rev 52(2):273–296
Sykes AO (1998) Comparative advantage and the normative economics of international trade policy. J Int Econ Law 1(1):49–82
Tangermann S (2014) Paper prepared for the conference on 'Challenges Facing the World Trade System' organized by Jagdish Bhagwati, Pravin Krishna & Arvind Panagariya Columbia University, New York, and Johns Hopkins University (SAIS), Washington DC, 29 September–2 October, pp 1–32
Tangermann S (n.d.) Agriculture: Food Security and Trade Liberalisation. https://sais.jhu.edu/sites/default/files/Tangermann_1.pdf
Tania S, Mapulanga-Hulston JK (2016) Examing the synergy between the right to food and agricultural trade policy. Afr J Int Comp law 24(2):299–326
Tkara Y (2012) Trade as a tool of diplomacy and global security. http://sam.gov.tr/wp-content/uploads/2012/02/YildizTugba.pdf
Tokarick S (2008) Dispelling some misconceptions about agricultural trade liberalization. J Econ Perspect 22(1):199–216
TRALAC (2019) The African Continental Free Trade Area: A Tralac Guide 4. https://www.tralac.org/documents/resources/booklets/3028-afcfta-a-tralac-guide-6thedition-november-2019/file.html
TRALAC (2025) Frequently Asked Questions: African Continental Free Trade Area (AfCFTA. Updated May 2025 available at https://www.tralac.org/documents/resources/faqs/5889-afcfta-frequently-asked-questions-updated-may-2025/file.html
Trauger A (2014) Toward a political geography of food sovereignty: transforming territory, exchange, and power in the liberal sovereign state. J Peasant Stud 41(6):1131–1152
Ukwandu D (2015) David Ricardo's theory of comparative advantage and its implication for development in Sub-Saharan Africa: a decolonial view. Afr J Public Aff 8(3):17–53
UN (2022a) United Nations Sustainable Development Goals Report, 2022. https://unstats.un.org/sdgs/report/2022/The-Sustainable-Development-Goals-Report-2022.pdf
UN (2022b) Towards Food Security and Sovereignty in Africa. https://www.undp.org/sites/g/files/zskgke326/files/202209/Towards%20Food%20Security%20and%20Sovereignty%20in%20Africa.pdf
United Nations Economic Commission for Africa (2018) African Continental Free Trade Area. https://au.int/sites/default/files/documents/33984-doc-qa_cfta_en_rev15march.pdf
UN (2023) Building Africa's Food Sovereignty and Resilience through Sustainable Investments, 2023. https://www.unfoodsystemshub.org/docs/unfoodsystemslibraries/stocktakingmoment/unfss2specialsessions/idtfaa%2D%2D-africa-special-session%2D%2D-un-food-systems-summit-2%2D%2D-policy-paper.pdf?sfvrsn=e19159a_3
United Nations Economic Commission for Africa (2017) The continental free trade area (CFTA) in Africa – A human rights perspective. https://www.ohchr.org/sites/default/files/Documents/Issues/Globalization/TheCFTA_A_HR_ImpactAssessment.pdf
United Nations Economic Commission for Africa "The Continental Free Trade Area (CFTA) in Africa –A Human Rights Perspective"https://www.ohchr.org/sites/default/files/Documents/Issues/Globalization/TheCFTA_A_HR_ImpactAssessment.pdf
Valdes V (1987) Agriculture in the Uruguay Round: interests of developing countries. World Bank Econ Rev 4(1):571–593
Valente FLS (2016) The corporate capture of food and nutrition governance revisited: a threat to human rights and people's sovereignty. Global governance/politics, climate justice and

Agrarian/social justice: linkages and challenges. An International Colloquium 4–5 February 2016, Colloquium Paper No. 62, pp 1–8
Van den Bossche P (2008) The law and policy of the World Trade Organisation: text, cases and materials. Cambridge University Press
Van der Mensbrugghe D, Beghin JC (2005) Global agricultural reform: what is at stake?. Staff General Research Papers Archive 12230, Iowa State University, Department of Economics
Wanki M, Gabriel P (2016) Comparative advantage, or competitive advantage in explaining agricultural trade?'. http://ageconsearch.umn.edu/bitstream/230031/2/2016SAEA_AgEconSearch_manuscript_AgriculturalTrade_SanAntonio_January22_2016.pdf
Warikandwa TV (2012) Enlarging the place of human rights and development in international trade regulation: an evaluation of the problems and prospects of incorporating a social clause in the legal framework of the World Trade Organization (LLD-Thesis University of Fort Hare, South Africa
Watkins K (1996) Free trade and farm fallacies: from the Uruguay Round to the World Food Summit. Ecologist 26(6):244–255
Weekes JM et al (2014) 'Leveraging trade agreements to succeed in global markets' The Canadian Agri-Food Policy Institute, pp 1–16
Will M (2017) Agricultural trade and food security. https://www.econstor.eu/bitstream/10419/163163/1/881174920.pdf
Winters L (2002) Trade liberalisation and poverty: the evidence so far. J Econ Lit 42(1):72–115
Wisborg P et al (2013) Farm workers and farm dwellers in Limpopo, South Africa: struggles over tenure, livelihoods and justice. https://core.ac.uk/download/pdf/62635743.pdf
Wise TA (2009a) Promise or pitfall? The limited gains from agricultural trade liberalisation for developing countries. J Peasant Stud 36(4):855–870
Wise TA (2009b) The limited promise of agricultural trade liberalization. Trade Working Papers 22787, East Asian Bureau of Economic Research
World Bank Unlocking Africa's Agricultural Potential. https://openknowledge.worldbank.org/server/api/core/bitstreams/3cbc1ec4-8400-5971-8b0b-6ada9679cec5/content
WTO (n.d.-a) Agriculture, export competition. https://www.wto.org/english/tratop_e/agric_e/ag_intro04_export_e.htm
WTO (n.d.-b) The GATT Years: from Havana to Marrakesh. http://www.wto.org/english/thewto_e/whatis_e/tif_e/fact4_e.htm
WTO (n.d.-c) Trade topics: Agriculture, Export Competition. https://www.wto.org/english/tratop_e/agric_e/ag_intro04_export_e.htm
WTO (n.d.-d) Understanding the WTO: the case for open trade. https://www.wto.org/english/thewto_e/whatis_e/tif_e/fact3_e.htm
Zahniser S et al (2015) NAFTA at 20: North America's Free-Trade Area and its impact on agriculture. Report from the Economic Research Service 2015 12 available at https://www.ers.usda.gov/webdocs/outlooks/40485/51265_wrs-15-01.pdf?v=708
Zidouemba PR, Mustapha SJ (2021) The African Continental Free Trade Area and the Trade Facilitation Agreement: some regional macroeconomic impacts. Int J Trade Global Markets 14(3):325–376

The AfCFTA Protocol on Competition Policy

An Opportunity for Effective Enforcement in Digital Markets?

Lulama Edith Gomomo

Abstract The emergence of digital markets has disrupted the enforcement of competition law and policy. Most jurisdictions are grappling with the unorthodox business models characterised by complex market structures, network effects, zero-pricing, multi-sided markets, and monetisation of data. The African Union (AU) conceded that anti-competitive practices may hinder trade liberalisation and sustainable development goals. The digital economy can stimulate economic growth, but high concentration of economic power and anti-competitive conduct by few dominant digital undertakings can increase inequality. But there is a lack of enforcement of competition policy at continental level. The AU has recently adopted the Protocol to the establishment of the African Continental Free Trade Area on Competition Policy (AfCFTA Protocol on Competition Policy) including provisions that distinctively regulate the digital markets. The chapter critically evaluates the AfCFTA Protocol on Competition Policy, whether it incorporates concepts that reflect the realities of the digital markets including, zero-pricing, multi-sided markets, and the small but significant non-transitory decrease in quality in competition analysis. It also explores the novel integration of the gatekeeper's ex-ante obligations and abuse of economic dependence to specifically deal with dominant digital platforms. Finally, it investigates the interface of competition, consumer protection, and data protection policies.

This contribution originated in a paper presented at the Society for Law Teachers of Southern Africa-2022 Conference, hosted by the University of Fort Hare on 10–16 July 2022.

L. E. Gomomo (✉)
University of Fort Hare, East London, South Africa
e-mail: lgomomo@ufh.ac.za

T. V. Warikandwa et al. (eds.), *Law and Policy of the African Continental Free Trade Area (AfCFTA)*, European Yearbook of International Economic Law,
https://doi.org/10.1007/978-3-032-01122-0_7

1 Introduction

This chapter critically evaluates the current review of traditional competition policy in the African Union (AU) within the architecture of the African Continental Free Trade Area (AfCFTA) to assess whether the adopted reforms reflect the realities of the digital markets.[1] Competition authorities face a range of challenges in digital markets due to unorthodox business models in the digital sector characterised by complex market structures, network effects, zero-price services, multisided-markets, and monetisation of data.[2] As the digital age develops, market definition becomes much more complex, particularly in relation to so-called zero-price markets and multisided markets.[3] Meanwhile, in leading competition law jurisdictions, the traditional relevant market definition has since evolved to accommodate the unique character of digital markets. The significant but small non-transitory increase in price SSNIP used to define a relevant market in abuse of dominance and merger control assessments has proved to be insufficient. The revisions include considering concepts such as zero-pricing and multi-sided markets and adapting the small but significant non-transitory increase in price (SSNIP) into a small but significant decrease in quality (SSNDQ) and in competition analysis.[4] Although these methods are developing and may have shortcomings, it is necessary to evaluate and adopt appropriate tools to regulate competition in the digital markets. Moreover, the gatekeepers' ex-ante obligations and the concept of economic dependence are integrated into the AfCFTA Protocol on Competition Policy to remove the requirement of dominance to effectively deal with dominant digital undertakings. The question is how will the two legal instruments be integrated and applied in practice? Furthermore, competition law and policy, consumer welfare, and data protection issues are increasingly intersecting. However, relevant competition policies and laws within the AfCFTA Regional Economic Communities (RECs) and State Parties are not adapted or coordinated in this regard. However, data is the backbone of digital markets; any enforcement strategy finds its basis in the knowledge and understanding of the use and processing of personal or business data. Thus, to regulate the digital sector effectively, the coordination of enforcement activities in competition, consumer welfare, and data protection is imperative.

It is reported that the number of functional national competition authorities who have joined the African Competition Forum has increased from a mere 13 countries in 2000 to 47 in 2020.[5] This growth is attributed to increasing influence of competition policy on the development agenda.[6] The adoption and ratification of the

[1] The terms competition policy and competition law are used interchangeably, unless otherwise stated.

[2] OECD (2018a, b), Radic et al. (2025), and International Center for Law & Economics (2024).

[3] Baker (2021); Knapstad (2024), pp. 412–413.

[4] Google Search (Shopping), AT.39740, para 242–246; Google Android, AT40099, paras 263–267.

[5] Bonakele and Kariuki (2022), p. 299.

[6] Bonakele and Kariuki (2022), p. 299.

AfCFTA Protocol (AfCFTA Agreement) is irrefutably the most recent ripple effect of the proliferation of competition laws in Africa.[7] Following the negotiation, signing, adoption and ratification of the AfCFTA Agreement most AU Member States have either revised their existing laws, or adopted new competition laws. But the enthusiasm did not extend to the adaptation of traditional competition law to effectively regulate the digital sector.

The AfCFTA Agreement also set the tone for negotiation and the adoption of a AfCFTA Protocol on Competition Policy.[8] On 19 February 2023, the AU Assembly of Heads of State and Government adopted a Protocol to the AfCFTA on Competition Policy (AfCFTA Protocol on Competition Policy). It establishes autonomous competition regime at continental level, and it also outlines and interprets AU's competition policy within the AfCFTA legal framework.[9] It will also be supplemented by future regulations.[10] Furthermore, it prohibits anticompetitive conduct with a continental dimension including cross border cartels, restrictive business practices, exemptions, abuse of dominance, abuse of economic dependence, and also has provisions on cross border mergers and acquisitions.[11] The pertinent question is whether the AfCFTA Protocol on Competition Policy has effectively addressed the existing gaps in traditional competition policy essential to effectively enforce competition in the digital markets.[12] To that end, the chapter prepositions that future regulations of the AfCFTA Protocol on Competition Policy must adopt robust enforcement strategies to effectively regulate the digital markets.

The chapter is structured as follows: Section 2 discusses the emerging importance of the interplay between trade, sustainable development, competition, and the digital economy in the AU within the framework of the AfCFTA regime. Section 3 provides a synopsis of competition regulation in digital markets in the AU as enforced in the AfCFTA RECs and State Parties. It commences by examining the evolution of the relevant market definition by incorporating concepts such as, zero-pricing, multi-sided markets, and the SSNDQ in the enforcement of digital markets in other leading jurisdictions. It also assesses whether AU's current competition legal framework through the AfCFTA RECs and State Parties has adapted its relevant market definition. Section 4 critically evaluates the AfCFTA Protocol on Competition Policy to assess whether it reflects the realities of the digital markets. First, it explores the novel integration of flexible enforcement tools that are incorporated in the AfCFTA Protocol on Competition Policy such as the gatekeeper's ex-ante obligations and the concept of abuse of economic dependence, which are inter

[7] Büthe and Kedogo Kigwiru (2020), p. 44.

[8] Art 7(1)(*c*) AfCFTA Protocol.

[9] Art 13 AfCFTA Protocol on Competition Policy.

[10] Art 19 AfCFTA Protocol on Competition Policy states that the Committee on Competition Policy shall develop and recommend Regulations for the effective implementation of this Protocol, including the procedures and powers of the Authority, for the consideration of the Council of Ministers.

[11] Arts 5, 6, 7, 8, 9, 10, and 11 AfCFTA Protocol on Competition Policy.

[12] The terms digital markets and digital sector are used interchangeably.

alia designed to exclude the legal requirement of dominance. Section 5 analyses the intersection of competition, consumer welfare and data protection policies, including the tensions that may exist and the scope of closer coordination to effectively regulate anticompetitive conduct in digital markets. It also proposes for an inclusion of an explicit provision formalising the interface between competition, consumer protection, and data protection policies within the impending regulations to the AfCFTA Protocol on Competition Policy.

2 The Interface Between Trade, Sustainable Development, Competition, and the Digital Economy

Initially, the AU overlooked the interface between trade, development, and competition. AU pursued trade liberalisation for regional development.[13] Development has since been replaced with the concept of 'sustainable development'.[14] Sustainable development entails development that meets the needs of the current generation without compromising the ability of future generations to meets their own needs.[15] The AfCFTA Agreement identifies the importance of the intersection of trade, sustainable development and competition.[16] This is explicitly articulated in the AfCFTA Agreement and reinforced in the AfCFTA Protocol on Competition Policy.[17] Anti-competitive practices have the potential to negate or undermine the gains of trade liberalisation and could hinder development.[18] The emergence of the digital economy has exacerbated the risk. One of the main objectives of the Agreement is to enhance trade liberalisation and the competitiveness of the economies of AfCFTA State Parties within the continent and the global market.[19] By definition, trade law and policy have an international focus, whereas competition law has national roots.[20] While competition law and policy focuses primarily on business anti-competitive actions that obstruct the effective operation of markets, trade policy promotes these aims mainly by removing of government-imposed barriers to trade.[21]

The AfCFTA Agreement formally establishes a continental-wide Free Trade Area.[22] At the core of this AfCFTA Agreement is an integrated African single

[13] Arts 3(*d*), 4(2)(*d*) of the Treaty Establishing the African Economic Community.

[14] Schaefer and Crane (2005), p. 77.

[15] Schaefer and Crane (2005), p. 77.

[16] Arts 3(*a*)–(*b*), (*d*), (*f*)–(*g*), 4(*a*)–(*e*) AfCFTA Protocol.

[17] Ibid; see also art 2(*a*)–(*b*), (*f*) AfCFTA Protocol on Competition Policy.

[18] Roberts et al. (2017), p. 264.

[19] Art 3(f) AfCFTA Protocol on Competition Policy; see also Okadia et al. (2021), p. 563.

[20] Anderson and Müller (2012).

[21] Anderson and Müller (2012).

[22] OECD (2004), p. 285. The African Continental Free Trade Agreement (AfCFTA) entered into force on 30 May 2019, but trading under the Agreement officially started in January 2021. A free

market.[23] It is anticipated that the AfCFTA single market will also constitute an integrated digital economy.[24] The term digital economy incorporates all economic activity reliant on significantly enhanced use of digital inputs including, digital technologies, digital infrastructure, digital services, and data.[25] The emergence and rapid rise of the digital economy presents developing countries with consequential several development opportunities, including an reversal of prevalent unemployment, inequality and poverty.[26]

The expansion of the digital economy is crucial to solving societal problems, including those related to achieving the United Nations Sustainable Development Goals adapted into the Africa Agenda 2063 (Agenda 2063).[27] However, António Guterres, the Secretary-General of the United Nations has also cautioned on the negative welfare effects caused by high level concentration in the digital sector, he said:

> Digital advances have generated enormous wealth in record time, but that wealth has been concentrated around a small number of individuals, companies and countries. Under current policies and regulations, this trajectory is likely to continue, further contributing to rising inequality. We must work to close the digital divide, where more than half the world has limited or no access to the Internet. Inclusivity is essential to building a digital economy that delivers for all.[28]

The AU has adopted Agenda 2063 as its blueprint for development.[29] Agenda 2063 outlines the continent's strategic framework that *inter alia* aims to deliver on its goals for inclusive and sustainable development.[30]

Anderson and Müller have long submitted that well-functioning markets are a *sine qua non* for development, economic growth and the reduction of poverty.[31] However, there are prevailing factors affecting developing countries which render their citizens inherently vulnerable to anticompetitive conduct by dominant

---

trade area is a clustering of countries within which tariffs and non-tariff trade barriers between the members are gradually decreased or generally abolished but with no common trade policy towards non-members or third-party countries. The United Nations Commission for Africa (UNECA) anticipates that AfCFTA will be a market of 1.2 billion consumers, which will reach 1.7 billion by 2030 with a combined GDP of 2.5 trillion US dollars, but equivalent to 6.4 trillion US dollars when measured in purchasing power parity terms.

[23] Art 3(a) AfCFTA Agreement; In February 2020, the African Union (AU) Assembly decided to include digital trade within the AfCFTA. Digital trade policy will be constituted into a Protocol that shall, upon entry into force, form an integral part of the AfCFTA Agreement, available at https://au-afcfta.org/trade-areas/digital-trade/.

[24] Ibid.

[25] OECD (2022a, b), p. 8.

[26] For a comprehensive discussion on the benefits accruing from the presence of dominant digital platform in developing countries, see UNCTAD (2019a, b).

[27] Royoa et al. (2022), p. 2.

[28] Guterres (2019).

[29] AU Agenda 2023.

[30] AU Agenda 2023.

[31] Anderson and Müller (2012).

undertakings platforms, these include high barriers to entry, lack of financial resources and expertise, underdeveloped markets, and a lack of competition culture.[32] The failure to curb anticompetitive conduct in the digital sector has a potential to shift distribution of wealth in society (including large to small micro enterprises and consumers) to few dominant digital undertakings.[33] Initially, the presence of a digital undertaking promotes competition in the market and can lower barriers to entry. But where the dominant digital undertaking due to tipping and network effects leads to high barriers to entry, competition can be restricted.[34]

Over the years, competition regimes have adopted a cautious approach towards enforcement of abusive conduct in the digital sector.[35] It could be that the digital markets were seen to be immature and in a state of evolution. The top five dominant digital platforms, the so-called GAFAM (Google, Amazon, Facebook (Meta), Apple, and Microsoft) are all US Tech corporations. They are among the most valuable undertakings in the world with a combined market value of almost seven trillion US dollars.[36] It is reasonable to assume that the US dragged its feet to create global champions. On the other hand, the European Union (EU) due to the 'fast moving' nature of digital markets, it was also reluctant.[37] Unsurprisingly, many developing countries, including the AfCFTA State Parties, also assumed a 'wait-and-see' approach.

A critical analysis of the conventional competition legal framework shows that it is not effective in curbing anti-competitive practices in digital markets.[38] The irony is that the infant start-up technology undertakings,[39] some of which faced stiff competition and barriers to entry into traditional bricks-and-mortar markets, had grown rapidly into dominant digital undertakings. Today, they are dubbed as 'tech giants' often associated with anti-competitive behavior hauled before policymakers, and competition authorities in various jurisdictions.[40]

The African digital platform users and consumers are vulnerable and unprotected due to a lack of appropriate competition enforcement in digital markets at the continental, regional and national levels. In 2022, five heads from leading competition jurisdictions in Africa, including Egypt, Kenya, Mauritius, Nigeria, and South Africa, announced a plan for cooperation in the regulation of competition and

[32] Aydin and Büthe (2016), pp. 15–26.

[33] The ongoing worldwide market inquiries and investigations relation to the distribution of media information through digital platforms (media houses are not paid for their content) and self-preferencing which affects online sellers and consumers alike on various digital platforms.

[34] Moss (2022), p. 537.

[35] Moss (2022), p. 537.

[36] Statista (2023).

[37] The term 'fast moving pace' in reference to digital markets' occupies most of the EU Commission's official documents.

[38] UNCTAD (2021), p. 10.

[39] The terms undertakings and firms are used interchangeably.

[40] Moss (2022), p. 35.

consumer welfare in digital markets;[41] they recognised that digital markets pose "considerable challenges for competition law enforcement and policy in terms of the unique competition issues that arise".[42]

Why competition regulation and enforcement at the continental level? Fox provides the most befitting response to this question, she says:[43]

> Africa needs a competition voice at the center, just as the European Union and the US each has a competition voice at the center. The central voice should speak to both internal-market (continent-wide) problems and global problems. Absent that voice, Africa will remain uncoordinated at home and a price-taker in the world. The developed world will continue to go first, setting the rules and foreseeing the outcomes with respect to all of the megamergers, world cartels, big tech abuses, and other global restraints that significantly impact Africa.

The United Nations Conference on Trade and Development (UNCTAD) has identified that digital markets are characterised by high concentration.[44] Among other interventions, UNCTAD has recommended a review of legal and policy frameworks, enforcement, and regulation to curb anti-competitive conduct in the digital sector.[45] UNCTAD has emphasised the compelling compulsion to address the adaptation of conventional legal provisions to deal with emerging business models in digital markets through the AfCFTA Protocol on Competition Policy.[46]

3 Adaptation of the Relevant Market in Zero-Price and Multi-Sided Digital Markets

3.1 The Relevant Market Definition

Defining the 'relevant market' is the first step in most competition investigations.[47] The relevant market definition is a valuable tool used by competition authorities to establish the boundaries of competition between undertakings,[48] to the exception of few matters.[49] The relevant market definition is important in assessing the substantial or appreciable restriction of competition of horizontal or vertical agreements, to establish the existence of a dominant position or when assessing concentration and

[41] Africa Heads of Competition Dialogues (2022).

[42] Africa Heads of Competition Dialogues (2022).

[43] Fox (2022), p. 326.

[44] Gachuiri (2020), pp. 1–28.

[45] Gachuiri (2020), pp. 1–28.

[46] Gachuiri (2020), pp. 1–28.

[47] Boshoff (2021), p. 115.

[48] Jones and Sufrin (2014), p. 61.

[49] EU (1997), para 9. The European Commission usually does not define a relevant market when assessing cartel agreements.

its effects on competition.[50] The concept of 'relevant market' is not the same as the 'market' which refers to the area where undertakings sell their products or services or the specific industry sector.[51] The relevant market is defined in relation to the relevant product market or geographic market. Traditionally, a relevant product market comprises all those products and/or services which are regarded as interchangeable or substitutable by the consumer, by reason of the products characteristics, their prices, and their intended use.[52] Whereas the relevant geographic market comprises the area in which the undertakings concerned are involved in the supply and demand of products or services, in which the conditions of competition are sufficiently homogeneous, and which can be distinguished from neighbouring areas because the conditions of competition are appreciably different in those area.[53]

Competition authorities, including those in Africa have reported defining the relevant market and determining dominance in digital markets as particularly challenging.[54] They often cite the inadequacy of SSNIP as a quantitative method to determine market in cases involving digital platforms.[55] Digital platform markets are often multi-sided in that they provide both priced-based and zero-price products and/or services. In these instances, SSNIP is not possible. The competition authorities often employ market definition based on the Hypothetical Monopolist Test (HMT) currently assessed through SSNIP. However, there is no hierarchy between the qualitative and quantitative measurements of the demand substitutability of the market.[56] Although there is no legal obligation to make use of the SSNIP test in the context of the market definition process, it is often adopted in most cases and is also gaining much importance.[57] In competition jurisdictions where the relevant market definition has evolved to consider zero pricing, the modification of SSNIP was achieved through amendment of legislation, revised guidelines, and/or legal precedent.

The relevant market definitions currently applied in the RECs and most State Parties are a replica of the recently repealed EU guidelines adopted in 1997.[58] Both the RECs and EU law apply demand substitutability of products and services which is price-centered, and often carries more weight in competition law analysis. However, in the *Topps* judgment, the EU General Court has since confirmed that the SSNIP test "is not the only method available to the European Commission (Commission) and said that the test may also prove unsuitable in certain cases, for example, where there are free goods or goods the cost of which is not borne by those

[50] EU (1997), para 3.

[51] EU (1997), para 7.

[52] EU (1997), para 7.

[53] EU (1997), para 8.

[54] UNCTAD (2019a, b), p. 3.

[55] UNCTAD (2019a, b), p. 3.

[56] Knapstad (2024), p. 11.

[57] Boshoff (2021), p. 115.

[58] EU (1997), para 12.

determining the demand".[59] The *Topp* judgement was decided two decades after the EU guidelines on market definitions were first published.

The EU is currently the leader in developing and testing the adapted legal instruments tools to effectively enforce competition policy in the digital markets. Since 1997, its concept of the relevant market has evolved through administrative decisions and legal precedent.[60] Previously, in traditional markets, in the absence of price data, the EU competition authorities resorted to use of qualitative evidence.[61] But, cases involving the zero-price digital platforms depend greatly on the correct definition of the relevant market.[62] The EU courts and the commission have since adopted the qualitative considerations regarding the various functionalities and size of the networks with respect to assessing products or services in digital zero-price markets.[63] Yet, most competition laws in AfCFTA RECs and State Parties were enacted and/or amended during this 20-year period, but the relevant market definition mainly relies on price.

On 8 February 2024, the EU Commission published its revised relevant market definition.[64] The new guidelines seek to inter alia align market definition to its decisions as well as the legal precedent.[65] The guidelines also incorporate the EU Commission's enforcement strategy in the digital sector.[66] They highlight the importance of a quantitative method like SSNIP, but acknowledge its limitation in zero-price digital markets.[67] Therefore, the EU Commission has opted to rely on qualitative characteristics of the relevant product or the SSNDQ test in assessing market definition in zero-price digital markets.

3.2 *Zero-Price Markets*

As mentioned above, modern competition law is firmly grounded in neoclassical economics, which is, in turn is centred on price theory.[68] Conventional competition enforcement tools based on neoclassical price theory are rendered obsolete in the regulation of competition policy in digital markets.[69] Pre-eminent competition law theorists have urged that without prices, there can be no markets and, consequently,

[59] *Topps Europe v Commission*, T-699/14, EU: T:2017:2, para 82.
[60] EU (1997), para 62.
[61] Mandrescu (2018), p. 255.
[62] Mandrescu (2018), p. 255.
[63] See also *M.7217 Facebook/WhatsApp*, para 24–33 and 51–61.
[64] EU (2024), para 30.
[65] EU (2024), para 30.
[66] EU (2024), para 30.
[67] EU (2024), para 30.
[68] Newman (2015), p. 149.
[69] Newman (2015), p. 154.

no market power.[70] It is argued that methodological weight dependence on positive prices has led competition law authorities to overlook potentially massive welfare harms.[71] The failure to meaningfully conceive zero-price markets as competition law "markets" led to a lack of or under-enforcement of competition policy.[72] It is equally true that the zero-price concept has been exaggerated to over emphasise the uniqueness of digital markets. Consequently, this also contributed to a lack of enforcement in the digital sector.

The use of zero-pricing is derived from traditional markets, it has often been adopted by undertakings in the context of tying practices, complementary products, two-sided or multi-sided markets and 'freemium' products or services.[73] Internet use increased significantly due to access to valuable free goods and services.[74] In recent years, digital undertakings have introduced free goods and services, including Google's search engine, Facebook, WhatsApp, Twitter, TickTok or other social networks, Wikipedia's online encyclopedia, YouTube's online video and music streaming services, and so forth.[75] Free goods and services often provide real benefits to consumers and are clearly pro-competitive.[76] However, it is an established fact that many zero-price products are not 'free' but rather incur costs for consumers in other ways.[77] The source of income for the monetary market is derived from the payment of subscription fees, advertising fees, software sales, and transaction costs for payment services, cloud services, or products. For dominant digital platforms among others, Amazon, Google, and YouTube, the advertising revenue is massive. For example, the free services provided by digital platforms provide data that is, in turn, harvested, customised, and sold to various customers. The information is sold to advertisers and other businesses, and this generates revenue. As the business expands, digital platforms need more and more access to data. Big data and access to Artificial intelligence (Al), Algorithms and harvesting through cloud technologies come into play. Subsequently, a digital platform shifts from being largely based on zero-pricing into a two-sided or multi-sided market.

Most jurisdictions have been gradually developing and reviewing their competition laws to incorporate zero pricing in competition analysis. As early as 1991, in the *Höfner & Elser v. Macrotron GmbH* case, the EU rejected the argument that a service that is "provided free of charge" is not subject to its EU competition rules and classified it as an economic activity.[78] In the *Google Shopping* decision, the EU

[70] Newman (2015), p. 154.

[71] Newman (2015), p. 154.

[72] Newman (2015), p. 154.

[73] Mandrescu (2018), p. 255.

[74] Gal and Rubinfeld (2016), p. 521.

[75] Gal and Rubinfeld (2016), p. 521.

[76] Gal and Rubinfeld (2016), p. 521.

[77] Jarman and Karaman (2020), p. 316.

[78] See *Höfner & Elser v. Macrotron GmbH*, C-41/90, [1991] ECR—(April 23, 1991), paras. 20–23; *Microsoft v Commission*, T-201/04, EU:T:2007:289, paras 966–970; *Cisco Systems, Inc. and Messagenet SpA v Commission*, Case T-79/12, EU:T:2013:635, paras 65–74.

Commission reiterated that general search free services constitute an economic activity.[79] Accordingly, the users of google search enter into a contractual relationship with its users through the acceptance of terms and conditions in exchange for data obtained per 'search query' for the use of the search engine.[80] In 2017, Germany revised its competition law to adapt its legal framework and tools to the realities of the digital markets; it introduced Section 18(2a) of the German Competition Act recognising free products and services provided by platforms as a market, stating that "the assumption of a market shall not be invalidated by the fact that a good or service is provided free of charge".[81]

3.3 Multi-Sided Markets

The concepts of zero-pricing and multisided markets are mutually significant in defining the relevant market in digital markets. An over-emphasis on zero-pricing as opposed to the concept of multi-sided markets creates another enforcement gap. A multi-sided market includes both monetary (price-based) and zero-pricing. The simplest form of a multi-sided market is a two-sided market. In the context of competition law, a multisided market is best defined as a market in which an undertaking act as a platform and sells different products to different groups of consumers while recognising that the demand from one group of customers depends on the demand from the other group(s).[82] For example, You Tube provides free upload of the content and access to its platform, but also sells its access without adverts to premium customers, and sells advertising space. Thus, You Tube draws two types of customers, zero-priced users and paying customers. Each group of You Tube customers depends on the other. This is the co-dependency that competition law authorities must acknowledge. It is important to characterise digital platforms as largely multi-sided markets. In the *Google Shopping* case cited above, the Commission considered that the general services constituted a multisided market.[83] The EU has taken the view that multi-sided markets, particularly the digital markets, must be defined in relation to their specific groups of users. In the *Google Shopping* case, the Commission identified general services as a two-sided market consisting of non-paying users/customers and paying users/customers who pay for advertising space.[84]

[79] Google Search (Shopping), paras 157–160.

[80] Google Search (Shopping), paras 157–160.

[81] UNCTAD (2019a, b), p. 6.

[82] OECD (2018a, b).

[83] Google Search (Shopping), para 159.

[84] Google Search (Shopping), para 159.

3.4 *Adaptation of a Price-Centered SSNIP into a Quality-Focused SSNDQ*

The prevailing recommended method for dealing with a zero-price market is to simply adapt the traditional competition law tools by substituting price with other competition parameters including, quality, choice and/or innovation.[85] This is considered to be a less disruptive approach.[86] It is submitted that since price and output do not play a decisive role in the zero-price market side of digital platforms, there is a strong case for competition law to adopt a quality consideration approach.[87] In the *Google Shopping* decision in 2017, the EU Commission did not use the SSNIP test in assessing the substitutability of Google's 'Comparison Shopping Services' with those of its competitors. The Commission said that the SSNIP test would not have been appropriate in the present case because Google provides its search services for free to users.[88] Instead, the Commission used qualitative evidence, i.e., the functionalities of the digital platforms compared.[89] Although Google painstakingly argued for the use of the SSNIP test, the Commission reiterated the legal position in the EU as follows:[90]

> The definition of the relevant market does not require the Commission to follow a rigid hierarchy of different sources of information or types of evidence. Rather, the Commission must make an overall assessment and can take account of a range of tools for the purposes of that assessment.

Mandrescu cautions that in the absence of conversion of SSNIP to SSNDQ, the market definition might be performed solely based on a qualitative evaluation of the functionalities of comparable digital platforms, as seen in the *Google Shopping* case.[91] He considers qualitative evaluation of the functionalities of digital platforms to be old-fashioned.[92] Although Mandrescu concedes that there is no legal obligation to rely on quantitative tools, nor do these possess a higher evidentiary value compared to qualitative evidence,[93] he nonetheless remains steadfast on the conversion of the SSNIP test into a quality centred assessment such as SSNDQ.[94] Accordingly, this would inevitability allow the application of the HMT quantitative assessment to be applied in cases involving zero-pricing and has a potential to lead

[85] OECD (2018a, b), p. 3.

[86] OECD (2018a, b), p. 3.

[87] OECD (2018a, b), p. 3.

[88] Google Search (Shopping), para 227.

[89] Google Search (Shopping), para 227.

[90] Google Search (Shopping), para 227.

[91] Mandrescu (2018), p. 255.

[92] Google Search (Shopping), para 159.

[93] Google Search (Shopping), para 159.

[94] Google Search (Shopping), para 159.

to a broader acceptance and understanding of non-price competition.[95] Thus, this suggests that a quantitative method is preferred because of its sense of credibility and predictability.

Quality assessment is most relevant in assessing substitutability in the digital sector since network effects can lead to tipping,[96] then monopolisation ensues to a 'the winner takes all' outcome.[97] Network effects could be a key contributor to amassing of monopoly power, in digital zero-markets, they have a potential to reduce demand substitution by consumers and creating barriers to entry that limit competitive constraints.[98] Consequently, consumers/digital platform users do not switch due to degradation of quality because of strong network effects.[99]

In the *Qihoo 360 v. Tencent* is the first judgement by the Supreme court of China on the Anti-Monopoly Law (AML). The case involved the definition of the relevant market in the zero-price digital market. The court critiqued the High court's use of the SSNIP test in defining the relevant product market, which led to its overstating of the substitutability between *social networking services* (SNS) and microblogs, and instant messaging (IM). The court found that there was a limitation of using the traditional HMT in internet-based instant messaging (IM) services featuring a "free" business model.[100] The court substituted the SSNIP test with the SSNDQ.[101] To assess demand substitution, the court actually relied on product characteristics, functions, quality, difficulty in acquiring the product, and other relevant factors.[102] It also comprehended that, when necessary, supply substitution should also be applied.[103] Therefore, the Court analysed the substitution between IM and Weibo, SNS, mobile text, messaging and email.[104] It also, noted that the focus of relevant geographic market definition is not whether it is feasible but whether or not foreign-based suppliers can and will enter China in a timely manner and act as effective competitive constraints in response to a small change in relative product quality an equivalent of the SSNDQ in the IM services available to users in China; recognising that the legal and regulatory restrictions imposed on foreign-based providers present real entry barriers in the provision.[105] In the end, the court concluded that the relevant market is the IM service market in China.

---

[95] Mandrescu (2018), p. 255.

[96] Moss (2022), p. 542.

[97] Competition Commission of South Africa (2020), p. 10.

[98] OECD (2022a, b).

[99] *European Commission Google Android*, Case AT.40099, paras 288–290.

[100] *Qihoo 360 v. Tencent* (pinyin: 2013); Zi (2017).

[101] Evans and Zhang (2014).

[102] Evans and Zhang (2014).

[103] Evans and Zhang (2014).

[104] Evans and Zhang (2014).

[105] Evans and Zhang (2014).

The EU Commission applied the SSNDQ test to assess of dominance in the relevant market in the *Google Android* decision.[106] The Commission found that SSNIP test would not produce a different outcome because of the Original Equipment Manufacturers' (OEMs) lack of substitutability.[107] The Commission assessed whether the OEMs would switch away from Android app stores to app stores for other licensable smart mobile operating systems in the event of a SSNDQ.[108] It was found that such a switch was not possible since when users buy a phone, the smartphone OS is already pre-installed.[109] Accordingly, consumers take various factors into account when buying a smartphone, including the smart mobile OS, the number of app stores available in smart mobile OS, the price of the device, battery life, quality of the device screen, quality of the camera, design of the device, and data storage available on the device. As such, it is unlikely that users would change their purchase behaviour and switch to devices based on non-licensable smart mobile OSs in the event of a small but significant SSNDQ. Therefore, the SSNDQ test proved the non-existence of substitutability based on the degradation of quality between Google Android smartphone OS and other PC or Phone OS.[110]

On appeal the General Court confirmed the EU Commission's *Google Android* decision and found that the SSNDQ test constitute relevant evidence for the purpose of defining the relevant market, it also reiterated that competition between undertakings can take place through other means including quality and innovation.[111] The EU Commission has confirmed this legal position in its recent notice on market definition and has adopted SSNDQ to assess quality degradation in assessing market definition in zero-price and multisided markets.[112]

4 Adaptation of the Relevant Market in Zero-Price and Multi-Sided Digital Markets in the AfCFTA RECS and State Parties

Until recently, the AU did not have a competition policy at continental level. As mentioned earlier, the continental dimension is currently outlined in the recently adopted AfCFTA Protocol on Competition Policy. However, at the regional level, the RECs have established Regional Competition Regimes (RCRs) to enforce cross-border anticompetitive conduct and regulate transnational mergers.[113] Since the late

[106] Evans and Zhang (2014).
[107] Evans and Zhang (2014).
[108] Evans and Zhang (2014), paras 288–290, 296.
[109] Evans and Zhang (2014).
[110] Evans and Zhang (2014), para 297.
[111] Google and Alphabet v Commission, T-604/18, EU:T:2022:541, paras 177 and 180.
[112] EU (2024).
[113] Büthe and Kedogo Kigwiru (2020), p. 46.

1980s, the AfCFTA State Parties have implemented contemporary competition laws at the national level.[114] The AfCFTA Protocol on Competition Policy is adopted at a time when competition authorities worldwide are crafting and testing new enforcement strategies dedicated at regulating the digital markets. The AfCFTA Protocol on Competition Policy also gives credence to these new developments.

The AU formally recognises eight RECs as its building block,[115] the Arab Maghreb Union (AMU), the Common Market for Eastern and Southern Africa (COMESA), the Community of Sahel-Saharan States (CEN-SAD), the East African Community (EAC), Economic Community of Central African States (ECCAS), the Economic Community of West African States (ECOWAS), Intergovernmental Authority on Development (IGAD), and the Southern African Development Community (SADC).[116] So far out of the eight, only COMESA, EAC and ECOWAS have adopted a supranational competition model and have established functional RCRs.[117] SADC has a cooperative arrangement,[118] whereas the AMU, CEN-SAD, ECCAS, and IGAD do not have enforceable competition policy provisions in their treaties.[119] Thus, the term RECs refers to some of the eight recognised AU regional economic arrangements which have adopted competition policy and have established functional RCRs, including COMESA, EAC, and ECOWAS operating within the architecture of the AfCFTA regime. Whereas the term State Parties includes AfCFTA contracting State Parties with competition laws and functional competition authorities.

The current legal instruments of the RECs and the national laws of State Parties mirror the traditional competition laws of developed nations, such as the EU and its Member States, Canada, the US and so forth.[120] Gal and Fox suggest that borrowing off-the-shelf rules is timesaving and cost effective.[121] Other benefits of legal transplant include increased legal certainty and an accustomed application and interpretation of the law.[122] All of these factors are essential for attracting Foreign Direct

[114] Büthe and Kedogo Kigwiru (2020), p. 46.

[115] Art 88 of the of the Treaty Establishing the African Economic Community of 1991 ("Abuja Treaty") read with the Protocol on Relations between the African Union (AU) and the RECs—The protocol aims to: strengthen the existing regional economic communities in accordance with the provisions of the Treaty; and promote the coordination and harmonisation of the policies, measures, programmes and activities of regional economic communities towards an efficient integration of the regional economic communities into the African Common Market among others. All RECs have signed the protocol except for AMU; Art 1(t) of AfCFTA Agreement.

[116] This is because the Abuja Treaty divides the AU into five regions, namely North Africa, West Africa, Central Africa, East Africa, and Southern Africa.

[117] Kigwiru (2023), p. 5.

[118] Southern African Development Community (2009).

[119] See the Arab Maghreb Union (AMU), Community of Sahel-Saharan States (CEN-SAD), Economic Community of Central African States (ECCAS), and Intergovernmental Authority on Development (IGAD).

[120] Art 5(b) of AfCFTA states that RECs' FTAs are the building blocks of the AfCFTA.

[121] Gal and Fox (2015), p. 301.

[122] Gal and Fox (2015), p. 301.

Investment (FDI).[123] However, legal transplant of competition policy and law in Africa often fails because amongst other things legislatures and their competition regulators do not keep abreast of current legal developments. Consequently, competition policies and laws within the AfCFTA regime remain old-fashioned and inadequate to protect the African digital platform user/consumer from anticompetitive conduct by dominant digital undertakings. It is the responsibility of the RECs to harmonise and coordinate the enforcement of competition policy at regional level, but they have not lived up to this expectation. Moreover, an exclusively price-centered relevant market definition currently adopted by the AfCFTA and State Parties is rendered obsolete if it is not properly aligned to the unique operations prevalent in the digital sector.

AU does not have continental legal precedent on competition policy at continental level which has adapted a traditional competition law to address anti-competitive practices in the digital sector? The AfCFTA Protocol on Competition Policy is not yet operational. The AfCFTA RECs and State Parties have been hesitant to adapt their competition laws to regulate digital markets effectively. In most instances where AfCFTA State Parties have been amended, or repealed their competition law, they fail to provide specific provisions addressing enforcement in digital markets. However, a new dawn is emerging, major economies like South Africa and Kenya have commenced with the review of their enforcement strategies, and the RECs are beginning to follow suit.

The AfCFTA RECs and the State Parties often define a relevant market in both its product/service and its geographic dimensions. However, the product/service market definition is often assessed based on price, it does not consider other competition parameters that are relevant in the digital sector such as quality and innovation. As mentioned earlier, in abuse of dominance cases involving digital platforms with zero-price services, the demand side cannot be assessed using the SSNIP test since it is a price-based assessment. COMESA, EAC and ECOWAS do not have revised relevant market definition to enforce competition law in the digital sector. The EAC Act of 2006 defines the concept of the relevant market as follows:[124]

> For the purpose of this Act, the area of the relevant market shall be determined by the substitutability of goods or services for consumers in light of their intended use, characteristics, and prices as well as by the substitutability of different sources of supply located in different regions.

On 16 May 2023, the EAC RCR concluded a Memorandum of Understanding (MOU) with the Competition Authority of Kenya (CAK) to inter alia collaborate on several activities including capacity building on enforcement of competition policy and law in the digital sector.[125] We suggest that the starting point should be the review of the legal instruments of both parties to modernise and harmonise the relevant market definition in the EAC REC. Kenya is a member of three RECs,

---

[123] Raslan (2017), p. 31.

[124] East Africa Competition Act, 2006.

[125] East Africa Community (2023).

including COMESA, EAC and IGAD. The Kenyan market is the most advanced economy in all these RECs and boasts the most functional and experienced competition regime. It is more urgent for Kenya to act against anticompetitive conduct in the digital sector. The main responsibility of the RECs through their established RCRs is to facilitate the harmonisation of the competition laws of their contracting State Parties. The harmonisation of competition law through the RECs is imperative, particularly to assist the less advanced competition regimes. This task will soon be shifted to the AfCFTA competition authority, but it can only achieve this through working together with the RCRs.

COMESA adopted its competition Regulations in 2004 (Regulation).[126] But the COMESA RCR only began to actively enforce the Regulations when it commenced operations in January 2013. On 2 April 2019, COMESA published its Market Definition Guidelines. Article 19 of the COMESA guidelines states:

> In determining whether an undertaking is in a dominant position, Article 18(2) of the Regulations provides that consideration shall be given to the following factors: a) relevant market defined in terms of the product and the geographic context.[127]

The COMESA does not have administrative decisions or legal precedents which revise the traditional relevant market definition. Notably, the CAK also published its updated guidelines in July 2019, just a few months after COMESA. But COMESA's guidelines do not meet the prevailing digital market realities. On the other hand, the 2019 CAK revised guidelines on market definition adopt a modern and progressive approach.[128] The CAK guidelines provide guidance on the adaptation of new concepts to the definition of the relevant market, including zero price, multi-sided markets and in digital markets.[129] The guidelines also identify the limitation of SSNIP in digital zero-priced markets due to the free services offered in digital markets.

In 2019, the CAK revised its guidelines on the definition of the relevant market. The guidelines provide for an expanded definition, including concepts such as multi-sided markets, non-priced markets, and digital markets.[130] The guidelines *inter alia* state:

> Multi-sided markets are platforms that coordinate the demand of distinct groups of customers whose presence in the market enables the supply of the product in the first instance. In multi-sided markets, distinct user groups (i.e. distinct demand systems) interact with each other through a common platform and the participation of at least one of these groups impacts the value of participation for other group(s).

It remains to be seen how the CAK will interpret these concepts in the enforcement of its competition laws in the digital markets. However, on multi-sided markets, the guidelines state, The Authority shall consider the multi-sided market approach to market definition in platforms. Additionally, it provides that it will refer to

---

[126] Common Market for Eastern and Southern Africa (COMESA) Regulation of 2004.

[127] Art 19 of COMESA guidelines.

[128] Competition Commission of Kenya (n.d.), paras 58–66.

[129] Competition Commission of Kenya (n.d.), paras 58–66; See also Dessemond (2019), p. 10.

[130] Competition Commission of Kenya (n.d.), paras 58–66.

precedents from other jurisdictions that have dealt with similar cases in carrying out the market definition and analysing competitive effects.[131] The paragraph on the digital market also states:[132]

> Most digital markets are multi-sided in nature. The Authority shall consider substitutability at one side of the market in contact with the wider market for the basic products. Additionally, this section shall be read in conjunction with multi-sided markets and non-price markets sections.

However, on 24 January 2024, the COMESA RCR published the Draft Competition and Consumer Protection Regulations (COMESA Draft Regulations) for public comment.[133] The COMESA Draft Regulations define the relevant product market in relation to a set of products or services that are considered as substitutes, both in terms of their characteristics and the geographic area where they are offered. The definition appears to be broad to include price and other competition factors such as quality and innovation. But this must be further clarified and confirmed in the revised market definition guidelines.

ECOWAS also defines the relevant product market based on price and use and does not have legal precedent where it has adopted a revised definition.[134] ECOWAS and its State Parties are staggering as compared to the rest of the continent in reviewing their legal instruments, particularly to enforcing competition law and policy in the digital markets.

As discussed above, SSNIP is limited in digital zero-price markets. The question that arises is, how should the AfCFTA RECs and State Parties accommodate competition assessment in digital zero-price markets? Thus far, there is no known case in RECs or in the AfCFTA State Parties that was decided using adapted relevant market definition based on SSNDQ. In the *GovChat v Facebook (WhatsApp)* interim relief matter, the South African Tribunal (Tribunal) did not apply SSNIP,[135] but a qualitative assessment based on the technological functionalities of various messaging functionalities.[136] The Tribunal identified a market for over-the-top (OTT) messaging applications, by distinguishing WhatsApp's technological functionalities from other services like SMS, MMS, USSD.[137] The Tribunal recognised OTT as the relevant market, along with WeChat, Facebook Messenger, and Snapchat.[138] The Tribunal established that WhatsApp was dominant in the OTT market on the grounds that: (1) 89% of all internet users in South Africa between the ages of 16 and 64 reported having used WhatsApp; (2) at least 58% of all mobile phone users in South

[131] Competition Commission of Kenya (n.d.), para 60.

[132] Competition Commission of Kenya (n.d.), para 66.

[133] COMESA Competition and Consumer Protection Regulations (COMESA Competition Draft Regulations) (2024).

[134] Economic Community of West African States (ECOWAS), Supplementary Act A/SA 1/12/08.

[135] *GovChat Proprietary Limited and Another v Facebook Inc. and Others* (IR165Nov20).

[136] Gumede and Manenzhe (2023), pp. 13–14.

[137] Gumede and Manenzhe (2023), pp. 13–14.

[138] Gumede and Manenzhe (2023), pp. 13–14.

Africa had downloaded WhatsApp; (3) WhatsApp comes pre-loaded on almost all Android smartphones; and (4) mobile networks in South Africa offer WhatsApp data bundles (GovChat v Facebook, 2020).[139]

Considering the above, it is important to critically evaluate whether the AfCFTA Protocol on Competition Policy has effectively addressed these concerns and other enforcement gaps that have an adverse impact on the regulation of competition in the digital markets.

5 A Critical Analysis of the AfCFTA Protocol on Competition Policy in Regulating Competition in the Digital Markets

The recently adopted AfCFTA Protocol on Competition Policy is the first attempt to regulate competition policy at the continental level. Article 1(h) provides for the principle of subsidiarity: it states "Conduct with a Continental Dimension" means any conduct, practice, merger, or agreement that has a significant effect on competition in a market of at least two State parties that do not share the same jurisdiction of the existing regional economic communities. The AfCFTA on Competition Policy confers concurrent jurisdiction to the AfCFTA Competition Authority and the RECs.[140] This will allow higher levels of implementation of the competition policy within the AfCFTA competition regime, to the RECs and down to the State Parties. State Parties will retain the national competence to enact and enforce competition law and have a right to achieve unique legitimate policy objectives.[141] The AfCFTA Protocol on Competition Policy greatly emphasises harmonisation of competition policy.[142]

5.1 The Adaptation of the Relevant Market in the AfCFTA Protocol on Competition Policy

A progressive all-encompassing AfCFTA Protocol on Competition Policy must adopt an expanded definition of relevant market to include the concepts of SSNDQ, multi-side markets and zero-pricing. This could be included in the future regulations. Like the Treaty of Functioning of the European Union (TFEU), the AfCFTA

[139] The Competition Commission of South Africa (CCSA) has referred to the Competition Tribunal for prosecution the social media giant, Meta Platforms Inc. (previously known as Facebook Inc.), and its subsidiaries, WhatsApp Inc. and Facebook South Africa.

[140] Art 20 AfCFTA Protocol on Competition Policy.

[141] Art 12(6) AfCFTA Protocol on Competition Policy.

[142] See the preamble to the Competition Act 89 of 1998, sec 2(1) (a), (d)–(g).

Protocol on Competition Policy does not define a relevant market. However, it has adopted specific competition provisions and modern concepts employed specifically to regulate digital markets. The relevant market definition forms part of AfCFTA's competition assessments. However, since most RECs and State Parties have not adapted their relevant market definition to include new concepts such as zero-pricing, multisided markets, and SSNDQ. It is important to provide these in the future regulations or guidelines to ensure uniformity to effectively regulate the digital sector in the AfCFTA single market. This will eliminate the Kenya-COMESA-EAC debacle, where the contracting State party's laws are more progressive than that of its RECs. This will also assist with the harmonisation of the laws at continental, regional and national laws. It is also important to build a specific technical capacity and competency on the implementation of adapted rules applicable in the regulation of the digital sector.

5.2 *Gatekeeper's Ex-Ante Obligations and Abuse of Economic Dependence*

The AfCFTA Protocol on Competition Policy has integrated novel power concepts such as the gate-keepers *ex-ante* obligations and the abuse of economic dependence. The AfCFTA Protocol on Competition Policy, to some extent, it mirrors the EU Digital Markets Act (DMA),[143] it also provides for the gatekeepers' ex-ante obligations to regulate the digital sector.[144] The EU DMA also sets qualitative threshold to designate gatekeepers.[145] However in the EU, a designated as a gatekeeper is required to proactively implement certain behaviours that make the markets more

[143] EU Regulation 2022/1925 of the European Parliament and of the Council of 14 September 2022 (Digital Market Act ("DMA"). On November 1, 2022, the DMA came into effect, and became operational on May 2, 2023. The undertakings offering key platform services were required to notify the EU Commission and submit all pertinent information within 2 months of that date, assuming they meet the quantitative thresholds. Recently, the EU Commission designated six gatekeepers, the GAFAM and Tick Tock/Bytedance), while Samsung was still under review available at https://ec.europa.eu/commission/presscorner/detail/en/ip_23_4328. But some platforms have since appealed the decisions.

[144] Art 11(4)(*a*)–(*i*) AfCFTA Protocol on Competition Policy.

[145] An undertaking meets the designation of a gatekeeper if (1) it generates EU revenues of at least €7.5 billion in each of the last 3 financial years or had an average market capitalisation of at least €75 billion in the last financial year, and the undertaking provides the same core platform service in at least three Member States; (2) In each of the last 3 financial years, the undertaking provides a core platform service with at least 45 million EU monthly active end users in the last financial year, and at least 10,000 yearly active EU business users. (3). The undertaking met the second criteria in each of the last 3 financial years; An undertaking that does not meet the quantitative threshold can still be designated as a gatekeeper if it meets a qualitative criterion including (1) A significant impact on the internal market; (2) it provides a specified service that is an important gateway for business users to reach end users; and (3) it enjoys an entrenched and durable position (or it is foreseeable that it will enjoy such a position in the near future).

open and contestable and at the same time refrain from engaging in unfair behaviour, as identified in the legislation. Whereas the AfCFTA Protocol on Competition Policy defines the term gatekeeper as:

> …an undertaking that has a significant impact on the Market, operates a core platform service that serves as an important gateway for business users to reach end-users, enjoys an entrenched and durable position in its operations or it is foreseeable that it will enjoy such a position in the near future.

The AfCFTA Protocol on Competition Policy does not define core platform service. It *inter alia* prohibits the following anti-competitive practices: imposing price or service parity clauses on platform business users, imposing anti-steering provisions or otherwise preventing business users from engaging consumers directly outside of a core platform,[146] the use of business platform user data to compete against its own business customer, abusive self-preferencing of services or products offered by the gatekeeper on a core platform,[147] placing restrictions on the portability of data or other actions that inhibit switching platforms for business and end-users, failing to identify paid ranking as advertising in search results and to allow paid results to exceed organic results on the first results page, combining personal data sourced from different services offered by the gatekeeper,[148] and requiring the pre-installation of gatekeeper applications or services on devices.[149] It is expected that the gatekeeper's provisions will be further articulated in the upcoming regulations to the AfCFTA Protocol on Competition Policy.

The AfCFTA Protocol on Competition Policy simultaneously adopts both *ex-post* and *ex-ante* provisions in a single legal instrument. The conventional *ex-post* or 'after-the-fact' enforcement requires extensive investigations that are both costly and time-consuming and are assessed on a case-by-case basis as currently applied in traditional competition matters.[150] Whereas *ex-ante* refers to 'before-the-fact', it proscribes the conduct through a set of obligations designed to regulate a specific sector (in this case, the digital sector), often without demonstrating harm to consumers.[151] The concern among the scholars is whether the assessment of the relevant market definition is a prerequisite in respect of the gatekeepers' obligations.[152] This has now been partially resolved in the EU communication document on the market definition stating that 'relevant market element' is not included in the EU DMA.[153] However, it remains to be seen how the EU and the AfCFTA competition regimes will enforce both the *post-ante* and *ex-ante* instruments in the digital sector.

146 Art 11(*a*) AfCFTA Protocol on Competition Policy.

147 Art 11(*b*) AfCFTA Protocol on Competition Policy.

148 Art 11(*c*) AfCFTA Protocol on Competition Policy.

149 Art 11(*d*) AfCFTA Protocol on Competition Policy.

150 Art 11(*d*) AfCFTA Protocol on Competition Policy.

151 See also Cani (2021), p. 271.

152 Cani (2021), p. 271.

153 European Commission Press Corner, available at https://ec.europa.eu/commission/presscorner/detail/en/qanda_23_6002.

In traditional competition law, in abuse of dominance, anticompetitive behaviors are directed to competitors (exclusion) or consumers (exploitation), but it is a prerequisite that competition in the relevant market be affected.[154] If the relevant market is not affected, in principle an abuse of a dominant position cannot be established.[155] Consequently, most competition jurisdictions refrain from regulating business-to-business dealings if the relevant market is not affected.[156] However, this disregards relative dominance and its possible effects on competition. Abuse of economic dependence, also known as an abuse of superior bargaining, was introduced to regulate abuse of relative dominance.[157] Abuse of economic dependence, refers to a situation where one party to a transaction in a position of relative strength as compared to another party abuses such a position.[158] Other competition regimes applying this type of an enforcement tool include France, Germany, Italy, Japan, Korea and so forth. Some critique that the abuse of economic dependence protects individual competitors, suppliers, or buyers that are in a position of dependence rather than protecting the competition in the market.[159]

The other recent trend is to introduce an economic dependence clause to address regulatory gaps in the digital sector.[160] In digital platforms, abuse of economic dependence occurs where there is no possibility of switching the service to another undertaking.[161] In a digitalised economy, the business entities or sellers are often integrated into a platform's ecosystem. Consequently, the business entities lose their autonomy and are instead subject to the platform's rules.[162] Once the digital platform reaches a level of influence and can no longer tolerate competition or internal brand competition, it can resort to exclusionary conduct by delisting products or simply demoting them in search ranking.[163] Competition-related issues with digital platforms arise against this backdrop, including self-preferencing, imitation of third-party products, free-riding on books and news, or other media content, and the compulsion of app developers to exclusively use platform payment systems.[164]

The advantage of the adoption of the gatekeeper's *ex-ante* list and the abuse of economic dependence concept is the negation of the requirement of dominance. The proof of dominance in the digital sector can be problematic due to the rapid speed of technological evolution and market innovation, which makes it difficult to

---

[154] Mor (2015), p. 157.

[155] Mor (2015), p. 157.

[156] Mor (2015), p. 158.

[157] Concurrence, available at https://www.concurrences.com/en/dictionary/abuse-of-economic-dependance.

[158] Ibid.

[159] Fox (2022), p. 34.

[160] Abuse of economic dependence definition, available at https://www.concurrences.com/en/dictionary/abuse-of-economic-dependance.

[161] Wakui (2022).

[162] Wakui (2022).

[163] Wakui (2022).

[164] Wakui (2022).

assess the boundaries of the market.[165] The AfCFTA Protocol on Competition Policy integrates the two remedies; it prohibits an undertaking, or a group of undertakings referred to as gatekeepers from abusing the relative position of economic dependence ("superior bargaining") over a customer or supplier if the conduct substantially affects the functioning and structure of competition in the market.[166]

The recently published COMESA Draft Regulations appear to harmonise its competition policy with the AfCFTA Protocol on Competition Policy. They also integrate the gatekeeper's provisions with the novel infringement of abuse of economic dependence.[167] Similar to its AfCFTA counterpart, the COMESA Draft Regulations also target both the unilateral and collective abuse of economic dependence by gatekeepers. They too apply to the dominant players in the digital sector who are referred to as gatekeepers without defining the term. However, the COMESA Draft Regulations explicitly make it clear that the requirement of dominance in the market is excluded in assessing abuse of economic dependence.[168] But there is no certainty as to whether the COMESA Draft Regulations have adopted a *post-ante* or *ex-ante* legal provisions in relation to gatekeepers, since it does not have a list of obligations. This will need to be clarified in future guidelines.

However, as outlined above, a plethora of interventions is necessary to effectively regulate competition in the market, including the adaptation of the relevant market definition to reflect the realities of the digital market, or the introduction of other enforcement tools such as the gate keepers' provisions and the novel abuse of economic dependence. But effective regulation of competition in digital markets requires an intersection of competition, consumer protection and data protection.

5.3 *Interface of Competition, Consumer Protection and Data Protection Policies*

In general, competition, consumer protection , and data protection laws and policies serve goals that are distinct but are also complementary. However, the AfCFTA State Parties trails behind, the adoption of effective consumer protection and data protection laws. Consumer protection and data protection laws have been at a slower pace than competition laws in the African continent.

Consumer protection law is used here to refer to the rules pertaining to protection of the interests of consumers. One of the proactive pillars adopted by competition jurisdictions in tackling enforcement challenges in digital markets is to consistently fill regulatory gaps beginning with addressing the interplay between competition, consumer protection, and data protection laws. Traditionally, competition policy

[165] Wakui (2022).

[166] Art 11 (1)–(3) AfCFTA Protocol on Competition Policy.

[167] Art 33(5) COMESA Draft Competition Regulation.

[168] Art 33(3) COMESA Draft Competition Regulation.

addresses market failures through regulation of anti-competitive conduct and merger control.[169] Although competition policy, in its application, uses the consumer welfare standard, which protects consumers, it is also the task of consumer welfare policy through the enacting the relevant law to protect consumers against the negative effects of the market failures of information and behavioural problems.[170]

The competition laws of the RECs like COMESA, EAC, and of most AfCFTA State Parties often combine competition and consumer protection provisions in a single legal instrument and are enforced by the same agency.[171] Although SADC did not adopt a supranational model, its arrangement is twofold, it has a Declaration on Regional Cooperation in Competition and Consumer Policies.[172]

The discussion on whether to integrate competition and consumer welfare policies is over; rather, the question is how to facilitate it.[173] More than a decade later, the debate is dominated by how to align competition, consumer, and data protection policies to regulate competition in digital markets effectively? The COVID-19 experience has shown that this omission can have huge negative effects on consumers and markets.[174] Practices such as hoarding and price gouging or overcharging of basic consumer products, price fixing especially of masks and sanitisers online and offline were among others reported in many countries.[175] The institutional design integrating competition and consumer protection laws depends on the needs of each economy. However, the EAC REC, together with its contracting State Parties including Burundi, Kenya, Rwanda, United Republic of Tanzania, and Uganda have adopted integrated competition and consumer welfare regimes. The EAC has no track record of dealing with cross-border consumer welfare cases or having an effective role in the coordination of such activities with its signatories.

Traditionally, data protection is regulated separately. But Big data, coupled with network effects, can confer market power and durable competitive advantage, especially in vertically integrated digital platforms.[176] There are obvious tensions between competition and data protection policies. The data protection laws prohibit the exploitation of users' personal data, whereas the competition law promotes data portability between service providers to curb monopolistic behaviour in digital platforms.[177] Data protection law aims to protect the right to privacy and data protection

---

[169] Kerber and Zolna (2022), p. 223.

[170] Kerber and Zolna (2022), p. 223.

[171] SADC Member States include Angola, Botswana, Comoros, Democratic Republic of Congo (DRC), E-Swatini, Lesotho, Madagascar, Malawi, Mauritius, Mozambique, Namibia, Seychelles, South Africa, Tanzania, Zambia and Zimbabwe. For example, Botswana, Tanzania, Zambia have a mixed system of competition and consumer welfare enforced by a single agency.

[172] Southern African Development Community Declaration on Cooperation in Competition and Consumer Policies (2021).

[173] OECD (2008), p. 4.

[174] OECD (2008), p. 4.

[175] OECD (2008), p. 4.

[176] CCSA (2023).

[177] See also Nebbia (2023), p. 516.

by giving data subjects control over their personal data and setting limits on the collection, use, and access to such information.[178] Personal data means any information relating to an identified or identifiable natural person ('data subject'); an identifiable natural person is one who can be identified, directly or indirectly, in particular by reference to an identifier such as a name, an identification number, location data, an online identifier or to one or more factors specific to the physical, physiological, genetic, mental, economic, cultural or social identity of that natural person.[179] This means that business data belonging to digital platform users is excluded from data protection laws. Competition law takes an interest in the use of user data in general to promote and protect competition in digital markets. It is suggested that access to user data is critical to curb the negative cost of strong network effects for competition and to promote contestability.[180] Data portability is often touted as the solution to grant competitors access to data necessary to compete in the market by enabling consumers to port their personal data between digital platforms.[181] But this will make dominant digital platforms more powerful and a potential national security threat as this will allow them to operate outside the purview of the regulators in the name of 'user consent' and 'promotion of competition'. Imagine a small technology company porting its data, which makes it competitive and unique as compared to a dominant digital platform like Facebook (which also owns WhatsApp and Instagram), and so forth; in the long run, will this influence competition? Data portability must be restricted; this must be mulled by the competition, and data protection regulators; they must work together to align their functions and guard against creating new gaps in the system. Kerber submits that lack of interaction in the development of policies on competition, consumer protection and data protection may be the cause for reduced effectiveness of enforcement of competition rules and the incentive for developing services which enhance privacy and, therefore, minimise potential for harm to the consumer.[182] Effective enforcement of competition law and policy in digital markets dictates that all existing gaps in the interconnected regulatory frameworks be bolted.

The ability of digital undertakings to collect massive data from customer users/customers and later make use of the information to their advantage and to self-preference has received much attention.[183] Self-preferencing is an act by which digital platforms will give favourable treatment to the services over those of its users/customers as such maintain their positions of dominance.[184] Self-preferencing causes two primary harms to third-party rivals and consumers:[185] First, it enables a

[178] Nebbia (2023), p. 516.

[179] Art 4, Regulation (*EU*) 2016/679 of the *European* Parliament and of the Council of 27 April 2016.

[180] OECD (2021), p. 40.

[181] OECD (2021), p. 40.

[182] Kerber and Zolna (2022), p. 281.

[183] Google Search (Shopping), AT.39740, para 242–246.

[184] Google Search (Shopping), AT.39740, para 242–246.

[185] Hanley (2021), CPI 4.

dominant digital platform to unfairly preserve and increase its market power by artificial reduction of the competitive position of other competing undertakings.[186] When this occurs, entry barriers in the relevant market may rise, which could reduce customer choice and raise the cost of doing business for third-party rivals.[187] Second, self-preferencing significantly reduces consumer choice for other products or services, and they miss out on potential innovation, and this may cause exclusion and foreclosure.[188] However, anti-competitive conduct in the digital market cannot be eradicated without an integrated approach to enforcement which is inclusive of competition, consumer welfare and data protection policies.

The AfCFTA Protocol on Competition Policy takes a bold step, though the details are not yet specific to regulate the anticompetitive conduct in the digital sector. However, effective enforcement will only be achieved through intersection of competition, consumer welfare and data protection policies. The integrated approach to enforcement in digital markets is only possible if AfCFTA State Parties adopt effective laws in the three regulatory pillars, including competition, consumer protection, and data protection. In the areas requiring interactions, the laws must be strictly coordinated to close all existing loopholes.

The upcoming regulations to the AfCFTA Protocol on Competition Policy are an opportunity to integrate enforcement of competition, consumer protection , and data protection laws for effective regulation of digital markets. However, this does not mean regulation of these laws in one legal instrument by a single agency. But a simple clause providing for coordination between these laws is a workable solution. This is much more important since the legal instruments of the RECs and State Parties are also deficient in harmonising and coordinating competition, consumer protection and data protection policies. At least, traditional competition laws of most AfCFTA State Parties acknowledge concurrent jurisdiction and cooperation between competition agencies and other sector regulators and public institutions.[189] But these many need to be broadly construed to create space for the much-needed cooperation between the competition, consumer protection welfare and data protection agencies.[190] The AfCFTA State Parties do not have effective coordinated concurrent arrangements- in cases where competition and consumer protection laws are under separate regulators. This defect can be cured by introducing explicit clauses within the AfCFTA Protocol on Competition Policy which formalises the interface between competition, consumer protection, and data protection laws.

However, the AfCFTA Protocol on Competition Policy has similar provisions on coordination, Arts 2(e) and 2(g) state:

---

186 Hanley (2021), CPI 4.

187 Hanley (2021), CPI 4.

188 Hanley (2021), CPI 4.

189 Compare the concurrent jurisdiction clause of Competition laws of Botswana, Namibia, Kenya, and South Africa.

190 Competition Act 12 of 2010.

> The objectives of this Protocol are to: provide a continental platform for research, information exchange, capacity building, training, consultation, cooperating, and coordinating on competition policy and law in Africa...manage the interrelationships of competition regimes and sectoral regulatory laws at the national, regional, and continental levels.

Whereas Art 15(g)(ii)(iii) provides as follows:

> The Authority, through the Investigative Body, shall administer and enforce the provisions of this Protocol and shall in particular: co-operate with: national and regional competition authorities.... sector regulators with or without concurrent competition jurisdiction.

Similar provisions are found in the laws of the RECs and State Parties.[191] The Kenyan Competition Act provides:

> 5(3) If a body charged with public regulation has jurisdiction in respect of any conduct regulated in terms of this Act within a particular sector, the Authority and that body shall—(a) identify and establish procedures for management of areas of concurrent jurisdiction; (b) promote co-operation; (c) provide for the exchange of information and protection of confidential information; and (d) ensure consistent application of the principles of this Act: Provided that in all matters concerning *competition* and *consumer protection*, if there is any conflict, disharmony or inconsistency, the determinations, directives, regulations, rules, orders and decisions of the Authority shall prevail [My emphasis].

The Nigerian Federal Competition Consumer Protection Act ("FCCCPA"), 2018 provides a similar provision in section 105 (2) and (4). Subsec 105 (2) establishes concurrent jurisdiction in cases where the law of another government agency affects competition and consumer protection matters. Whereas subsec (4) deals with concurrent jurisdiction between the competition authorities and government agencies or sector regulators dealing with competition and consumer matters. Sec 3A(1)(a)(b) of the South African Competition Act 89 of 1998 ("Act"), which states:

> In so far as this Act applies to an industry, or sector of an industry, that is subject to the jurisdiction of another regulatory authority, which authority has jurisdiction in respect of conduct regulated in terms of Chapter 2 or 3 of this Act, this Act must be construed as establishing concurrent jurisdiction in respect of that conduct. (b) The manner in which the concurrent jurisdiction is exercised in terms of this Act and any other public regulation, must be managed, to the extent possible, in accordance with any applicable agreement concluded in terms of sections 21(1) (h) and 82(1) and (2).

Traditionally, this section is interpreted to refer to regulatory bodies responsible for specific industries, such as the banking sector, telecommunications sector, and so forth including other public regulated activities such as consumer protection, financial conduct, etc. with a bearing on competition policy. Competition regulators work with several sector regulators; industry sector or public regulators tend to have specific broader aims and sometimes may align with the promotion of competition. Competition and Consumer Protection can both deal with competition related matters, but data protection laws do not regulate competition policy in any specific sector, they focus on privacy and data protection. However, the activities such as the

[191] Art 9(2)(*j*)—COMESA Competition Regulations; EAC 42(1)(*i*); section 105 of the Nigerian Federal Competition and Consumer Protection Act, 2018.

data protection impact on competition. The Nigerian FCCPA is broadly construed to cover data protection agencies insofar as this relates to competition and consumer protection matters.

The Competition Commission of South Africa (CCSA) has concurrent jurisdiction with several independent sectoral regulators and is also tasked with the cooperation mandate.[192] The CCSA has concluded Memoranda Agreements (MOAs), among others, with the National Consumer Commission and the Information Regulator (a data protection agency).[193] Although the Information Regulator does not have jurisdiction on competition matters, but its activities may impact on competition, thus the CCSA has interpreted sec 3(A1) broadly. Regrettably, the MOAs are broadly crafted and need to be revised to include specific clauses pertaining to the core cooperation areas in the digital sector. This cooperation also serves as a form of advocacy to various industries and the consumer/digital platform users. However, the lack of specific cooperation areas could be because the CCSA and the other parties have an arrangement to form a Joint Working Committee ("the Committee") constituted by representatives of both Regulators is to be established pursuant to the MOA and shall function on an ongoing basis.[194] The Committee is responsible for facilitation and management of cooperation and consultation in respect to matters dealt with by each Regulator in terms of the MOA. The Committee can also propose, when necessary, any amendment or supplementation to the MOA.

We submit that the Committee constituting the CCSA, National Consumer Commission, and the Information Regulator or similar joint institutions in the continent, should collaborate, be proactive and identify the specific areas of cooperation. Thus, a future regulation of the AfCFTA Protocol on Competition Policy must adopt a specific, explicit provision dealing with the interface between competition, consumer welfare and data protection. This is more important in an environment where there is no competition in the law culture, and digital enforcement is not necessarily a priority. This would force the regulators to work together and consistently close existing gaps. We propose an explicit provision in the future regulations of the AfCFTA Protocol on Competition Policy to reflect the increasing interplay between public functions, which require multiple cooperation arrangements. An example of a general provision could be as follows:

> (a) In so far as this Protocol applies to any matter that is subject to the jurisdiction of another public body which may have an impact on enforcement of competition policy, it must be construed as establishing cooperation arrangements between the Authority and the other public body. (b) The manner in which the cooperation arrangement is exercised in terms of this Protocol between the Authority and any other public body must be managed, to the extent possible, in accordance with any applicable agreement concluded in terms of this Protocol.

---

[192] Sec 3(1A) (b), and 82(1) (2).

[193] CCSA, Memorandum of Agreement between the CCSA, and the National Consumer Commission, Government Gazette, Notice Number 1624 in Gazette 45649, 17 December 2021.

[194] See Burger-Smidt and Mathebula (2022).

The AfCFTA competition regime is best suited for the task of coordination and harmonisation of policies; it will strengthen the RECs by providing capacity building in competition, consumer protection and data protection policies. A continental body will have a responsibility to deal with each State Party, considering its level of economic development and strengthen coordination at all levels.

6 Conclusion

We have established that to effectively regulate competition in the AfCFTA single market, it is essential to have a competition regime at the centre. An AfCFTA-spearheaded competition policy at the continental level will serve as the bedrock to ensure uniformity and coordinated enforcement strategy to deal with anti-competitive conduct and control high concentration of market power in digital markets. However, this is not possible if modern enforcement tools are not adopted in the AfCFTA Protocol on Competition Policy and implemented at all levels. Although qualitative evidence might be sufficient in assessing competition analysis in zero-price markets, a quantitative method like SSNDQ is necessary for credibility and predictability and can be supplemented with qualitative evidence.

The AfCFTA single market constitutes mainly developing countries. It is expected that anticompetitive business practices will be regulated in both the dominant and start-up tech undertakings, but the latter could benefit from exemptions.

There must be a focus on the capacity building of the competition authorities, through training and practical application of the new concepts. Therefore, test cases must be identified in various regions of the continent. The novel integration of both the gatekeeper's *ex-ante* obligations with the abuse of dominance reinforces the removal of the abuse of dominance requirement in cases involving dominant digital platforms. This attests to the ongoing adaptation of traditional competition policy within the AU through the AfCFTA competition regime. Competition and consumer protection laws are intersecting. However, the policy makers must not downplay the intersection of competition and data protection policies; greater interaction between the two will yield more protection for digital platform users/consumers. Advocacy on giving of consent in data platforms must take centre stage. This means that competition authorities must also review their expertise, except for economist and lawyers, they will need highly trained data scientists and information technology personnel.

There is a need for further research on specific theories of harm occurring in the digital sector in so far as these affect developing countries, the AfCFTA single market, the RECs, and the State Parties. AfCFTA competition regime must be at the forefront of research initiatives aimed at deriving economic value from dominant digital markets for the benefit of the citizens of individual State Parties. Market conduct research should focus on the pro-competitiveness and inclusion in digital markets, and by deploying proactive strategies which include monitoring of killer acquisitions, use of user data, user terms and conditions on various dominant digital undertakings, especially those that are vertically integrated or serve a dual market role.

Documents, Cases, and Acts

AfCFTA Protocol on Competition Policy adopted by the AU Assembly during its 36th Ordinary Session held from 18 to 19 February 2023 in Addis Ababa, Ethiopia
Arab Maghreb Union (AMU), Community of Sahel-Saharan States (CEN-SAD), Economic Community of Central African States (ECCAS), and Intergovernmental Authority on Development (IGAD)
AU Agenda 2023, available at https://au.int/en/agenda2063/goals, accessed 27 January 2024
Cisco Systems, Inc. and Messagenet SpA v Commission, Case T-79/12, EU:T:2013:635, paras 65–74
COMESA Competition and Consumer Protection Regulations (COMESA Competition Draft Regulations) available at https://comesacompetition.org/wp-content/uploads/2024/01/CCC-Draft-Proposed-Amendments-the-Regulations-shared_stakeholders.pdf
COMESA Competition Regulations 2004
COMESA Draft Competition Regulation 2023
Common Market for Eastern and Southern Africa (COMESA) Regulation of 2004
Competition Act 12 of 2010
Competition Act 89 of 1998
Competition Commission of Kenya, Revised Guidelines on Relevant Market Definition. https://www.cak.go.ke/sites/default/files/Guidelines%20on%20Relevant%20Market%20Definition%20(1).pdf
East Africa Community press release, 16 May 2023. https://www.eacompetition.org/resources/view/the-east-african-competition-authority-and-the-competition-authority-of-kenya-sign-bilateral-agreement
East Africa Competition Act 2006
Economic Community of West African States (ECOWAS), Supplementary Act A/SA 1/12/08
EU 1997 Market Definition Notice, OJ 372 1997 https://eur-lex.europa.eu/legal-content/EN/TXT/PDF/?uri=CELEX:31997Y1209(01)
EU Market Definition Notice, https://eur-lex.europa.eu/legal-content/EN/TXT/?uri=CELEX:52024XC01645
EU Regulation 2022/1925 of the European Parliament and of the Council of 14 September 2022
European Commission Google Android, Case AT.40099
European Commission Press Corner. https://ec.europa.eu/commission/presscorner/detail/en/qanda_23_6002
Google and Alphabet v Commission, T-604/18, EU:T:2022:541, paras 177 and 180

GovChat Proprietary Limited and Another v Facebook Inc. and Others (IR165Nov20)
Höfner & Elser v Macrotron GmbH, C-41/90, [1991] ECR—(April 23, 1991), paras. 20—23
Memorandum of Agreement between the CCSA, and the National Consumer Commission, Government Gazette, Notice Number 1624 in Gazette 45649, 17 December 2021
Microsoft v Commission, T-201/04, EU:T:2007:289, paras 966–970
Nigerian Federal Competition and Consumer Protection Act 2018
Qihoo 360 v. Tencent (pinyin: 2013) Min San Zhong Zi (No. 4) Stanford Law School China Guiding Cases Project, English Guiding Case (EGC78), (2017) Edition, https://web.archive.org/web/20170415194016/http://www.crai.com/sites/default/files/publications/China-Highlights-Qihoo-360-v-Tencent-0215_0.pdf
Regulation (EU) 2016/679 of the European Parliament and of the Council of 27 April 2016
Southern African Development Community Declaration on Cooperation in Competition and Consumer Policies. https://www.sadc.int/sites/default/files/2021-08/SADC_Declaration_on_Competition_and_Consumer_Policies.pdf
Statista, 'Google, Amazon, Meta, Apple, and Microsoft (GAMAM)'—Statistics & Facts. https://www.statista.com/topics/4213/google-apple-facebook-amazon-and-microsoft-gafam/#topicOverview
Topps Europe v Commission, T-699/14, EU: T:2017:2
Treaty Establishing the African Economic Community ("Abuja Treaty"). https://au.int/en/treaties/treaty-establishing-african-economic-community
Treaty Establishing the African Economic Community of 1991

References

Africa Heads of Competition Dialogues (2022) Joint statement of the Heads of Competition Authorities Dialogue on regulation of digital markets. https://www.compcom.co.za/wp-content/uploads/2022/02/Joint-Statement-of-the-Heads-of-Competition-Authorities-Dialogue-on-Regulation-of-Digital-Markets.pdf
Anderson RD, Müller AC (2012) Competition policy and poverty reduction: a holistic approach. World Trade Organization staff working paper ERSD-2018-12. https://www.wto.org/english/res_e/reser_e/ersd201302_e.pdf
Aydin U, Büthe T (2016) Competition law & policy in developing countries: explaining variations in outcomes; exploring possibilities and limits. Law Contemp Probl 79(4):15–26
Baker M (2021) Competition in the digital economy: an African perspective. https://www.bakermckenzie.com/en/-/media/files/insight/publications/2021/07/baker-mckenzie-competition-in-the-digital-economy.pdf
Bonakele T, Kariuki F (2022) Some opening words for the special issue. Rev Ind Organ 60(3):299
Boshoff WH (2021) South African competition policy on excessive pricing and its relation to price gauging during the covid-19 disaster period. South Afr J Econ 89(1):112–140

Burger-Smidt A, Mathebula N (2022) Data privacy meets competition law: a new dawn for the regulators. https://www.werksmans.com/wp-content/uploads/2022/02/Data-privacy-meets-competition-law-A-new-dawn-for-the-regulators-Legal-Brief-01.pdf
Büthe T, Kedogo Kigwiru VK (2020) The spread of competition law and policy in Africa: a research agenda. Afr J Econ Law 1:42–72
Cani F (2021) A new kid on the block: how will competition law get along with the DMA? J Eur Competition Law Pract 12(4):271–272
CCSA (2023) Online intermediation platforms market inquiry, final report. https://www.compcom.co.za/wp-content/uploads/2023/07/CC_OIPMI-Final-Report.pdf
Competition Commission of South Africa (CCSA) (2020) Competition in the digital economy: version. http://www.compcom.co.za/wpcontent/uploads/2021/03/Digital-Markets-Paper-2021-002-1.pdf
Dessemond EG (2019) Restoring competition in winner took all markets. UNCTAD research paper 40. https://unctad.org/system/files/official-document/ser-rp-2019d12_en.pdf
Evans DS, Zhang VZ (2014) Qihoo 360 v Tencent: first antitrust decision by the Supreme Court. In: Zhang VY (ed) Competition policy in Asia: essay on recent development. Competition Policy International
Fox EM (2022) Integrating Africa by competition and market policy. Rev Ind Organ 60(3):305–326
Gachuiri E (2020) African Continental Free Trade Area phase II negotiations: a space for a AfCFTA Protocol on Competition Policy? https://unctad.org/system/files/official-document/ser-rp-2020d15_en.pd
Gal MS, Fox EM (2015) Drafting competition law for developing jurisdictions: learning from experience. In: Gal MS, Mor B, Drexl J, Fox EM, Geber DJ (eds) The economic characteristics of developing jurisdiction: their implications for competition law, law and economics research paper series working paper no. 14-11
Gal MS, Rubinfeld DL (2016) The hidden costs of free goods: implications for competition law enforcement. Antitrust Law J 80:521–562
Gumede S, Manenzhe P (2023) Competition regulation for digital markets: the South African experience. Afr J Inf Commun 31:1–19
Guterres A (2019) Secretary-General of the United Nations, digital economy report. https://pdf4pro.com/amp/download?data_id=68bff2&slug=digital-economy-report-unctad
Hanley DA (2021) How self-preferencing can violate Section 2 of the Sherman Act' CPI 4. https://www.competitionpolicyinternational.com/how-self-preferencing-can-violate-section-2-of-the-sherman-act/
International Center for Law & Economics (2024) Digital competition regulations around the world. 16 May 2024. https://laweconcenter.org/spotlights/digital-competition-regulations-around-the-world
Jarman S, Karaman DD (2020) The regulation of zero-price markets by the competition authorities in the USA and the EU. Competition Regul Netw Ind 21(4):315–343
Jones A, Sufrin B (2014) EU competition law - text, cases and materials, 5th edn. Oxford University Press, Oxford
Kerber W, Zolna KK (2022) The German Facebook case: the law and economics of the relationship between competition and data protection law. Eur J Law Econ 54(2):217–250
Kigwiru VK (2023) Supranational or cooperative? Rethinking the African Continental Free Trade Area Agreement Competition Protocol institutional design. J Antitrust Enforcement 12(1):98–125
Knapstad T (2024) Digital dominance: assessing market definition and market power for online platforms under Article 102 TFEU. Eur Competition J 20(2):412–436
Mandrescu D (2018) The SSNIP test and zero-pricing strategies. Eur Competition Regul Law Rev 2(4):244–257
Mor B (2015) Abuse without dominance in competition law: abuse of economic dependence and its interface with abuse of dominance. Working paper 15(15) Max Planck Institute for Innovation and Competition

Moss DL (2022) Toward a coherent approach to market power in the digital sector: complexity, growth through acquisition, and remedies. Antitrust Bull 67(4):536–551
Nebbia P (2023) The interaction of competition, consumer and data protection laws: a few comments inspired by the recent case law of the Court of Justice of the European Union. ERA Forum 23(4):516
Newman JM (2015) Antitrust in zero-price markets: foundations. Univ Pa Law Rev 164:149–206
OECD (2004) Glossary of statistical terms. https://stats.oecd.org/glossary/glossary.pdf
OECD (2008) Policy round tables: the interface between competition and consumer. https://www.oecd.org/daf/competition/40898016.pdf. Accessed 27 Jan 2024
OECD (2018a) Quality considerations in the zero-price economy - note by the European. https://www.oecd.org/competition/quality-considerations-in-the-zero-price-economy.htm
OECD (2018b) Rethinking antitrust tools for multi-sided platform. https://www.oecd.org/daf/competition/Rethinking-antitrust-tools-for-multi-sided-platforms-2018
OECD (2021) Ex ante regulation of digital markets. Competition Committee Discussion Paper. https://www.oecd.org/daf/competition/ex-ante-regulation-andcompetition-in-digital-markets.htm
OECD (2022a) OECD handbook on competition policy in the digital age. https://www.oecd.org/daf/competition/oecd-handbook-on-competition-policy-in-the-digital-age.pdf
OECD (2022b) The evolving concept of market power in the digital economy, OECD competition policy roundtable background note. http://www.oecd.org/daf/competition/the-evolving-concept-of-market-power-in-the-digital-economy-2022.pdf
Okadia F, Wa-Kyendo E, Njeru M, Jattani D, Kemboni L (2021) Designing an AfCFTA-driven continent-wide competition policy around the regional economic communities. Antitrust Bull 66(4):556–575
Radic L, Manne GA, Auer D (2025) Regulate for what? A closer look at the rationale and goals of digital competition regulations. 1 April 2025. https://laweconcenter.org/spotlights/digital-competition-regulations-around-the-world/
Raslan AA (2017) The diffusion of competition law in Africa: theoretical perspectives on the policy transfer process. Unpublished LLD thesis, University College London
Roberts S, Vilakazi T, Simbanegavi W (2017) Competition, regional integration and inclusive growth in Africa: a research agenda. In: Roberts S, Klaaren J, Valodia I (eds) Competition law and economic regulation in Southern Africa. Wits University Press, Johannesburg, pp 263–287
Royoa MG, Diepa L, Mulliganb J, Mukanga P, Parikha P (2022) Linking the UN Sustainable Development Goals and African Agenda 2063: understanding overlaps and gaps between the global goals and continental priorities for Africa. World Dev Sustain 1:100010
Schaefer A, Crane A (2005) Addressing sustainability and consumption. J Micromarketing 25(1):76–92
Southern African Development Community (2009) Competition policy. https://www.sadc.int/document/sadc-declaration-competition-and-consumer-policies-2009
UNCTAD (2019a) Competition issues in the digital economy. https://unctad.org/system/files/official-document/ciclpd54_en.pdf
UNCTAD (2019b) Digital platforms and value creation in developing countries: implications for national and international policies. https://unctad.org/system/files/official-document/tdb_ede4d2_en.pdf5-8
UNCTAD (2021) Strengthening consumer welfare and competition in the digital economy. https://unctad.org/system/files/official-document/tdrbpconf9d4_en.pdf
Wakui M (2022) On market power and economic dependence. https://one.oecd.org/document/DAF/COMP/WD(2022)61/en/pdf

Competition Enforcement for Fair-Trade Practices in the AfCFTA Market

Ignatious Nzero and Chidochashe Nicolette Ncube

Abstract Multilateral trade seeks to promote market access and in turn economic growth and improved standards of living of the citizens. This is because they will have access to cheaper and quality goods and services including those produced outside their domestic markets. Similarly, domestic producers and suppliers will be motivated to innovate so as to effectively compete with quality and cheaper imports that will have unrestricted access to domestic markets. However, whereas trade liberalisation through the rules aimed at reducing barriers to trade have had significant impact on national spheres, the same cannot be said of the private spheres. Within the private spheres, private business enterprises through anti-competitive practices have eroded the gains of trade by distorting trade and erecting barriers to trade. The place of competition enforcement within the trading system has been a subject of debate for some time. The establishment of the AfCFTA and the adoption of competition system within the continental trading system have aided impetus to this debate. This chapter largely argues that the AfCFTA through its competition agreement, is a welcome development to the African economy for there exists strong mechanism such as capacity building and strengthening of national competition authorities to ensure that they become building block for regional and then continental integration.

I. Nzero (✉)
Faculty of Law-Zimbabwe Open University, Zimbabwe and Competition Law and Policy, Mergers and Acquisitions Consultant, Harare, Zimbabwe

C. N. Ncube
Faculty of Law, University of Western Cape, Cape Town, South Africa

T. V. Warikandwa et al. (eds.), *Law and Policy of the African Continental Free Trade Area (AfCFTA)*, European Yearbook of International Economic Law,
https://doi.org/10.1007/978-3-032-01122-0_8

1 Introduction

The establishment of the African Continental Free Trade Area (AfCFTA)[1] in 2019 marked a landmark development for the continental trading system. AfCFTA aim to enable the free flow of goods and services across the African continent and boost trading position of Africa in the global market,[2] has been hailed as one of the flagship projects of the African Union (AU) Agenda 2063: *The Africa We Want.*[3] It is the largest free trade area binding together 55 countries of the AU and eight Regional Economic Communities (RECs) to create a single market for the continent. AfCFTA is a critical mechanism to advance regional integration. It will contribute to the establishment of regional value chains in Africa. The AfCFTA mandate is to eliminate trade barriers and boost intra-Africa trade.[4] AfCFTA was established to advance trade in value-added production across all service sectors of the African economy.[5]

The goals of AfCFTA mirror those of the existing multilateral trading system promoted by the World Trade Organisation (WTO).[6] The principles of the multilateral trading system as contained in a variety of agreements under the auspices of the WTO, have gone a long way in reducing tariff barriers[7] and non-tariff barriers (NTB),[8] there is a new threat emerging from private businesses who are not members of the multilateral trading system. Private business in a bid to acquire and strengthen market shares, engages in anti-competitive practices that have the potential to prevent, restrict and distort competition and in the process negate the benefits of trade.

Competition policy is meant to promote and maintain a competitive market structure through the regulation and prohibition of business practices that actually or have the potential to prevent, restrict or distort competition. Given the nexus

---

[1] Agreement Establishing the African Continental Free Trade Area (AfCFTA), was signed at Kigali, Rwanda on 21 March 2018 and entered into force on 30 May 2019 after 24 Member States deposited their instruments of Ratification following a series of continuous continental engagements since 2012.

[2] Art 3 of AfCTA Agreement 'General Objectives.'

[3] It was launched at the 12th Extraordinary Session of the AU Assembly of Heads of States and Government in Niamey, Niger in July 2019.

[4] Art 3 of AfCTA.

[5] Trade under AfCTA commenced on 1 January 2021.

[6] The World Trade Organisation (WTO) was established by the Marrakesh Agreement of 1994 to replace the General Agreement on Tariffs and Trade (GATT) that has been in force since 1947. The WTO is an intergovernmental organization that regulates and facilitates international trade. See the Marrakesh Agreement Establishing the World Trade Organisation ("WTO Agreement") of 15 April 1994 1867 UNTS 154. See further Oatley (2019).

[7] A tariff barrier is an obstacle to trade as a result of a tax imposed on the import or export of goods. See art 1 of General Agreement on Tariffs and Trade; Text of The General Agreement Geneva, July 1986.

[8] NTMs are policy measures, other than ordinary customs tariffs, that can potentially have an economic effect on international trade in goods, changing quantities traded, or prices or both. See United Nations Conference on Trade and Development (2020), p. 13.

between competition enforcement and trade, it is important to explore the relationship between the multilateral and regional trading systems and competition systems. These are not the same as much as they have some common goals: economic efficiency for the benefit of consumers. The adoption of the AfCFTA had added a voice to the debate as to whether competition enforcement can fit within the trading system and if so, what dimension must it take. This chapter explores this question and related issues and argue that there is a role for competition enforcement within the trading system and the adoption of the AfCFTA competition system is a welcome development.

To advance the above thesis, the chapter will first present a discussion on the relationship between competition and trade. The aim is to build a foundation for understanding the context of the AfCFTA competition system which will then be discussed as provided under the AfCFTA Competition Protocol. Here, an analysis will be made of the objectives and dimension of the Protocol where it will be argued that there is enough evidence to suggest that the Protocol will aid towards the advancement of global welfare through promoting regional and continental integration that is essential for building economic relations. It will further be argued that through seeking to build and strengthen the capacity of national competition authorities, the Protocol will make a significant contribution to effective competition enforcement in Africa which will enhance trade through reducing and eliminating barriers that arise from anti-competitive practices.

2 Competition Enforcement for Trade Promotion

Competition broadly denotes all mechanism that are designed to increase inter firm rivalry[9] and eliminates barriers to the proper operation of market forces.[10] Policies that are related with the firm behaviour are concerned with horizontal and vertical agreements such as cartels or restrictive business arrangements.[11] Policies that are related to the structure of the market are concerned with regulation of business combinations (mergers and acquisitions) that might have an impact on the competitive structure of the market. Competition policy encompasses measures related to the behaviour of firms and those related to the structure of the markets.[12]

The principles of the global trading system are contained in a variety of agreements that are under the auspices of the World Trade Organisation (the WTO). These agreements deals with specific aspects of global trade amongst them as

[9] See generally, Wish and Bailey (2021), p. 1.

[10] Market forces are those factors that influence the price and availability of goods and services on the market. They include the forces of supply and demand. Market forces pushes the prices up when supply declines and demand rises and drive prices down when supply grows or demands slows.

[11] Examples are exclusive dealings with resellers.

[12] Singh and Dhumale (1999); Ljubownikow and Hwee Ang (2020); Kolmar (2021); Everest-Phillips (2009), p. 48.

agriculture,[13] trade in services,[14] investments and banking,[15] government procurement,[16] food sanitation regulations,[17] and intellectual property.[18] These agreements are characterised by simple common principles that run through all of them. These principles underpin the multilateral trading system.

Promoting fair competition is one of the principles of the multilateral trading system. To this end, the WTO has been described as a 'free trade' institution.[19] This statement is not entirely accurate for the WTO does allow for use of restrictive practices in justifiable circumstances.[20] Tariffs are allowed in limited circumstances. Given that the WTO is not necessarily an unlimited 'free trade' institution, it can thus be accurately described as a system of rules dedicated to open, fair and undistorted competition. The existence of these rules regulates when competition can be defined as being fair thereby allowing market access.

The WTO trading system hinges on such principles as non-discrimination which encompasses the the Most-Favoured Nation rule requiring WTO member to apply the same conditions on all trade with other WTO members,[21] and the National Treatment rule which provides that a member must 'grant someone a special favour and you have to do the same for all other WTO members.'[22] The National Treatment rule requires that imported goods be subjected to same treatment as domestically produced ones upon entering the market of the host.[23] These rules are designed to secure fair conditions of trade.

Anti-dumping[24] and subsidies[25] are amongst the rules adopted by the WTO which have a bearing on competition and trade. Dumping is a practice 'by which products of one country are introduced into the commerce of another country at less than the normal value of the products'[26] to gain market share. Similar goods produced at normal cost must compete with those dumped on importing market. The dumped goods will thus enjoy favourable conditions since they will be cheaper. This in turn

[13] WTO Agreement on Agriculture (1995).

[14] WTO, The General Agreement on Trade in Services (GATS) (1995).

[15] WTO, The Agreement on Trade-Related Investment Measures (TRIMS) (1995).

[16] WTO, The Agreement on Government Procurement (GPA) (2012).

[17] WTO, The Agreement on the Application of Sanitary and Phytosanitary Measures (the 'SPS Agreement') (1995).

[18] WTO, The Agreement on Trade-Related Aspects of Intellectual Property Rights (TRIPS) (1995).

[19] See generally, Lumina (2008), pp. 20–40.

[20] See generally Art XX of GATT.

[21] Hoekman (2002), p. 43. The MFN provides that WTO members 'has to grant the most favourable conditions under which it allows trade in a certain product type to all other WTO members.' See also in general Van den Bosche and Prevost (2016), pp. 13–48.

[22] WTO (n.d.-b) Principles of the trading system. https://www.wto.org/english/thewto_e/whatis_e/tif_e/fact2_e.htm#seebox.

[23] Hoekman (2002), p. 42.

[24] See generally Art VI of GATT on Anti-dumping and countervailing measures.

[25] See WTO Agreement on Subsidies and Countervailing Measures (1995).

[26] GATT, art VI.

distorts competition and leads to slow to no economic growth, job losses and declining standards of living in the importing market. Anti-dumping measures are thus permitted to counter this practice.[27] These are additional import duties calculated to compensate for damage caused by unfair trade (dumping).

State subsidies are another practice that has similar negative effects to competition and trade. A subsidy is "financial contribution" by a government which provides a benefit.[28] The National Treatment principle requires that the host market treats imports under the same conditions as domestic goods and services. This ensures that there is fair competition between imported goods and domestically produced ones. However, where a government subsidies domestic production, these domestically produced goods and services will have been produced cheaper thus can be sold or offered at a cheaper price compared to similar imports. This causes unfair competition and distorts trade. Whilst for the domestic producer and consumers, there might appear to be some benefits but in actual fact the practice destroys the motivation to innovate.

Dumping and subsidies are complex issues. However, the rules attempt to establish what is fair or unfair and how governments can respond particularly by imposing anti-dumping measures.

Competition law and policy have merged as a significant element of global trade in recent years. Multilateral trade has resulted in a substantial decrease in adverse tariff rate on imports.[29] It has similarly led to the abolishment of various non-tariff barriers (NTBs). Internal trade's main objective is to reduce the adverse effects of tariff and abolish NTBs.

The multilateral trading system has witnessed significant gains been recorded in the reduction and elimination of barriers to trade. However, these gains have mostly been recorded within the public and national spheres. In the context of private business, whose conduct can distort trade, they have not been as significant gains as within the national spheres in dealing with trade distorting conduct by private enterprises. Competition law and policy is designed to deal with anti-competitive business practices such as Restrictive Business Practices (RBPs) which erects barriers to trade. Competition law and policy thus seeks, in the main, to prevent corporate businesses from reducing the efficiency of market systems.[30] Its aim is to keep entities forming cartels or monopolies as well as from abusing a dominant market position and ensuring that mergers and acquisitions (corporate combinations) are subjected to proper scrutiny. This scrutiny constitutes competition enforcement.

In a market where entities compete, there is motivation to innovate to produce quality and sufficient goods and products to outcompete rivals and gain and maintain market shares. Anti-competitive practices often limit competition and defeat the

[27] GATT, art VI.

[28] Art I of the Agreement on Subsidies and Countervailing measures.

[29] See WTO (2023).

[30] This goal is mainly advanced by the Chicago Scholars or Chicagoans. See generally Bork (1993), pp. 90–106; Posner (1981), pp. 13–115, and Corradi and Nowag (2023) pp. 32–47.

incentive to innovate so as to be efficient and reduce prices and improve consumer welfare.

Within the context of trade, anti-competitive practices act as trade barriers that distort trade. Whereas global welfare and promote peaceful co-existence amongst trading nations, anti-competitive practices may reduce global welfare and may invariably lead to conflict amongst nations.

Since its first introduction by the United States in 1890 with the enactment of the Sherman Antitrust Act[31] to prohibit cartels and vertical agreement, competition laws and policies have been adopted in numerous individual national jurisdictions.[32] Competition systems have developed from being national to supranational with the European Union's adoption of a supranational competition system that regulate anti-competitive practices, mergers and acquisitions (concentrations) having trans-border effects.[33] Various attempts have been made at international level to establish a multilateral competition agreement on competition policy *albeit* unsuccessfully.[34] Despite the failure to establish a competition system at international level, it is accepted that competition laws and policies can be a platform for the creation of competitive markets at international level. The adoption o competition policies and establishment of enforcement mechanism at national level is thus a requirement for building a global competitive market.

The OECD which 'is an international organisation that works to build better policies for better lives' with a 'goal is to shape policies that foster prosperity, equality, opportunity and well-being for all'[35] not only recommends that its members adopts a competition system, but requires members to co-operate in order to restrain anti-competitive practices that have transborder effects, that is, having competitive effects on more than one country.[36]

Competition law and policy have remained active discussion topics at international organisations. The WTO, the largest multilateral trading organisation, has a working group studying the subject.[37] The framework agreements of the WTO include aspects of promoting fair trade thereby encouraging competition.[38] The

---

[31] Ch. 647, 26 Stat. 209 (1890) (Codified as amended at 15.U.S.C ss1-7 (1892).

[32] By 2007, the United Nations Conference on Trade and Development (UNCTAD) had documented 165 competition systems across the globe. See UNCTAD (2007).

[33] The European competition system is premised on arts 101 to 109 of the Treaty on the Functioning of the European Union (TFEU). See *Consolidated version of the Treaty on the Functioning of the European Union*, 26 October 2012, OJ L. 326/47–326/390; 26.10.2012, available at: https://www.refworld.org/docid/52303e8d4.html.

[34] The topic of establishing a multilateral agreement on competition policy has been considered extensively by the Organisation of Economic Cooperation and Development (0ECD) and the UNCTAD.

[35] OECD, About OECD, available at https://www.oecd.org/about/.

[36] See OECD (1986).

[37] See WTO (n.d.-a) Interaction between Trade and Competition Policy', available at https://www.wto.org/english/tratop_e/comp_e/comp_e.htm.

[38] See WTO TRIMS dealing with agreements that reduces the risk of foreign investment, such as investment protection agreements and other agreements that do away with government erected

OECD has published several proposals.[39] Various sub-regional groupings are also examining the possibility of adopting a transborder competition system.[40]

The creation of Free Trade Areas (FTAs) which a geographic region whose members have entered into a free trade agreement aimed at enhancing cooperation in areas of economic growth and integration,[41] in various parts of the globe have given impetus to the establishment of a multilateral competition system. These include the Free Trade Area of the Americas (FTAA)[42] and of late the African Continental Free Trade Area (AfCFTA). These bodies are not intranational competition authorities but rather trading blocks. The significance of the relationship between competition enforcement and trading bodies lies in the fact that competition law and policy are increasingly becoming important subjects for discussion within these bodies. The AfCFTA has added another voice to this debate on the need to an effective multilateral agreement necessary to necessary to forestall or eliminate these new kinds of trade barriers.

3 The African Continental Free Trade Area (AfCFTA)

Generally, a free trade area (FTA) seeks to enhance economic integration within its market. AfCFTA is no exception to this established goal. To add to the growing subject of promoting trade through reducing trade barriers, AfCFTA identified competition law and policy as a central tool. To this end, a separate instrument has been established in the form of the AfCFTA Protocol on Competition Policy.[43]

barriers to foreign firms. Also see WTO TRIPS) dealing with intellectual property.

[39] One of the most significant OECD publication in this regard is the Recommendation of the Council for Co-operation between Member Countries in Areas of Potential Conflict between Competition and Trade Policies (1986).

[40] MERCOSUUR, Group of Three, the North American Free Trade Agreement (NAFTA) and the Asia-Pacific Economic Cooperation (APEC).

[41] See O'Sullivan and Sheffrin (2003), p. 453; Ajewumi et al. (2024), p. 2783; Mindaye et al. (2025); Ishikawa (2021), p. 24.

[42] The FTAA was a proposed agreement to eliminate or reduce the trade barriers among all countries in the Americas, excluding Cuba. However, the parties failed to reach an agreement by the set deadlines resulting in the failure to implement it.

[43] The Protocol To The Agreement Establishing The African Continental Free Trade Area On Competition Policy (hereinafter the AfCFTA Protocol on Competition Policy or the Protocol), was adopted by the AU Assembly during its 36th Ordinary Session held from 18 to 19 February 2023 in Addis Ababa, Ethiopia. (Herein after the Protocol). The Protocol will enter into force 30 days after the deposit of the 22nd instrument of Ratification of the Protocol.

3.1 The AfCFTA Protocol on Competition Policy

The Protocol is an agreement by State Parties to ensure that competition contributes towards the AU objectives of trade, inclusive growth, industrialisation, innovation and sustainable economic development in Africa.[44] An effective implementation of the Protocol, which is largely dependent on State Parties' capacity and willingness, will aid in the creation of a fair and competitive business environment in Africa. This is through the promotion of competition to address restrictive business practices that distort markets and disrupt trade.

Micro-Small, and Medium -sized Enterprises (MSMEs) have been recognized by the AU as key to the achievement of the Agenda 2063 Goals.[45] Through the AU S Small and Medium Enterprises Strategy, the AU aims 'to develop competitive, diversified, and sustainable economies underpinned by dynamic, entrepreneurial, and industrial sectors that generate employment, reduce poverty, and foster social inclusion.' Thus the effective implementation of the Protocol will benefit MSMEs from a fair and competitive business environment. Restrictive business practices and other forms of anti -competitive behaviours deprive MSMes an opportunity to partake in economic activities as they are excluded from markets.

Improved consumer welfare is one of the benefits of competition.[46] Competition pushes producers and suppliers to produce and supply cheap and quality goods and services in sufficient quantities. This entails that they have to innovate in order to improve the quality of their products and services on the market. The Protocol's implementation will thus benefit consumers across the continent that will enjoy the goods and services produced not only in their domestic markets, but across borders.

3.2 The Objectives of the Protocol on Competition Policy

The Protocol seeks to create a single African Competition regime. This is a clear indication of the continent's desire to have a unitary competition system. The establishment of such a system is meant to ensure that members not only promote free trade principles but also recognise the threat that anti-competitive practices poses to the attainment of trade goals. The question however remains as to whether the multilateral approach to competition is the ideal route? It has been argued, on one hand, against the idea that what is ideal is the adoption of bilateral rather than multilateral

---

[44] See in general the AU Agenda 2063 Goals.

[45] In 2019, the AU Executive Council developed and adopted the African Union Small and Medium Enterprises Strategy. The Strategy was endorsed by the Heads of State and Government during the 17th Extraordinary Summit on Industrialization and Economic Diversification on 25th November 2022 in Niamey, Niger.

[46] See generally Whish et al. (2021), p. 1; Everest-Phillips (2009) p. 47; Thorelli (1954), p. 171; Fox (1997), p. 1.

agreements whose scope would be confirmed to cooperation between national competition policy enforcement authorities.

On the other hand, it has been argued for, that a multilateral approach such as the intranational law system of the EU, which the Protocol proposes, with the need to adopt common rules by all countries and international cooperation between competition enforcement authorities. It is submitted that developing economies like those constituting AfCFTA are better served by adopting an intranational competition system. This will also aid in their integration agenda given that their individual markets share common features that will make adoption of common rules and enforcement mechanism easier.

The Protocol also seeks to promote competition within the AfCFTA so as to improve market efficiency, inclusive growth and structural transformation of the African economy. This stated objective encompasses the tradition economic efficiency dimension of competition. This perspective views the goal of competition of the promotion of economic efficiency through which growth is achieved. It has increasingly been accepted that competition systems are designed to achieve many other goals beyond market efficiency. It is submitted that by transforming the African economy for the better, other socio-political challenges that the continent is currently facing can also be addressed.

Significantly, the Protocol boldly seeks to ensure that gain from the AfCFTA trade liberation is not undermined by anti-competitive business practices. This is a confirmation of the nexus between trade and competition enforcement. Trade has a positive effect on economic growth and global welfare. Anti-competitive practices have the potential to negate the positive effects of trade. Thus, competition enforcement within the trade matrix will ensure that the trade benefits are not eroded by anti-competitive practices.

One factor that will make or break the Protocol is the capacity of State Parties to effectively enforce competition rules within their jurisdictions as well as cooperate should a transaction have a cross border effect. The Protocol aim to develop and strengthen the capacity of States to deal with anti-competitive business practices. These practices emanate from domestic markets and spreads across the borders, region, and continent. The ability of national competition authorities to identify and control anti-competitive business practices is essential to the effectiveness of AfCFTA's bid to establish a single and effective competitive system. Whereas most individual African nations have established competition systems, very few pass the test of being effective.[47] They either suffer from institutional deficiencies associated with lack of independence to effectively enforce and sanction anti-competitive behaviours[48] or have inadequate and inappropriate frameworks[49] or simply lack the

---

[47] An effective competition system is one that is provides adequate and relevant regulatory framework and enforcement mechanism capable of dealing with any challenges that the system might face. See Singh and Dhumale (1999) p. 8. See also Kububa (2007).

[48] See generally Zogbhi (2009), pp. 89 and 96. See further OECD (2004).

[49] See generally Zogbhi (2009), pp. 89 and 96. See further OECD (2004).

resources.[50] The capacity building and strengthening objectives is thus a welcome development. This ties in with the OECD recommendations on capacity building for national competition authorities to ensure competition enforcement benefits global trade.

Closely related to the objective of capacity building and strengthening competition enforcement institution is the Protocol's proclamation that it seeks to act as a 'continental platforms for research, information exchange, capacity building, trading, consultation, cooperation and coordination on competition policy and law in Africa.' This again, it is submitted, is a welcome development given that most African competition systems are very much in their infancy compared to such jurisdictions as the US and the EU that adopted competition systems much earlier and as such had developed experience in enforcement. In Africa, competition systems were adopted largely as part of broader economic reforms thus very late.[51]

The Protocol further state as its objective the promotion of economic integration and sustainable development Africa as well as the management of interrelationships of national, regional and continental competition regimes and sector regulatory laws. This objective clearly shows that the Protocol is established with a mandate to further foster the AU's broader integration and peaceful co-existence values. Regional economic blocks form the basis for a wider continental integration. Given that these regional communities have been in existence long before AfCFTA, the experience gained, and relationships build thereon can be very useful to AfCFTA. Members of these blocks share more than economic relations but deep rooted cultural and political ties upon which regional value chains can be established and strengthened. These will in turn enable investment flows and job creation-pillars of the global welfare enhancement of trade.

3.3 *Guiding Principles Dimensions of the AfCFTA Competition Protocol*

3.3.1 Application of the Protocol

The Protocol applies to businesses conduct with a continental dimension and to all economic activities by enterprises that have a significant impact on competition in the AfCFTA market.[52] There are three aspects to the Protocol's application.

First it applied to business conduct with a continental dimension.[53] This means business activities whose effects are felt within the African continent are subjected to the regulatory purview of the Protocol.

[50] See generally Zogbhi (2009), pp. 89 and 96. See further OECD (2004).

[51] Kavacic (1997–98), p. 403; Hatzenberg (2002); Kamala and Lipimile (2021).

[52] Art 3(1) of the Protocol.

[53] Art 3(1)(b).

The second element is that the Protocol applies to all economic activities by enterprises. This is further qualified by the proviso that these enterprises can either be 'private or public entities that are involved in the production of, or the trade in goods, or the provision of services.'[54] The Protocol first clearly state that either private or public enterprises are subject to its application. This entails that the ownership or control of the enterprise in question is not the determinant of the Protocol's applicability. Both private and public enterprises are equally subject to the Protocol for as long as they are involved in economic activities. This ensures that anti-competitive practices perpetrated by even State Owned or Controlled entities are subjected to regulatory scrutiny. This is a significant pronouncement given that state erected barriers are one of the major contributors to the creation of uncompetitive domestic markets that are stumbling blocks to market access and trade liberalisation.

The protocol has a proviso that makes reference to 'economic activities'. It is submitted that the phrase 'economic activity' that is subject to the Protocol is assigned its ordinary meaning of the production of, or the trade in goods, or the provision of services. This is broad to capture any such activity that have the potential to impact on the defined market and impede continental trade.

The third element of the application provision is that the economic activity having a continental dimension must have a significant effect on the competition.[55] It is important to note that what is subject to the Protocol's application are not every economic activities by either the private or public enterprise with a continental dimension but rather those that have a significant impact on competition in the AfCFTA market. There is a need to define the affected market which in this case is the geographic market under the AfCFTA. Then the activity in question must have a significant impact on the competitive structure of the said market. This can be interpreted as meaning that it must have not necessarily actually caused harm to the market but likely have the potential to negatively affect the competitive structure of the market through hampering competition or reducing it where it exists. The significant impact thus is a degree to which the activity in question have impeded or lessen competition thereby negatively impacting the competitive structure of the said market but not any mere prevention or reduction in competition.[56]

The Protocol excludes from its application labour-related issues, collective bargaining agreements or matters falling within jurisdictions of national competition authorities. A few issues can be said about this statute of limitation. It is a common practice to exclude labour issues from competition statutes. This is meant to protect a constituency that is largely viewed as weak when it comes to protecting themselves during corporate transactions.

The Protocol does not apply to matters where national competition authorities have jurisdictions. This entails that should a matter be exclusively under the

[54] Art 3(1)(a).

[55] Art 3(1)(a) and (b) of the Protocol.

[56] See *International Shoe.Co.v FTC*, 280 U.S 291 at 298, 50 S.St. 89, 74 L ED, 431 (1930).

purview of national competition authorities; it lacks the continental dimension for its effects will not be transboundary. The challenge is when a transaction has national effects that are not necessarily transboundary but also independently affect another market. This becomes an issue where the different markets that are affected by the transaction in nature have different rules in dealing with it. A case in question is mergers that end up being subject to regulatory scrutiny in more than one jurisdiction. The transaction can be approved in one and be blocked in another.[57] This unfortunate scenario can be avoided if AfCFTA State Parties adopt shared common competition law rules and principles.

3.3.2 AfCFTA Protocol and Regional Competition Agreements

The AfCFTA Protocol is coming into force when several regional competition arrangements are already in existence.[58] The question is how will it relate to these arrangements? There is potential of conflict in application between the Protocol and these regional agreements given that the market to which they both apply is the same. The Protocol however makes it clear that in the event of there being a conflict in application, it shall take precedence.[59] This follows that as much as national competition authorities have exclusive jurisdiction over matter having national effects, once those have a regional dimension, the jurisdiction is handed over to the regional authority that will do the same once the matter exhibits a continental dimension.

3.3.3 Dimensions of the AfCFTA Competition Protocol

In order to promote competition within the AfCFTA market, the Protocol regulates and prohibits business that are deemed to be anti-competitive, restrictive and incompatible with the proper functioning of the AfCFTA.[60] Regulating implies that the Protocol does not adopt a blanket condemnation of practices that have an impact on competition. It adopts a rule of reason enforcement approach where a practice/

---

[57] This was the case in the *Boeing/McDonell-Douglas* merger which was approved in the US but faced challenges in the UE. See further Stock (2014), pp. 825-9-09.

[58] For example, art 25 of the Protocol on Trade in the Southern African Development Community (SADC) Region (1996), gives effect to the SADC Declaration on Regional Cooperation in Competition and Consumer Policies (2009) and requires Member States to implement measures that foster competition and prohibit unfair business practices. In 2004 the COMESA Competition Regulations and Competition Rules were adopted to prohibit anti-competitive practices within the COMESA Common Market, to establish a merger control regime for cross-border cases and to address other competition law and consumer protection matters.

[59] Art 3(3) of the Protocol.

[60] Part II of the Protocol.

transaction is subjected to scrutiny to determine whether it has any competition effects or gains and thereafter weighs if the gains outweigh the effects.[61]

Generally, the rule of reason approach is adapted to anti-competitive business practices. The Protocol identifies the following anti-competitive practices:

(i) Agreements between enterprises, decisions by organisations of enterprises and concerted practices between enterprises that prevent, restrict or distort competition in the AfCFTA market.
(ii) Mergers and acquisitions[62] that prevent, restrict or distort competition in the AfCFTA market, especially when they give rise to or strengthen a dominant market position.[63] Enterprise combinations in the form mergers and acquisitions distort trade through negative effects on the competitive structure of the market.
(iii) Abuse of dominance- abuse of a dominant position in the AfCFTA market either by a single enterprise or a combination thereof is another behaviour identified by the Protocol as an anti-competitive practice requiring regulation.[64] The existence of a dominant position in its own is not an anti-competitive practice. However, is when a dominant entity abuses its market dominance that is when it becomes a competition concern. An entity abuses its dominance by engaging in practices that negatively alters the competitive structure of the market.[65] This includes any conduct that is designed to artificially alter the functioning of market forces.[66]
(iv) Abuse of economic dependence and any other anti-competitive practices.[67] Realising that even enterprises that are not dominant can negatively influence the competitive structure of the market,[68] the Protocol brought such behaviours under its purview as anti-competitive practices. Furthermore, reference to the 'ant other anti-competitive practices' is a catch-all-proviso that is meant to capture any practices besides those mentioned for as long as it amounts to a conduct that prevents, restricts, or distorts competition.

The Protocol also provides for the adoption of the *per se* approach to enforcement whereby transactions/practices are condemned on their mere existence for that is

[61] See generally Hovenkamp (2018), pp. 81–167.

[62] A merger is any situation which arises where one or more enterprises acquires the whole or part of the business of another. See Nzero (2013), p. 13. See further art 1 of the AfCFTA Protocol.

[63] See Landes and Posner (1981), p. 937.

[64] Art 9 of the Protocol.

[65] *Hoffman- La Roche & Co. AG v Commission* . Case 85/76 [1979] ECR 416.

[66] Entities abuse their dominance position if they use their positions to fix prices, restrict output or favour one supplier over others. See generally Continental Can Co. Inc., v Commission [1973] ECR 215, [1973] CMLR 199, para.26.

[67] Art 11 of the Protocol.

[68] See for instance Airtours/First Choice OJ [2000] L93/1, [2000] 5 CMLR 494 and upon appeal Case T- 342/99 Airtous v Commission [2002] ECMR II-2585, [2002] ALL ER (EC) 783.

enough to harm the competitive structure of the market.[69] Generally anticompetitive business practices are subjected to the rule of reason approach whereas restrictive business practices are subject to the per se approach.

The following practices are categorised as prohibited under the Protocol;

(i) Horizontal business practices.[70] These are agreements between enterprises operating at the same level in the supply chain. These kinds of practices are easy to prevent, restrict and distort competition within a market through cartels[71] hence they are *per se* prohibited. There are no any offsetting benefits therefrom.
(ii) Vertical business practices.[72] These are agreements between businesses operating at different levels of production, distribution or supply the effect thereof is to prevent, restrict or distort competition in the AfCFTA market. Given that vertical business practices equally negate the benefits of competition and thereby distort trade, it is equally important that they are prohibited. Their most profound effects are that they foreclose the market through exclusionary and discriminatory dealings that denies those that are not parties thereto market access.[73]

In addition to regulating and prohibiting anti-competitive and restrictive business practices, the Protocol also applies to practices that are incompatible with the proper functioning of the AfCTA. These are practices that distort trade as a result of them either being anti-competitive or restrictive in nature. The net single or combined effect of these is that trade is distorted. Anti-competitive or restrictive practices create barriers to market entry which hinders market access. The significance of this provision is that enterprises cannot engage in any practice that distorts, prevent or restrict competition in the AfCFTA market.

4 Conclusion

Multilateral agreements promote international competition through, *inter alia*, limiting the use of such protectionist policies as the use of export subsidies that gives domestic producers an unfair competitive advantage over their foreign competitors. The adoption of multilateral competition within the AfCFTA is a welcome development that has the potential to attain both public and private goals. AfCFTA as a continental trade institution seeks to promote continental welfare through ensuring

[69] See Bork (1965), p. 226.

[70] Art 6 of the Protocol.

[71] The Protocol refers to these as "Concerted Practices" which are defined in article 1 as meaning 'cooperative or coordinated conduct between undertakings, achieved through direct or indirect contact, that replaces their independent action, but which does not amount to an Agreement.'

[72] Art 7 of the Protocol.

[73] See generally Salop (2001), Chap. 12.

that citizens of the African economy have access to quality and affordable goods and services. However, these benefits have increasingly been threatened by anti-competitive practices of private businesses. Competition policy as a public policy tool seeks to restrain private businesses from acting in ways that distorts markets operations to the detriments of the consuming public in stark contrast to what trade seeks to achieve. The adoption of competition rules within AfCFTA is a plausible development that if effectively implemented, will mend the bridges between trade and competition.

References

Agreement Establishing the African Continental Free Trade Area was signed at Kigali, Rwanda on 21 March 2018 and entered into force on 30 May 2019

Airtours/First Choice OJ [2000] L93/1, [2000] 5 CMLR 494 and upon appeal Case T- 342/99

Airtous v Commission [2002] ECMR II-2585, [2002] ALL ER (EC) 783

Ajewumi OE, Afolabi JA, Joe-Akunne (2024) Regional trade agreements and economic integration in Africa: assessing the impact of the African continental free trade area (AfCFTA). World J Adv Res Rev 23(03):2783–2801

Bork RH (1965) The rule of reason and the per se concept: Price fixing and market division part 1. Harv Law Rev 74:226

Bork R (1993) The antitrust paradox: a policy at war with itself (with a new introduction and epilogue). Basic Books, New York

Consolidated version of the Treaty on the Functioning of the European Union, 26 October 2012, OJ L. 326/47–326/390; 26.10.2012. https://www.refworld.org/docid/52303e8d4.html

Continental Can Co. Inc., v Commission [1973] ECR 215, [1973] CMLR 199

Corradi M, Nowag J (2023) Policies at the intersection between competition and corporate law. In: Corradi M, Nowag J (eds) Intersections between corporate and antitrust law. Global competition law and economics policy. Cambridge University Press, Cambridge

Everest-Phillips M (2009) Tackling the 'tyranny of vested interests'. In: Mehta PS, Evenett SJ (eds) Politics Triupms Economins? Political Economny and the implementation of competition law and economic regulation in developing countries. CUTS international, Jaipur

Fox EM (1997) Towards world antitrust and market access. Am J Int Law 91(1):1–25

General Agreement on Tariffs and Trade; Text of The General Agreement Geneva, July 1986

Hatzenberg T (2002) Competition Policy in SADC. Annual Forum, Glenburn Lodge, Muldersdrift, South Africa

Hoekman B (2002) Chapter 6. The WTO: functions and basic principles. In: Aaditya M, Development PE (eds) Trade, and the WTO: a handbook. University of Colorado Press, Boulder

Hoffman- La Roche & Co. AG v Commission. Case 85/76 [1979] ECR 416

Hovenkamp HJ (2018) The rule of reason. Florida Law Rev 70:81–167

International Shoe Co v FTC, 280 U.S 291 at 298, 50 S.St. 89, 74 L ED, 431 (1930)

Ishikawa K (2021) The ASEAN economic community and ASEAN economic integration. J Contemp East Asia Stud 10(1):24–41

Kamala D, Lipimile G (2021) Harmonization and integration in Africa: the case of competition law and policy. In: Amao O, Olivier M, Magliveras KD (eds) The emergent African union law: conceptualization, delimitation, and application. Oxford University Press, Oxford

Kavacic WE (1997–98) Creating new competition policy in transition economies. Brooklyn J Int Law 23(2): 403

Kolmar M (2021) Firm behaviour under perfect competition. In: Principles of microeconomics. Classroom companion: economics. Springer, Cham

Kububa AJ (2007) Criteria for evaluating the effectiveness of competition authorities. Presentation by the Zimbabwean Competition and Tariff Commission Executive Director at the Intergovernmental Group of Experts on Competition Law and Policy. Geneva, 17–19 July 2017
Landes WA, Posner RA (1981) Market power in antitrust cases. Harv Law Rev 94:937
Ljubownikow G, Hwee Ang S (2020) Competition, diversification and performance. J Bus Res 112:81–94
Lumina C (2008) Free trade or just trade? The World Trade Organisation, human rights and development (part 1). Law Democracy Dev 12(2):20–40
Marrakesh Agreement Establishing the World Trade Organisation ("WTO Agreement") of 15 April 1994, 1867 UNTS 154
Mindaye M, Migliardo C, Ferede T (2025) Heterogeneous effects of free trade areas (FTAs) on trade in Africa. Springer Nature Bus Econ 5(71):1–24
Nzero I (2013) Corporate Restructurings in Zimbabwe: A Legal Analysis of the Regulation of Corporate Mergers and Acquisitions in Zimbabwe. LLD Doctoral Thesis. Pretoria: University of Pretoria
O'Sullivan A, Sheffrin SM (2003) Economics: principles in action. Pearson Prentice Hall, New Jersey
Oatley T (2019) International Political Economy, 6th edn. Routledge, New York
OECD (1986) Recommendation of the Council for Co-operation between Member Countries in Areas of Potential Conflict between Competition and Trade Policies (1986). https://legalinstruments.oecd.org/en/instruments/OECD-LEGAL-0228
OECD (2004) Challenges and Obstacles faced by competition authorities in achieving greater economic development through the promotion of competition. Contribution from the Fair Trade Commission of Jamaica, Session 11
Posner RA (1981) The economics of justice. Harvard University Press, Harvard
Salop SC (2001) Analysis of F analysis of foreclosure in the EC guidelines on vertical restraints. In: Hawk BE (ed) Annual proceedings of the Fordham corporate law institute. Fordham Corporate Law Institute, Manhattan
Singh A, Dhumale R (1999) Competition Policy, Development and Developing Countries. South Centre Trade Related Agenda (T.R.A.D.E) Working Paper 7
Stock EJ (2014) Explaining the differing U.S and EU positions on the Boeing/McDonnell-Douglas merger avoiding another near-miss. Univ Pa J Int Econ Law 20(4):825–909
The Protocol To The Agreement Establishing The African Continental Free Trade Area On Competition Policy adopted by the AU Assembly during its 36th Ordinary Session held from 18 to 19 February 2023 in Addis Ababa, Ethiopia
Thorelli BH (1954) The Federal Antitrust Policy: Origination of an American tradition (Norstedt Stockholm, Baltimore).
UNCTAD (2007) Guidebook on competition systems. UN, New York
United Nations Conference on Trade and Development (2020) Non-Tariff Measures: Definitions and basic facts. In *A* Practical Guide to the Economic Analysis of Non-Tariff Measurer
Van den Bosche P, Prevost D (2016) Rules on non-discrimination. In: Essentials of WTO law. Cambridge University Press, Cambridge
Wish R, Bailey D (2021) Competition law. Oxford University Press, Oxford
WTO (2023) Tariffs applied by WTO members have almost halved since 1996. https://www.wto.org/english/blogs_e/data_blog_e/blog_dta_13apr23_e.htm#:~:text=For%20example%2C%20the%20largest%20decrease,in%201996%20to%207.6%20per
WTO (n.d.-a) Interaction between Trade and Competition Policy. https://www.wto.org/english/tratop_e/comp_e/comp_e.htm
WTO (n.d.-b) Principles of the trading system. https://www.wto.org/english/thewto_e/whatis_e/tif_e/fact2_e.htm#seebox
WTO Agreement on Agriculture (1995)
WTO Agreement on Subsidies and Countervailing Measures (1995)
WTO The Agreement on Government Procurement (2012)

WTO The Agreement on the Application of Sanitary and Phytosanitary Measures (1995)
WTO The Agreement on Trade-Related Aspects of Intellectual Property Rights (1995)
WTO The Agreement on Trade-Related Investment Measures (1995)
WTO The General Agreement on Trade in Services (1995)
Zogbhi V (2009) Strategic priorities of competition and regulatory agencies in developing countries. In: Mehta, Evenett (eds) Politics thumps economics? Political economy and the implementation of competition law and economic regulation in developing countries. CUTS international, Jaipur

Developing the Africa Continental Free Trade Area Through the Banking Industry: A Law and Economics Perspective

Tapiwa Victor Warikandwa

Abstract The African Continental Free Trade Area (AfCFTA) Agreement is one of the flagship initiatives of the African Union's Agenda 2063's first ten-year implementation plan. The full implementation of AfCFTA is equivalent to the establishment of a continental market, which would need concerted measures to decrease all trade costs and restrictions. The significance of banks in the successful development of the African economy, and hence in the expansion of the African economy, cannot be overstated. One of the most important functions of banks in Africa and other African economies is to provide the necessary capital to facilitate the establishment of businesses of all sizes in order to stimulate the economy's development and growth. In this chapter, it will be argued that in the context of the AfCFTA, financial institutions, especially banks, play a key role in Africa's trade finance policy execution. Banks offer the necessary financial assistance to promote intra-economic activity. They leverage businesses and have a financial mediation role aimed at ensuring the survival and success of businesses. However, the chapter will indicate the challenges which banks operating on the African continent are likely to face in their attempts to finance trade for purposes of driving forward the AfCFTA.

T. V. Warikandwa (✉)
University of Venda, Limpopo, South Africa, and University of Botswana, Gaborone, Botswana
e-mail: Warikandwat@ub.ac.bw; Tapiwa.Warikandwa@univen.ac.za

T. V. Warikandwa et al. (eds.), *Law and Policy of the African Continental Free Trade Area (AfCFTA)*, European Yearbook of International Economic Law,
https://doi.org/10.1007/978-3-032-01122-0_9

1 Introduction

The African Continental Free Trade Area Agreement[1] has emerged as one of the African Union's much anticipated strategic economic growth and trade expansionist project.[2] Prior to the AfCFTA, a couple of notable flagship economic growth initiatives such as the New Partnership for Africa's Development[3] and the Pan-African Investment Code[4] have received significant plaudits but none has come to the level of the AfCFTA.[5] The AfCFTA focuses on promoting investment (both intra-African and foreign investment),[6] facilitating trade,[7] reducing non-tariff and tariff barriers[8] as well as leveraging other factors that will significantly increase the continent's competitiveness in the twenty-first century global economic environment. Implementing the AfCFTA is likely to be a costly exercise which would require significant trade financing.[9] It is with regards to trade financing that banks become a crucial component to the realisation of growing trade and investments on the African continent, in the context of the AfCFTA. Banks play a key role in expanding Africa's economy as they are the main source of lines of credit for small, medium and large businesses.[10] The marginalised youth and women who want to participate in trade activities on the continent will want to access lines of credit to finance their projects. Banks are the ideal financial institutions to provide the requisite capital aimed at establishing and growing businesses which will lead to growth in intra-African trade, economic growth and sustainable development on the continent. This chapter will argue that financial institutions such as banks are the foundation upon which the AfCFTA's finance policy will be premised and executed. Banks have the

[1] African Continental Free Trade Agreement (AfCFTA) 21st March 2018.

[2] See the Preamble of the AfCFTA Agreement.

[3] The New Partnership for Africa's Development (NEPAD) is a policy framework approved by the African Union's Heads of State and Government Summit on the 23rd of October 2001. NEPAD is a comprehensive strategic framework for socio-economic development. It was introduced to address the political and socio-economic problems facing the continent. Much was expected from the NEPAD but it appears to have delivered little in so far as driving the African continent's quest to realise sustainable growth. See Schell-Kerr (2009), p. 15. Schell-Kerr once stated the following: "While indigenous ownership and involvement is vital to the economic and political transformation of Africa, the NEPAD, as it stands now, does not provide the much needed answers to Africa's problems".

[4] Mbengue and Schacherer (2017), p. 414. See also Adenekan (2024).

[5] See Fofack (2024). See also African Business (2023), Shikwati (2024) and Erasmus (2023).

[6] See the preamble of the AfCFTA Agreement. See art 3(c) of the AfCFTA Agreement.

[7] Art 3(a)-(c) of the AfCFTA Agreement.

[8] Art 4(a) of the AfCFTA Agreement.

[9] ElMaayergi (2024). Statement by Mr. Haytham ElMaayergi, Afreximbank's Executive Vice President, Global Trade Bank, Abuja 8 August 2024. See also International Finance Corporation (2024) IFC Partners with Deutsche Bank to Boost Trade Finance in Africa with a Focus on Small, Fragile and Conflict-Affected Countries. World Bank Group Press release 28 June 2024; and Knowles (2023).

[10] Art 28(1) of the AfCFTA Agreement.

capacity to finance capital intensive industrial sectors such as infrastructure, agriculture, telecommunications, manufacturing, energy, oil and gas, amongst others. Banks can also finance critical sectors such as education and health. In principle, banks can provide the appropriate financial injection to businesses to promote intra-economic services related to supplying consumer services and manufacturing of goods.

It is therefore not in doubt that banks on the African continent and beyond will play a leading role in the success or failure of the AfCFTA in so far as the implementation of its policy and realisation of key objectives as set in Articles 3 and 4 of the agreement establishing the AfCFTA is concerned. Africa will not achieve its economic development or succeed in its structural transformation initiatives without accessing trade finance. Akinwumi A, Adesina the President of the African Development Bank underscored the significance of trade finance when he stated that, "Trade finance is an important instrument for influencing Africa's long term economic development and structural transformation. It can play a cross sectoral role to facilitate delivery of the Bank's 'High 5' strategic priorities to 'Power and Light Up Africa', 'Feed Africa', 'Industrialise Africa', 'Integrate Africa', and 'Improve the quality of life of the people of Africa'".[11] This chapter thus reinforces the argument that whilst the AfCFTA Agreement (and its protocols) on paper seeks to facilitate trade in general, promote intra-Africa trade specifically, attract foreign direct investment, and realise sustainable economic growth and development on the continent, all these objectives will remain a pipe dream if banks do not finance trade in Africa.

2 Banks and Their Key Role in Trade Financing for the Success of the AfCFTA

Intra-Africa trade on the African continent has remained significantly low.[12] This development has been fuelled by the evident fact that most businesses (specifically small and medium enterprises) lack access to trade finance.[13] This pattern is worsened when one considers that informal traders, who contribute to a significant share of intra-Africa trade, are financially excluded as they cannot access lines of credit from formal banking institutions.[14] This implies that failure to access trade finance is an Achilles heel and thus an inhibiting factor to trade on the African continent. Further, considering the devastating effects of financial shocks induced by the COVID-19 pandemic, a development which delayed the implementation of the AfCFTA, some businesses still face challenges in accessing trade finance due to

[11] African Development Group (n.d.). See also Oramah (2021), p. 24.

[12] Ngwu and Ojah (2024), pp. 1–16.

[13] World Bank (n.d.). See also Zuzana et al. (2020), pp. 1–24.

[14] Ngwu and Ojah (2024), pp. 1–16.

perceived potential risks and losses that are projected to occur. Without trade financing, businesses, in particular small and medium enterprises (SMEs) will not be able to grow.[15] Export capacity is likely to remain stagnant as will intra-Africa trade. In fact, post-COVID-19, there is greater need for availing sustainable trade finance in order to boost the AfCFTA. Questions have been raised as to the potential for success of the AfCFTA after the devastating effects of COVID-19 which led to widespread business closures on the African continent, especially SMEs.[16] Some large businesses are still recovering from the COVID-19 induced economic shocks. Trade financing could go a long way in accelerating such recovery and building the required resilience for businesses to build back better and drive the AfCFTA forward. Banks are thus an ideal source for trade financing for SMEs and other businesses on the continent.

Banks are important institutions which play the role of leveraging businesses.[17] They have a financial mediation role which is aimed at ensuring the survival and success of businesses. Banks, in performing their financial leveraging role, can nevertheless be limited by government induced and politically stimulated restrictions on credit allocations.[18] Such restrictions can be in the form of inadequate supervisory policies relating to matters such as restrictions on insider trading/activities and capital standards.[19] Further, the restrictions could centre on incompetent management of credit risk or poor credit decisions.[20] These restrictions however do not weaken the argument that efficiency in market-based economies, as envisaged by the African Union in launching the AfCFTA,[21] is facilitated by credit provision through financial institutions, in particular banks.[22]

However, the restrictions imposed on banks due to governmental and political interferences in Africa, a development which can hamper trade financing on the continent, can be mitigated by complying with the Basel III framework for banks which are active internationally.[23] The Basel III framework refers to an international regulatory framework for banks that is aimed at maintaining and ensuring a healthy banking system which is crucial for trade financing.[24] The Basel III standards were implemented post the 2007–2008 financial crisis which prompted European and other international leaders to adopt international banking standards that are sound and aimed at ensuring that banks survive any crises.[25] In 2024, the Council of the

[15] Ngwu and Ojah (2024), pp. 1–16.

[16] PWC (2020).

[17] Agostino et al. (2024), p. 345.

[18] Jaïdi et al. (2024), pp. 1–18.

[19] Jaïdi et al. (2024), pp. 1–18.

[20] Jaïdi et al. (2024), pp. 1–18.

[21] See the Preamble of the AfCFTA Agreement.

[22] Oramah (2021), p. 24.

[23] European Banking Authority (n.d.).

[24] Gottschalk et al. (2022), p. 249.

[25] Ranjit (2009), pp. 1–38.

European Union announced Basel III reforms aimed at increasing banks' resilience to economic shocks.[26] Through the Basel III regulatory framework for internationally active banks, microeconomic prudential rules have been surrounded by a macro-prudential layer that seeks to target systemic risks affecting the banking sector.[27] Standards for liquidity coverage were also established to cater for concerns related to liquidity shortages during economic shocks.[28] Measures aimed at limiting risk taking behaviours by banks, such as the deploying of the leverage ratio and the implementation of extended disclosure requirements, have set the basis for banks to limit risk taking behaviours and empower market discipline. It is therefore anticipated that banks operating on the continent can thus manage the challenges posed by policy directives of banks in African countries. Through the Basel III framework, banks maintain the pedestal on regular assessment of their fitness and propriety.[29] More significantly banks also maintain control in areas of risk management, audit, internal controls and behavioural standards on governance.[30] These monitoring measures will assist banks to carefully and prudentially manage the leveraging they have.

It is nevertheless important to point out that whilst the Basel III framework will help banks operating in Africa to manage their risk in order to promote trade financing for the purpose of the success of the AfCFTA, the framework has been subject to some fair measure of criticism. Such criticism centres on the effectiveness of the Basel III framework to address idiosyncratic and systematic risks.[31] In principle, questions have been raised about the fundamental underpinnings of the Basel III Framework's prudential rules. It may be argued that the reforms to the Basel III framework will render banks operating in Africa capable of maintaining their high leveraging hence enabling them to extend credit to businesses for trade purposes. The benefits by the Basel III framework in so far as financial systems' stability and resilience cannot be outweighed by the criticisms. The success of the AfCFTA is dependent on the ability of business, especially SMEs, to access trade financing in order to increase investment and grow intra-African trade.

---

[26] Kroszner and Robins (2024), pp. 1–58.

[27] Amorello (2016), p. 21.

[28] Chen et al. (2022).

[29] Basel Committee on Banking Supervision (2010), pp. 1–77.

[30] Basel Committee on Banking Supervision (2015), pp. 1–43. See also Nguyen and Dang (2022), pp. 1–14.

[31] The criticisms centre on the complexities of the Basel III requirements, the inadequate capturing of a significant number of off-balance sheet risks, calculating capital requirements on the basis of internal model-based regulation, and the perceived inadequacies of disclosure requirements. See Amorello (2016), pp. 24–27.

3 Challenges Faced by Banks in Performing the Trade Financing Role in Africa

Banks operating on the African continent are likely to face challenges in their attempts to finance trade for purposes of driving forward the AfCFTA. Their effectiveness in trade financing is likely to be hampered or obstructed by institutional failures. Such institutional failures could include but are not limited to a slow process of how the courts adjudicate over recovery processes.[32] Inadequate data coordination and integration in banks in Africa is also another challenge that stands as a significant stumbling block to intra-African trade as opposed to trade financing.[33] Banks in Africa do not *per se* have a centralised financial system at their disposal.[34] This may be a challenge in so far as banks' effort to collect data on foreign investors applying for credit is concerned. This is the case in matters concerning foreign investors who want to apply for credit to conduct business outside their home countries is concerned. There is therefore need for dedicated AfCFTA financial regulations aimed at increasing access to capital as well as promoting movement of capital within a business community.

Recent developments in the aftermath of the greylisting of South Africa by the Financial Action Task Force (FATF) in February 2023 for failure to comply with international standards around preventing money laundering has emerged as a challenge to the AfCFTA objectives, especially in the Southern Africa Development Community (SADC).[35] Cross-border investment has been adversely affected for South African investors due to imposition of foreign exchange controls. The foreign exchange controls have been imposed due to perceived deficiencies in South Africa's anti-money laundering and counter-terrorist financing frameworks. It is therefore now difficult for investors in South Africa to navigate the complexities posed by the greylisting on attempts aimed at attracting foreign direct investment in the country and complying with the exchange-control regulations imposed.[36] South Africa therefore has to take the necessary steps to address the shortcomings raised by the FATF in a period of 12 months of observation to enable investors to participate in cross-border investments without restrictions. Banks have been given a key role to ensuring that exchange-control regulations are complied with through processes such as Know-Your-Customer and Know-Your-Business. South Africa is a major trade actor on the continent. It would be difficult to realise the AfCFTA's trade objectives with South Africa operating under the greylisting measures imposed by

[32] See for example Delicate Debt Collectors (Pty) Ltd v Director-General of the Department of Labour and Others (65869/2020) [2022] ZAGPPHC 348 (25 May 2022). See also Bosio (2023), pp. 1–47.

[33] Hartzenberg (2011), pp. 1–27. See also United Nations Economic Commission for Africa (2017), pp. 1–170.

[34] Iddrisu and Danquah (2024).

[35] Fabricius (2024).

[36] Investec (2024). See also Theobald et al. (2022), pp. 1–36.

the FATF. There is therefore need for South Africa to address the concerns of the FATF to advance the AfCFTA objectives in the SADC region.

Another notable challenge for the banks in Africa is the absence of a Model Law for Factoring to enable trade finance in Africa.[37] Factoring refers to a type of debt financing and financial transaction in which a business can sell its outstanding invoices or receivables to a third party at a discount in order to trade. Factoring is a facilitator to trade and not a loan.[38] SMEs, for example may need to identify alternative sources of funding to capitalise their trade and investment objectives. Factoring is largely a non-bank alternative source of trade financing. Factoring provides immediate capital to a business based on future income attributed to amounts due on existing invoices. The invoices therefore act as a record of the credit extended to customers for payment that is yet to be received but is due.[39] The African Export-Import Bank has registered its support for factoring in Africa by signing deals to provide lines of credit amounting to EUR 23 million to enable companies to expand factoring activities in Africa.[40] Access to finance remains a challenge to SMEs as banks consider them risky to lend money to. However, should factoring prove to be a success, mainstream banking services may end up being limited to large businesses which may lead to the closure of banks on the continent.[41] Alternative sources of trade financing could lead to international banks shutting down in Africa. There are already notable concerns around bank closures on the continent, more specifically foreign owned banks.

4 Risk Mitigation for Banks

Banks in Africa, in trying to advance lines of credit to finance trade must be cognizant of the poor credit culture of African businesses. Some businesses in Africa thrive on inefficiencies inherent in institutional structures to default without consequences.[42] This implies that fixed servicing obligations imposed by banks with respect to debt repayment might not be recovered from cash flows generated by a business's assets. Gaps in debt servicing are likely to be created by fluctuations in derived revenues or the need to write-down the value of selected business assets.[43] This may lead to the writing off of some interests of equity holders in order to meet a business' debt servicing obligations. Regrettably, fragile internal business

[37] The African Capacity Building Foundation (2021), pp. 1–43.

[38] See the UNIDROIT Model Law on Factoring 2023 published by the International Institute for the Unification of Private Law, Rome Italy.

[39] Chen (2024).

[40] Afreximbank (2023).

[41] Tomusange (2015), pp. 1–164. See Klapper (2005), pp. 1–39.

[42] Ezeh and Lu (2019), pp. 1–51.

[43] Drehmann and Juselius (2012), pp. 1–15.

structures and stunted investment in such structures is likely to reduce the risk appetite required to harness the benefits of the AfCFTA. Banks in Africa therefore need to implement policies aimed at maximizing the potential gains of the AfCFTA whilst in the process limiting the inherent risks associated with lending.

5 The Role to Be Played by Central Banks in Trade Financing

The fact that African banks have taken more risk in order to fund trade and that more loans should be given to businesses, especially SMEs, might be evidence that central banks in Africa have a strong commitment to achieving the objectives of the AfCFTA.[44] Strong mitigating measures, such as reviewing minimum capital, leverage, and gearing ratio requirements, may be necessary in response to these financial developments in order to boost bank liquidity and make sure the banks are in a position to sufficiently meet the financial (loan) needs of businesses and AfCFTA objectives.[45]

Strong safety nets are required to shield banks from macroeconomic shocks that could lead to a spike in the volatility of some important indicators, including interest rates, inflation, currency rates, capital flows, and loan defaults, among others. This is supported by a wealth of evidence. Poorly built safety nets may lead to excessive risk-taking; and instability within the banking and larger economic environment, vice versa. Banks must ensure that money and deposits are allocated effectively and as cheaply as possible for investments.[46] They must carry out this vital function by making sure that money borrowed from other companies and extra money invested by households are given to institutions who want to borrow it. However, banks become highly indebted in an effort to maximise the profits from credit intermediation. African central banks must reassess existing regulatory measures, including minimum criteria for funding big exposures, liquidity, leverage, and bank capital, in order to offset the possible risk of banks supplying the necessary finance to leverage the AfCFTA.[47] These actions could make more loanable capital available to companies in Africa as well as other economic enterprises.

[44] African Development Bank (2017), pp. 1–88.

[45] See arts 3 and 4 of the AfCFTA Agreement.

[46] Elekdag et al. (2024), pp. 1–46.

[47] United Nations (2022), pp. 1–208.

6 Recommendations

To address challenges associated with trade financing in Africa, in order to realise the central objectives of the AfCFTA, a few recommendations are proposed. The availability of a centralised financial system and efficient bank cooperation are prerequisites for the successful execution of the AfCFTA's trade finance policy.[48] In order to facilitate banks' credit intermediation processes, the Technical Directorate of the AfCFTA is urged to walk the talk by accelerating the process of financial data integration at the continental level.[49] Additionally, effective collaboration will ensure a swift integration of the various financial markets. The current digital initiatives and integrations ought to be planned and executed strategically in order to significantly reduce the level of risk in the business environment, enhance the relationship between banks and businesses, and expedite loan approvals to generate employment and business expansion opportunities.[50] African banks need to make sure their policies about proper bank risk monitoring are implemented correctly.[51] This is because, although they protect banks that are known for their highly effective and efficient operations, they may be in dire straits due to loan defaults resulting from their support of AfCFTA businesses.[52] The risk-adjusted returns on loans must be high to justify the capital required by banks to approve those loans. More investors may be needed in the banking industry to shore up respective capitals to meet recurring financial needs of existing customers; and AfCFTA prospects.[53] Lastly banks must build capacity in research to have better appreciation of business needs of borrowers; and to design bespoke products to meet those needs.[54]

7 Conclusion

Africa's banks are urged to devote sufficient funds, including time, to research and development in order to help identify the appropriate degree of leverage that is ideal for striking a meaningful balance between debt and equity financing.[55] Modern banks nevertheless have to believe that funding research is essential to their continued operations, faster development and expansion, and ability to compete internationally.[56] Banks remain a vital cog for realising the success of the AfCFTA in

[48] Ebenezer (2023). See also Oramah (2021), p. 24.

[49] Ebenezer (2023); Oramah (2021), pp. 24–25.

[50] Ebenezer (2023). See also Osei et al. (2023), pp. 1–18; Uddin et al. (2023), pp. 1–22.

[51] Ebenezer (2023), p. 149; Hargarter and Vuuren (2018), pp. 1–27; Odubuasi et al. (2022), p. 51.

[52] Oramah (2021), pp. 24–25.

[53] Ebenezer (2023).

[54] Ebenezer (2023).

[55] Ebenezer (2023).

[56] Ebenezer (2023).

Africa. Even if there are proposals to adopting a Model Factoring Law to create alternative avenues for trade financing, formal banking remains the best and safe option for accessing trade finance. Policy makers in Africa must thus ascertain how they will engage banks to ensure that they continue to proactively finance trade not just for large business but SMEs as well.

References

Adenekan VO (5 January 2024) A Critical appraisal of the Pan-African Investment Code's Influence on the AfCFTA Investment Protocol. Transnational Dispute Manag

Afreximbank (13 June 2023) Afreximbank Signs Factoring deals of EUR 23 million to Boost Factoring in Africa. https://www.afreximbank.com/afreximbank-signs-factoring-deals-or-eur-23-million-to-boost-factoring-in-africa

African Business (7th May 2023) Africa Day 2023: Accelerating implementation of the AfCFTA. African Business

African Continental Free Trade Agreement (AfCFTA) 21st March 2018

African Development Bank (2017) Trade Finance in Africa: Overcoming Challenges. September 2017, pp. 1–88

African Development Group (n.d.) Trade Finance Program. https://www.afdb.org/en/topics-and-sectors/initiatives-partnerships/trade-finance-program

Agostino M, Errico L, Rondinella S, Trivieri F (2024) Leverage and SMEs financial stability: the role of banking competition. J Econ Financ 48:345–376

Amorello L (2016) Beyond the horizon of banking regulation: what to expect from Basel IV, vol 58. SSRN, pp 21–38

Basel Committee on Banking Supervision (2010) Basel III: a global regulatory framework for more resilient banks and banking systems. Bank for International Settlements:1–77

Basel Committee on Banking Supervision (2015) Guidelines: corporate governance principles for banks. Bank for International Settlements:1–43

Bosio E (June 2023) A Survey of Judicial Effectiveness: The Last Quarter Century of Empirical Evidence. World Bank Group: Governance Global Practice, pp. 1–47

Chen P (2024) Guide to Factoring: What is Invoice Factoring and How it Works, Hubble Financial 21 February 2024

Chen T, Lee C, Shen C (2022) Liquidity indicators, early warning signals in banks, and financial crises. North Am J Econ Finance 62:101732

Delicate Debt Collectors (Pty) Ltd v Director-General of the Department of Labour and Others (65869/2020) [2022] ZAGPPHC 348 (25 May 2022)

Drehmann M, Juselius M (2012) Do debt service costs affect macroeconomic and financial stability. https://www.bis.org/pul/qtrpdf/r_qt1209e.pdf

Ebenezer AM (2023) Banking industry and effective development of the AfCFTA. The B&FT Online 4 April 2023

Elekdag S, Emrullahu D, Naceur SB (2024) Does FinTech Increase Bank Risk Taking. International Monetary Fund, Working Paper 24/17, pp. 1–46

ElMaayergi H (8 August 2024) Afreximbank to double intra-African trade financing to $40 billion by 2026. Statement by Mr. Haytham ElMaayergi, Afreximbank's Executive Vice President, Global Trade Bank, Abuja

European Banking Authority (n.d.) The Basel Framework: The Global Regulatory Standards for Banks. https://www.eba.europa.eu/activities/basel-framework-global-regulatory-standards-banks

Ezeh A, Lu J (July 2019) Transforming the Institutional Landscape in Sub-Saharan Africa: Considerations for Leveraging Africa's Research Capacity to Achieve Socioeconomic Development. Center for Global Development, Policy Paper 147, pp. 1–51

Fabricius P (8 March 2024) South Africa struggles to get off the FATF grey list. Institute for Security Studies, https://issafrica.org/iss-today/south-africa-struggles-to-get-off-the-fatf-grey-list
Fofack H (23 February 2024) The Future of African Trade in the AfCFTA. Brookings
Gottschalk R, Castro LB, Jiajun X (2022) Should National Development Banks be subject to Basel III? Rev Polit Econ 34(2):249–267
Hargarter A, Vuuren v (2018) Conduct risk in south African banks: aligning regulatory compliance with business sustainability. South Afr Bus Rev 22:1–27
Hartzenberg (2011) Regional integration in Africa. World Trade Organisation Economic Research and Statistics Division, TRALAC, pp 1–27
Iddrisu AM, Danquah (2024) The financial inclusion agenda: examining the role of conventional banks in deepening access to formal credit. Econ Syst 48(2):101202
International Finance Corporation (28 June 2024) IFC Partners with Deutsche Bank to Boost Trade Finance in Africa with a Focus on Small, Fragile and Conflict-Affected Countries. World Bank Group Press release
Investec (2024) South Africa's journey off the greylist. https://www.investec.com/en_za/focus/economy/its-official-south-africa-greylisted-html
Jaïdi L, Byiers B, El Yamani S (2024) Fostering Investment and Inclusivity in Africa's Continental Free Trade Area. Policy Center for the New South, Africa-Europe Relations: A Balanced Narrative and Reality Check, Policy Brief No. 182, pp. 1–18
Klapper L (May 2005) The Role of Factoring for Financing Small and Medium Enterprises, World Bank Policy Research Working Paper 3593, pp. 1–39
Knowles M (25 October 2023) The digital bridge for Africa's trade finance gap. Absa Corporate and Investment Banking
Kroszner RS, Robins NR (5 February 2024) White Paper on Basel III Endgame Proposal. Booth School of Business, University of Chicago, pp. 1–58
Mbengue MM, Schacherer S (2017) The 'Africanization' of international investment law: the pan-African investment code and the reform of the international investment regime. J World Investment Trade 18(3):414–448
Nguyen QK, Dang VC (2022) The impact of risk governance structure on bank risk management effectiveness: evidence from ASEAN countries. Heliyon 8(10):1–14
Ngwu F, Ojah K (2024) Intra-Africa trade and the need to rethink the neo-liberal approach. Transnatl Corp Rev 16(4):1–16
Odubuasi AC, Ofor NT, Ilechukwu FU (2022) Enterprise risk management, risk committee, and earning capacity of African banks: a comparative approach. Mod Econ 13:51–68
Oramah B (2021) Afreximbank in the era of the AfCFTA. J Afr Trade 8(2):24–35
Osei LK, Cherkasova, Oware KM (2023) Unlocking the full potential of digital transformation in banking: a bibliometric review and emerging trend. Future Bus J 9(30):1–18
PWC (2020) COVID-19 and the African Continental Free Trade Area: Key Considerations. https://www.pwc.com/ng/en/pdf/covid19-key-considerations-afcfta.pdf
Ranjit L (2009) Why Basel II failed and why any Basel III is doomed. GEG Working Paper, No. 2009/52. University of Oxford, Global Economic Governance Programme (GEG), Oxford, pp 1–38
Schell-Kerr L (2009) Global governance initiative: a critique of the new Partnership for Africa's development (NEPAD). Federal Governance 6(1):1–17. 15
Shikwati J (2 May 2024) A Beacon of Hope or a Failed Project? The Continental Free Trade Area (AfCFTA). Friedrich Naumann FoundationPotsdam
Erasmus G (2023) What is the Mandate of the AfCFTA? Is it changing? TRALAC 13 August 2023
The African Capacity Building Foundation (2021) Factoring in Africa to support trade development: Challenges and opportunities for growth through capacity development. Occasional Paper, Harare, Zimbabwe pp. 1–43
The New Partnership for Africa's Development (NEPAD) is a policy framework approved by the African Union's Heads of State and Government Summit on the 23rd of October 2001

Theobald S, Baloyi N, Montalto PA (2022) Sword of Damocles: South Africa's FATF Grey Listing. Intellidex Researching Capital Markets and Financial Services, Business Leadership South Africa pp. 1–36

Tomusange RL (2015) Factoring as a financing alternative for African small and medium-sized enterprises. Walden dissertations and doctoral studies collection. Walden University, Minneapolis, pp 1–164

Uddin MH, Mollah S, Islam N, Ali MH (2023) Does digital transformation matter for operational risk exposure? Technol Soc Change 197:1–22

UNIDROIT Model Law on Factoring, 2023 published by the International Institute for the Unification of Private Law, Rome Italy

United Nations (2022) Bridging the Finance Divide. Financing for Sustainable Development Report 2022, Inter-agency Task Force on Financing for Development, pp. 1–208

United Nations Economic Commission for Africa (2017) Bringing the continental free trade area about: assessing regional integration in Africa VIII. Addis Ababa, pp. 1–170

World Bank (n.d.) Trade Obstacles to SME participation in trade. https://www.wto.org/english/res_e/booksp_e/wtr16-4_e.pdf

Zuzana B, Kangoye, Yogo T, Urbain T (2020) Access to finance among small and medium-sized enterprises and job creation in Africa, GLO discussion paper, no. 665. Global Labour Organization (GLO), Essen, pp 1–24

The (F)Law Behind the Pan-African Online Payment System

Dunia P. Zongwe

Abstract This chapter discusses Pan-African Payment and Settlement System (PAPSS), a first-ever continent-wide online payment system. Today, cross-border payments require third currency, usually a hard currency, such as the United States dollar or the Euro, which takes time, increases transaction costs, and poses risks that parties will disagree over exchange rates. The PAPSS aims to make it easier for individuals and businesses to buy goods and services online in local currencies. Afreximbank set up the PAPSS as one of the five instruments specially designed to implement the African Continental Free Trade Area Agreement. However, unless Afreximbank or the PAPSS provides the monetary infrastructure necessitated by deeper levels of regional economic integration, they will doom the PAPSS to fail. Scholars have not yet probed the law and economics behind this digital platform, nor has anyone examined how the system will interact with the electronic transactions laws and payment-and-settlement systems (PSS) of the municipal laws of the African Union. Yet understanding this legal and policy framework, if any, can prevent major disputes from arising a few months or years down the line. The author argues that the biggest flaw of the PAPSS is that it lacks a proper law. This (f)law renders the PAPSS unnecessarily cloudy and complex, while inducing traders to stay away from the PAPSS and weakening public confidence in this payment platform.

I thank the participants for their questions, comments, and suggestions at the Zimbabwe Chapter of the Federation of African Law Students (FALAS) on May 25th, 2023; at Midlands State University in Zimbabwe on February 21st, 2022; and at the Institute for African Development (IAD) at Cornell University in the United States on February 17th, 2022, where I presented earlier drafts of this chapter remotely.

D. P. Zongwe (✉)
School of Law, University of Namibia, Windhoek, Namibia

T. V. Warikandwa et al. (eds.), *Law and Policy of the African Continental Free Trade Area (AfCFTA)*, European Yearbook of International Economic Law,
https://doi.org/10.1007/978-3-032-01122-0_10

1 Introduction

This chapter delves into the recently launched, first-ever continent-wide online payment system. Formally launched by the African Export-Import Bank (Afreximbank) in June 2019, the Pan-African Payment and Settlement System (PAPSS) aims to make it easier for individuals and businesses to buy goods and services in local currencies through online transactions.

Afreximbank has set the PAPSS in motion to assist the African Continental Free Trade Area (AfCFTA). The idea behind the PAPSS is to ease and increase commerce among individuals and businesses within the AfCFTA by domesticating payments for goods and services. In so doing, the PAPSS will reduce transaction costs and exchange rate risks. However, the law and the technology behind the PAPSS remain a mystery.

Most people paid rapt attention to the advent of PAPSS, but until now no one looked into the law behind this digital payment system, nor has anyone examined how the system will interact with the electronic transactions laws and payment-and-settlement systems (PSS) of the municipal laws of the African Union (AU). Yet this knowledge can prevent market failures and major disputes from arising a few months or a few years down the road. Today, cross-border payments require third currency, usually a hard currency, such as the United States (US) dollar or the Euro, which takes time, increases transaction costs, and poses risks that parties will disagree over exchange rates. Moreover, the payment system of each country falls under the sovereignty of those countries. Therefore, a PAPSS that would not entail the assent or accession of the countries where it will operate should expect complaints, disputes, and inevitably litigation.

While the PAPSS clearly constitutes a payment system, much less clarity exists concerning the technology that the Afreximbank will use and the legal framework that underlies the PAPSS. This poses a major problem because if cybercriminals can easily hack the technology, the PAPSS will not achieve its very noble and legitimate purposes of increasing intra-African trade. Under that scenario, traders cannot rely on the technology, leaving in place the existing system that depends on third-party currencies to mediate cross-border trade in Africa, with all the costs and inconvenience that such system carries with it. If people use payment instruments suboptimally or if governments poorly design the systems to process those instruments, these systems will negatively impact their stability and hamper economic growth and development.[1] As the World Bank explained it, a weak payment system may:

> severely hamper the stability and developmental capacity of an economy; its failures can result in inefficient use of financial resources, inequitable risk-sharing among agents, actual

[1] World Bank (2011). See also Crawford (2011), p. 4—(mentioning that payment systems allow a country's financial and commercial sectors to operate smoothly). See further and in general Chang-Tam et al. (2024), pp. 441–455; Beck et al. (2018), pp. 162–186; Aguilar et al. (2024), pp. 1–31.

> losses for participants, and loss of confidence in the financial system and in the very use of money.[2]

Ergo this chapter seeks to shed light on the technology and the law behind the PAPSS, highlights the strengths and weaknesses of such technology and law, and offers recommendations on how Afreximbank or the AU can overcome the challenges and strengthen its advantages. To uncover the key legal and economic aspects of PAPSS in general and in relation to domestic laws of AU member states, the author organized this chapter in five parts. Following the introduction, the first section gives the background to the adoption of the PAPSS and the currency conundrum that has plagued the PAPSS since its inception. Second, the chapter describes the legal framework for the PAPSS and how it interfaces with the laws on electronic transactions and the PSSs of AU member states. Then, the chapter relies on the 'publicness' or public values of global administrative law (GAL) to assess that framework (in the third section) and on perspectives from economics to tackle the questions whether this digital payment system has managed to make traders trust it and whether it enables traders to credibly commit (in the fourth section). Lastly, the chapter puts forward suggestions as to how Afreximbank or the AU could bridge the gaps as well as the (f)law that the chapter canvassed.

Overall, the author argues that the biggest flaw of the PAPSS is that it lacks a proper law. This (f)law renders the PASS unnecessarily cloudy and complex, while inducing traders to stay away from the PAPSS and weakening public confidence in this payment platform.

Nevertheless, the PAPSS holds great promise for intra-African trade after the AfCFTA Agreement came into force on May 30th, 2019. Experts estimate that the PAPSS will help AU member states save about 5 billion US dollars in payment transaction costs every year.[3] All the same, if the experts do not bring out and assess the law and the economics behind the PAPSS, cross-border intra-African payments will not only confront high transaction costs; they will incur huge litigation costs too.

2 The PAPSS, the AfCFTA, and Africa's Currency Conundrum

The PAPSS will realize a long-cherished idea of building the United States of Africa. In the process, it will serve as a template for the payment systems of member states. In that sense, the PAPSS is most welcome, though jurists have not yet written on this continent-wide payment system.

The idea to create a United Sates of Africa came into the minds of the forerunners and pioneers of pan-Africanism. Unfortunately, decades of failed and externally driven development models blighted this pan-African project. Against this

---

[2] World Bank (2011), p. xv.

[3] Wass (2019), Oramah (2023), Yadeka (2024), Everington (2024) and Emejo (2025).

backdrop, the AfCFTA and the PAPSS promise better days for the people and commerce on the continent. In particular, the PAPSS forms part of the crux of the dream to build "an Africa we want".[4]

The advent of the PAPSS would not have the same meaning, consequence, and significance if it did not connect with the AfCFTA. This free trade area thus provides the natural context for the PAPSS.

2.1 *The African Continental Free Trade Area*

In 2018, Heads of State and Government in Africa gathered in Kigali, Rwanda, to sign the African Continental Free Trade Area (AfCFTA) Agreement, the world's biggest free trade area by membership. Later, in 2019, the AfCFTA Agreement reached the threshold of signatures required for it to come into force when the Gambia became the 22nd nation to ratify the Agreement. As of August 2020, all African states, except Eritrea, have signed the AfCFTA Agreement and 28 have ratified it.[5] For the 24 countries that had then ratified it, the AfCFTA Agreement formally entered into force on May 30th, 2019. Members of the AU decided that the Secretariat of the AfCTA will sit in Accra, Ghana—a fitting tribute to the contribution of Ghanaian leader Kwame Krumah to the vision and design of pan-Africanism.

The AU played a crucial role in the drafting and the adoption of the AfCFTA Agreement. The Agreement seeks to create one single market boasting a combined gross domestic product of 2.5 trillion US dollars and covering 1.2 billion consumers.[6] This initiative should help Africa regain some of the market share it lost after her share shrank from 4.3% of world trade in 1970 to 2.4% in 2018.[7] Furthermore, Africa trades more with the outside world than with herself. Unlike Europe where intra-regional trade accounts for 69% of total trade and Asia where it accounts for 59%, intra-African trade only accounts for a mere 16% of total trade.[8]

It bears mentioning that the AfCFTA Agreement is not a complete document. While it provides for several major aspects of regional and international trade such as trade in goods and rules of origin, it does not deal with other major aspects of trade, for example, foreign investments. Also among the outstanding issues, states have yet to negotiate tariffs and rules of origin. Crucially, they still have to decide which sectors to open or close—a process that may prove long.[9] The AU delegates

---

[4] Arnoldi (2019), (quoting Afreximbank President Oramah).

[5] TRALAC (2024).

[6] Fofack (2019), p. 33; Thomas (2022).

[7] Fofack (2019), p. 32.

[8] Fofack (2019), p. 32.

[9] Fofack (2019), p. 32; Wass (2019).

will address these outstanding areas of regional trade during the second phase of the negotiations and drafting of the AfCFTA Agreement.

Another piece missing from the AfCFTA Agreement pertains to the payment system to facilitate intra-African commerce. While this area does not always feature regional trade agreement, in the context of Africa this matter covers an area that AU negotiators cannot dispense with. This piece missing from the AfCFTA puzzle relates to the question as to how and with which currency traders in AU member states can pay for goods and services.

2.2 *The Pan-African Payment and Settlement System*

2.2.1 Launch of the PAPSS

On July seventh, 2019, in Niamey, Niger, Afreximbank President Benedict Oramah launched the Pan-African Payment and Settlement System (PAPSS) at the 12th Extraordinary Summit of AU Heads of State. That Summit officially kick-started the operational phase of the AfCFTA Agreement.[10] Afreximbank will manage and operate the PAPSS. In late June 2020, it advertized the position of Head of the PAPSS, who will work from Cairo, Egypt.[11]

Afreximbank set off the PAPSS to fill the gaps in the modalities of transacting among African nations. Oramah told the Summit of AU Heads of State gathered in Niamey that the PAPSS will enable each AU country to use its local currency to transact business online.[12] The PAPSS marks the first time Africa established a continent-wide digital payment system.

2.2.2 Benefits of the Payment Platform

The PAPSS aims to offer individuals, businesses, and governments a digital payment platform that will allow them to trade in African currencies. To attain that goal, this digital platform cuts down on "the foreign currency content of intra-African trade payments".[13] It will release the continent from heavily relying—as it very often does—on hard currencies in intra-Africa trade payments. Indeed, cross-border payments in Africa typically involve a third currency, such as the US dollar or the Euro, which slows down transactions and makes them expensive.[14] (Actually, the

---

[10] TRALAC (2024).

[11] See Head, PAPSS (2020).

[12] TrendsNAfrica (2019) The Pan-African Payment and Settlement System (PAPSS) Launched, (12 July 2019), http://trendsnafrica.com/2019/07/12/the-pan-african-payment-and-settlement-system-papss-launched/.

[13] Jere (2019) (quoting Afreximbank President Benedict Oramah).

[14] TrendsNAfrica (2019). See also Wass (2019).

US dollar already serves in practice as the world's reserve currency.[15]) In that fashion, the PAPSS will save Africa more than 5 billion US dollars in payment transaction costs every year.[16]

Afreximbank President Oramah pointed out that, as the continent renews its efforts to jolt its members into developing industries and value chains to boost trade and investments within the region, it must address "the economic costs of effecting so many payments in scarce foreign exchange".[17] With the PAPSS, AfCFTA member states will pay with US dollars only to settle trade deficits.[18] Just like the continent resorted to the US dollar to overcome exchange constraints, the PAPSS strives to defragment cross-border payments.

Two other benefits deserve mention. First, the PAPSS will formalize a big portion of the estimated 50 billion US dollars trade that takes place informally.[19] It will also defragment Africa's economies.[20]

Ultimately, the PAPSS seeks to defeat underdevelopment. As Afreximbank President Oramah said, by enabling Africans to pay for goods and services in their local currencies, the digital platform will "deal a fatal blow to the underdevelopment of Africa".[21] The continent's underdevelopment results from the fragmentation of its economies[22] and the continuing colonial model that consists in extracting natural resources for export to the industrialized nations.[23]

2.3 *The Relation Between the AfCFTA and the PAPSS*

The Afreximbank collaborated with the AU to set up the PAPSS, alongside a 1.7 billion US dollars adjustment facility,[24] to support the AfCFTA. Observers expect the PAPSS to boost trade among AU members.[25] One of the big questions that emerge when analyzing the PAPSS concerns the manner in which it formally relates and interacts with the AfCFTA or the AU? To start, since Afreximbank does not

[15] Rickards (2014), pp. 1–2, 137, 149–150, 208, and 24 (predicting the demise of the US dollar and extending that prediction to the international monetary system because the US serves in practice as the linchpin, as the world's reserve currency).

[16] Wass (2019).

[17] As quoted by Jere (2019).

[18] TrendsNAfrica (2019) and Wass (2019).

[19] Wass (2019); Fofack (2019), p. 34; Aderonmu (2023); Kamau (2025).

[20] Fofack (2019), p. 33.

[21] Jere (2019); Arnoldi (2019).

[22] Fofack (2019), p. 33; Arnoldi (2019).

[23] Fofack (2019), pp. 32–33.

[24] The facility aims to enable states to adjust through an orderly transition if they lose tariff revenue significantly after implementing the AfCFTA Agreement. TrendsNAfrica (2019), Arnoldi (2019), Wass (2019), African Review (2021) and Afreximbank (2025).

[25] See Wass (2019).

form part of the AU structures, how will it enforce and monitor the functioning of the PAPSS? More importantly, will Afreximbank wield the power to oblige AU member states to abide by the PAPSS rules? And what will it do if an AU member state does not comply with the rules? or will it obtain the mandate to resolve the disputes that will inevitably erupt regarding the operations and functioning of the PAPSS? These questions merit appropriate answers if the AU and Afreximbank do not want to see the PAPSS embroiled in wasteful disputes and litigation. This chapter only speaks to some of these concerns. Further research will be needed to unravel and resolve the remaining questions.

3 Payment Systems and Online Technologies

Today, payment systems cannot dispense with digital technologies. Information and communication technologies (ICTs) have become ubiquitous in payment systems. Likewise, Afreximbank counts on innovating finances and on digital technologies to address exchange and liquidity constraints and to boost cross-border trade.[26] In this section, accordingly, the chapter zooms in on the payment function, payment systems, digital technologies, and the risks regarding online payments.

3.1 Payment

To understand how the PAPSS will work in practice, trade experts must demarcate the scope of its operations. They achieve this by clearly underlining the type of activity it is engaged in, namely payments.

Trade experts must also keep in mind the definition of 'payment' because of the risks that exist that people will confuse what amounts to a payment and other types of business transactions. For example, people can easily confuse payment and banking. Though the two intersect, they are by no means identical. These risks of confusion increase further in countries such as South Africa where only banks offer payment services or instruments.[27] For instance, an instant money function on a phone does not technically amount to 'banking'; it merely constitutes a payment. On the other hand, if the phone's owner deposits cash or money with a deposit-taking institution and transact with the deposited money online through his phone, his transaction would qualify as 'banking', and not merely as payment.

Afreximbank and the managers of the PAPSS should make sure that they do not mistake payment for banking, or vice versa, if they wish to avoid being dragged in disputes or questions that have nothing to do with the scope of their activities.

[26] Fofack (2019), p. 34; Ashiadey and Njoku (2024); Fintechview (2025); Musumba (2025).

[27] Shamraev (2019), pp. 61–62.

Payment systems have historically lain at the heart of banking.[28] But, here again, the two do not amount to one and the same thing. 'Banking' refers to the intermediation between savers and borrowers. It entails borrowing and saving. By contrast, 'payment' does not entail the intermediation between savers and borrowers; rather it involves a movement of money from one person to another. What about 'payment systems'?

3.2 Payment Systems

3.2.1 Definition

A 'payment system' refers to the infrastructure set up to transfer monetary value between parties discharging obligations they owe to each other. The system comprises institutions, instruments, rules, procedures, and technical means.

Even if payment systems have long formed part of the core of banking, central banks and commercial banks eventually lost interest in them. After payment technology stabilized, central banks and commercial banks treated payment system issues as less important and left it to subunits of their ICT departments to handle them.[29] In the mid-1980s, however, states started to attach greater weight to payment systems reform.[30]

3.2.2 Their Growing Role in the Economy

A World Bank report noted that payment systems have "moved from the *backroom* to the *boardroom*" to emphasize the growing awareness among all finance institutions that well-functioning payment systems support the finance sector and the real economy.[31] Interbank, money and capital markets cannot function without an efficient payment system.[32] For that reason, the World Bank concluded that payment systems constitute a key component of a country's finance infrastructure.[33]

The Great Recession of 2007–2009 led governments across the globe to realize that payment systems can help them prevent or manage systemic risks. Many governments reckoned the huge volume of payments made every year and came to view the relations between payment service providers as "extremely important" in

[28] World Bank (2011), p. xv.
[29] World Bank (2011), p. xv.
[30] World Bank (2011), p. xv.
[31] World Bank (2011), p. v.
[32] World Bank (2011), p. xv.
[33] World Bank (2011), p. v.

protecting the health of the economy and controlling system risk.[34] Many experts have also lauded payment systems as an effective way of ensuring financial inclusion.[35]

The movement of payment systems up governments' lists of priorities also results from the increasing attention paid by bank boards to the automation of banking operations and services, and their impact on bank income and profits.[36] Payment systems have shifted from narrow channels for transferring funds to a much wider integrated network for transferring other forms of value.[37] They serve in effecting retail payments, thereby playing a leading role in enabling more and more people to access finance.

3.2.3 How They Function

Central banks typically oversee, operate and regulate national payment systems. This role seems to suggest that the law could hold the central bank liable if someone hacks the PAPSS, if the trading parties litigate about the value of their transaction because they disagree over the true exchange rate, or if the system fails.

Payment systems involve three types of activities usually: paying, clearing, and settling. Likewise, the PAPSS constitutes a centralized market-infrastructure that enables AfCFTA member states to clear and settle intra-African commerce payments.

In addition to the payment function, which this chapter explained above, payment systems perform a 'settlement' function. Clearing involves updating the accounts of the trading parties (i.e., transmitting, reconciling, and—in some cases—confirming payment orders) before the actual transfer of money (i.e., settlement).[38] A settlement completes a payment by actually transferring money to the payee. Central bank clearing resorts to a third party—known as the clearinghouse—to clear trades.

[34] Crawford (2011), pp. 3–4.

[35] See for example Komba (2013), p. 35 (explaining that, although only 12.4% of the adult population enjoy formal financial inclusion in Tanzania, mobile payment services have financially included 41% of the adult population); Porteous (2013), pp. 67–68 (discussing the example of Ghana, which reformed its payment systems and which, notably, established the Ghana Interbank Payment and Settlement System (GhiPSS)—as a separate subsidiary of the central bank—to manage electronic payments in the country); World Bank (2011), p. v (stating that creating networks and systems for retail payments can have a substantial role to play in increasing access to financial services in developing countries).

[36] World Bank (2011), p. v.

[37] World Bank (2011), p. v.

[38] Bank for International Settlements (2003), p. 13.

3.2.4 Payment Systems Law

Almost invariably, the payment and settlement functions of commerce are heavily regulated by law. This holds true for municipal law as much as it does for international trade. Payment systems law denotes[39]:

> the evolving body of law that governs the relations of persons making a payment of money ("payers"), persons receiving money payments ("payees") and persons facilitating those transactions ("payment services providers").

Approaching trade finance through the eyes of payment systems law offers fresh and deep insights into the mechanisms devised to finance cross-border money payments. Traditionally, experts and scholars would approach trade finance through the law governing *the instrument* or the device used to make payments (for example, cash, bills, cheques, notes, electronic fund transfers (EFTs), a card of some sort, or letters of credit).[40] If parties used cheques to pay for goods and services, they would classify their transactions as falling under the law of negotiable instruments. Alternatively, they would tackle trade finance questions through *the service provider*, such as a bank.[41] If a payment involves a bank, the experts and scholars would categorize the transaction as falling under banking law. Still other experts would analyze trade finance through the *relations of the parties.* Thus, depending on the nature of those relations, they would conclude that the transaction belongs to the law of contract, the law of debtor and creditor, the law of consumer protection, and so on.[42]

Rarely, will experts and scholars view these transactions as part of the payment systems law. The advantage of seeing these transactions through the lens of payment systems law lies in the broader perspective and deeper understanding that come when one looks at payment as a *system,* and not merely as an instrument, a group of service providers, or a type of relation between parties.

Presumably, each and every AU member state has its own laws on payment and settlement. In 2010, about 70% of the 139 countries surveyed by the World Bank affirmed that their laws cover settlement finality, netting, and electronic payment processing.[43] The questions that this chapter addresses concern the legal framework for the PAPSS and, perhaps more crucially, the manner in which the PAPSS relate to the 55 national payment and settlement laws on the continent.

[39] Crawford (2011), p. 1.

[40] Crawford (2011), p. 1.

[41] Crawford (2011), p. 1.

[42] Crawford (2011), p. 1–2.

[43] World Bank (2011), p. vi.

3.2.5 Issues in the Payment Systems Laws

Country-level payment system laws grapple with a host of drawbacks. Municipal laws do not often provide for a zero hour rule, the enforceability of security interest in pledged collateral or repurchase agreements ("repo"), and the protection of collateral pledged in a payment or other type of settlement system.[44] In particular, developing countries do not often provide for consumer protection and competition issues.[45]

By contrast, the European Union (EU) boasts the strongest and most complete legal system for payment systems, especially securities settlement.[46] This achievement may tempt Afreximbank to benchmark PAPSS norms against the EU payment system law. However, Afreximbank should bear in mind that, unlike the PAPSS, the wheels of the EU payment system are oiled by a monetary union. Indeed, the Euro shields EU members from the exchange rate risks that the AU members using the PAPSS will run.

Specifically, the PAPSS may face the capacity issues that individual AU members confront. Evidence suggests that income levels and geographical location correlate with levels of payment system development.[47] This evidence implies that, insofar as the PAPSS will interact with the payment systems of individual AfCFTA member states, it will likely struggle with similar capacity constraints.

4 Technology of Payment Systems

Payment systems nowadays almost always work with digital technologies. One hundred years ago, most people paid for goods and services in cash.[48] Merchants financed their businesses and settled their accounts with bills of exchange.[49] As banks proliferated, people began to pay most debts for goods and services by cheque.[50] Over time, bank accounts replaced wallets and purses in making or receiving payments.[51] Later, new services supplanted the cheque, including notably direct deposits, pre-authorized debits credit, and debit credit.[52] These new services

[44] World Bank (2011), p. vi.

[45] World Bank (2011), p. vi.

[46] World Bank (2011), p. vi.

[47] World Bank (2011), pp. xi–xii.

[48] Kazachenok and Lavrentyeva (2019), p. 333; Crawford (2011), p. 2; Allcock (2025).

[49] Crawford (2011), p. 2.

[50] Crawford (2011), p. 2.

[51] Crawford (2011), p. 2.

[52] Crawford (2011), p. 2.

intensified transfers between bank accounts as a major means of receiving and making payments.[53]

Today, people buy goods and services through electronic means, and much less with cash, not to mention the nearly defunct cheque. While digital technologies have exponentially increased the efficiency of payment systems, they have also increased the risk and incidence of cybercrimes, including identity theft, fraudulent payments, and other crimes committed through the medium of digital technologies.

The advent of the Internet has caused electronic commerce and Internet-based global trade to sprout. That said, some people may still manipulate information. And, although these manipulations do not go beyond transmission delays, they still undermine the performance of international trade.[54] Chang and others note that traders consider letters of credit (L/C) secure and effective in paying for goods and services, and that they used L/C to build trust.[55] However, Chang and others point out that confirmations on L/C documents and logistics information during payment have made L/C more inconvenient and thus decreased the usefulness of L/C.[56]

The vast majority of countries (i.e., 116 out of 139 countries) apply a secure and world-class real-time gross settlement (RTGS) system that allows them to significantly reduce systemic risk, when compared to former systems for processing large-value payments, such as cheque systems.[57] For retail payments, automated clearinghouses (ACHs) facilitate commercial and person-to-person payments, and as such they tremendously impact the overall efficiency of a country's payment system.[58] From a regional perspective, including Sub-Saharan Africa, states tend to use cheque systems alongside RTGS systems as well.[59]

5 Centralizing Online Payments

The technology used to effect online payment has definitely and dramatically increased the efficiency of commerce and commercial law. It has also enhanced the ease of doing business in all the countries that adopted these technologies.

Online technologies have helped addressed some of the issues that plagued traditional cross-border payments. These issues include intermediaries; opaque information; trust; and tedious confirmations on traceability of goods, cash, and

[53] Crawford (2011), p. 2.

[54] Chang et al. (2019), p. 1712.

[55] Chang et al. (2019), p. 1712.

[56] Chang et al. (2019), pp. 1712–1713.

[57] World Bank (2011), pp. vi–vii.

[58] World Bank (2011), p. ix.

[59] World Bank (2011), p. vii.

information flows.[60] These issues severely hinder the efficiency of traditional payment methods.[61] Emerging technologies, especially blockchain, offer ways to overcome these issues.

5.1 *Centralized Technologies*

The technologies most often deployed in financing trade centralize payments. Currently, the entire financial system depends on centralized trusted intermediaries.[62] Varma outlines these intermediaries as follows[63]:

> Central counter parties (CCPs) guarantee trades in exchanges; central securities depositories (CSDs) settle securities; the Society for Worldwide Interbank Financial Telecommunication (SWIFT) intermediates money transfers globally; CLS Bank settles foreign exchange transactions; a few banks dominate correspondent banking; and an even smaller number of banks render custodial services to large investment institutions.

Before the financial crisis of 2007–2008 and the Eurozone crisis of 2010–2012, people deemed these centralized intermediaries safe, unlikely to fail, or too big to fail.[64] After those crises, they no longer saw these intermediaries the same way. Instead, some experts looked to alternatives, including decentralized technologies such as blockchain.

5.2 *Decentralized Technologies: Blockchain*

While Afreximbank presents the PAPSS as a "centralized"[65] payment infrastructure, centralized systems remain vulnerable to cybercrimes. In repeated instances, cybercriminals have hacked the computers of large financial institutions.[66]

Reacting to these cybercrimes against the hubs of finance, a few scholars have suggested that traders utilize blockchain to ease and finance cross-border trade.[67] Blockchain serves as a distributed ledger (or database) for recording information relating to transactions.[68] This technology underpins Bitcoin and other cryptocurrencies. Those who propose Blockchain to finance cross-border trade insist that

---

[60] Chang et al. (2019), p. 1712.

[61] Chang et al. (2019), p. 1712.

[62] Varma (2019), p. 1.

[63] Varma (2019), p. 1.

[64] Varma (2019), p. 1.

[65] Head, PAPSS (2020).

[66] Varma (2019), p. 1.

[67] See, e.g., Chang et al. (2019), p. 1713; Varma (2019), p. 1.

[68] Chang et al. (2019), p. 1713.

finance institutions can use them in several industries, such as payment and settlement, securities issuance, clearing and settlement, derivatives, trade repositories, and credit bureaus.[69]

Still, blockchain poses a major engineering problem. Even where blockchain technology can apply to a financial industry feasibly, it will encounter barriers that are legal, regulatory, institutional, and commercial.[70] And it may take years before policymakers can remove those barriers.[71] Furthermore, blockchain remains "immature", and experts cannot confidently predict whether it will succeed when applied outside of its only proven domain of cryptocurrencies.[72]

These concerns become even more pressing when the technologies employed to facilitate online payments cover a territory as vast as an entire continent. Like Oramah enthused, the idea of the PAPSS consists in making cross-border payments not only easier and cheaper, but safer as well.[73] For that reason, Afreximbank and the AU acted wisely when they decided to make the PAPSS a centralized payment infrastructure. Nonetheless, they still have not said what technology will support the PAPSS.

6 The Law and the Rules That Should Govern the PAPSS

The PAPSS has not yet published a law to regulate it. And this absence of clear legal frameworks confronts the pan-African body with its biggest loophole. It exposes gaps in the institutionalization of the PAPSS. To make matters worse, even when a law governs electronic commerce and payment systems such as the PAPSS, it tends to lack flexibility, which also give rise to gaps.[74]

One serious defect concerns the rules that distribute the losses among parties if fraud in e-commerce occurs. This question has become a matter of controversy.[75] Who should bear the losses in those cases? Either trading party, the financial institution, the central bank,[76] the payment systems management body, Afreximbank (i.e., the PAPSS), or a combination of the above? Parties may also lock horns over the extent of such liability when it attaches to either or both parties.[77]

[69] See, e.g., Varma (2019), p. 2.

[70] Varma (2019), p. 2.

[71] Varma (2019), p. 2.

[72] Varma (2019), p. 9.

[73] Arnoldi (2019).

[74] See Kazachenok and Lavrentyeva (2019), p. 333.

[75] See Olowokere (2019), p. 60.

[76] If the law tasks the central bank with managing the country's payment system.

[77] For example, under the law in Nigeria, where fraud in e-commerce happens, the consumer has unlimited liability. See Olowokere (2019), p. 60.

Conflict of laws complicates the question of liability. Here, if in an instance of intra-African e-commerce payment fails, conflicting provisions in the laws of the parties may make it hard for an adjudicator to determine who picks up the tab. For example, if the law in State A stipulates that the consumer bears the loss whereas the law in State B attributes liability to the financial institution, then a situation may arise whereby a consumer sues a bank in State B while the bank sues the consumer in State A. Both parties may win their respective case in the state where it commenced action and both may thus end up seeking to enforce the judgment in the courts of the other country.

This hypothetical scenario may not unfold precisely like this in the real world. Still, it underscores the necessity for Afreximbank and the AU to legislate on the allocation of risks and the extent of liability when a risk materializes.

6.1 How the PAPSS Compares to Other African Regional Payment Systems

Afreximbank and the AU may draw on regional payment systems to come up and design the law that governs the PAPSS. In particular, the AU may take a few pages from books in Southern and East Africa. Members of regional economic communities (RECs) have introduced at least two other payment systems, one covering Southern Africa and the other applying to both Southern and East Africa.

The PAPSS could implement a system similar to the SADC Integrated Regional Electronic Settlement System (SIRESS), but the PAPSS will encounter obstacles related to the exchange rate risks arising from its use of different currencies. On July 22nd, 2013, the SIRESS started to operate in the four countries of the Common Monetary Area (CMA)—a currency union that pegs the Namibian dollar, the Lesotho loti, and the eSwatini lilangeni one-to-one to the South African Rand.

The SIRESS represents the first step towards a common electronic cross-border payment system across SADC.[78] This system created a regional interbank settlement system. However, at the time of its establishment, the SIRESS had not yet introduced any capability for clearing low-value EFTs, and card and ATM transactions; nor had it built any capability for settling securities.[79] Whereas cheques and paper-based systems cleared money between seven and 21 working days, the SIRESS allows banks across borders to clear money within the same working days.[80]

However, unlike the PAPSS, the SIRESS relies on one currency, the South African Rand, which anchors the monetary policies of the other CMA members, namely Namibia, Lesotho, and eSwatini (formerly 'Swaziland'). It means that the SIRESS denominates transactions in the CMA in South African Rands.

---

[78] Wentworth (2013), p. 1.

[79] Wentworth (2013), p. 1.

[80] Wentworth (2013), p. 2.

The Common Market for Eastern and Southern Africa (COMESA) founded the Regional Payment and Settlement System (REPSS). Contrary to the SIRESS, the REPSS will better serve as a model for the PAPSS because it deals with multiple currencies that COMESA has not pegged to any one of those currencies. The REPSS empowers COMESA members to transfer and receive funds within the region faster, more cheaply and more safely.[81]

Nonetheless, unlike the SAPSS and the SIRESS, the REPSS denominates transactions in US dollars.[82] Hence, the REPSS cannot fully guide or inspire the SAPSS because the REPSS does not domesticate transactions.

Given the sheer size of the countries whose transactions the PAPSS will mediate, Afreximbank may find it exceedingly difficult to process cross-border payments internally. Afreximbank would display great wisdom if it hires the services of CLS Bank or a similar firm to process, clear, and settle foreign exchange transactions within the AfCFTA.

6.2 *The Necessity to Pass a Law on the PAPSS*

The launch of the PAPSS has been made with fanfare and understandable optimism and enthusiasm. However, people know less about the legal framework governing the PAPSS. Worse still, a possibility exists that the PAPSS may operate in the absence of any such framework, which could lead to a host of far-reaching negative consequences for trade within the African continent.

Payment systems come short in the sense that some aspects of those systems evolve outside any legal framework. As Crawford observed, no coherent body of law avails the state to govern the relations of persons using the new payment methods in the way that the law of negotiable instruments regulated bills, cheques, and promissory notes for several hundred years; and in the way that the law of money still governs cash.[83]

The law is a powerful tool that makes transactions and promises credible and safe. Inversely, the absence of a legal framework creates a situation where actors in business cannot commit credibly or transact safely. Hence, the necessity to have a legal framework and, in the absence of any framework, the necessity to build one. In fact, an efficient payment system cannot dispense with a sound and appropriate legal framework.[84] Above all else, therefore, *Afreximbank and the AU should craft and publish a law on the PAPSS.*

Obviously, the municipal laws governing and regulating online payment systems do not extend beyond the territory of the state. Extending such laws beyond the

[81] Wentworth (2013), p. 3.

[82] See Ssonko (2016), p. 205.

[83] Crawford (2011), p. 4.

[84] World Bank (2011), p. 1.

territory would violate international law and the sovereignty of the states on which such extended laws will encroach.

This reality entails that the AU must work closely with the Afreximbank and the PAPSS to come up with rules that AU member states will adopt, incorporate and apply domestically and in their transactions with fellow AU member states.

6.3 Five Broad Recommendations for the PAPSS

In light of the aspects of the PAPSS that this chapter has touched upon earlier, what features should the PAPSS model endorse? This section puts forth five general recommendations for the PAPSS. First and foremost, Afreximbank will have to pass and clarify the law behind the PAPSS as this will go a long way in building trust and convincing individuals, businesses, and governments to accept and implement this online payment system. This transparency, required by the 'publicness'[85] of the PAPSS as a global administrative structure, will dramatically contribute to the stability, sustainability, and integrity of the continent-wide payment system.

As far as it concerns technologies, this chapter recommends that the PAPSS adopts RTGS (with or without a cheque system alongside) and centralized trusted intermediaries. Thirdly, the PAPSS should enlist the CLS Bank or similar firms to clear and settle the foreign exchange involved in AfCFTA commerce. Furthermore, Afreximbank should establish a forum or mechanisms for settling disputes regarding the PAPSS. Perhaps, it should formally take advantage of the AfCFTA's dispute settlement mechanism for its own purposes.

These recommendations will not address all the issues surrounding the PAPSS. In the following lines, this chapter will only discuss the safety and efficiency of payment systems, the distribution of loss, and the extent of liability.

6.4 Recommendations on Specific Key Issues

6.4.1 Safety and Efficiency

The law regulating the PAPSS can draw on the existing laws on payment systems. The ideal pursued by these laws aims to build safe and efficient payment systems. Thus, safety and efficiency constitute the two prime goals targeted by payment systems laws. These laws also seek to mitigate risks in financial markets. Domestic payment system (for example, RTGS systems) and global payment infrastructure (especially, CLS Bank) enabled authorities to react immediately and absorb shocks.[86]

[85] See von Bogdandy et al. (2008), p. 1375.

[86] World Bank (2011), p. xii.

An efficient payment system reduces the cost of exchanging goods and services.[87] The technical efficiency of a payment system determines the efficiency with which people use transaction money and the risks associated with its use.[88]

Safety closely relates to trust. The fortunes of PAPSS hinges on whether individuals, businesses, and governments in Africa will *trust* this system. Trust, in turn, will depend on whether the PAPSS employs a secure technology and whether the law governing it creates certainty.

6.4.2 Distribution and Extent of Liability

Afreximbank should make the financial institution liable for losses caused to any party when the payment system malfunctions or fails. If the PAPSS law attached liability to Afreximbank or PAPSS itself, this liability would increase the likelihood that either body will go bankrupt. For similar reasons, consumers will struggle to shoulder that liability as they may find themselves incapable of affording to pay those costs. Financial institutions, including banks, may stand in a better position to foot the bill, but they do not have much capacity to prevent losses from arising in the place.

A national central bank, on the other hand, can both prevent and bear the losses more cheaply than the parties to an intra-African transaction and a financial intermediary. To put it simply, a country's central bank serves as the cheapest cost avoider.

7 Conclusion

This chapter has dealt with the PAPSS, which Afreximbank launched to complement and support the AfCFTA. This payment system will throw a lifeboat to intra-African trade and, in this regard, it may prove as essential to cross-border commerce in Africa as the blood that keeps a body's circulatory system alive.

Scholars have not yet addressed the legal aspects of the PAPSS, although these questions have become vital and pressing with the coming into force of the AfCFTA. If scholars and trade experts do not carry out research and assessment of the PAPSS soon, the AU and the managers of the PAPSS may end up grappling with major problems and litigation that they could have anticipated and avoided if such research and assessment had been conducted by trade experts.

This chapter took a first bite at this matter with the hope of igniting further debate on this golden opportunity to bolster the ideals of the AfCFTA and pan-Africanism more generally. It has sought to unpack the legal aspects of the technology and

[87] World Bank (2011), p. xv.

[88] World Bank (2011), p. xv.

actual functioning of the PAPSS. It has done so by looking at the background to the PAPSS through its relationship, intimate and congenial, with the AfCFTA. It has then analyzed the payment systems that form the subject matter of national and regional payment systems. It has also sought to fathom the laws that regulate the digital dimensions and technologies behind such payment systems.

The chapter advanced the thesis that, above all, Afreximbank and the AU should enact a law to circumscribe the operations of the PAPSS because the lack of legal framework exposes the PAPSS to clashes and litigation that may set it back or bankrupt it. More importantly, this chapter outlined some provisions that should guide the PAPSS in executing its mandate. It has, in general, recommended that the PAPSS work closely with the AU and draws on the regional and national payment systems for inspiration in designing the legal framework of the PAPSS. By doing so, this chapter wishes to buttress the PAPSS and its goals.

After having tried countless and fruitless development models and suffered the ravages of the COVID-19 pandemic, Africa cannot afford to fail. For Africa, this may be her last chance to survive and thrive in this globalized world. Deeper intra-African trade within the AfCFTA can improve the lives of people in Africa and help in forging a collective African identity, while fulfilling the dreams of the fathers of pan-Africanism. And, by domesticating cross-border commerce payments, the PAPSS can effectively contribute to the construction and consolidation of an African economic commonwealth.

References

Aderonmu F (11 September 2023) Formalizing Africa's Informal Sector through the AfCFTA: An Opportunity for Economic Transformation. https://jpia.princeton.edu/news/formalising-africas-informal-sector-through-afcfta-opportunity-economic-transformation

Afreximbank (6 March 2025) KCB Group and Bank of Kigali launch Pan-African Payment and Settlement (PAPSS), enabling seamless and affordable cross-border payments across Africa. https://afreximbank.africa-newsroom.com/press/kcb-group-and-bank-of-kigali-launch-panafrican-payment-and-settlement-system-papss-enabling-seamless-and-affordable-crossborder-payments-across-africa?lang=en

African Review (2021) Afreximbank and AfCFTA announce operational roll-out of PAPSS. https://africanreview.com/finance/banking-a-finance/afreximbank-and-afcfta-announce-operational-roll-out-of-papss

Aguilar A, Frost J, Guerra R, Kamin S, Tombini A (July 2024) Digital Payments, informality and economic growth. BIS Working Papers No. 1196, https://www.bis.org/publ/work1196.pdf

Allcock S (1 January 2025) The Evolution of Payment Systems: From Cash to Digital Wallets. https://socialequality.org.uk/news/the-evolution-of-payment-systems-from-cash-to-digital-wallets

Arnoldi M (9 July 2019) Afreximbank Commits to Extensive African Continental Free Trade Area Support (Polity), https://www.polity.org.za/article/afreximbank-commits-to-extensive-african-continental-free-trade-area-support-2019-07-09

Ashiadey BY, Njoku ECA (12 September 2024) Digital solutions to drive compliance trade—Afreximbank. https://thebftonline.com/2024/09/12/digital-solutions-to-drive-compliance-trade-afreximbank/

Beck THL, Pamuk H, Ramrattan R, Uras B (2018) Payments instruments, finance and development. J Dev Econ 133:162–186

Chang SE, Yi-Chian C, Wu T (2019) Exploring Blockchain Technology in International Trade: business process re-engineering for letter of credit. Ind Manag Data Syst 119:1712–1733
Chang-Tam RJ, Caldera-Gutiérrez V, Caldera AAC (2024) Mobile payment technology trending tool for economic development: a systematic literature review. In: Mansour N, Bujosa Vadell LM (eds) Green finance and energy transition. Contributions to finance and accounting. Springer, Cham
Crawford B (2011) The future of payment law. Can Bus Law J 50(1):201
Emejo J (11 April 2025) Tinubu Lauds Afreximbank for Advancing Africa's Trade through AfCFTA, PAPSS. https://www.arise.tv/tinubu-lauds-afreximbank-for-advancing-africas-trade-through-afcfta-papss-initiatives/
Everington J (18 December 2024) PAPSS paves the way for intra-African trade efficiency. https://www.thebanker.com/content/9cd65e99-2065-5009-a2ca-32fa3adead9d
Fintechview (18 June 2025) Emerging trends & opportunities in Africa's trade finance landscape. https://fintechview360.com/emerging-trends-opportunities-in-africas-trade-finance-landscape-talk-with-afreximbank/
Fofack H (19 December 2019) Africa's Quest for a Bigger Role in Global Markets. International Trade Forum. International Trade Centre
Head, Pan African Payment & Settlement System (PAPSS) (2020) – Cairo, Egypt, https://www.afreximbank.com/careers/vacancies/international-job/head-pan-african-payment-settlement-system-papss-cairo-egypt/
Jere RJ (15 July 2019) Afreximbank $1 Billion Adjustment Facility for AfCFTA, New African, https://newafricanmagazine.com/19145/
Kamau M (2025) African Payments System PAPSS Plans to Launch FX Market Platform this year: A Game Changer for Intra-African Trade. https://serrarigroup.com/african-payments-system-papss-plans-to-launch-fx-market-platform-this-year-a-game-changer-for-intra-african-trade/
Kazachenok OP, Lavrentyeva AV (2019) New digital payment facilities: an analysis of institutional and legal regulation. In: Popkova EG (ed) Ubiquitous computing and the internet of things: prerequisites for the development of ICT. Dokuman PUB, pp 333–340
Komba KJ, (2013) Enhancing Financial Inclusion Through Proportionate and Regulatory Framework in Tanzania, in Policy Memoranda
Musumba V (14 April 2025) Afreximbank delivered exceptional 2024 financial performance, cementing its position as a systematic pan-African trade finance institution. https://www.afreximbank.com/afreximbank-delivered-exceptional-2024-financial-performance-cementing-its-position-as-systematic-pan-african-trade-finance-institution/
Olowokere EN (2019) A comparative analysis of civil liability in electronic payment systems under the U.S. and Nigerian Laws. J Law Policy Globalisation 82:60
Oramah BO (2023) Afreximbank revolutionises intra-african payments and trade integration. https://thebftonline.com/2023/06/22/afreximbank-revolutionises-intra-african-payments-and-trade-integration/
Porteous D (2013) Mobile Financial Services in Africa: the next generation. In: Beck T, Maimbo SM (eds) Financial sector development in Africa: opportunities and challenges. World Bank, Washington, pp 67–68
Rickards J (2014) The death of money: the coming collapse of the international monetary system. Penguin, New York
Shamraev A (2019) Legal and regulatory framework of the payment and e-money services in the BRICS countries. BRICS Law J 6(2):60–81
Ssonko GW (2016) Lowering the cost of doing business in Africa: leveraging the COMESA regional payments and settlement system (REPSS). J Payments Strategy Systems 10:205
TrendsNAfrica (2019) The Pan-African Payment and Settlement System (PAPSS) Launched (12 July 2019) TrendsNAfrica. http://trendsnafrica.com/2019/07/12/the-pan-african-payment-and-settlement-system-papss-launched/

Thomas D (18 May 2022) What you need to know about the African Continental Free Trade Area. African Business. https://african.business/2022/05/trade-investment/what-you-need-to-know-about-the-african-continental-free-trade-area

Trade Law Centre (TRALAC) (2024) Status of AfCFTA Ratification, https://www.tralac.org/resources/infographic/13795-status-of-afcfta-ratification.html

Varma JR (2019) Blockchain in finance. J Decision Makers 44(1):1–11

Von Bogdandy A, Dann P, Goldmann M (2008) Developing the publicness of public international law: towards a legal framework for global governance activities. German Law J 9(11):1375–1400

Wass S (9th July 2019) Africa's Continent-Wide Payment and Settlement System Launched, Global Trade Law Review, https://www.gtreview.com/news/africa/africas-continent-wide-payment-and-settlement-system-launched/

Wentworth L (August 2013) SADC Payment Integration System. European Centre for Development Policy Management

World Bank (2011) Payment systems worldwide: a snapshot: outcomes of the global payment systems survey 2010 v (2011). World Bank Group, Washington DC

Yadeka J (2024) PAPSS and AfCFTA: A New Era for Cross-Border Trade in Africa. https://www.linkedin.com/pulse/papss-afcfta-new-era-cross-border-trade-africa-joanna-yadeka-ukzze

The Causes and Effects of Poor Customs Administration on the Successful Implementation of the African Continental Free Trade Area Agreement (AfCFTA): The Need to Digitalise Customs Procedures in Africa

Bella Morufa Ngobeni

Abstract Customs play a significant role in trade. They ensure that domestic trade laws are complied with and implement controls that secure revenue. Nonetheless, many African countries are notoriously known to have bad customs environments. Their borders are gridlocked with manual customs operations which consequently induce time delays at borders, customs offices charging excessive customs fees, goods being in transit for long durations, and unscrupulous payments received by people tasked with regulating customs operations and measures at border crossings. As a result, Africa is considered one of the most expensive continents to trade in and with. The excessive administration at borders, police roadblocks, and checkpoints are considerable barriers that make it difficult to trade within and outside the continent. The effectiveness and coherence of custom measures have a significant influence on the growth of trade in the continent, and the advancement of the African marketplace. It is then the purpose of this chapter to investigate the effects of the continent's poor custom efficiency on the realisation of the African Continental Free Trade Area Agreement and to show the need to digitalise custom procedures and ensure better enforcement of customs laws, as means of improving the custom inefficiencies in Africa.

B. M. Ngobeni (✉)
University of Limpopo, Mankweng, South Africa
e-mail: bella.ngobeni@ul.ac.za

T. V. Warikandwa et al. (eds.), *Law and Policy of the African Continental Free Trade Area (AfCFTA)*, European Yearbook of International Economic Law,
https://doi.org/10.1007/978-3-032-01122-0_11

1 Introduction

The general understanding of what entails the customs authority of any country is that is it an administrative government agency tasked with the responsibility of charging and collecting customs duties.[1] The customs authority is entrusted with the enforcement and administration of the laws protecting and collecting import income, and its scope of function extends to regulating the movements of goods into, through, and out of a country, and advancing trade in the greater international market.[2]

Adequate customs administrative procedures play a vital role in protecting a country's trade and economic interests.[3] For many developing African countries, import duties contribute considerable revenue to the government, contrasting with domestic taxes.[4] At the same time, customs administration procedures are also responsible for continental and international trade facilitation and compliance, prohibiting harmful and dangerous substances, and safeguarding the cultural heritages of African countries.[5]

African countries are ill-famed to have bad customs environments.[6] Their border posts are congested with inefficacious customs administrative procedures which negatively affect the continent's performance in trade.[7] The causes of this inefficiency largely relate to bureaucracy and corruption at border posts, restrictive regulations, manual customs management systems, lack of cooperation and connectedness between African countries, lack of transparency, and misreporting.[8] Consequently, the aftermath of these gridlocks is congestion, elevated logistics costs, excessive delays in the transit of goods, and contraband goods moving through some of the border checkpoints.[9]

One of the grand objectives of the African Continental Free Trade Area Agreement (AfCFTA) is to establish a single market of goods, services, and investments, and to improve the continent's economic competitiveness in the grand global market.[10] To realise this objective, there exists a need to improve the continent's customs performance. In improving that, countries need to ensure proper enforcement of customs laws and their customs administration procedures ought to move away from those that are conventional, to those that are modernised by digitalisation. In effect, modernised customs administration systems will ensure that the continent's customs operations are effective, efficient, and aligned with those entrenched in international standards.[11]

---

[1] Erasmus (2022); Lux (2023).

[2] Gordhan (2007), p. 51; Azcárraga (2022); Rbehat and Marafi (2024).

[3] International Trade Council (2022).

[4] International Trade Council (2022), p. 55.

[5] Widdowson (2007), p. 31.

[6] Ngobeni (2023), p. 11.

[7] African Development Bank Group (2013).

[8] Ntabazi (2010), p. 30; Canon (2019), p. 94; Chibira (2021a, b); Rbehat and Marafi (2024), p. 7.

[9] Chibira (2021a, b).

[10] African Continental Free Trade Area Agreement (AfCFTA) Preamble.

[11] Kouamo (2020).

2 The Causes of Penurious Customs Administrations in Africa

Trading in Africa has endured long before the establishment of national borders. This suggests that cross-border trade has been the main source of income for many African households. The AfCFTA is an ambitious experiment to integrate African trade. Its bold goals are to transform the economies of its member states by increasing and ensuring the swift movement of goods and services while focusing on developing other areas of the continent's economic activities.[12] Poor customs efficiency stands in the way of achieving the goals of the AfCFTA. As such, member states, together with their customs agencies ought to ensure that goods and services move without any hassle. The following subparagraphs discuss the causes of poor customs administration.

2.1 Corruption at Border Posts

Corruption at border posts has been a long-established global problem that is continuing despite the many legal literature, regulations, and international norms. It involves money-pursuing practices such as theft, fraud, and bribery, as well as other subtle activities which include tax evasion, nepotism, misreporting, under-invoicing, and inconsistent and discriminatory discretion.[13] The continent's customs administration has been labelled by business executives to be one of the leading corrupt sectors. This is a result of the lasting effects of colonialization and is considered one of the primary contributors to the continent's economic development challenges.[14] The contemporary factors which make the continent's borders prone to corruption are:

2.1.1 Administration Cartels and Discretionary Power

Customs administration officers are susceptible to corruption as a result of their line of work. They enjoy wide discretionary power on the admissibility of imports and exports in a particular country and have the exclusive responsibility and authority to decide on the level at which taxes and duties are charged. As a result, they target high-value cargo and impose burdensome requirements, to which clients end up offering bribes to avoid them.

[12] The African Continental Free Trade Area (AfCFTA) Secretariat 2023 available on https://au-afcfta.org/about/.

[13] Muzurura (2019), p. 105.

[14] Ali et al. (2020), p. 80.

2.1.2 Geographical Dispersion[15]

In Africa, most customs borders are located in remote areas where there is inadequate staff complement, limited resources, and poor levels of infrastructure. This makes it difficult to supervise customs administration officers, despite their powers to decide on the admissibility of goods entering into, through, and out of a country. This challenge allows them to extract bribes from border clients as there are weak controls and little to no supervision.

2.1.3 High Tariffs and Complex Clearance Policies[16]

The leading role of customs administration officers is to ensure that domestic policies are implemented at border posts. Customs regulations in some African countries are outdated and often contradictory, and customs clients are mostly unable to establish clearly what regulation requires of them.[17] Excessive tariffs and domestic customs regulations which are complex and burdensome propagate unscrupulous behaviour. Here, customs administration officers tend to offer, in return for an incentive, reduced import and export charges to customs clients, and to speed up their transactions.

2.1.4 Pressure from Organised Crimes

Customs administration officers have the duty to ensure that illicit consignment, wildlife, and persons are not allowed entrance into a country. These banned activities are very lucrative and mostly comprise criminal syndicates. Given the financial stakes, customs administration officers are offered bribes to facilitate the entrance of contraband into a country.[18]

2.1.5 Size and Type of Border Configuration

The magnitude of a border post influences the scale and the nature of the corruption it faces. At small border posts, corruption is in the form of favours that customs administration officers make for those whom they have relations with. The payment of bribes is conducted at social settings such as gyms, bars, parks, etc. Larger borders are characterised by sufficient workers, resources, infrastructure, and

---

[15] Warf (2017), pp. 22–23; Luke and Walters (2023), pp. 357–377; Flory and Nyaronga (2025), pp. 18–39.

[16] Mitchell (2014), p. 4; Mgeni (2025), p. 142.

[17] Kouamo (2020).

[18] Chene (2018).

ordinarily have anti-corruption mechanisms. Therefore, unscrupulous dealings would require more financial and advanced schemes, which would demand the involvement and cooperation of customs administration officers and guards.[19]

2.2 *Manual Customs Administration Procedure*

Customs administration procedures are regarded as effective and efficient if they are fast, accessible, simple, and predictable to other customs agencies.[20] As highlighted above, customs administrations play an important role in charging and collecting customs duties, taxes, and revenue on behalf of the government. In an era where there are high levels of trading transactions due to globalisation, some border posts in Africa are still characterized by outdated manual operations.[21] Manual customs operations are susceptible to human manipulation and often result in the delay of transit of goods. The clearing of goods at border posts requires the exchange of information with businesses and other customs agencies. Manual customs systems make it difficult for customs administrators to track individual transactions and follow up on errors. In many instances, audit evidence is 'mistakenly' erased or it is subjected to improper storage.[22] Consequently, manual customs administration consumes a lot of time and money, and the effect of it is that it undermines the competitiveness of African border ports, in contrast with their trading partners.[23]

2.3 *Lack of Transparency*

Article X of the Marrakesh Agreement[24] requires member states of the World Trade Organisation to publicize their customs regulatory frameworks. This is to allow their trading peers to be able to challenge any customs administration decision at

[19] Chene (2018).

[20] Olyanga et al. (2022), p. 43.

[21] Ancharaz (2018).

[22] Ondlek (2019), p. 13.

[23] Bassa et al. (2021), p. 43.

[24] Art X(1) reads "Laws, regulations, judicial decisions and administrative rulings of general application, made effective by any contracting party, pertaining to the classification or the valuation of products for customs purposes, or to rates of duty, taxes or other charges, or to requirements, restrictions or prohibitions on imports or exports or on the transfer of payments therefor, or affecting their sale, distribution, transportation, insurance, warehousing inspection, exhibition, processing, mixing or other use, shall be published promptly in such a manner as to enable governments and traders to become acquainted with them. Agreements affecting international trade policy which are in force between the government or a governmental agency of any contracting party and the government or governmental agency of any other contracting party shall also be published. The provisions of this paragraph shall not require any contracting party to disclose confidential infor-

border posts and to be notified if there have been changes to the regulations.[25] The essence of customs administration is transparency. It is fundamental to international trade in that it allows traders to truly appreciate the constraints and conditions of entering or passing through a specific country, and have a great degree of certainty in their business with customs authorities.[26]

The customs laws, regulations, guidelines, and procedures have been identified as a fundamental risk area for unscrupulous activities at border posts. This is because, in many African countries, these are not easily accessible. This negatively affects border clients as they are often uninformed of their rights and duties in certain countries, therefore making them vulnerable to illegal advances from customs administration officers.[27]

2.4 *Lack of Inter-agency Cooperation*

To attain the AfCFTA goals, there must be cooperation between the customs authorities of its member states. Articles 4 and 14 of the Agreement Establishing the African Continental Free Trade Area calls for member states to cooperate and collaborate for the purposes of customs clearance, transit coordination, and border controls.[28] The long transit time of goods and layed customs clearance at African borders are not only a result of the existing manual systems of administration but are also the effects of the lack of inter-agency cooperation.[29] Border clients are expected to abide by the many distinct laws of the countries in which they enter and exit, including the "behind-the-border" processes of each country. An example of this is the current Kenya-Uganda trade dispute. Although Uganda serves as an important destination for Kenyan exports (which shows the significance of their trade relationship), Uganda's dependence on Kenya for sea access to import petroleum products

mation which would impede law enforcement or otherwise be contrary to the public interest or would prejudice the legitimate commercial interests of particular enterprises, public or private."

[25] UNCTAD (2009).

[26] UNCTAD (2009).

[27] Kouamo (2020).

[28] Ugaz and Sun (2019). Part II Art 4 of the Agreement Establishing the African Continental Free Trade Area reads "For the purposes of fulfilling and realizing the objectives set out in Art 3, State Parties shall: (a) progressively eliminate tariffs and non-tariff barriers to trade in goods; (b) progressively liberalise trade in services; (c) cooperate on investment, intellectual property rights and competition policy; (d) cooperate on all trade-related areas; (e) cooperate on customs matters and the implementation of trade facilitation measures; (f) establish a mechanism for the settlement of disputes concerning their rights and obligations; and (g) establish and maintain an institutional framework for the implementation and administration of the AfCFTA". Furthermore, Part IV Art 14 reads "State Parties shall take appropriate measures including arrangements regarding customs cooperation and mutual administrative assistance in accordance with the provisions of Annex 3 on Customs Cooperation and Mutual Administrative Assistance".

[29] Kouamo (2020).

has of late become difficult. This strain is a result of Kenya refusing to issue Uganda with a passage license, which restricts its ability to operate at Kenyan ports for fuel imports intended to go to Uganda.[30] With many African border posts comprising diverse actors with conflicting interests and mandates,[31] this lack of inter-agency cooperation hampers trade facilitation and continental integration as countries only want to serve themselves, forgetting the bigger objective of the AfCFTA.

2.5 *Inconsistent and Complex Policies*

Countries in Africa have different trade and customs administration policies that suit their individual fiscal needs.[32] The differing and complicated customs administration policies make it difficult for the continent to reap the prospective benefits of the AfCFTA. Complicated customs policies act as obstacles that dissuade businesses from engaging in African trade, which in effect hinders the continent's intra-African and international trade participation.[33] For example, excessive customs administration policies make it difficult for exporters from poor nations to participate in continental trade. The lack of uniform customs administration policies in Africa is a serious barrier to the efforts of the AfCFTA.[34]

2.6 *Lack of Effective Regional Customs Transit Guarantee Schemes*

Africa's lack of effective regional customs transit guarantee schemes (RCTG schemes) has been established to be one of the major reasons why the continent experiences poor customs administration and low levels of trade facilitation. An RCTG scheme is defined to be a program that has been designed by a region to facilitate and ensure the swift movement of goods and provide a sense of customs

---

[30] Cannon and Mogaka (2022), p. 1.

[31] International Trade Centre (2020).

[32] Muftan (2023), p. 65. Ismail notes that "Despite the important obligations placed on the Council of Ministers under the AfCFTA, it has no autonomy of direct regulatory authority over the state parties. The Council of Ministers cannot also harmonize trade rules or directly influence or enforce changes in the state parties' regulatory frameworks. How would the AfCFTA then achieve harmonization of trade rules among the state parties? There is a need for considerable institutional expansion and adjustment in the AfCFTA's institutional powers, particularly as relates to the Council of Ministers as the engine room for implementation of the AfCFTA. There is a need to grant this body greater autonomy to be able to galvanize implementation of the AfCFTA in terms of trade facilitation, liberalisation, and economic integration. The wording of the provision of the AfCFTA to the effect that state parties shall take measures as are necessary to implement the decisions of the Council of Ministers, is too lax and obviously not self-executing."

[33] Drinkwater and Robinson (2023), p. 1.

[34] Kouamo (2019), p. 120.

security and guarantee between trading countries. In Africa, only the Common Market for Eastern and Southern Africa (COMESA) region has developed and implemented an RCTG scheme, wherein member states are issued an RCTG bond which permits them to travel throughout the region for the purposes of trade.[35] In this region, the implementation of the RCTG scheme has proven to increase competition amongst traders and has reduced transit costs and cargo dwell times.[36]

3 The Effects/Consequences of Penurious Customs Administrations in Africa

3.1 Corruption at Border Posts

The consequences of corruption at border posts are those that affect the continent's current and prospective development. Corruption impedes the continent's economic growth in that inefficient customs administration distorts Africa's competitiveness in international trade and it sabotages its governance.[37] Poor governance entails weak customs institutions, poor application of customs procedures and guidelines, and inadequate regulations, all of which further encourage corruption. From a social point of view, corruption at border posts enables customs administration officers to use this platform to extort traders of money or anything of commercial value for self-gain and enrichment. This is a case of expertise and talent turning into money-seeking activities. Depending on the ranks of these officers, should they be found guilty of this misconduct, this offence is usually 'swept under the rug' or they are charged with a minor sentence, in contrast with the nature of the misdeed committed. From a political viewpoint, this may give rise to political instability.[38] Here, uproar may ensue driven by people who are outraged by unscrupulous activities. These unrests may cause border posts to stop operating, thus further delaying the transit of goods and people into, through, and out of a specific country. From an economic perspective, businesses are reluctant to trade with countries that require them to pay additional amounts at border posts, to the already existing tariffs. This affects the overall revenue that a country acquires from customs duties[39] and the country's potential to receive foreign investments, and the ability to trade globally.[40] An example of the costs of corruption at border posts is a report in Nigeria which showed that in a period of less than three months, the cost of corruption incurred, as a result of corruption at border posts, amounted to over eighty thousand US dollars.[41]

[35] Dorra (2017), p. 45.

[36] Namasaka (2020).

[37] Mlambo et al. (2019), p. 42.

[38] Mlambo et al. (2019), p. 43.

[39] Muzurura (2019), p. 106.

[40] Muzurura (2019), p. 107.

[41] Chene (2018).

3.2 Inconsistent and Complex Policies

The business of importing and exporting involves considerable documentation which differs according to the varied policies of African countries. Businesses are required to understand and comply with these differing regulations, which can be very challenging and frustrating. For example, in some countries, certain product categories are overly regulated and require complex legal documentation to be furnished, as opposed to other countries with much more relaxed regulations. Inconsistent and complicated regulations impede trade between African countries, and international trade at large. The lack of consistency in the customs policies of African countries results in failed customs procedures, which has the effect of disrupting the movement of goods, business people, and services in Africa.[42]

3.3 Manual Customs Administrations

Manual customs administration comprises of physical inspection of cargo and direct interactions between customs administration officers and traders.[43] Traders are required to complete many contracts and forms which include tax payment contracts, inspection contracts, manifest contracts, etc. With these interactions occurs the handing of documents, the physical admissibility of goods, and the charging of duty, all of which are time-consuming and costly. Manual customs administration involves a lot of paperwork, which results in possible information inaccuracies and provides opportunities for fraud, corruption, misreporting, and arbitrary decision making.[44] In addition, manual customs administration limits the exchange of information with other customs administration agencies, which leads to a lack of coordination, transparency, and confidence between trading countries.[45]

3.4 Lack of Transparency

The poor publication of customs regulations increases the trade barriers that already exist. Having the privilege of knowing what is required of traders in other territories allows them to know what can or cannot be imported into other countries, the documentation that is required, and the tariffs they can expect to pay for their cargo.[46] This predictability creates a sense of stability in the trading market and traders are

[42] KPMG (2022).

[43] Addo and Avgerou (2021), p. 16.

[44] Tan and Sundarakani (2020), p. 203.

[45] Santra and Bardhan (2021), p. 1666.

[46] Norouzi and Fani (2021), p. 52.

allowed to prepare, beforehand, what will be required at border posts. In addition to the lack of predictability that is caused by the lack of transparency, poor knowledge, understanding, and enforcement of regulations causes corruption. Traders are not informed of their rights, leaving them exposed to abuses caused by border officials.[47]

3.5 Lack of Inter-agency Cooperation

Each customs administration authority has distinct prerequisites for verifying and clearing goods at border posts. They each have different customs duty tariffs, and procedures for inspecting cargo, and require different documentation. All these validation measures are unique to each country's needs.[48] The lack of inter-agency cooperation, synergy, and sharing of information often breeds inter-agency rivalry. Where there is no cooperation and connectedness between customs agencies, distrust and competitiveness are born. This happens especially when the customs procedures of one country are very thorough, as compared to those of its trading partners, and cause delays in the transit of goods from another country.[49] Some countries may consider this as deliberate sabotage and may become hostile in admitting the exports of that country.

4 International Instruments Regulating Customs Administration Procedures

4.1 Arusha Declaration on Customs Integrity[50]

The Arusha Declaration is the principal instrument aimed at increasing the levels of integrity in global customs administration. It is designed to prevent unscrupulous dealing at border posts. The Declaration acknowledges the important role of domestic customs administration, which is to collect revenue, facilitate trade, and protect the community on behalf of their government. It also notes that integrity is an

[47] Larson (2019), p. 384.

[48] Liu et al. (2022), p. 13.

[49] Olomu et al. (2019), p. 13.

[50] The Arusha Declaration of the Customs Co-operation Council Concerning Integrity in Customs, 2003. The African countries who have members of the Customs Co-operation Council (World Customs Organization) are Algeria, Angola, Benin, Botswana, Burkina Faso, Burundi, Cameroon, Cape Verde, Central African Republic, Chad, Comoros, Congo, Cote d,Ivoire, Democratic Republic of Congo, Djibouti, Egypt, Eritrea, Ethiopia, Gabon, Gambia, Guinea, Guinea-Bissau, Kenya, Lesotho, Liberia, Libya, Madagascar, Malawi, Mali, Mauritania, Mauritius, Morocco, Mozambique, Namibia, Niger, Nigeria, Rwanda, Sao Tome and Principe, Senegal, Seychelles, Sierra Leone, Somalia, South Africa, South Sudan, Sudan, Swaziland, Tanzania, Togo, Tunisia, Uganda, Zambia and Zimbabwe.

important value that the customs authority of all nations should possess, as the lack of it limits the effectiveness of customs administration. It asserts that corruption at border posts can be tackled if the political will of the governments of all nations is committed against it, and there is a comprehensive national effort to combat it.

The Declaration reveals the need for the establishment of effective domestic customs administration programs. It declares that these programs should encompass and address the ensuing crucial factors:

4.1.1 Regulative Framework

The declaration notes that custom legislation, formalities, and guidelines of all trading nations should be, to the greatest extent possible, harmonised and simplified to ensure that custom procedures at border posts are administered without any unreasonable delays and burdens. This would require the adoption of international conventions, instruments, and standards aimed at reducing and eliminating trade delays and burdens. The rates in which duty is charged ought to be moderated, to ensure compliance with internationally agreed principles, and exemptions to these principles should be minimized.

4.1.2 Leadership and Commitment

The Declaration affirms that the head of customs of any particular country, together with their executive management team, are responsible for corruption prevention. These managers ought to possess qualities such as accountability and strong leadership, and should exude an unequivocal focus on integrity. An example of a country implementing this is Sierra Leone, whose National Revenue Authority is currently establishing an Internal Audit Unit at border posts, to intensify oversight and control of all goods coming into, and through the country.[51]

4.1.3 Transparency

The Declaration asserts that the business of customs administrators and their customs clients should be certain and predictable. This would require customs legislation, guidelines, and formalities to be made public, and accessible, and be applied in a manner that is consistent and uniform.[52]

[51] WCO (2020).

[52] The Arusha Declaration of the Customs Co-operation Council Concerning Integrity in Customs, 2003.

4.1.4 Automation

The Declaration reveals that the computerisation or digitalisation of customs administrations and procedures can assist in eliminating unscrupulous dealings at border posts. This is because the automation of customs administration will monitor and provide a trail of dealings between customs clients and customs administrators. This will all assist in the reviewing of administrative decisions and will increase the level of accountability for customs officials.

4.1.5 Reform and Modernisation

The Declaration shows the need for customs administration to reform and modernise their systems. This is for the reason that corruption at border posts thrives in situations where manual and outdated procedures are employed. In such situations, customs clients often offer 'incentives' to customs administrators in an attempt to avoid the lengthy procedures at checkpoints. Modernised systems will ensure that official requirements are not circumvented and that all aspects of customs operations and performance are effective. One of the countries implementing this is Ethiopia, who, after its latest organisational restructuring process, has made it a point that all customs administration officers are aware and understand these changes, so that their morale is not affected.[53]

4.1.6 Human Resource Management

The Declaration prescribes that in order to eradicate corruption at border ports, member states should establish and implement adequate human resource procedures and policies. The Declaration provides that appropriate policies and procedures are those that:

1. Provide customs officials with decent salaries and working conditions, so that they are able to live a standard life;
2. Employ and keep customs officials who possess high levels of integrity;
3. Ensure that customs officials are rotated, relocated and deployed to different positions, to avoid them occupying susceptible positions for long intervals;
4. Provide continual training and developmental programs aimed at reminding and reinforcing the importance of being ethical and professional;
5. Introduce suitable performance appraisal and management systems, which monitor the work of customs officials and ensure that they maintain professional integrity in their line of work.[54]

[53] WCO (2020).

[54] The Arusha Declaration of the Customs Co-operation Council Concerning Integrity in Customs 2003.

Other factors include audit and investigation, code of conduct, morale and organisational culture, and relationship with the private sector.[55]

4.2 *International Convention on the Simplification and Harmonisation of Customs Procedures*[56]

Previously known as the Kyoto Convention, this instrument is the blueprint for efficient customs procedures in contemporary trade. The Convention aims to eliminate the distinction between customs procedures and the practices of customs clients that have a negative impact on international trade. It further seeks to contribute to international trade by promoting trade facilitation and ensuring that customs procedures are simplified and harmonised, without compromising legally accepted standards on customs administration. The Convention narrates several essential principles governing customs procedures. Those relevant to customs procedures are:

1. Transparent and predictable implementation of customs and transit procedures;
2. Simplified and systematized declaration of goods and supporting documents;
3. Uncomplicated procedures for customs officials and clients;
4. Maximum reliance on information technology for customs administration;
5. Minimal manual customs control measures, to ensure obedience to regulations.

The Convention prescribes that an instrument that embodies the mentioned principles and objectives that member states are obliged to apply will pilot a high level of simplified and harmonised customs procedures, which will contribute to the facilitation of global trade.

4.3 *International Convention on the Harmonized Commodity Description and Coding System*[57]

This convention is a successful instrument designed and established by the World Customs Organisation. It contributes to the harmonisation of global customs and trade administrations by ensuring that member states make use of a uniform system

---

[55]The Arusha Declaration of the Customs Co-operation Council Concerning Integrity in Customs 2003.

[56]The International Convention on the Simplification and Harmonisation of Customs Procedures. The African countries that have ratified this convention are those which are member states of the Customs Co-operation Council.

[57]The International Convention on the Harmonized Commodity Description and Coding System, 1988. The African member states are Angola, Algeria, Botswana, Burundi, Comoros, Djibouti,

of gathering information, describing, and coding of goods in trade, for the purposes of charging and collecting customs duties.[58] The usage of this instrument is not limited to the charging of customs tariffs, but it also acts as a basis for collecting international trade statistics, trade negotiations, collection of internal taxes, monitoring controlled goods, and assisting the governments of member states to be able to categorise the goods that are being traded, amongst many other purposes.[59]

4.4 WTO Agreement on Customs Value[60]

Alike to the International Convention on the Harmonized Commodity Description and Coding System, this instrument serves as the methodology used by member states to value goods for the purposes of duty collection. The agreement sets forth objective and uniform international principles on how imported goods should be valued, taking into consideration existing and prospective commercial realities.[61] It acknowledges that the source of customs valuation should be the transaction price of the imported goods valued, being the actual price of goods fixed by the exporting country, instead of justifications that are fictitious or arbitrary.[62] Where it is impossible to determine customs value on the basis of the actual price, methods such as the transactional value or similar or identical goods, the deductive value method, or the fall-back method are used.[63]

Egypt, Eritrea, Eswatini, Ethiopia, Kenya, Lesotho, Libya, Madagascar, Malawi, Morocco, Mauritius, Mozambique, Namibia, Rwanda, Seychelles, Somalia, South Africa, South Sudan, Sudan, Tanzania, Tunisia, Uganda, Zambia, and Zimbabwe.

[58] World Customs Organisation available on https://www.wcoomd.org//media/wco/public/global/pdf/topics/nomenclature/activities-and-programmes/30-years-hs/hs-compendium.pdf.

[59] Ibid, p. 18.

[60] Agreement on Implementation of Art VII of the General Agreements on Tariffs and Trade, 1994. The African countries which are member states to this agreement are Angola, Benin, Botswana, Burkina Faso, Burundi, Cameroon, Cabo Verde, Central African Republic, Chad, Congo, Cote d'Ivoire, Democratic Republic of Congo, Djibouti, Egypt, eSwatini, Gabon, Gambia, Ghana, Guinea, Guinea-Bissau, Kenya, Lesotho, Liberia, Madagascar, Malawi, Mali, Mauritania, Mauritius, Morocco, Mozambique, Namibia, Niger, Nigeria, Rwanda, Senegal, Seychelles, Sierra Leone, South Africa, Tanzania, Togo, Tunisia, Uganda, Zambia, and Zimbabwe.

[61] Ibid Preamble and Objectives of General Agreement on Tariffs and Trade.

[62] Ibid Art 1.

[63] Art 2 and Note to Art 7. Identical goods refers to "the requirement that the identical goods should be exported at or about the same time as the goods being valued could be flexibly interpreted; identical imported goods produced in a country other than the country of exportation of the goods being valued could be the basis for customs valuation; customs values of identical imported goods already determined under the provisions of Articles 5 and 6 could be used." Similar goods refer "to the requirement that the similar goods should be exported at or about the same time as the goods being valued could be flexibly interpreted; similar imported goods produced in a country other than the country of exportation of the goods being valued could be the basis for customs valuation; customs values of similar imported goods already determined under the provisions of Arts 5 and 6

For the purposes of customs administration, the agreement is said to provide predictable and stable means of collecting duty, thus ensuring that international trade is facilitated in a manner that is transparent and in compliance with domestic regulations. The agreement also provides a platform for the customs authority of member states to enquire about the accuracy and authenticity of any declaration, statement, or document presented to them for the purposes of correct and complete customs valuation.[64]

4.5 *WCO SAFE Framework of Standards*[65]

This framework recognises the importance and functions of customs administrations, being to regulate the movement of goods into, through, and out of a country, to facilitate trade, and to collect revenue. The objectives of the SAFE Framework are:

1. To prepare, develop, and strengthen customs administration to ensure that it copes and keeps up with the ever-evolving world of trade;
2. To enhance the collaboration between customs administrators of member nations to improve their abilities to discern high-risk consignment through the speedy exchange of information and harmonised methods of goods recognition;
3. To fortify the relationship and cooperation between customs administrations and businesses globally.

4.6 *WTO Trade Facilitation Agreement*[66]

The Trade Facilitation Agreement was promulgated to improve global trade efficiency and to motivate economic growth. This came after the World Trade Organisation saw the need for member states to effectively cooperate on customs compliance issues and trade facilitation. This agreement aims to simplify trade facilitation and customs procedures and prompt the swift clearance and movement of goods at border gates while improving transparency.

could be used." Deductive methods refers to "the requirement that the goods shall have been sold in the "condition as imported".

[64] Ibid Art 17.

[65] World Customs Organization Safe Framework of Standards (2018).

[66] WTO Trade Facilitation Agreement. The African countries that have ratified this instrument are Angola, Benin, Botswana, Burkina Faso, Burundi, Cabo Verde, Cameroon, Central African Republic, Chad, Congo, Cote d'Ivoire, Djibouti, Ecuador, Egypt, Eswatini, Gambia, Ghana, Guinea, Guinea-Bissau, Kenya, Lesotho, Liberia, Madagascar, Malawi, Mali, Morocco, Mozambique, Namibia, Niger, Nigeria, Papua New Guinea, Rwanda, Senegal, Sierra Leone, Seychelles, South Africa, Tanzania, Togo, Tunisia, Uganda, Zambia, Zimbabwe.

The Agreement requires member states to publish information relating to customs regulations and procedures to all parties with which they are acquainted to, without any discrimination.[67] The Agreement further requires state parties to avoid burdensome documentation requirements and formalities at border gates, unless they are necessary to identify the goods in transit and to ensure the satisfaction of transit requirements.[68] In addition, the Agreement encourages member states to make information relating to their average release time of goods available to their trading partners.[69]

4.7 Agreement Establishing the African Continental Free Trade Area

As already mentioned in the chapter, one of the objectives of the AfCFTA is to establish a single market of goods, services, and investments, and to enhance the continent's economic competitiveness in the grand global market. This agreement arises from one of the African Union's Agenda 2063 aspirations, being the creation of a continental market that allows for the free and swift movement of goods, services, people, and capital, all which are important for economic integration and transformation. In order for this to be realised, the Agreement prescribes that there be a reduction or progressive elimination tariff and non-tariff barriers to trade.[70]

On the matter of customs administrations, the Agreement requires that there be cooperation between member states on matters regarding customs and the implementation of trade facilitation measures.[71] Annex 4 of the Agreement, which focus on trade facilitation, aims to provide harmonised and simplified logistical and trade procedures which could potentially fasten the transit, import and export processes. In addition, the object of this Annex is also to accelerate the movement, clearing and releasing of goods at the borders of member states.[72] In order to achieve this, the Annex provides guidelines on matters such as:

1. How customs regulations, data, documentation, rates and fees should be published;[73]
2. The number of enquiry points that should be established by member states and the time of response;[74]

[67] Art 1 of the WTO Trade Facilitation Agreement.

[68] Art 11 of the WTO Trade Facilitation Agreement.

[69] Art 6 of the WTO Trade Facilitation Agreement.

[70] Preamble of the Agreement Establishing the African Free Trade Area.

[71] Art 4 of the Agreement Establishing the African free Trade Area.

[72] Art 2 of Annex 4 of the Agreement Establishing the African Continental Free Trade Area.

[73] Art 4 of Annex 4 of the Agreement Establishing the African Continental Free trade Area.

[74] Art 5 of Annex 4 of the Agreement Establishing the African Continental Free Trade Area.

3. How, when, and what should be contained in rulings;[75]
4. The submission of import documentation;[76] to name a few.

Annex 8 of the Agreement[77] regulates the transit of goods. Its scope of application extends to all transitors, mail, modes of transport, or any ship that carries goods between two states.[78] The Annex provides directions on matters such as:

1. The approval of the modes of transport;[79]
2. The licensing of transitors and carriers of goods;[80]
3. Indemnity from customs charges;[81]
4. Transit procedures,[82] to name a few.

A protocol, which forms part of the set of agreements within the AfCFTA, has been introduced to clarify the digital trade environment in Africa.[83] The objectives of this protocol are to establish a uniform regulatory framework that enables and encourages digital trade in the continent. It places emphasis on promoting digital trade between the AfCFTA member states and enhances cooperation on digital matters, including customs administration, thus creating a digital trade ecosystem that is trusted, secure and transparent.[84]

5 Recommendations and Conclusion

On the issue of corruption, this study has established that the discretionary powers held by customs administration officers are one of the causes of corruption at border points. Their functions include the assessment of the origin of goods, valuation and classification of goods, examining cargo, issuing of various licenses, and the administration of concessions, amongst many others. The discretionary powers to perform these functions are afforded to customs officials, regardless of their rankings.[85] This study recommends that in order to reduce the discretionary powers of customs officials, the AfCFTA ought to have Pre-Shipment Inspections (PSI) as a mandatory prerequisite for member states trading under the Agreement. PSI is a program where an independent surveillance company is hired to conduct inspections on cargo

[75] Art 6 of Annex 4 of the Agreement Establishing the African Continental Free Trade Area.
[76] Art 7 of Annex 4 of the Agreement Establishing the African Continental Free Trade Area.
[77] Annex 8 of the Agreement Establishing the African Continental Free Trade Area.
[78] Art 3 of Annex 4 of the Agreement Establishing the African Continental Free Trade Area.
[79] Art 4 of Annex 4 of the Agreement Establishing the African Continental Free Trade Area.
[80] Art 5 of Annex 4 of the Agreement Establishing the African Continental Free Trade Area.
[81] Art 8 of Annex 4 of the Agreement Establishing the African Continental Free Trade Area.
[82] Art 9 of Annex 4 of the Agreement Establishing the African Continental Free Trade Area.
[83] The Digital Trade Protocol of the African Continental Free Trade Area.
[84] Stuart (2024).
[85] Abdul et al. (2019), p. 225.

before it leaves a country of origin. A PSI inspector is appointed and entrusted with the responsibility of verifying the value and classification of a shipment before it exits a specific country, to ensure that the products meet the requirements of the destination market, and issue reports for import and billing.

The findings of the valuation and classification are then shared with the receiving country.[86] With this program, the excessive discretionary powers of customs administrators will be limited as cargo would have already been verified, and the inspector would have ensured that the goods are in line with the customs regulations of the importing country. The African countries that are currently voluntarily utilizing this program are Kenya, Tanzania, Mozambique, Uganda, and Egypt to name a few. Secondly, in order to eliminate corruption at border points, the governments of African countries ought to raise awareness of the corrupt activities taking place at border gates. The awareness can be in the form of codifying and reporting rent-seeking activities that constitute corruption. Customs administration officers are conscious of the unscrupulous activities happening at border checkpoints but may elect to protect each other or be scared to speak up. With the government raising awareness, customs administration officers will be aware of the government's knowledge of corrupt activities and this may encourage them to desist from partaking in them, or motivate that such matters be reported.[87]

Thirdly, this chapter recommends that the provisions of AfCFTA should require its member states to prioritize the elimination of corruption at border points in their countries and that they furnish evidence of actions taken in that regard. The agreement should also require that contracting parties implement and incorporate into their national customs regulations the provisions of the Arusha Declaration of Customs Integrity and other anti-corruption instruments binding African states, and ensure that the instruments are implemented. To ensure implementation, the governments of member states should see to it that these provisions are publicized and accessible to its members, and those trading with it.[88] Fourthly, African countries should establish and implement strategic plans which are aimed at combatting corruption at border ports. These strategic plans should include each country's vision and mission, together with action plans to eliminate corruption. This strategic plan should serve as a guide to be followed by customs administration officers, to ensure that there is an increase in internal control of customs procedures.[89]

Lastly, on how digitalisation can be used to combat corruption in Africa, the study recommends that the Government of the member states of the AfCFTA should introduce crowd sourced electronic systems that enable truck drivers and traders to report any corrupt advances or activities occurring at border posts. For better accessibility, the system should be in the form of a mobile application, and with every report entered, the legal authorities should be alerted of such activities and the

[86] Ali et al. (2020), p. 10.

[87] Abdul et al. (2019), p. 226.

[88] Odusote and Aduak (2022), p. 331.

[89] Abdul (2019), p. 225.

perpetrators be held accountable. A country that has implemented a system of this nature is Nigeria, whose Trade Route Incident Mapping System is used as a whistle-blowing tool against bribe-seeking harassment from customs officials.[90]

On the issue of manual customs administration, it is important that the continent advances from outdated customs procedures to those that are electronic in nature.[91] Given the growth of e-commerce under the AfCFTA, it is important for customs administration to keep up with the 21st-century world of trade. Digital customs administration procedures drive trade facilitation. This is because electronic customs administration procedures expedite trade-related procedures, which then reduce the transit time of goods and other barriers to cross-border trade. For example, in the Asian agricultural trade industry, there is evidence that the shift from manual customs administration procedures to electronic customs administration procedures has increased the number of exports by 9.7 percent.[92] Additionally, it has been projected that should a region fully implement digital customs administration procedures, it would gain over two hundred and fifty-seven billion dollars in exports yearly.[93]

Digital customs administration procedures are more transparent, as compared to manual systems, and are less vulnerable to corruption as there is less physical contact between customs administration officers and traders.[94] The added advantages of digitalizing customs administration procedures are:

1. Digital customs administration promotes the easy access and uniform application of customs regulations in the continent.
2. Digital customs administration procedures provide fast cargo clearance which reduces congestion at border ports and the cost of conducting cross-border trade.
3. Digital customs administration procedures can detect irregularities and illegal consignments using data collected by customs administration officers.
4. Digital customs administration procedures increase accountability as they provide an audit trail of cargo admitted into a country.
5. Digital customs administrations enable the sharing of information with other customs administration authorities in the continent.[95]

On the challenge of lack of transparency, this chapter has already established that many African countries lack automated customs administration processes, which makes it difficult for continental customs administrations to effect information sharing and risk identification. The paper recommends that the customs authorities of African countries should initiate open and transparent relationships with other customs agencies and the private sector. These relationships can be fostered first by

[90] NANTS Regional Trade Advocacy Series (2020), p. 13.

[91] Suyunov and Fakhriddinova (2022), p. 699.

[92] de Castro and Kornher (2022), p. 1.

[93] Gichuki and Msiska (2022).

[94] Apiko et al. (2020).

[95] Ancharaz (2018).

publishing and communicating existing and new regulations.[96] All the entities partaking in customs transactions should be well acquainted with their rights and obligations.[97]

On the issue of lack of inter-agency cooperation, this chapter acknowledges that the customs authorities of African countries lack synergy, especially where the requirements for verifying and clearing goods at border posts are concerned. To remedy this issue, this chapter recommends that African countries ought to adopt a comprehensive system that allows for the harmonisation of customs policies and procedures, whilst also making way for the automated streamline of data sharing.[98] The initiative referred to is one that is empowered by the International Convention on the Simplification and Harmonisation of Customs Procedures and the International Convention of the Harmonized Commodity Description and Coding System, which will ensure that customs procedures are uniform and simplified and that the system used in describing and coding goods is the same throughout the continent. The recommended system will also assist in aiding the issue of inconsistent and complex policies in customs administration in that policies will be integrated into one. This will ensure that there is customs administration cooperation between African states.[99]

In conclusion, the purpose of this chapter was to investigate on the effects of poor customs administration efficiency on the implementation and realisation of the African Continental Free Trade Area Agreement. The chapter found that the causes of Africa's poor customs administration processes lead to an opaque trading environment, which discourages businesses from participating in cross-border trade and severely threatens the success of the AFCFTA. Unfortunately, customs administrations cannot be isolated from intra-African and international trade. Its pivotal role of regulating the movement of goods into, through, and out of a country cannot be done away with. Thus, for as long as the border posts are infected with poor customs administration procedures, the possibility of reaping the benefits of the AFCFTA may as well be kissed goodbye.

References

Abdul SL, Yusoff H, Mohamed N (2019) Factors that might lead to corruption: a case study in Malaysian government. Int J Financ Res 10(3):216–229

Addo A, Avgerou C (2021) Information technology and government corruption in developing countries: evidence from Ghana customs. MIS Q 45(4):16

African Development Bank Group (2013). https://www.afdb.org/en/news-and-events/border-posts-checkpoints-and-intra-african-trade-challenges-and-solutions-12377

---

[96] Nguyen et al. (2019), p. 356.

[97] Kouamo (2019), p. 62.

[98] Zain (2020).

[99] Njinkeu and Powo Fosso (2006).

Agreement Establishing the African Free Trade Area 2019
Agreements on Tariffs and Trade, 1994
Ali M, Fjeldstad O, Shifa AB (2020) European colonization and the corruption of local elites. J Econ Behav Organ 179(C):80–100
Ancharaz SD (2018) Best practices in digital customs in East and Southern Africa. https://www.wcoesarocb.org/wp-content/uploads/2018/09/best-practices-in-digital-customs-in-east-and-southern-africa.pdf. Accessed 4 May 2023
Apiko P, Wooley S, Byiers B (2020) The promise of the African Continental Free Trade Area. https://ecdpm.org/work/the-promise-of-the-african-continental-free-trade-area-afcfta
Arusha Declaration of the Customs Co-operation Council Concerning Integrity in Customs, 2003
Azcárraga AAP, Matsudaira T, Montagnat-Rentier G, Nagy J, Clark RJ (2022) Customs matters: strengthening customs administration in a changing world. International Monetary Fund, Washington DC
Bassa L, Kwateng KO, Kamewor FT (2021) Paperless customs clearance and business supply chains. Mar Econ Manag J 4(1):42–58
Cannon BJ, Mogaka S (2022) Rivalry in East Africa: the case of the Uganda-Kenya crude oil pipeline and East Africa crude oil pipeline. Extr Ind Soc J II:1–7
Chene (2018) M Corruption at Borders. https://knowledgehub.transparency.org/assets/uploads/helpdesk/Corruption-at-borders-2018.pdf
Chibira E (2021a) Improving border efficiency in Sub-Saharan Africa: the need to look beyond the border' operations. https://www.tralac.org/blog/article/15328-improving-border-efficiency-in-sub-saharan-africa-the-need-to-look-at-beyond-the-border-operations.html
Chibira E (2021b) Improving customs efficiency: what are the gains and for whom? Tralac 24 August 2021. https://tralac.org/blog/article/15329-improving-customs-efficiency-what-are-the-gains-and-for-whom.html
COMESA. https://www.tralac.org/news/article/14912-comesa-launches-regional-customs-transit-guarantee-scheme-mobile-app.html
De Castro ABR, Kornher L (2022) The effect of trade and customs digitalization of agrifood trade: a gravity approach. Q Open 3(1):qoac037
Dorra HA (2017) African economic integration: assessing the Tripartite Free Trade Area: a critical case study. Unpublished LLM dissertation, The American University of Cairo
Drinkwater S, Robinson C (2023) The impact of customs and trade regulations on the operation of African firms. J Bus Res 165(C):1–9
Erasmus G (2022) When will the AFCFTA be customs-ready. https://www.tralac.org/blog/article/15478-when-will-the-afcfta-be-customs-ready.html
Flory OO, Nyaronga GJ (2025) Enhancing economic growth through transport corridors: a case study of the central corridor transit transport facilitation agency. Afr Dev Finance J 8(III):18–39
Gichuki N, Msiska F (2022) Customs digitalization and deepening Inta-COMESA Trade. https://www.comesa.int/wp-content/uploads/2022/01/CUSTOMS-DIGITALIZATION-AND-DEEPENING-INTRA-COMESA-TRADE.pdf
Gordhan P (2007) Customs in the 21st century. World Cust J 1(1):49–54
International Trade Centre (2020) Getting down to business: making the most of the WTO Trade Facilitation Agreement. https://unctad.org/system/files/non-official-document/wto-technical-note_ch08a08_en.pdf
International Trade Council (2022) Decoding the role of customs in international trade. https://tradecouncil.org/decoding-the-role-of-customs-in-international-trade/
Kouamo JA (2019) Modernisation of customs regulations and practices to combat customs offences in France, South Africa and Cameroon. Published LLD thesis, North West University
Kouamo JA (2020) Customs modernization in Africa and related challenges. https://www.tralac.org/blog/article/15053-customs-modernisation-in-africa-and-related-challenges.html
KPMG (2022). https://kpmg.com/xx/en/home/insights/2022/04/the-challenges-of-cross-border-international-trade.html
Larson P (2019) Corruption, gender equality and logistics performance. Int J Logist Manag 31(2):381–397

Liu Y, Zhou Z, Yang Y (2022) Verifying the smart contracts of the port supply chain system based on probabilistic model checking. MDPI Syst J 10(19):1–20

Luke R, Walters J (2023) Logistics challenges and opportunities in Africa in the 2020s. In: Merkert R, Hoberg K (eds) Global logistics and supply chain strategies for the 2020s. Springer, Cham

Lux M (2023) The ambitious reform package proposed by the EU Commission. Global Trade Cust J 18(11/12):399–425

Mgeni CP (2025) Elimination of non-tariff measures under AfCFTA: implication for trade facilitation and food sector development in East African Community. East South Afr J Agric Econ Dev 13(1):142–163

Mitchell UPP (2014) The relationship between tariffs, corruption, and growth in developing countries. https://www.uakron.edu/economics/academics/senior-projects/2014/Upp-M-SeniorProject2014.pdf

Mlambo D, Mubecua M, Mpanza S (2019) Corruption and its implications for development and good governance: a perspective from post-colonial Africa. J Econ Behav Stud 11(1):39–47

Muftan I (2023) Overview of the African Continental Free Trade Area (AFCFTA) and challenges of implementation: Nigeria and South Africa's implementation as case studies. Unpublished LLM dissertation, University of British Columbia

Muzurura J (2019) Causes, dissemination channels, and consequences of corruption in Zimbabwe, searching for kryptonite solution. Humanit Soc Sci Lett 7(2):105–122

Namasaka M (2020) COMESA launches regional customs transit guarantee scheme mobile app. https://www.tralac.org/news/article/14912-comesa-launches-regional-customs-transit-guarantee-scheme-mobile-app.html

NANTS Regional Trade Advocacy Series (2020) Combating corruption along Nigeria-ECOWAS trade routes through TRIMS. ECOWAS Vanguard 4(1):13

Ngobeni B (2023) Expected challenges and drawbacks faced by SADC countries as a result of the proposed Tripartite Free Trade Area Agreement. (Unpublished)

Nguyen VD, Aquino PG, Hong LE (2019) A critical analysis of customs-business partnership compliance with the import and export enterprises with customs law and regulation. Utopia y Praxis Latinoamericana 24(5):349–358

Njinkeu D, Powo Fosso B (2006) Intra-African Trade and Regional Integration. https://www.afdb.org/fileadmin/uploads/afdb/Documents/Knowledge/09484259-EN-INTRA-AFRICAN-TRADE-AND-REGIONLA-INTEGRATION.PDF

Norouzi N, Fani M (2021) Globalization and the oil market: an overview on considering petroleum as a trade commodity. J Energy Manag Technol 6(1):52–64

Ntabazi SM (2010) Combating corruption in customs through trade facilitation: case of East African Community. Unpublished LLM dissertation, University of Pretoria

Odusote G, Aduak Y (2022) Implementing the African Continental Free Trade Area Agreement (AfCFTA) and the Challenges of Corruption in Africa. OJPS 12(1):321–336

Olomu B, Oladimeji AD, Adewumi E (2019) Border security issues and challenges of the Nigeria customs service. Int J Latest Res Humanit Soc Sci 2(3):10–19

Olyanga AM, Shinyeka IMB, Ngoma M, Nkote IN, Esemu T, Kamya M (2022) Export logistics infrastructure and export competitiveness in the East African Community. Mod Supply Chain Res Appl J 4(1):39–61

Ondlek W (2019) Effects of risk management systems on customs declaration violations at Kilindini Port, Mombasa, pp 1–70

Rbehat AM, Marafi HB (2024) The role of customs process in facilitating international trade. Saudi J Bus Manag Stud 9(1):7–14

Santra B, Bardhan KM (2021) Automation of the maritime sector is expected to boost global trade's competitiveness and resilience. Int Res J Mod Eng Technol Sci 3(12):1665–1675

Stuart J (2024) The Digital Trade Protocol of the AfCFTA and digitally-driven development in Africa. https://www.tralac.org/blog/article/16306-the-digital-trade-protocol-of-the-afcfta-and-digitally-driven-development-in-africa.html

Suyunov A, Fakhriddinova R (2022) Improvement of customs control forms is key to simplification of customs procedures. Galaxy Int Interdiscip Res J 10(3):698–706

Tan WK, Sundarakani B (2020) Assessing blockchain technology application for freight booking business: a case study from technology acceptance model perspective. J Global Oper Strateg Sourc 14(1):203

The African Continental Free Trade Area (AfCFTA) Secretariat (2023). https://au-afcfta.org/about/

The Digital Trade Protocol of the African Continental Free Trade Area 2024

The International Convention on the Harmonized Commodity Description and Coding System, 1988

The International Convention on the Simplification and Harmonisation of Customs Procedures 1999

Ugaz P, Sun S (2019) Making Africa cross-border trade cheaper, easier and faster: highlights from the first African forum for national trade facilitation committees. https://unctad.org/news/making-african-cross-border-trade-cheaper-easier-and-faster-highlights-first-african-forum

UNCTAD Economic Development in Africa (2009) Strengthening regional integration for Africa's development. https://unctad.org/board-action/economic-development-africa-strengthening-regional-economic-integration-africas

Warf B (2017) Geographies of African corruption. PSU Res Rev 1(1):20–38

WCO (2020) WCO Revised Arusha Declaration: putting integrity back in the spotlight. https://mag.wcoomd.org/magazine/wco-news-91-february-2020/wco-revised-arusha-declaration-putting-integrity-back-in-the-spotlight/

Widdowson D (2007) The changing role of customs: evolution or revolution. World Cust J 1(1):31–37

World Customs Organisation (n.d.). https://www.wcoomd.org//media/wco/public/global/pdf/topics/nomenclature/activities-and-programmes/30-years-hs/hs-compendium.pdf

World Customs Organization Safe Framework of Standards (2018). https://www.wcoomd.org/-/media/wco/public/global/pdf/topics/facilitation/instruments-and-tools/tools/safe-package/copy-of-safe-framework-of-standards.pdf

Zain S (2020) Corrupting trade: an overview of corruption issues in illicit wildlife trade. https://files.worldwildlife.org/wwfcmsprod/files/Publication/file/3m48phx0ap_Introductory_Overview_Corrupting_trade_An_overview_of_corruption_issues_in_illicit_wildlife_trade.pdf

The Feasibility of an African Monetary Union to Fully Implement the AfCFTA

Gerda van Niekerk

Abstract As outlined in Agenda 2063, the African Union believes that a successful monetary union on the African continent is an essential prerequisite for the full implementation of the AfCFTA. The challenges of forming a monetary union and the convergence criteria to create such must be investigated to determine whether an African Monetary Union is feasible. Challenges include the formulation of a shared monetary policy and the establishment of a common central bank as well as a single currency for Africa. Achieving a small deficit in the current account and a common interest rate for all African countries may also be problematic. The author argues that an African customs union is more achievable than an African monetary union, and the focus in Africa should preferably be on the former. This would be in accord with the AfCFTA agreement that determines in Article 3(d) that one of the general objectives of the AfCFTA is to lay the foundation for establishing a Continental Customs Union.

1 Introduction

The African Economic Community was established in the Abuja Treaty of 3 June 1991.[1] In the Treaty, it is envisioned that member states will establish an African Monetary Union through the harmonisation of regional monetary zones.[2] The strategy document drawn up in 2013 by the African Union Commission and the Association of African Central Banks, indicates progress made in the monetary

[1] African Union (1991).

[2] Art 44(2)(g) of the Treaty Establishing the African Economic Community.

G. van Niekerk (✉)
University of Limpopo, Polokwane, South Africa
e-mail: gertruida.vanniekerk@ul.ac.za

T. V. Warikandwa et al. (eds.), *Law and Policy of the African Continental Free Trade Area (AfCFTA)*, European Yearbook of International Economic Law,
https://doi.org/10.1007/978-3-032-01122-0_12

policy and budget policies of various countries in Africa.[3] The African Union's Protocol on the Establishment of the African Monetary Fund was adopted on 27 June 2014 and the date of the last signature was 28 June 2019.[4] The African Union ("AU") believes that a successful monetary union on the African continent is feasible, and it is set as a target.[5]

2 Agenda 2063

Already in 2012 with the Action Plan for Boosting Intra-African Trade ("BIAT"), it was envisioned that BIAT would address the main challenges of "regional and continental integration in Africa, with the specific aim of unlocking the benefits of trade for sustainable growth and economic development".[6] In 2013 the AU Heads of State and Government adopted Agenda 2063 in Addis Ababa.[7] Agenda 2063 underlined the importance of African unity and having more economic networks between African states to enable Africa to develop its full potential.[8] This blueprint and master plan for transforming Africa underlines the importance of promoting African unity and the formation of economic relations between African states to expand Africa into an economic powerhouse.[9]

Agenda 2063 set out seven aspirations for Africa's prosperity and well-being so that Africa will be more economically successful and dynamic in 2063 than in 2013.[10] To achieve Aspiration Two, "An integrated continent politically united and based on the ideals of Pan-Africanism and the vision of Africa's Renaissance", three goals were set.[11] These goals envision a united Africa, either as a federation or as a confederation; continental financial and monetary institutions to be established; and world-class infrastructure to crisscross Africa.[12] It was anticipated in Agenda 2063 that an Africa Customs Union be established in 2019 as an anchor of the governance

[3] African Union Commission and Association of African Central Banks (2013).

[4] African Union (2018a, b).

[5] Art 19(b) Constitutive Act of the African Union 11 July 2000; African Union (2018a, b), p. 1; Moustafa and El-Shal (2024), p. 111.

[6] Fofack and Mold (2021), p. 3.

[7] African Union (2018a, b).

[8] Jazbhay (2019), p. 26; Odeku and Rikhotso (2023), p. 112.

[9] Odeku and Rikhotso (2023), p. 112; Jazbhay (2019), p. 26.

[10] African Union and Economic Commission for Africa (2015), pp. 13, 14 and 29.

[11] African Union and Economic Commission for Africa (2015), p. 15.

[12] African Union and Economic Commission for Africa (2015), p. 15. The various aspirations are broken up into goals necessary to achieve the aspiration and priority areas are set to focus on. Priority areas for these goals are frameworks and institutions for a United Africa, financial and monetary institutions, and communications and infrastructure connectivity.

structure of a United Africa.[13] The establishment of an African Monetary Union by 2025 was set as a further milestone for attaining the aspirations in Agenda 2063.[14]

The African Continental Free Trade Agreement (AfCFTA) was envisaged in Agenda 2063 and was signed in March 2018, bringing 54 countries together to form a single market to enhance African integration, challenging hindrances, and barriers to intra-Africa trade.[15] Market fragmentation historically constrained growth and economic development in Africa.[16] The AfCFTA presented an opportunity for African economies to fast-track their transformation and integration into the broader economy of the world.[17] It further seeks to provide business unity among African states and form a single market for goods and services, which will be facilitated by the movement of persons to participate in economic activities.[18] A free trade area for all African states will promote Africa's economic integration and development.[19]

In Agenda 2063, it was envisioned that the transition to a continental Customs Union should be accelerated with a Common External Tariff scheme, increased investment in market and trade infrastructure, promoting and strengthening multi-stakeholder platforms, and streamlining coordination mechanisms to promote a common African position on agriculture-related international trade negotiations and partnership agreements.[20]

To analyse whether a monetary union in Africa is viable and would be a feasible pre-requisite for fully implementing the AfCFTA, the challenges of forming a monetary union in Africa and the convergence criteria to create a monetary union must be analysed and considered.

3 Monetary Union and Convergence Criteria

Saka, Onafowokan and Adebayo refer to a monetary union as a full or nearly complete monetary integration between countries, where these countries' monetary policy and exchange rates are controlled to achieve common economic objectives.[21] According to De Lhoneux and Louis, a monetary union in Europe implied that a

[13] African Union and Economic Commission for Africa (2015), p. 36.

[14] African Union and Economic Commission for Africa (2015), pp. 149 and 165.

[15] Agreement Establishing the African Continental Free Trade Area available at https://au.int/sites/default/files/treaties/36437-treaty-consolidated_text_on_cfta_-_en.pdf, accessed on 15 July 2023.

[16] Fofack and Mold (2021), p. 1.

[17] African Union and Economic Commission for Africa (2015), p. 1; Olayiwola (2020).

[18] Art 2 AfCFTA.

[19] African Union and Economic Commission for Africa (2015), p. 1; Nubong (2021), p. 125.

[20] African Union and Economic Commission for Africa (2015), pp. 13, 14 and 29.

[21] Saka et al. (2015), p. 232; Kempf (2022), p. 395; Bamigbola (2024).

single currency would be used as well as a single external and internal monetary policy with a single European Central Bank.[22]

Convergence criteria are a set of macroeconomic indicators that focus on price stability and sound finances in a country and as such include monetary convergence and fiscal convergence criteria.[23] These criteria are implemented to measure whether countries are economically ready to become part of a monetary union, especially when these countries have different monetary and fiscal policies.[24] The process of convergence is described by Afxentiouw, as "a process which unifies technological and non-rival domains, preparing institutionally and structurally laggard countries to catch up with those at the forefront."[25]

Key indicators of monetary convergence are inflation, interest rates and foreign exchange and indicators of fiscal convergence are budget deficit and public debt.[26] The relevance of monetary convergence criteria declines after the monetary union has been established because of the adoption of a single currency, but the fiscal convergence criteria will still be critical after the monetary union has been established because if not coordinated between countries in the monetary union, it could undermine the monetary union.[27]

In 1992 convergence was an issue in Europe and many debates on this topic took place, leading to the Maastricht Treaty.[28] The question was asked whether convergence is a precondition for a monetary union or whether it is the consequence of such.[29] Masson believes that convergence of inflation and the need for the same real capital income before a monetary union is formed is not necessary and also not always possible.[30]

The convergence criteria set in the Maastricht Treaty as preconditions to a monetary union were fiscal criteria of a 3 percent ceiling on deficits as a ratio to Gross Domestic Product (GDP) and a 60 percent discretionary ceiling on gross

---

[22] De Lhoneux and Louis (1990), p. 11; Le Cacheux (2018), p. 49; Ryan and Loughlin (2018), p. 709; James (2023), p. 51.

[23] De Grauwe (1996), p. 1094; Saka et al. (2015), p. 232; Tweneboah and Eshun (2023), p. 2.

[24] De Grauwe (1996), p. 1094; Saka et al. (2015), p. 232; Afxentiou (2000), p. 246; Fontana and Kamara (2023), p. 58.

[25] Afxentiou (2000), p. 248.

[26] Saka et al. (2015), p. 232; De Grauwe (1996), p. 1095; Ocran (2022), p. 23.

[27] Saka et al. (2015), p. 232; Kebalo and Zouri (2022), p. 30; Fe et al. (2024), p. 1.

[28] Masson (1992), p. 181; Afxentiou (2000), p. 245; Also see paragraph IV below on the European Monetary Union.

[29] Masson (1992), p. 181; De Grauwe (1996), p. 1094; Afxentiou (2000), p. 248.

[30] Masson (1992), p. 181.

government debt.[31] Other criteria that were set were caps on the inflation rate measuring it in terms of the lowest inflation rate.[32] Since the global financial crisis in 2008, government debt of countries in the European Union ("EU") is not allowed to exceed 60% of GDP and the deficit on the government's current account is not allowed to be higher than 3% in any fiscal year.[33]

Some authors believe that a true monetary union entails that the countries in the zone only use a single currency and thus have a common monetary policy with a single central bank[34] while other authors opine that a monetary union only requires a common monetary policy without a single currency and where capital control is free.[35] When countries use multiple currencies, it raises problems of currency conversion and comparing the value of goods using different currencies as the various currencies can be a barrier to trade between the countries, whereas a single currency results in better commercial affiliation between countries and reduces exchange rate instability and inflation volatility and supports economic growth.[36]

4 European Monetary Union

The accomplishments of the EU with the Euro as a strong single currency underline the possibility of higher economic growth and development through monetary integration.[37] Convergence processes derived from the EU are often followed across the globe to achieve monetary integration so that the goals of promotion of trade, more business opportunities, unhindered movement of people between countries, and the dismantling of barriers are achieved.[38] Asongu, Nwachukwu and Tchamyou in analysing proposed African monetary unions, opined that lessons from the European Monetary Union ("EMU") should be considered for application in Africa.[39]

[31] Masson (1992), p. 184. "According to 1992 data, only France, Denmark, and Luxembourg satisfied all the criteria. Several countries, in particular Italy, Greece, and Portugal, needed substantial fiscal and inflation adjustment in order to meet the criteria. For instance, in Italy, the general government balance in 1992 was a little over 10 percent of GOP, the debt ratio was 110 percent of GOP, and the inflation rate was about 5112 percent for the year"; Vourexakis (2011), p. 2.

[32] Masson (1992), p. 184; Afxentiou (2000), p. 248.

[33] Vourexakis (2011), p. 2.

[34] Afxentiou (2000), p. 252; Saka et al. (2015), p. 232; De Lhoneux and Louis (1990), p. 11.

[35] Masson (1992), p. 172; Saka et al. (2015), p. 232.

[36] Saka et al. (2015), p. 233.

[37] Saka et al. (2015), p. 230.

[38] Saka et al. (2015), p. 230.

[39] Asongu et al. (2017), p. 880.

4.1 Process Followed to Become the EMU

The dream of a monetary union for the African continent has many similarities with the dream that existed in Europe before the EMU was established in 1992.[40] This gradual process of establishing the EMU over forty years will be outlined below.

The Treaty that established the European Economic Community ("EEC"), was signed in Rome on 25 March 1957, officially known as the EC Treaty, and entered into force on 1 January 1958.[41] To harmonize the monetary policies of the EU, article 105 of the EC Treaty required member states to coordinate their economic policies and to provide for cooperation between their appropriate administrative departments and between their central banks.[42] A Monetary Committee with advisory status was set up.[43] Each member state appointed 2 members to this Committee who had the task of promoting the coordination of the policies of the member states in the monetary field for the functioning of the common market.[44]

The Committee of the Governors of the Central Banks of Member States was created on 8 May 1964 by a Council decision wherein the governors were authorised to collaborate and exchange information.[45] A Council decision of 22 March 1971 obliged the Member States and central banks to co-ordinate their monetary and borrowing policies.[46] In 1972, the Heads of State of various countries approved the objective of gradual realisation of a monetary union.[47] In 1979 the Exchange Rate Mechanism was set up and that marked the first state of the European Monetary System.[48] In 1989 the Delors Report, requested by the European Council, proposed concrete stages towards a monetary union.[49] The report set out the conditions for a monetary union, namely total and irreversible convertibility of currencies; complete liberalisation of capital transactions; full integration of banking and other financial markets; the elimination of margins of fluctuation, and the irrevocable locking of exchange rate parities.[50]

The first stage in achieving the EMU started on 1 July 1990 after a decision by the European Council that exchange control in the EEC would be abolished,

---

[40] Vourexakis (2011), p. 1; Afxentiou (2000), p. 245.

[41] Scheller (2004).

[42] Art 105 EC Treaty.

[43] Scheller (2004), p. 21.

[44] Art 105 EC Treaty.

[45] De Lhoneux and Louis (1990), p. 9.

[46] De Lhoneux and Louis (1990), p. 9. Decision no. 71/142.

[47] De Lhoneux and Louis (1990), p. 8.

[48] Vourexakis (2011), p. 1.

[49] De Lhoneux and Louis (1990), p. 10.

[50] De Lhoneux and Louis (1990), p. 11.

liberalising capital movements between countries.[51] The EC Treaty was amended by the Treaty on European Union (EU Treaty), which was signed in Maastricht on 7 February 1992 (the "Maastricht Treaty") to establish the European Community from what was previously the EEC.[52] The treaty set down the criteria and final timetable for a full EMU in Europe by 1999/2002 as proposed by the 1988 Delors Commission Report.[53] In the Maastricht Treaty, it was agreed that various convergence criteria had to be satisfied by countries before entry into the union.[54] Convergence criteria that had to be satisfied were inflation convergence, interest rate convergence, no devaluation of the currency two years before entry into the union, and budgetary norms such that the deficit in the government's current account should not exceed 3% in any fiscal year budget as that could threaten price stability.[55] To adhere to the inflation convergence criteria, many countries like Spain and Italy applied strict disinflationary policies based on the German model until 1992.[56] De Lhoneux and Louis mentioned that the three most necessary conditions for a monetary union, using a single currency, are the following:

> total and irreversible convertibility of currencies; complete liberalisation of capital transactions and full integration of banking and other financial markets; elimination of margins of fluctuation and the irrevocable locking of exchange rate parities.[57]

The second stage of the EMU began on 1 July 1990 when the European Monetary Institute, as a predecessor for the ECB, was established and exchange controls were abolished.[58] The third stage of the EMU began in 1999 when the irrevocable fixing of conversion rates of the currencies used by the countries in the Eurozone was adopted and ceased to exist with the adoption of a single currency.[59]

The expanding proposed membership of the European Community (EC) and the European Monetary Union (EMU) led thereto that the European currency

[51] De Lhoneux and Louis (1990), p. 9; Vourexakis (2011), p. 1.

[52] Scheller (2004), p. 21; See also Treaty on European Union.

[53] Vourexakis (2011), p. 1.

[54] De Grauwe (1996), pp. 1091 and 1095.

[55] De Grauwe (1996), pp. 1093 and 1096.

[56] De Grauwe (1996), p. 1096.

[57] De Lhoneux and Louis (1990), p. 11.

[58] Vourexakis (2011), p. 1.

[59] Vourexakis (2011), p. 1.

(that was only named the Euro later and introduced on 1 January 1999) becoming a dominant world currency.[60]

4.2 Comments on Convergence Criteria in the EMU

It was suggested that less emphasis should be on convergence requirements and more on ensuring that the future European Central Bank maintained price stability.[61] Some authors proposed that countries that do not satisfy the convergence requirements should be accepted into the union, without any decision-making power in the ECB.[62]

The criteria of a deficit not larger than 3% is seen as a responsible budget economy but also very rigid in its implementation.[63] This is a criterion that will be difficult to adhere to for African countries. For example, South Africa's deficit for 2021 was 11.2% of GDP and 4.9% of GDP in 2024.[64] This would mean that South Africa would not be accepted into the monetary union at this stage, even considering the nominal GDP per capita in South Africa is the third highest in Africa.[65]

A problem that developed in the EMU, is that some countries refinanced their debt because of shortcomings like too much public spending, unproductive use of capital inflows, and loss of competitiveness.[66] These challenges could be faced in monetary unions in Africa. Member countries would have to adjust by implementing structural reform and budget consolidation.

Ideas that worked in forming the European Money Union, would not necessarily work in Africa, considering the smooth functioning of governance and judicial infrastructure that existed in the member states that became part of the EMU and that do not exist as such in all states in Africa.[67] Nevertheless, one can learn valuable lessons from the process followed in forming the EMU.

---

[60] Masson (1992), p. 181.

[61] De Grauwe (1996), p. 1099.

[62] Gros (1995), p. 21; De Grauwe (1996), p. 1099.

[63] De Grauwe (1996), pp. 1093 and 1096.

[64] National Treasury (2024).

[65] Statista (2023).

[66] Weber (2011), p. 236. Weber was the former president of the Deutsche Bundesbank and a visiting professor of economics at the University of Chicago Booth School of Business.

[67] Honohan and Thorsten (2007), p. 25.

5 Trade Agreements, Free Trade Areas, Regional Economic Communities, Customs Unions and Monetary Unions in Africa

The connection between trade agreements, free trade areas, regional economic communities, customs unions, and monetary unions in Africa, will be explored below.

Pelkmans referred to five stages of the integration theory, namely the free trade area, the customs union, the common market, the economic union and total economic integration.[68] He defined an economic union as the combination of a common market with some degree of harmonising of economic policies to remove discrimination due to disparities in the policies.[69] He regards these stages as distorted and twisted and labels them as "the dichotomy of economic integration theory".[70] He opines that the first three stages, namely that of a free trade area, a customs union, and a common market refer to economies where member governments do not intervene in the markets but only agree to break down distortions to obtain a free market over a larger economic space and are thus steps of pure market integration.[71] He regards the last two stages of economic union and total economic integration as pure forms of policy integration.[72]

A parallel initiative to the AfCFTA, the African Union Free Movement of Persons Protocol, was signed by the African Union in 2018, to decrease barriers for Africans in crossing borders by promoting free movement of persons over borders between African countries.[73] When cross-border movement becomes easier, it would add to trade, investment, cultural understanding, and scientific cooperation between countries in Africa.[74] Some regional blocs allow cross-border movements, even passport-free cross-border travel.[75]

There are many trade agreements in Africa, including African regional economic communities and unions, such as the West African Economic and Monetary Union, East African Community, and Southern African Development Community. Some countries are members in several economic communities and unions. The free trade areas, regional economic communities, customs unions, and monetary unions that were formed in Africa will be referred to below.

[68] Pelkmans (1980), pp. 334 and 343. A common market consists of one economic space in which goods, payments, corporate stock, bonds and other liquid and illiquid debt certificates, loans, labour services, services of the free professions, patents, and licences can all move freely.

[69] Pelkmans (1980), p. 334.

[70] Pelkmans (1980), p. 334.

[71] Pelkmans (1980), p. 334.

[72] Pelkmans (1980), p. 334.

[73] Hirsch (2023), p. 1.

[74] Hirsch (2023), p. 1.

[75] Hirsch (2023), p. 3.

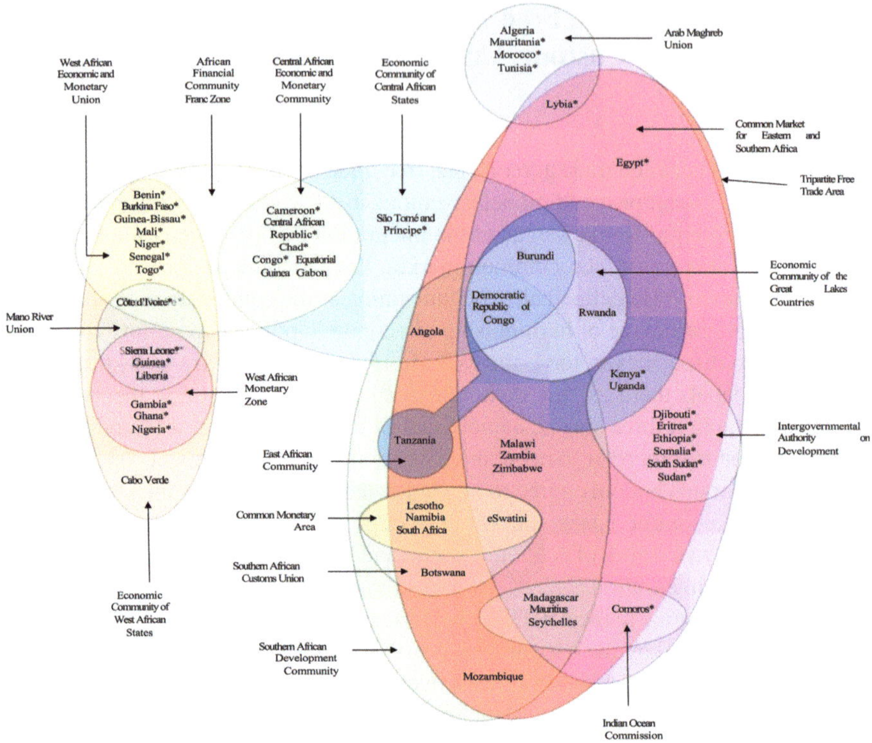

Source: Adapted from Economic Integration in Africa in Abrego ML et al. 'The African Continental Free Trade Area: Potential Economic Impact and Challenges'

5.1 *Free Trade Area*

A Free Trade Agreement (FTA) between countries is an agreement to reduce trade barriers like tariffs on imports and exports or the movement of goods and services across borders, with the prospect that it will lead to increased economic growth for the countries involved in the agreement.[76]

There is strength in numbers, therefore countries in Africa have a responsibility to be unified to address economic challenges as a group.[77] Half of the extremely poor people globally live in Sub-Saharan Africa, while only a small share of production and trade in the world comes from this region.[78] Considering that 54 of the 55 members of the African Union are part of the AfCFTA, it will be the largest free

[76] Daniel (2021), p. 11.

[77] Odeku and Rikhotso (2023), p. 112.

[78] Kassa et al. (2022), p. 3; Odeku and Rikhotso (2023), p. 113.

trade area in the world and present an opportunity for reform in the production and trade in Africa so that African firms can participate stronger in regional markets, leading Africa to catch up with the rest of the world.[79] Coulibaly, Rojas, Kee, and Mirza analysed the tariff barriers for trading in Africa in manufactured products and found that they are very high, thus the AfCFTA is a welcome initiative to promote trade in Africa by the possibility of breaking down tariffs.[80]

The AfCFTA negotiations were planned to take place in three phases where phase one, negotiations on trade in goods and services, are completed.[81] Phase two negotiations on investment, intellectual property rights, and competition policy are well on course and then phase three on digital trade and women and youth in trade will follow.[82]

5.2 *Regional Economic Communities*

More than 15 Regional Economic Communities ("RECs") with overlapping memberships already existed in Africa in 2019.[83] This is proof of the realisation of leaders in African states that isolation and poor relationships between states should be addressed to achieve higher economic growth and to form a basis for wider African integration.[84]

RECs are defined in the AfCFTA as the eight RECs recognised by the AU, namely, the Arab Maghreb Union ("UMA"); the Common Market for Eastern and Southern Africa ("COMESA"); the Community of Sahel-Saharan States ("CEN-SAD"); the East African Community ("EAC"); the Economic Community of Central African States ("ECCAS"); the Economic Community of West African States ("ECOWAS"); the Intergovernmental Authority on Development ("IGAD") and the Southern African Development Community ("SADC").[85] Other monetary unions in Africa include the West African Monetary Union ("UEMOA"), East African Monetary Union ("EAMU"), Southern African Monetary Union ("SAMU") and African Monetary Union ("AMU"). UEMOA was formed in 1964, incorporating countries that used the British Pound as currency[86] and other countries that had the CFA Franc from France as legal tender.[87]

[79] Kassa et al. (2022), p. 3; Odeku and Rikhotso (2023), p. 113.

[80] Coulibaly et al. (2022), p. 58.

[81] International Institute for Sustainable Development (2021).

[82] Daniel (2021), p. 44.

[83] Daniel (2021), p. 12.

[84] Odeku and Rikhotso (2023), pp. 114 and 117; Lehloenya and Mpya (2016), p. 95.

[85] Art 1(t) AfCFTA; African Union (2023).

[86] Saka et al. (2015), p. 231. The Anglophone countries are The Gambia, Ghana, Nigeria and Sierra Leone.

[87] Saka et al. (2015), p. 231. The Francophone countries are Benin, Burkina Faso (Upper Volta), Cote d'Ivoire, Guinea, Mali, Niger, Senegal and Togo.

The challenges are to transition from RECs to full implementation of the AfCFTA, to build the necessary institutions and follow up on regional strategies.[88]

5.3 *Customs Unions*

One of the general objectives of the AfCFTA is to lay the foundation for the establishment of a Continental Customs Union at a later stage, leading to a single African market for goods and services where people can freely move across the continent.[89] Deeper integration in the RECs is necessary to involve more African countries, and that could be achieved through amongst others, customs union arrangements.[90] Some authors propagate the need for a roadmap to develop AfCFTA into a continental customs union.[91]

Existing customs unions in Africa are the Southern African Customs Union ("SACU"), ECOWAS, CEMAC, and the EAC.

The SACU consists of South Africa, Botswana, Lesotho, Namibia, and Swaziland, which is a group of states that have agreed to charge the same import duties, based on those applicable in South Africa, and to allow free interchange of goods in the customs area, except for spirits, beer, and fortified wine.[92] SACU was governed for more than sixty years by the Customs Agreement of 29 June 1910.[93] On 12 December 1969 a new agreement, the Customs Union Agreement between the Governments of South Africa, Botswana, Lesotho, and Swaziland was signed.[94] This new agreement brought about a new economic partnership based on a review of what a customs union's purposes and consequences should be.[95] In 1986 the agreement was amended to give more independent monetary control to Lesotho and Swaziland.[96] In 2002, after South Africa's democracy in 1994 and the independence of Namibia, a new agreement, the 2002 SACU Agreement, was signed by the

[88] Kassa et al. (2022), p. 25.

[89] Art 3(d) AfCFTA. In art 1(j) AfCFTA it is determined that a customs union means the Customs Union at the continental level through adopting a common external tariff, as provided by the Treaty Establishing the African Economic Community of 1991; Daniel (2021), p. 8.

[90] Luke and Mabuza (2018), p. 1.

[91] Luke and Mabuza (2018), p. 6.

[92] Ramolefe and Sanders (1973), p. 83.

[93] Customs Agreement: Union of South Africa - Territories of Basutoland, Swaziland and the Bechuanaland Protectorate (Potchefstroom) High Commissioner's Notice 65 of 29 June 1910; Ramolefe and Sanders (1973), p. 83.

[94] Government Gazette of the Republic of South Africa, Regulation Gazette 1212 vol 54 2584 of 12 December 1969, Government Notice R3914; Ramolefe and Sanders (1973), p. 89.

[95] Ramolefe and Sanders (1973), p. 89.

[96] Fagbayibo (2013), p. 37; African Union and Economic Commission for Africa (2015), p. 185.

countries and this agreement implemented a joint-decision-making administrative body, the Secretariat, to oversee the SACU.[97]

The two most advanced regional blocks in Africa, according to Hirsch, are the EAC and ECOWAS.[98] Fifteen West African states signed a treaty on 28 May 1975 to establish ECOWAS.[99] ECOWAS was founded in 1975 and had a vision to become a single monetary zone.[100] Some of the objectives of the 1975 Treaty included the elimination of customs duties, the free movement of persons, capital, and services, and the harmonisation of agricultural and industrial policies.[101] In 1990 the Treaty was reviewed, and a new Treaty was agreed to in 1993.[102]

The EAC Treaty was signed in Kampala, Uganda on 6 June 1967 and was inaugurated in Arusha on 1 December 1967.[103] The EAC incorporated the EASCO.[104] The countries in the EAC have been moving towards adopting regional passports and citizens of Kenya, Rwanda and Uganda move freely between the three countries using either their national identity cards or the EAC passport because of the removal of mobility restrictions enacted by the Heads of State in 2013.[105] Free movement has enabled the EAC to make significant progress around social integration.[106] Kenya, Rwanda, and Uganda have also facilitated the right of establishment, the right of residence and access to the labour market for their citizens across the three states.[107] The Africa Visa Openness Report 2022 reports that 27% of all intra-African travel routes require no visa at all for citizens of African countries.[108]

The main distinction between customs unions and free trade areas is a common external tariff that exists in the case of a customs union where countries in a free trade area maintain their external tariff regimes.[109] Tariffs are the fees collected by a country's customs authorities.[110] The AfCFTA is a free trade agreement and not a customs union and thus member countries negotiate tariffs individually with countries outside the agreement and possibly at different rates.[111] In a customs union, all

---

[97] Fagbayibo (2013), p. 38; Alden C and Soko M (2005), pp. 370–371.

[98] Hirsch (2023), p. 3.

[99] Fagbayibo (2013), p. 34.

[100] Saka et al. (2015), p. 231. ECOWAS comprises of 15 countries in West Africa, namely Benin, Cote d'lvore, Gambia, Guinea, Liberia, Nigeria, Burkina Faso, Cape Verde, Ghana, Guinea-Bissau, Mali, Niger Senegal, Sierra Leone and Togo. Read more in paragraph VI below on the challenges experienced by ECOWAS to become a monetary union.

[101] Fagbayibo (2013), p. 35; Art 2 ECOWAS Treaty.

[102] Fagbayibo (2013), p. 35.

[103] Fagbayibo (2013), p. 41.

[104] Fagbayibo (2013), p. 41.

[105] Hirsch (2023), p. 3.

[106] Hirsch (2023), p. 3.

[107] Hirsch (2023), p. 4.

[108] Hirsch (2023), p. 4; Marinov (2014), p. 166.

[109] Clausing (2000), p. 419; Daniel (2021), p. 13.

[110] Daniel (2021), p. 11.

[111] Daniel (2021), p. 3.

members are bound by the rates as negotiated under the customs union.[112] Furthermore, the free movement of goods and services in an FTA is only allowed if the goods and services have originated within the FTA, whereas the free movement of all goods and services is allowed in a customs union.[113]

Doing away with tariffs between countries in Africa will lead to a bigger market on the continent that will allow participants to benefit from the economies of scale because of the larger market.[114] Where countries are unable to agree on a common external tariff, it would be more feasible to form a free trade area than a customs union.[115] It was found that when the average of the member countries' previous tariff levels are set as the common external tariff under a customs union, it will distort the market less, than when the member countries in an FTA maintain their tariff levels at levels before forming the FTA.[116]

5.4 Monetary Unions

Monetary unions were referred to in paragraph III above. In this paragraph, reference will be made to the monetary unions established in Africa. When a monetary union is compared with a customs union, it is seen that the former applies to more than just goods. It extends to the free movement of money and workers between member countries, which a customs union does not imply.

The CFA franc zone where the CFA franc is used as currency, consists of two monetary unions, namely the West African Economic and Monetary Union (WAEMU) which was built on the West African Monetary Union founded in 1973,[117] and the Central African Economic and Monetary Union (CAEMC)[118] both founded in 1994. A study done on convergence in the CFA zone, UEMOA, and CEMAC, found the absence of any convergence in the CEMAC zone; the UEOMOA and CFA zones reflect absolute convergence in liquid liabilities, banking activity, financial activity and financial size, although no form of convergence exists for inflation and GDP growth.[119] It is suggested by Asongu that member states in these monetary

[112] Daniel (2021), p. 13.

[113] Clausing (2000), p. 419; Daniel (2021), p. 13; Krueger (1997), p. 169. Rules of Origin specify the requirements that must be met for good to be regarded to originate in each country.

[114] Kassa et al. (2022), p. 3.

[115] Clausing (2000), p. 432.

[116] Clausing (2000), p. 420.

[117] International Monetary Fund (2023). The member countries in WAEMU are Benin, Burkina Faso, Côte D'Ivoire, Guinea-Bissau, Mali, Niger, Senegal and Togo.

[118] International Monetary Fund (2023). The member countries in CAEMC are Cameroon, Central African Republic, Chad, Republic of Congo, Equatorial Guinea and Gabon.

[119] Asongu (2012), p. 20.

unions should work on harmonising their differences so that monetary policies will be more effective.[120]

6 The Challenges of Forming a Monetary Union in Africa and the Convergence Criteria to Create a Monetary Union

There will always be challenges when countries consider forming monetary unions. Africa is no different from other regions in the world that envisaged the dream of a monetary union or that successfully formed such a union. Economic and monetary union in Africa could imply complete freedom of movement of persons, goods, services, and capital and fixed exchange rates. This could happen even before a single currency is accepted. To achieve it, would require a common monetary policy as well as compatibility with other economic policies of member states, especially in fiscal policies.

There are a few common objectives for a monetary policy for any country. These objectives will also apply to a shared monetary policy in a monetary union. These objectives include relative stability of the price level, the balance of payments equilibrium, optimal and relatively stable economic growth, and a high and relatively stable level of employment and utilisation of resources in general.[121]

The IMF opines that for more economic growth that could lead to the reduction of poverty in the countries that are included in these monetary unions, the governments should focus more on providing essential public services such as roads, bridges, schools health care, and education and less on being directly involved in the production, which private enterprise can do better than governments.[122]

ECOWAS had a vision to become a single monetary zone with one currency and a common Central Bank to accelerate socio-economic development in the region, but this vision has not been realised.[123] Despite various programmes of intervention like the ECOWAS Monetary Cooperation Programme that had the objective of improving the payments system under the West Africa Clearing House (now West African Monetary Agency—WAMA), and the adoption of a surveillance mechanism to monitor how member states coordinated their macro-economic and fiscal policies, these goals were not met because of obstacles like the problematic meeting of the strict convergence criteria and conducting effective monetary and fiscal policies.[124]

---

[120] Asongu (2012), p. 20.

[121] De Jager (2006), p. 164.

[122] International Monetary Fund (2023) 2.

[123] Adu et al. (2022), p. 13; Saka et al. (2015), p. 231.

[124] Saka et al. (2015), p. 231.

Saka, Onafowokan and Adebayo analysed convergence criteria in a proposed monetary union with a study of ECOWAS from 2000 to 2010.[125] They analysed the convergence criteria and the degree of convergence for the economies having such monetary union plans.[126] They found that there needs to be economic cooperation through policies that can enhance a vision of well-integrated economies as it is difficult to maintain a monetary union without effective fiscal policy mechanisms and political support.[127] Obstacles for countries addressing the convergence criteria are political will and commitment; lack of policy coordination and harmonization; different levels of development; distrust and suspicion between member countries; inadequate financial market and infrastructure; regulation and supervision problems and how to conduct effective monetary and fiscal policies.[128] According to the authors, the theory of convergence is in line with the neoclassical growth model, explaining that convergence exists when the income per capita in a weak economy increases more rapidly than that in a strong economy.[129] They found that there was convergence in income levels among the countries although the economic growth of the countries was at different levels.[130]

Some writers evaluated the impact of a single currency in ECOWAS and found that the trade gain from using a single currency is limited where countries are not closely integrated, and labour and capital cannot easily move between the countries.[131] It was found that non-tariff barriers such as transportation links and the cost of transport as well as customs checkpoints on highways and ports as well as customs being bureaucratic, had a huge effect on trade integration.[132]

For member states to create a real monetary union, there are essential requirements that must be met. Some of these requirements pose challenges for the African continent to become a monetary union.

6.1 The First Challenge: A Shared Monetary Policy

There are a few common objectives for a monetary policy for any country. These objectives will also apply to a shared monetary policy in a monetary union. These objectives include relative stability of the price level, balance of payments

[125] Saka et al. (2015), p. 239.
[126] Saka et al. (2015), p. 231.
[127] Saka et al. (2015), p. 231.
[128] Saka et al. (2015), p. 231.
[129] Saka et al. (2015), p. 235.
[130] Saka et al. (2015), p. 238.
[131] Adu et al. (2022), p. 15.
[132] Adu et al. (2022), p. 15.

equilibrium, optimal and relatively stable economic growth, and a high and relatively stable level of employment and utilisation of resources in general.[133]

Various pointers can be set as long-term monetary policy objectives of a shared monetary policy. Firstly, the primary monetary policy objective is the maintenance of stability of the price level of the applicable currency.[134] This should be conducted within an inflation-targeting framework where price stability as an objective focuses on the value of the currency.[135] The primary objective of the South African Reserve Bank ("SARB") is the protection of the value of the South African currency in the interest of balanced and sustainable economic growth in South Africa.[136] This constitutes the whole or forms part of the primary objective of the central banks of a vast number of countries all over the world.[137] In South Africa, the Government sets an explicit inflation target for the economy and the central bank acts independently to achieve the target, using instruments at its disposal to achieve this goal as well as the goal of price stability.[138]

Rules for sound public finances are of particular importance in a monetary union since the incentives for excessive borrowing are even greater in a monetary union than they are anyway. Weber mentioned that unsound public finances are the Achilles' heel of a monetary union.[139]

6.2 *The Second Challenge: A Small Deficit in Current Account*

A deficit on the government's current account not higher than 3% will be difficult to adhere to for African countries.[140]

6.3 *The Third Challenge: The Inflation Rate*

The criteria of an inflation rate measuring it in terms of the lowest inflation rate of countries concerned would be a problem in Africa since for example, the inflation rate in Benin was 1.5%, South Africa's 3.8%, Ethiopia's 28.3%, and Egypt's 38% in 2022/2023. For all the countries in Africa to be successful in obtaining inflation rates of 1.5% or even 5% would be unattainable at this stage. Very strict

[133] De Jager (2006), p. 164; Afxentiou (2000), p. 247.

[134] Panos Ibid at 250.

[135] De Jager (2006), p. 165.

[136] Sec 3(1) South African Reserve Bank Act 90 of 1989.

[137] De Jager (2006), p. 165.

[138] De Jager (2006), p. 165.

[139] Weber (2011), p. 239.

[140] De Jager (2006), p. 165.

disinflationary policies would be necessary to obtain such lower inflation rates and that would give rise to more unemployment which already is a big challenge in Africa.[141]

7 Conclusion

The AU has ambitions for Africa beyond AfCFTA, including a Customs Union and a Monetary Union.[142] To form a monetary union in Africa, the formulation of a shared monetary policy, a small deficit in the current account of all the countries as well as a common inflation rate will be necessary.

From the above analysis of the requirements for establishing a monetary union, it is shown that the success of regional monetary integration depends on improving efficiency in resource allocation through the development of competitive, market-based economies, shared monetary policy objectives, coordinated economic policies, macroeconomic policies geared towards financial stability and redistribution mechanisms to help less developed member states catch up. The hopes that exist that AfCFTA would lead to the establishment of a monetary union in Africa seem impossible at this stage. This contribution argues that an African Customs Union is more achievable than the dream of an African Monetary Union, and the focus should not be on the latter. This would be in accordance with the AfCFTA agreement that determines in Article 3(d) that one of the general objectives of the AfCFTA is to lay the foundation for the establishment of a Continental Customs Union at a later stage.

The major goals of the AfCFTA are to build a unified continental market for goods and services with unrestricted trade and investment, opening the door to faster creation of the Customs Union.

For regional integration in Africa, leading countries, namely Ethiopia (as leader of COMESA), Nigeria (as leader of ECOWAS) and South Africa (as leader of SADC), should take the lead in the integration process because of the advantage their sizes (based on population and GDP) give.[143] Export of products from African countries can be more diversified to include more than just the traditional exports such as coffee and cocoa, to expand to fruit and vegetables, wood and products from wood and chemicals.[144] This diversification can happen through regional cooperation, leading to regional and continental integration in Africa, and unlocking the benefits of trade for sustainable growth and economic development.

[141] Afxentiou (2000), p. 250.

[142] See sec IV(b) above.

[143] Coulibaly et al. (2022), p. 58.

[144] Ibid at 57.

References

Abego ML, de Zamaroczy M, Gursoy T, Nicholls GP, Perez-Saiz H, Rosas J (2020) The African Continental Free Trade Area: potential economic impact and challenges. https://www.imf.org/en/Publications/Staff-Discussion-Notes/Issues/2020/05/13/The-African-Continental-Free-Trade-Area-Potential-Economic-Impact-and-Challenges-46235

Adu R, Litsios I, Baimbridge M (2022) ECOWAS single currency: prospective effects on trade. J Int Money Finance 126:1–19

African Union (1991) Treaty Establishing the African Economic Community. https://au.int/sites/default/files/treaties/37636-treaty-TREATY_ESTABLISHING_THE_AEC-compressed.pdf

African Union (2000) Constitutive Act of the African Union. https://au.int/sites/default/files/pages/34873-file-constitutiveact_en.pdf

African Union (2018a) Protocol on the Establishment of the African Monetary Fund. https://au.int/en/treaties/protocol-establishment-african-monetary-fund

African Union (2018b) What is Agenda 2063? https://au.int/en/agenda2063

African Union (2023) Regional Economic Communities. https://au.int/en/recs

African Union and Economic Commission for Africa Assessing Regional Integration in Africa (2015) Agenda 2063 – The Africa We Want – Framework. https://au.int/sites/default/files/documents/33126-doc-framework_document_book.pdf

African Union Commission and Association of African Central Banks (2013) Joint AUC-AACB Strategy on the Establishment of the African Central Bank. https://au.int/sites/default/files/pages/32815-file-african_central_bank_joint_strategy_e.pdf

Afxentiou PC (2000) Convergence, the Maastricht criteria, and their benefits. Brown J World Aff 7:245–254

Agreement Establishing the African Continental Free Trade Area. https://au.int/sites/default/files/treaties/36437-treaty-consolidated_text_on_cfta_-_en.pdf

Alden C, Soko M (2005) South Africa's Economic Relations with Africa: Hegemony and its Discontents. J Mod Afr Stud 367:370–371

Asongu SA (2012) Real and monetary policy convergence: EMU crisis to the CFA zone. AGDI Working Paper, No. WP/12/033, African Governance and Development Institute: Yaoundé

Asongu SA, Nwachukwu J, Tchamyou V (2017) A literature survey on proposed African monetary unions. J Econ Surv 31:878–902

Bamigbola S (2024) Currency unions: definition, evolution, applications. https://www.supre-money.com/encyclopedia/currency-union

Clausing KA (2000) Customs unions and free trade areas. J Econ Integr 15:418–435

Coulibaly S, Rojas AF, Kee HL, Mirza D (2022) Nontariff measures and services trade restrictions in global value chains. In: Coulibaly S, Kassa W, Zouvak AG (eds) Africa in the new trade environment: market access in troubled times. Post-Print hal-03810306, HAL

Customs Agreement: Union of South Africa - Territories of Basutoland, Swaziland and the Bechuanaland Protectorate (Potchefstroom) High Commissioner's Notice 65 of 29 June 1910

Daniel M (2021) Trade Unions and Trade: A Guide to the African Continental Free Trade Agreement (AfCFTA). https://www.tradeunionsinafcfta.org/reports_and_publicat/trade-unions-and-trade-afcfta/. Accessed 15 July 2023

De Grauwe P (1996) Monetary union and convergence economics. Eur Econ Rev 40:1091–1101

De Jager J (2006) The South African Reserve Bank: an evaluation of the origin, evolution and status of a Central Bank (Part 2). SA Merc Law J 18:159–174

De Lhoneux E, Louis J (1990) Towards a European System of Central Banks. J Int Bank Law 5:8–14

Fagbayibo B (2013) Common problems affecting supranational attempts in Africa: analytical overview. Potchefstroom Electron Law J 16:31–69

Fe DC, Konin AC, N'Guessan AMM (2024) Economic convergence in the West African Economic and Monetary Union: a new analysis. Cogent Econ Finance 12(1):1–20

Fofack H, Mold A (2021) The AfCFTA and African trade – an introduction to the Special Issue. J Afr Trade 8:1–11

Fontana G, Kamara MSH (2023) Towards monetary union in the Economic Community of West African States (ECOWAS): better policy harmonisation and greater intra-trade are needed. J Policy Model 45(1):58–73
Gros D (1995) Towards a credible excessive deficits procedure. Centre for European Studies, Brussels, pp 1–21
Hirsch A (2023) Free movement of people across Africa: regions are showing how it can work. The Conversation 19 January 2023, pp 1–4
Honohan P, Thorsten B (2007) Making finance work for Africa. World Bank, Washington, DC
International Institute for Sustainable Development (2021) AfCFTA Protocol on Investment was concluded' Investment Treaty News, April 2021. https://www.iisd.org/itn/en/2022/12/26/afcfta-protocol-on-investment-was-concluded/
International Monetary Fund (2023) The Fabric of Reform. https://www.imf.org/external/pubs/ft/fabric/backgrnd.htm. Accessed 1 Oct 2023
James H (2023) Monetary union and the single currency. In: Adamski D, Amtenbrink F, de Haan J (eds) The Cambridge handbook of European monetary, economic and financial integration. Cambridge law handbooks. Cambridge University Press
Jazbhay AH (2019) African powerhouses: a Decolonial critique of Nigeria and South Africa's perceived economic and political strengths in the modern world-system. In: Tella O (ed) Nigeria-South Africa relations and regional hegemonic competence. Springer, pp 25–42
Kassa K, Edjigu HT, Zeufack AG (2022) The promise and challenge of the African Continental Free Trade Area. In: Coulibaly S, Kassa W, Zoufack AG (eds) Africa in the new trade environment: market access in troubled times. World Bank Group, Washington DC, pp 1–28
Kebalo L, Zouri S (2022) Monetary agreements reform and issue of the key fiscal convergence in the West African Economic and Monetary Union (WAEMU). J Econ Integr 37(1):30–53
Kempf H (2022) The fate of a monetary union. In: Monetary unions. Springer texts in business and economics. Springer, Cham
Krueger AO (1997) Free trade agreements versus customs unions. J Dev Econ 54:169–187
Le Cacheux J (2018) Single market and single currency: intended and unintended effects. In: Creel J, Laurent É, Le Cacheux J (eds) Report on the State of the European Union. Palgrave Macmillan, Cham
Lehloenya PM, Mpya MN (2016) Exploring the citizen inclusiveness and micro-economic empowerment aspects of regional integration in Africa. Law Democr Dev 20:91–105
Luke D, Mabuza Z (2018-11) The Tripartite Free Trade Area and the African Continental Free Trade Area: the case for consolidation. Addis Ababa, United Nations Economic Commission for Africa, pp 1–6
Marinov E (2014) Economic integration theories and the developing countries. https://eprints.nbu.bg/id/eprint/4653/1/15%20Marinov%2C%20E.%202014.%20Economic%20Integration%20Theories%20and%20the%20Developing%20Countries.pdf
Masson PR (1992) Exchange rate policy in a monetary union. In: Barth RC, Chong-Huey W (eds) Approaches to exchange rate policy. International Monetary Fund, Washington DC, pp 172–186
Moustafa E, El-Shal A (2024) An African exchange rate mechanism in the era of an African Continental Free Trade Area. In: Ocran MK, Abor JY (eds) The Palgrave handbook of international trade and development in Africa. Palgrave Macmillan, Cham
National Treasury (2024) Budget Review 21 February 2024. https://www.treasury.gov.za/documents/National%20Budget/2024/review/FullBR.pdf
Nubong GF (2021) Developmental regionalism and the success prospects of Africa's Continental Free Trade Area (CFTA): lessons from Africa's early integration experience. Afr Rev 13:123–138
Ocran MK, Sheefeni JPS, Oduro-Afriyie E (2022) Inflation, interest rates, and exchange rates in Africa. In: Abor JY, Adjasi CKD (eds) The economics of banking and finance in Africa. Palgrave Macmillan studies in banking and financial institutions. Palgrave Macmillan, Cham
Odeku KO, Rikhotso T (2023) African Continental Free Trade Area (AfCFTA): an impetus for Intra-African Trade Integration. J Afr Foreign Aff 10:111–131

Olayiwola W (2020) Governing the interface between the African Continental Free Trade Area and Regional Economic Communities Free Trade Areas: issues, opportunities and challenges. ECA Publications, Addis Ababa

Pelkmans J (1980) Economic theories of integration revisited. J Common Market Stud 18:333–354

Ramolefe AMR, Sanders AJGM (1973) The structural pattern of African regionalism. Comp Int Law J South Afr 6:82–105

Ryan J, Loughlin J (2018) Lessons from historical monetary unions - is the European monetary union making the same mistakes? Int Econ Econ Policy 15:709–725

Saka JO, Onafowokan IA, Adebayo AA (2015) Analysis of convergence criteria in a proposed monetary union: a study of the economic community of West African States. Int J Econ Financ Issues 5:230–239

Scheller HK (2004) The European Central Bank: history, role and functions. https://www.ecb.europa.eu/pub/pdf/other/ecbhistoryrolefunctions2004en.pdf. Accessed 12 Dec 2023

Statista (2023) African countries with the highest Gross Domestic Product (G) in 2022 22 September 2023. https://www.statista.com/statistics/1120999/gdp-of-african-countries-by-country/DP

Tweneboah G, Eshun R (2023) Integration of macroeconomic fundamentals in the West African Monetary Zone: a multi scale perspective. Cogent Soc Sci 9(1):1–19

Vourexakis A (2011) 'What are the Benefits and Challenges of the Economic and Monetary Union?' Interstate – J Int Aff 1:1–2

Weber AA (2011) Challenges for monetary policy in the European Monetary Union. Fed Reserve Bank St. Louis Rev 93:235–242

The Interplay Between Tax and the African Continental Free Trade Area (AfCFTA)

Lessons from the World Trade Organisation (WTO)

Jeffrey Owens, Ruth Wamuyu, and Rhodah N. K. Nyamongo

Abstract Despite having similar underlying principles, that is the elimination or reduction of barriers to trade, international tax and trade law have traditionally evolved separately Even so, these disciplines are intrinsically linked. First, while multinationals consider an array of factors when selecting an investment location, tax benefits and incentives, all factors remaining constant, influence the attractiveness of a location. Therefore, offering more attractive tax incentives based on the location or origin of investors would have a distortive effect on international trade. In addition, double taxation of investment income would impede the free movement capital. In this way, tax would constitute a barrier to trade. Unsurprisingly, this has led to an increase in tax related cases at the World Trade Organisation (WTO) dispute settlement body, which confirms that despite protests from tax policymakers and exemptions under trade laws, tax laws may be subject to WTO rules. In respect to the AfCFTA, the question arises on how African countries should react to the inevitable interaction between the two disciplines. In this regard, this chapter aims to evaluate the potential tax implications of the AfCFTA, considers the treatment of tax under WTO and specifically analyses the arguments raised in the tax-related cases at the WTO dispute settlement body. It considers the lessons from the WTO cases and proposes a regional response to the interaction between tax and trade.

J. Owens
OECD Centre for Tax Policy and Administration, and Vienna University Global Policy Center, Institute for Austrian and International Tax Law, Vienna University of Economics and Business, Vienna, Austria

R. Wamuyu (✉) · R. N. K. Nyamongo
Institute for Austrian and International Tax Law, Vienna University of Economics and Business, Vienna, Austria
e-mail: ruth.wamuyu.maina@wu.ac.at; rhodah.nyamongo@wu.ac.at

T. V. Warikandwa et al. (eds.), *Law and Policy of the African Continental Free Trade Area (AfCFTA)*, European Yearbook of International Economic Law,
https://doi.org/10.1007/978-3-032-01122-0_13

1 Introduction

While international tax and trade law have a similar underlying objective, which is to facilitate cross border trade and investment through elimination or reduction of barriers, these disciplines have traditionally evolved separately.[1] The two are architecturally distinct with "different structural and practical foundations which rarely interact."[2] Despite these fundamental differences in approach and structure, they are intrinsically linked.[3] First, tax benefits and incentives influence the attractiveness of a location for investment.[4] Therefore, multinationals would select locations offering the highest tax incentives in order to reduce their tax expense, all other factors remaining constant. Tax incentives based on the location or origin of investors would have a distortive effect on international trade. Second, double taxation of investment income would impede the free movement of capital as it increases the financial burden on investors and in turn reduces the ability to trade across borders.[5]

International trade agreements aim to eliminate measures that constitute barriers to trade by applying two fundamental principles: (i) states shall not treat domestic investors more favourably than foreign investors (national treatment (NT) obligation); and (ii) states should not treat investors from one state less favourably than investors from another state (most-favoured nation (MFN) obligation).[6] Tax measures may in some instances contradict these fundamental principles which may result in state-to-state conflicts where for example, tax measures are used to further protectionist policies.[7] To mitigate this risk the World Trade Organization (WTO) adopted a number of legal texts, most notably the Agreements on Subsidies and Countervailing Measures and Agreement on Trade-Related Investment Measures that prohibit tax measures which hinder trade liberalisation and advance protectionist measures.[8] This has led to an increase in tax related cases at the WTO dispute settlement body which confirms that despite protests from tax policymakers and exemptions under trade laws, both direct and indirect taxes are subject to WTO rules.[9] The conflicts arising in this respect are often difficult to settle as they require balancing the sovereign right to tax and trade liberalisation objectives.[10]

---

[1] For a detailed discussion on the nuanced differences in respect to the theoretical, structural, and practical elements of the laws see Farrell (2013), chapter 2, Van Thiel (2023), p. 213; Rubini (2023), p. 204.

[2] Lijun et al. (2021), pp. 267–294.

[3] Owens and Zhan (2018), pp. 1–8.

[4] Owens and Zhan (2018), pp. 1–8.

[5] See Farrell (2013), chapter 2.

[6] The Sovereign Power to Tax (2008), pp. 51–60.

[7] Daly (2016), pp. 1–54; Shome (2021), p. 53.

[8] Daly (2016), p. 3.

[9] See for instance the *United States - Tax Treatment for "Foreign Sales Corporations"* case discussed in Sect. 3.4.1.

[10] The Sovereign Power to Tax (2008), pp. 51–60.

At a regional level, states entering free trade areas agree to relinquish aspects of their sovereignty, including in respect to taxation, to pursue greater economic integration. For the European Union (EU), for example, efforts have been made to harmonize indirect taxes.[11] Though harmonization of direct taxes lags behind, Member States are required to comply with the principles and rules under the Treaty on the Function of the European Union (TFEU) specifically, the free movement principles and the state aid rules. The EU's approach to taxes recognises that if left unchecked, taxes may be barriers to trade and therefore, there is a need to consider regional harmonization of taxes.

The AfCFTA aims to establish a single market for goods and services that is facilitated through free movement of people and capital, eliminate tariff and non-tariff barriers to trade and establish a customs union.[12] Similar to the WTO agreements, the AfCFTA contains both the MFN and NT principles, dispute settlement mechanisms and exemptions to these principles. In respect to taxes, the Agreement does not contain the typical carve-outs seen under WTO Agreements though it does refer to these agreements in certain instances. Despite these carve-outs, experience at the WTO indicates that it is not possible to exclude taxation from the ambit of trade agreements. The question now arises on how African states will react to the inevitable interaction between the two disciplines. The AfCFTA may present an opportunity for harmonization of tax policy measures similar to the progress seen in the EU.

This chapter aims to evaluate the potential tax implications of the AfCFTA, considers the treatment of tax under WTO and specifically analyses the arguments raised in the tax-related cases at the WTO dispute settlement body. It considers the lessons learnt from the WTO cases and proposes a regional response to the interaction between tax and trade. This chapter is structured as follows: Sect. 2 considers the WTO treatment of taxation specifically, the impact of tax carve-outs and tax-related case law. Section 3 reviews the treatment of taxation under the AfCFTA highlighting the carve-outs that exist and the rules on subsidies and countervailing measures. Section 4 identifies the lessons learnt from the WTO experience and translates this into the AfCFTA context. Section 5 gives the conclusion and recommendations for the future interaction between AfCFTA and taxation with a focus on increased regional cooperation in regard to taxation and dispute settlement.[13]

---

[11] Fact sheet on the European Union, Indirect Taxation. https://www.europarl.europa.eu/factsheets/en/sheet/81/indirect-taxation.

[12] Art 3, of the AfCFTA Agreement of 2019.

[13] See policy briefs on the AfCFTA based on a joint research by the African Tax Administration Forum and the WU Global Tax Policy Centre on "The Tariff Revenue Implications of the AfCFTA" and "Understanding the Overlaps between Trade and Investment Obligations and Tax Measures." Though this chapter does not specifically tackle the interaction between taxation and investment agreements, UNCTAD have prepared a guide for tax policymakers, "International Investment Agreements and their Implications for Tax Measures" and the World Investment Report 2022 which may also be relevant for the reader.

1.1 *WTO Treatment of Taxation*

1.1.1 Development of the Relationship Between WTO and Taxation

The WTO Member States entered into agreements that cover goods, services and intellectual property rights.[14] These agreements set out "the principles of liberalization, and the permitted exceptions."[15] They contain commitments by states to eliminate trade barriers including lowering customs tariffs, lay out the dispute settlement procedure, offer special and differential treatment for developing states, set out non-discrimination obligations and provide mechanisms for annual reporting.[16] The history of the development of the relationship between WTO and taxation is considered in two phases: pre-1994 (trade under the General Agreement on Tariffs and Trade, 1947) and post-1994 (establishment of the WTO).

From 1948 to 1994, the General Agreement on Tariffs and Trade (GATT), signed in 1947, was the source of world trade rules though it was intended to be a provisional agreement and organization.[17] Pre-1985, the GATT was rarely invoked with respect to domestic tax rules.[18] The exception to this was the case instituted by the European Community and Canada against the United States (U.S.) on the grounds that its Domestic International Sales Corporation (DISC) regime was inconsistent with GATT obligations.[19] Corporations qualifying for this regime were "not subject to U.S. federal income tax on its current or retained export earnings."[20] These taxes were deferred without attracting interest for the period of deferral, contrary to the "general practice in the case of late payment of corporation income tax."[21] The U.S national treasury promoted the use of DISC and issued reports on increased exports as a result of the regime.[22] These characteristics of the regime led the panel to conclude that the DISC was an export subsidy that violated GATT obligations, a decision the U.S. disputed.[23] The U.S. filed counterclaims against exemption systems

[14] See GATT 1994, General Agreement on Trade in Services (GATS) and Trade-Related Aspects of Intellectual Property Rights (TRIPS).

[15] World Trade Organisation (2015), Chapter 2.

[16] World Trade Organisation (2015), Chapter 2.

[17] The GATT years: from Havana to Marrakesh. Available at https://www.wto.org/english/thewto_e/whatis_e/tif_e/fact4_e.htm.

[18] McDaniel (2001), p. 1627.

[19] United States Tax Legislation (DISC) Report of the panel presented to the council of representatives on 12 November 1976 (L/422-23S/98). Available at http://www.sice.oas.org/dispute/gatt/73discec.asp.

[20] United States Tax Legislation (DISC) Report (1976).

[21] United States Tax Legislation (DISC) Report (1976).

[22] McDaniel (2001), p. 1627.

[23] McDaniel (2001), p. 1627. For details on the United States arguments against the panel report see: General Agreement on Tariffs and Trade, Council of representatives: Report on Work Since the Thirty-First Session, L/4440, 18 November 1976.

adopted by European states.[24] However, these counterclaims were unsuccessful because the systems were applied to transactions that originated in the states not just foreign transactions.[25] In response to this case, the 1979 GATT Subsidies/Countervailing Measures Agreement expanded the definition of tax related export subsidies to include exemptions, deferrals and remissions targeted at exports.[26] In addition, the Agreement clarified that where an interest is charged on the deferred tax, it would not be considered an export subsidy.[27] In order avoid further objections to the DISC regime, the U.S. introduced an interest charge on the deferred tax in 1984. Therefore, though not as prevalent, during the pre-1994 period, the interaction between tax and trade had already existed and there were growing tensions over tax sovereignty and trade obligations, evident from the objections raised by the U.S.

As seen in the DISC case, tariffs and indirect taxes were subject to the GATT since its inception. However, only upon the conclusion of other multilateral agreements, following the eight-year-long Uruguay Rounds of negotiations, did this extend to direct taxation.[28] This followed growing concerns over the use of tax policies to further protectionist ideologies which hindered actualisation of trade liberalisation objectives.[29] This was particularly concerning as tariff barriers declined and states opted to adopt more non-tariff barriers which included taxes.[30] The multilateral agreements signed at the conclusion of the Uruguay round included the Agreement on Subsidies and Countervailing Measures (SCM), the Agreement on Agriculture and, the Agreement on Trade-Related Investment Measures (TRIMs).[31] In addition to the multilateral agreements, the WTO Trade Policy Review Mechanism (TPRM) ensures compliance with WTO agreements and provides for monitoring of tax policies, practices and measures of member states, including those not yet covered under WTO rules but which may still influence free trade and have effects similar to tax or non-tax measures prohibited by existing rules.[32] Therefore, while international trade and tax law evolved separately, from as far back as 1970s, there has been an appreciation that tax measures may potentially act as barriers to trade.

---

24 McDaniel (2001), p. 1628.

25 McDaniel (2001), p. 1628.

26 McDaniel (2001), p. 1628.

27 McDaniel (2001), p. 1628.

28 Daly (2000), p. 1056.

29 Daly (2000), p. 1056.

30 Daly (2000), p. 1056.

31 Daly (2000), p. 1056.

32 Daly (2000), p. 1056.

1.2 *Treatment of Tax Under Specific WTO Agreements*

1.2.1 GATT

A key foundation of the GATT is the obligation for non-discrimination expressed in the MFN and NT clauses. The MFN clause bars member states from granting preferential treatment of goods from any trading partners to the detriment of other trading partners. This therefore mandates that states must extend immediately and unconditionally any preferential treatment afforded to goods originating in or destined for one state to all other contracting states.[33] The NT obligation bars member states from applying "internal taxes and other internal charges, and laws, regulations and requirements affecting the internal sale, offering for sale, purchase, transportation, distribution or use of products, and internal quantitative regulations requiring the mixture, processing or use of products in specified amounts or proportion"[34] to domestic or imported products with the intention of protecting the domestic market. Contracting states are also barred from imposing, directly or indirectly, internal taxes or other internal charges to imported products in excess to those imposed on like domestic products.[35] In addition, states are required to ensure that imported products "shall be accorded treatment no less favourable than that accorded to like [domestic] products in respect of all laws, regulations and requirements affecting internal sale, offering sale, purchase, transportation, distribution or use."[36] Contracting states are allowed to impose a charge equivalent to an internal tax on the grounds that it is consistent with Article III (2)[37] of the Agreement. However, contracting states may rely on Article XX on general exceptions to defend the application of specific internal taxes if these were considered necessary to "secure compliance with laws or regulations which are not inconsistent with the provisions of [the] Agreement."[38]

The applicability of GATT on indirect taxes is generally agreed upon, given that the nature of these taxes makes them susceptible to border adjustments. However, while other WTO agreements discussed below clearly extend to direct and indirect taxation, the applicability of GATT to direct taxes continues to be a subject of international discourse.[39] Some authors argue that the Agreement's non-discrimination obligations relate only to indirect taxes charged on goods and do not impact income

[33] Art I: General Agreement on Trade and Tariffs (GATT). See also Daly (2000), p. 1057.

[34] Art III (1): General Agreement on Trade and Tariffs (GATT).

[35] Art III (2): GATT.

[36] Art III (4): GATT.

[37] This bars states from imposing internal taxes or other internal charges to imported products more than what is applied to domestic products.

[38] Art XX (d): GATT.

[39] For articles arguing that GATT applies only to indirect taxes see for example Pitschas (1995), p. 478.

taxes.[40] Other authors argue that direct taxes often have an impact on the pricing of products and in this way would have an indirect impact on the price of products seemingly contradicting the provisions of Article III (2).[41] More recent cases have affirmed the conclusion that the GATT NT obligation does extend to direct tax measures, see for instance the panel report in the United States – Tax treatment for Foreign Sales Corporations (FSC), discussed below, where the panel noted that:

> …. Thus, nothing in the plain language of the provision specifically excludes requirements conditioning access to income tax measures from the scope of application of Article III, which deals with "national treatment on internal taxation and regulation.[42]

1.3 *General Agreement on Trade in Services (GATS)*

Like GATT, the GATS includes MFN and NT obligations. However, unique to this agreement is that these obligations are extended to cover the treatment of both services and service suppliers. Under Article II, member states are required to accord immediately and unconditionally to both services and service suppliers of any other member states treatment that is no less favourable than that it accords to like services and service suppliers of any other state (MFN obligation). However, a measure inconsistent with this obligation may be adopted if it is listed in and meets the conditions of the Annex on Article II Exemptions.[43] In addition, tax measures covered under a bilateral treaty for the avoidance of double taxation or within similar binding provisions in other international agreements are excluded from application of the MFN obligation.[44]

Article XVII requires member states to "accord services and service suppliers of any other member, in respect of all measures affecting supply of services, treatment no less favourable than it accords to its own services and service suppliers."[45] Tax measures and tax incentives aimed at ensuring "equitable or effective imposition or collection of direct taxes in respect of services and service suppliers of other

[40] For an analysis of the different arguments see Beyer (2018), p. 548.

[41] Beyer (2018), p. 548.

[42] Panel report, United States – Tax Treatment for "foreign sales corporations" Recourse to Art 21.5of the DSU by the European Communities, WT/DS108/RW, 2001, para. 8.142.

[43] According to the Annex on Art II Exemptions, the Council for Trade in Services shall review all exemptions granted for a period of more than 5 years, examining whether the conditions creating the need for the exemption still prevail and determining the date of any further review. In any case, such exemptions should not exceed a period of 100 years and are subject to negotiation in subsequent trade liberalizing rounds.

[44] Art XIV (e), GATS.

[45] Art XVII (1) General Agreement on Trade in Services (GATS).

members"[46] are excluded from application of the NT obligation. This includes measures which:[47]

(i) apply to non-resident service suppliers in recognition of the fact that the tax obligation of non-residents is determined with respect to taxable items sourced or located in the Member's territory; or
(ii) apply to non-residents in order to ensure the imposition or collection of taxes in the Member's territory; or
(iii) apply to non-residents or residents in order to prevent the avoidance or evasion of taxes, including compliance measures; or
(iv) apply to consumers of services supplied in or from the territory of another Member in order to ensure the imposition or collection of taxes on such consumers derived from sources in the Member's territory; or
(v) distinguish service suppliers subject to tax on worldwide taxable items from other service suppliers, in recognition of the difference in the nature of the tax base between them; or
(vi) determine, allocate or apportion income, profit, gain, loss, deduction or credit of resident persons or branches, or between related persons or branches of the same person, in order to safeguard the Member's tax base.

These exceptions are subject to the condition that such measures are not applied in a manner that constitutes unjustifiable or arbitrary discrimination between member states or a disguised restriction on trade in services.[48]

1.4 Agreement on Subsidies and Countervailing Measures (ASCM) and Agreement on Trade-Related Investment Measures (TRIMs): Impact of the Agreements on Tax Incentives and Benefits

As mentioned in Sect. 1, tax reliefs and fiscal incentives may influence the selection of an investment location, all other factors remaining constant.[49] This has posed concerns in so far as such reliefs and incentives provide opportunities for tax arbitrage between jurisdictions, heightened tax competition and facilitated tax evasion.[50] Certain subsidies and trade-related investment measures including tax incentives constitute protectionist measures which are antithetic to the promotion of trade and economic development. These concerns were already noted in GATT 1947 that contained basic rules on subsidies under Article XVI. This provision requires members

[46] Art XIV (d) GATS.
[47] The Sovereign Power to Tax (2008), pp. 51–60; GATS, p. 295.
[48] Art XIV, GATS.
[49] Owens and Zhan (2018), p. 1.
[50] Owens and Zhan (2018), p. 1.

who implement subsidies, including income or price support, that have a direct or indirect impact on exports or imports report the subsidy to the contracting states.[51] In addition, export subsidies on primary products would only be allowable where they do not result in the state having more than an equitable share of the world export trade.[52] States were barred from implementing export subsidies on any product other than primary products that met the requirements set out.[53] As discussed in Sect. 2.1 the US-DISC case found that certain measures constituted export subsidies. Therefore, tax measures have long fallen under the definition of subsidies.

There was a substantial modification of the subsidies provisions following negotiations at the Uruguay round where negotiators reviewed Article VI and XVI of GATT with the aim of improving "GATT disciplines relating to all subsidies and countervailing measures that affect international trade."[54]As such, the new Agreement on Subsidies and Countervailing Measures (ASCM) was adopted. The Agreement regulates the provision of subsidies and provides for countervailing measures to offset harm caused by subsidized imports. This built on the existing GATT provisions and went a step further by providing a definition of a subsidy. Only specific subsidies, those available only to an enterprise or industry or group of industries or enterprises, are subject to the ASCM.[55] The agreement divides specific subsidies into three categories: prohibited subsidies (export and local content subsidies), actionable subsidies (not prohibited but subject to challenge because of adverse effect on the interests other member states) and non-actionable subsidies.[56] A subsidy is deemed to exist if:[57]

(a) (1) there is a financial contribution by a government or any public body within theterritoryofaMember(referredtointhisAgreementas"government"),i.e.where:

  (i) a government practice involves a direct transfer of funds (e.g., grants, loans, and equity infusion), potential direct transfers of funds or liabilities (e.g., loan guarantees;
  (ii) government revenue that is otherwise due is foregone or not collected (e.g., fiscal incentives such as tax credits);
  (iii) a government provides goods or services other than general infrastructure, or purchases goods;
  (iv) a government makes payments to a funding mechanism, or entrusts or directs a private body to carry out one or more of the type of functions

[51] Art XVI (1), GATT 1947.

[52] Art XVI (2), GATT 1947.

[53] Art XVI (4), GATT 1947.

[54] Launching of Uruguay Round: The most complex and ambitious programme of negotiations ever undertaken by GATT, GATT Newsletter Focus No. 41, October 1986. Available at https://docs.wto.org/gattdocs/q/GG/GATTFOCUS/41.pdf at p. 4.

[55] Art 2, Agreement on Subsidies and Countervailing Measures (ASCM).

[56] See Arts 3, 5, 6 and 8, ASCM for a breakdown of the three categories. For a summary of the ASCM provisions see also Michalek (2004), pp. 25–38.

[57] Art 1 (1.1), ASCM.

illustrated in (i) to (iii) above which would normally be vested in the government and the practice, in no real sense, differs from practices normally followed by governments; or

(a) (2) there is any form of income or price support in the sense of Article XVI of GATT 1994; and

(b) a benefit is thereby conferred.

This applies to both direct and indirect tax measures.[58] Therefore, any specific tax credits or incentives offered on the condition of exportation or local content requirements would be prohibited. In addition, if specific tax incentives or credits are not prohibited subsidies but they cause adverse effects[59] to the interests of other members, they may be challenged. However, it is more difficult to prove that an actionable subsidy results in adverse effects, which explains why tax measures have rarely been challenged on these grounds.[60]

As part of the Uruguay round, negotiators agreed to an examination of existing GATT provisions "related to trade restrictive and distorting effects of investment measures [and] elaborate as appropriate, further provisions that may be necessary to avoid such adverse effects."[61] This resulted in the adoption of the Agreement on Trade -Related Investment Measures (TRIMS) which only applies to measures affecting trade in goods. The Agreement prohibits member states from applying measures that are inconsistent with provisions of GATT on national treatment (Article III) and the general elimination of quantitative restrictions (Article XI). Though no definition of "trade-related investment measures" is provided, the annex to the Agreement provides an illustrative list of measures inconsistent with Article III (4) and Article XI (1) of GATT. The prohibited measures can be categorized into benefits that are conditional upon local content requirements; restrictions on a firm's ability to import conditional upon its export performance; foreign exchange balancing requirements or restrictions; and domestic sales requirements involving restrictions on exports.[62] Measures that are inconsistent with Article III and XI of the GATT can be mandatory or enforceable under domestic law for which compliance is necessary for Member States to obtain the advantage.[63] Although the term

[58] Annex I of the ASCM on the illustrative list of export subsidies refers to both direct and indirect incentives offered subject to exportation. "Indirect taxes" are defined as sales, excise, turnover, value-added, franchise, stamp, transfer, inventory, and equipment taxes, border taxes, and all taxes other than direct taxes and import charges. "Direct taxes" are defined as taxes on wages, profits, interest, rents, royalties, and all other forms of income, and taxes on the ownership of real property The agreement however excludes refunds or remission of duties or indirect taxes on goods upon exportation.

[59] Arts 5 and 6 of the ASCM define adverse effects.

[60] Daly (2016), p. 21.

[61] Launching of Uruguay Round: The most complex and ambitious programme of negotiations ever undertaken by GATT, GATT Newsletter Focus No. 41, October 1986. Available at https://docs.wto.org/gattdocs/q/GG/GATTFOCUS/41.pdf at p. 4.

[62] Daly (2016), p. 25.

[63] Annex to the Agreement on Trade Related Investment Measures.

advantage is not defined, it is understood to encompass all types of advantages, including tax relief.[64] TRIMS does not prevent states from attaching export performance requirements to tax or non-tax incentives for investment[65] nor does it prevent local ownership requirements or requirements on the amount and type of research and development activities to be carried out locally.[66]

Article XV of GATS notes the potential distortive impact of subsidies and calls on member states to have further negotiations to develop multilateral agreements that prevent these negative effects.[67] However, progress in this respect has been limited and a special agreement on subsidies for services has yet to be adopted.[68] In the meantime, subsidies on services are regulated by GATS as they are subject to the MFN and NT obligations under the agreement.

1.5 Tax-Related Cases at the WTO Dispute Settlement Body

1.5.1 Direct Tax: United States – Tax Treatment for "Foreign Sales Corporations"

The European Communities (EC) challenged the U.S. tax exemptions for foreign sales corporations (FSC) in respect of their export-related foreign-source trade income. This regime was enacted to repeal the previously challenged deferral system under the DISC regime and replace it with a partial exemption system.[69] According to the Panel, the carve out of foreign source income attributable to exports from the worldwide income tax system as allowed by the FSC constituted a prohibited subsidy contingent on exporting, violating Article 3(1)(a) of the ASCM.[70] The fact that the U.S. carved out an exception from the way it normally taxed income from exports rendered this measure an export subsidy.[71] Additionally, this measure was inconsistent with the obligations of the U.S. under Articles 3 and 8 of the Agreement on Agriculture. The Panel recommended that the U.S. withdraw the FSC subsidies without delay. On appeal, the Appellate Body (AB) upheld the panels classification of the tax treatment of FSC as an export subsidy under the ASCM.[72]

---

[64] Daly (2016), p. 26.

[65] Daly (2016), p. 26. In addition, such requirements are provided for under the ASCM.

[66] Daly (2016), p. 26.

[67] Art XV, GATS.

[68] Grosso (2008).

[69] Turki (2010).

[70] Panel Report, United States – Tax Treatment for "Foreign Salles Corporations", WT/DS108R, 1999.

[71] Panel Report, United States – Tax Treatment for "Foreign Salles Corporations", WT/DS108R, 1999, para. 7.122.

[72] Appellate Body Report: United States – Tax Treatment for "Foreign Sales Corporations", WT/DS108/AB/R, February 2000.

In response to the AB report, the U.S. enacted the FSC Repeal and Extraterritorial Income Exclusion Act of 2000 (the "ETI" Act) to phase out the FSC benefits. The ETI Act however provided benefits that were conditional upon the sale of goods outside the U.S. and the use of less than 50% imported inputs. The EC challenged this measure requesting for authorisation to take appropriate countermeasures and suspend concessions. The Panel for the EC Article 21.5 application, compared Article III:4 GATT and Article XVII of GATS (regulating the national treatment under GATS) and pointed out that one of the general exceptions under GATS allows states to deviate from the national treatment obligation 'provided that the difference in treatment is aimed at ensuring the equitable or effective imposition or collection of direct taxes in respect of services or service suppliers of other Members.'[73] According to the panel, there would be no need to impose such a requirement if direct taxation is excluded from the scope of the GATS in the first place.[74] As such, the panel confirmed that direct tax measures were subject to the NT obligations in GATS. The AB, upholding the Panel's finding, stated that the ETI Act still granted subsidies conditional on export performance.[75] The U.S. argued that the ETI Act was a method of avoiding double taxation of "foreign sourced income" under the fifth sentence of footnote 59 of the ASCM. However, the AB held that the ETI measure was not confined to exemption of "foreign-source income" and certain aspects extended exemptions to domestic-source income, contrary to the intention of footnote 59.[76] Additionally, the AB upheld that the ETI Act, by attaching access to the tax exemption to the use of domestic products, affected the internal use of imported products as compared to like domestic products within the meaning of Article III:4 of GATT.[77] The AB found that this resulted in less favourable treatment of imported products and was therefore inconsistent with the NT obligation.[78]The ETI Act included certain transitional rules extending the application of the prohibited FSC provisions. The AB therefore upheld the Panel's finding that the US had failed to implement the DSB's recommendations to withdraw the export subsidies (FSC) and could find no legal basis for extending the period for the withdrawal of the subsidies.[79] The U.S. later enacted new legislation, the American Jobs Creation Act (AJCA) 2004 to repeal and replace the FSC/ETI. The AJCA maintained prohibited FSC and ETI subsidies through transitional and indefinite grandfathering measures. In response, the EC filed its second Article 21.5 of DSU application, where the AB found that the U.S. had failed to fully implement fully the DSB recommendations

[73] Art XIV (d) GATS.

[74] Panel Report, *US – FSC (Article 21.5 – EC)*, para. 8.143.

[75] Appellate Body Report: United States- Tax Treatment for "Foreign Sales Corporations" Recourse to Article 21.5 of the DSU by the European Communities WT/DS108/AB/RW, January 2002.

[76] Appellate Body Report: United States (2002) para. 185.

[77] Appellate Body Report: United States (2002) para. 213.

[78] Appellate Body Report: United States (2002) paras. 220–222.

[79] Appellate Body Report: United States (2002) para. 231

and rulings to withdraw prohibited subsidies and to bring its measures into conformity with its obligations.[80]

1.5.2 Tariffs and Sales Taxes: Indonesia – Certain Measures Affecting Automobile Industry[81]

The measures in dispute (as challenged by EC, Japan and the US) were "The 1993 Programme" which provided import duty reductions or exemptions on imports of automotive parts based on the local content percent and "The 1996 National Programme" which provided benefits such as luxury tax exemption or import duty exemption to qualifying cars (including local content) or Indonesian car companies.[82] The purpose of these programmes was to assist the development of the domestic car industry. According to the Panel, the 1993 Programme constituting the local content requirement violated Article 2(1) of the TRIMS Agreement—these measures were trade-related investment measures because they were intended to increase investment in the domestic industry and had local content requirements that, by definition favor domestic products.[83]As provided in the illustrative list in the Annex to TRIMS, the tax and treaty benefits were contingent on meeting the local content requirement and therefore, these measures were a violation of Article 2.1 of TRIMS Agreement.[84] The Panel also found that the sales tax benefits related to the measures violated the NT obligation under Article III:2 of GATT noting that an imported motor vehicle would be taxed in excess of a like domestic vehicle and imported vehicles that are directly or substitutable domestic vehicles were not similarly taxed to protect the domestic industry.[85] In addition, the exemptions accorded to Korean imports were found to be in violation of Article I:1 of GATT as they were not accorded "unconditionally" to "like" products from other member states.[86] Finally, the tariff and luxury sales exemptions offered through the national car programme were found to be specific subsidies under Article 1 and 2 of the ASCM and

---

[80] Appellate Body Report: United States- Tax Treatment for "Foreign Sales Corporations" Second Recourse to Article 21.5 of the DSU by the European Communities, WT/DS108/AB/RW2, February 2006 at para. 96.

[81] Panel Report: Indonesia – Certain Measures Affecting the Automobile Industry, WT/DS54R; WT/DS55R; AT/DS59R; WT/DS64R, July 1998.

[82] WTO, Summary of the key findings of the dispute: Indonesia – Certain Measures Affecting the Automotive Industry. Available at https://www.wto.org/english/tratop_e/dispu_e/cases_e/1pagesum_e/ds55sum_e.pdf.

[83] Panel Report: Indonesia – Certain Measures Affecting the Automobile Industry, (1998) para. 14.80–14.82.

[84] Panel Report: Indonesia – Certain Measures Affecting the Automobile Industry, (1998), para. 14.90–14.91.

[85] Panel Report: Indonesia – Certain Measures Affecting the Automobile Industry, (1998), para 14.116.

[86] Panel Report: Indonesia – Certain Measures Affecting the Automobile Industry, (1998), para 14.147.

caused serious prejudice to the interests of the EC through price undercutting of the Indonesian vehicle owing to the tariff and tax benefits.[87]

1.5.3 Internal Taxes: Japan – Taxes on Alcoholic Beverages

The measure in dispute was the Japanese Liquor Tax Law that established a system of internal taxes applicable to all liquors at different tax rates depending on which category they fell within. The domestic liquor, *shochu*, was taxed at a lower rate than vodka, other white spirits, cognac, rum, and whisky. The complainants, Canada, the EC, and the US alleged that this tax system discriminated against the spirits exported to Japan in violation of Japan's obligations under the Article III of GATT on NT.[88]

With regards to the first sentence of Article III: 2 on like products, the AB upheld the Panel's finding that imported vodka and domestic shochu were like products and vodka was taxed in excess of shochu in violation of the provision.[89] With regards to Article III: 2 second sentence, the AB held that shochu and whisky, brandy, rum, gin, genever, and liqueurs were directly competitive and substitutable and that these products were not similarly taxed so as to afford protection to domestic production in violation of Article III:2.[90]

1.5.4 Defensive Tax Measures: Argentina – Measures Relating to Trade in Good and Services

Argentina adopted 'blacklisting' measures in response to the Panama paper scandal.[91] Panama challenged eight financial, taxation, foreign exchange and registration measures imposed by Argentina on states classified as 'non-cooperative' jurisdictions.[92] The main question in this case was whether Argentina could differentiate between services and services suppliers from cooperative and non-cooperative jurisdictions. The panel found that these measures were inconsistent with the MFN obligation under Article II: 1 of the GATS because difference in treatment was

---

[87] Panel Report: Indonesia – Certain Measures Affecting the Automobile Industry, (1998), para 14.255–14.256.

[88] For further details on the factual background see: Panel Report: Japan – Taxes on Alcoholic Beverages, WT/DS8/R; WT/DS10/R; WT/DS11/R, July 1996.

[89] Appellate Body Report: Report: Japan – Taxes on Alcoholic Beverages, WT/DS8/AB/R; WT/DS10/AB/R; WT/DS11/AB/R, October 1996 at pp. 22–23.

[90] Appellate Body Report: Report: Japan – Taxes on Alcoholic Beverages (1996), pp. 25–30.

[91] This was a 2016 investigation that was centred on more than 11.5 million financial and legal records that exposed systems that enabled crime, corruption, and wrongdoing, hidden by offshore companies. Available at https://www.icij.org/tags/panama-papers/.

[92] Panel Report: Argentina – Measures Relating to Trade in Goods and Services, WT/DS453/R, September 2015, p. 15.

based on origin of the services and service suppliers—that is whether originating jurisdiction was cooperative or non-cooperative.[93] In addition, the tax measures did not fall within the exceptions under Article XIV (c) of GATS because their application constituted arbitrary and unjustifiable discrimination.[94] On appeal, the AB reversed the Panel's finding on likeness on the basis of an error by the Panel in applying the 'likeness' test, however, it refrained from explicitly taking a position on whether cooperative and non-cooperative jurisdictions service providers are 'like'.[95] The AB also found that the Panel had adopted an erroneous legal standard in regard to "treatment no less favorable" which if applied, meant that "regulatory aspects" identified by the implementing state could convert "less favorable treatment" to "treatment no less favorable."[96] Though the AB failed to give further insight on the issue of likeness, the case affirms that that any differentiation between services and services suppliers must be justifiable and should not lead to interference with trade obligations.

1.6 Conclusion

What is clear from these cases, is that both direct and indirect tax measures have and continue to be challenged at the WTO. States retain the right to determine internal taxes subject to the obligations under the WTO agreements. In cases where there is differential treatment, states must ensure that such treatment is justifiable under the exceptions provided within WTO agreements. Though the WTO is not able to force a state to change its laws, the agreements allow for retaliatory measures for non-compliance.[97] Similar concerns are evident in agreements that are structured in the same way as WTO agreements. In any case, states entering into trade agreements must accept the "constraints" on tax sovereignty to realize the benefits which international trade accords.[98]

[93] Panel Report: Argentina – Measures Relating to Trade in Goods and Services (2015) para. 8.

[94] Panel Report: Argentina – Measures Relating to Trade in Goods and Services (2015) para. 8.2 (d).

[95] Appellate Body Report: Argentina – Measures Relating to Trade in Goods and Services, WT/DS453/AB/R, April 2016.

[96] Appellate Body Report: Argentina – Measures Relating to Trade in Goods and Services (2016) para. 6.151.

[97] Schott (1996), p. 6.

[98] Schott (1996), p. 6.

2 The AfCFTA Treatment of Taxation

The AfCFTA legal texts cover trade in goods, trade in services, investment, intellectual property rights and competition policy.[99] Notably, in the event of any conflict or inconsistency between the AfCFTA and any regional agreement, the AfCFTA takes precedence to the extent of this specific inconsistency.[100]Article 3 of the AfCFTA Treaty outlines the general objectives of the AfCFTA which include the creation of a single market for goods and services and the movement of persons; creation of a liberalised market for goods and services; contribution to the movement of capital and natural persons and facilitate investments and the establishment of a Continental Customs Union. More specifically, Article 4(a) envisions specific outcomes including the progressive elimination of tariffs and non-tariff barriers to trade in goods; progressive liberalisation of trade in services; co-operation on all trade-related areas and co-operation on customs matters and the implementation of trade facilitation measures. These objectives will inevitably impact both direct and indirect taxation matters that may have an impact on the operationalisation of the AfCFTA.

The more immediate impact of the AfCFTA is the reduction of tax revenue. The actual revenue loss will vary from state to state depending on a state's reliance on tariff and import duties revenue from intra-African trade.[101] Therefore, smaller landlocked states are likely to see higher levels of revenue loss. In any case, the long-term economic benefits of the AfCFTA are expected to mitigate these initial revenue losses.[102] A more medium to long-term concern for states will be the interaction between trade obligations within AfCFTA agreements and domestic tax measures. This section considers the main obligations and the treatment of taxation under the AfCFTA legal framework.

Similar to the WTO, the key tenets of the AfCFTA are the principles of non-discrimination (NT and MFN) and reciprocity which are aimed at eliminating trade distortions.[103] AfCFTA member states are obliged to accord to each other, on a reciprocal basis, preferences that are no less favourable than those accorded to non-member third party states.[104] Further, and in line with the MFN treatment under the protocol on trade in goods, state parties can conclude or maintain preferential trade arrangements "with third parties provided that such arrangements do not impede or frustrate the objectives of [the] protocol, and that any advantage, concession or priv-

[99] Art 6, AfCFTA Agreement.

[100] Art 19(1), AfCFTA Agreement.

[101] The Tariff Revenue Implications of the African Continental Free Trade Area: A Joint Research Initiative of African Tax Administration Forum and the WU Global Tax Policy Center, Institute for Austrian and International Tax Law, WU (Vienna University of Economics and Business) at p. 7. Doi: file:///C:/Users/rmaina/Downloads/ATAF_Tariff_Policy_ENG_V2.pdf.

[102] Ibid, p. 7.

[103] Art 5, AfCFTA Agreement. On the removal of trade distortions see Daly (2016), p. 3.

[104] Art 18(1), AfCFTA Agreement.

ilege granted to [third parties] under such arrangements [are] extended to other state parties on a reciprocal basis."[105] For trade in services, state parties are obliged to "accord immediately and unconditionally to services and service suppliers of any other state party, treatment that is no less favourable than treatment that it accords to like services and service suppliers of any third party."[106] Additionally, state parties are obliged to extend any preferential treatment accorded to third parties under a subsequent preferential agreement, in accordance with Article V of GATS, to all other state parties on a reciprocal and non-discriminatory basis, provided that the agreement does not impede objectives of the Protocol.[107]

With regards to national treatment, state parties are obliged to accord products imported from other state parties' treatment that is no less favourable than that accorded to like domestic products of national origin after the imports have been cleared by customs.[108] Similarly, for trade in services, state parties shall extend to services and service suppliers of any other state party treatment that is no less favourable than what is applicable to domestic like services and service suppliers.[109] A state party would meet this requirement by "according to services and service suppliers of any other state party either formally identical treatment or formally different treatment to what it applies to its own like services and service suppliers."[110] Treatment would be regarded as less favourable if it alters the conditions of competition in favour of domestic services or service suppliers of the state party in comparison to and to the detriment of the like foreign services or service suppliers.[111]

2.1 *Tax Carve-Outs*

2.1.1 Protocol on Trade in Goods

Member states are required to progressively eliminate import duties or charges and not to impose any new duties on goods originating from other state parties.[112] According to Article 7(3) of the Protocol, import duties include any duty or charge of any kind imposed on or in connection with importation but does not include the following:

i) charges equivalent to internal taxes imposed consistently with Article III (2) of GATT 1994 and its interpretative notes in respect of like or directly competitive

[105] Art 4 (2), Protocol on Trade in Goods.
[106] Art 4(1), Protocol on Trade in Services.
[107] Art 4(2), Protocol on Trade in Services.
[108] Art 5, Protocol on Trade in Goods.
[109] Art 20, Protocol on Trade in Services.
[110] Art 20(2), Protocol on Trade in Services.
[111] Art 20(3), Protocol on Trade in Services.
[112] Art 7(1), Protocol on Trade in Goods.

or substitutable goods of the state party or in respect of goods from which imported goods have been manufactured or produced in whole or in part,

ii) antidumping or countervailing duties imposed in accordance with Articles VI, and XVI of GATT 1994 and the WTO Agreement on SCM and Article 17 of this Protocol which provides for the same, and

iii) duties or levies imposed in relation to safeguards, in accordance with Articles XIX of GATT 1994, the WTO Agreement on Safeguards and Articles 18 and 19 of this Protocol; and

iv) other fees or charges imposed consistently with Article VIII of GATT 1994.

For purposes of protecting an infant industry that has strategic importance domestically and having taken reasonable steps to overcome difficulties related to the industry, state parties may impose measures to protect such an industry on a non-discriminatory basis and for a specified period.[113]

2.1.2 Protocol on Trade in Services

Notwithstanding the MFN rule, the Protocol permits state parties to conduct negotiations and agree to liberalisation of trade in services for specific sectors or sub-sectors in accordance with the Protocol.[114] However, the states shall afford other member states an opportunity to negotiate such preferences on a reciprocal basis.

Similar to GATS, the Protocol permits the adoption or enforcement of measures that are inconsistent with NT provided that such difference in treatment is aimed at ensuring *equitable or effective* imposition or collection of direct taxes in respect of services or service suppliers of other states parties.[115] Footnote 7 of the Protocol provides an illustrative list of measures that are aimed at ensuring equitable or effective imposition or collection of direct taxes which is identical to the GATS list under footnote 6.

Additionally, parties can also adopt or enforce measures inconsistent with MFN obligation where the difference in treatment results from an agreement on avoidance of double taxation or the provisions on the avoidance of double taxation in other international agreements or arrangements to which the state parties are bound.[116]

[113] Art 24(1), Protocol on Trade in Goods.

[114] Art 4(3), Protocol on Trade in Services.

[115] Art 15 (d), Protocol on Trade in Services.

[116] Art 15 (e), Protocol on Trade in Services.

2.2 *Rules on Subsidies and Countervailing Measures*

The Protocol on Trade in Services provides for the issuance of subsidies by state parties. State parties are permitted to use subsidies in relation to their development programmes.[117] In the event that a state party finds that it is adversely affected by a subsidy of another state party, it may request consultations with the latter and such requests shall be accorded sympathetic consideration.[118]

Member states are permitted to apply anti-dumping and countervailing measures in accordance with Annex 9 on Trade Remedies and the AfCFTA Guidelines on Implementation of Trade Remedies in accordance with relevant WTO Agreements.[119] The implication of this is that such provisions must be WTO compatible, thus should there be any ambiguities in the AfCFTA Guidelines, member states may refer to the WTO law for clarification.[120]

Key to the operationalisation of the above provisions of the AfCFTA and specifically to the trade in goods is Annex 5 on Non-Tariff Barriers which provides a mechanism for the identification, categorisation, and progressive elimination of NTBs within the AfCFTA. Presently, the AfCFTA has an online mechanism open to all African business sectors for reporting of any obstacles encountered when trading goods across intra-African borders which could include ad hoc fees at the border.[121]

3 Lessons from the WTO Experience

3.1 *Potential Impact on Direct and Indirect Tax Measures*

The non-discrimination clauses in the AfCFTA broadly mirror those contained in the WTO Agreements. For the MFN obligation, the AFCFTA protocol on trade in services provides a carve out for agreements on avoidance of double taxation (DTTs).[122] This is similar to the treatment in GATS. This exemption is however not available under the AfCFTA protocol on trade in goods. Again, this is identical to GATT and may assume that goods will generally be subjected to indirect taxes which are not covered under DTTs. However, based on the analysis of the WTO case law above, both direct and indirect taxes have been challenged under GATT. Therefore, direct tax measures covered by DTTs may be challenged under the AfCFTA protocol on trade in goods. Members may rely on the exceptions provided under Article 26 of this protocol to justify discriminatory measures.

[117] Art 17 (1), Protocol on Trade in Services.

[118] Art 17 (2), Protocol on Trade in Services.

[119] Art 17, Protocol on Trade in Goods.

[120] Erasums (2021).

[121] Available at https://www.tradebarriers.africa/ on 8 September 2023.

[122] Art 15 of the Protocol on trade in services.

For the NT obligation, the protocol on trade in goods makes direct reference to Article III of the GATT.[123] Specifically, the provision extends the NT obligation to all "measures affecting the sale and conditions for sale of [products] in accordance with Article III of GATT 1994."[124] Though no direct reference is made in Article 20 of the protocol on trade in services, the wording is similar to Article XVII of the GATS on NT. Therefore, it can be concluded that in both cases, the experience at the WTO in respect to taxation measures and the NT obligation will be relevant in the interpretation of the AfCFTA provisions. States can therefore expect the application of the NT obligation to extend to both direct and indirect taxes.

3.2 Potential Impact on Defensive Tax Measures

The *Argentina – measures relating to trade in goods and services* case, discussed in Sect. 3.4.4, shows the potential interaction between domestic defensive measures and trade obligations. Within the AfCFTA context, the agreement does not completely prohibit member states from implementing discriminatory measures. The agreement recognises instances where setting aside economic freedoms is allowable in order to attain certain goals.[125] A key exception under the protocol in trade in services is that measures may be inconsistent with the NT obligation if they are aimed at the *equitable and effective* imposition or collection of direct taxes.[126] The illustrative list of measures aimed at equitable and effective imposition of direct taxes is similar to the provisions under GATS one of which is the prevention of tax evasion and avoidance. However, similar to GATS, these exceptions are subject to the condition that the measures do not constitute a means of arbitrary or unjustifiable discrimination, which means that they should not be in excess of what is necessary to achieve their objectives. For instance, it would be difficult to defend defensive measures imposed on a member state's services and service suppliers on the grounds of preventing tax evasion or avoidance where there is an existing agreement on exchange of information between the states. Therefore, states will be required to review the necessity and effectiveness of any proposed defensive measures. Given the existing challenges at the WTO and similarities with WTO obligations, AfCFTA member states will need to evaluate and test any existing or new conditions to ensure that they meet the obligations and conditions under the AfCFTA.

[123] Art 5 of the Protocol on trade in goods.

[124] Art 5 of the Protocol on trade in goods.

[125] The list of exceptions to the obligations under the AfCFTA are under Arts 15–16 of the Protocol on trade in services, and Arts 26–27 of the Protocol on trade in goods.

[126] Art 15 (d) GATS.

3.3 Treatment of Tax Incentives

Unlike the WTO provisions on subsidies, the AfCFTA seems to have a more pragmatic approach to subsidies. There appears to be a contradiction between the AfCFTA commitment to establishing a single market and removing protectionist measures on the one hand, and its more pragmatic approach to subsidies on the other hand. From the WTO perspective, states have adopted more detailed guidelines on the regulation of subsidies. This pragmatic approach to the regulation of subsidies under AfCFTA may negatively impact less developed member states as they liberalize trade because the more developed states have established industries and have the financial capacity to offer subsidies making it easier for them to penetrate the weaker market. To reduce this risk the AfCFTA allows for implementation of domestic measures aimed at protecting infant industries that have strategic importance for a state.[127] It is important to note that trade integration efforts in Africa have historically been hindered by the implementation of import substitution policies aimed at protecting infant industries.[128] Even so, there are circumstances where infant market protection policies have been successfully implemented and achieved their goals.[129] As the guidelines on measures to protect infant industries are developed, it is important to balance two main objectives - safeguarding less developed states on the one hand and preventing the negative impact of certain protectionist measures on the other hand. The WTO detailed guidance on subsidies and protection of economies in early development may serve as guidance for the AfCFTA.[130] In addition, implementation of the AfCFTA offers an opportunity for states to rethink domestic tax incentive regimes to bring them into compliance with trade obligations as well as considering whether they remain fit for purpose.

3.4 Tax Related Disputes

The AfCFTA protocols on trade in goods and services provide exceptions that states may rely on to justify discriminatory tax measures which are similar to the exceptions available under the WTO. However, the many tax-related cases under the WTO dispute settlement body lead to two important conclusions. One, tax measures are subject to the obligations under trade agreements and may indeed be found to be in violation of these obligations. Two, while there are exceptions that states may rely on to justify inconsistent tax measures, these cannot be seen as a means for unjustifiable or arbitrary discrimination. States must therefore ensure that domestic tax measures are fit for purpose and are not excessive. AfCFTA member states are

---

[127] Art 24, Protocol on Trade in Goods.

[128] ElGanainy (2023), p. 22.

[129] See Harrison and Rodríguez-Clare (2009).

[130] See Art XVIII of GATT on governmental assistance to economic development.

bound by similar provisions and must therefore appreciate that there is potential for tax measures to be challenged. This means that going forward, it is necessary for tax policymakers to understand the obligations set out in the AfCFTA and ensure that any policies adopted are not in violation of these obligations or where they may be discriminatory, they are justified under the exceptions provided.

4 Conclusion and Recommendations

Indeed, the AfCFTA will have a transformative impact for African countries. Not only does it offer the opportunity for countries to competitively integrate into the global value chain but can also lead to a reduction in poverty and promote inclusion.[131] World Bank estimates that the successful implementation of the Agreement will elevate 30 million people from extreme poverty, raise real income gains for African economies by 7 percent, and significantly boost intra continental exports by more than 81 percent by 2035.[132] These benefits will result from the reduction in tariffs and implementation of trade facilitation measures which ultimately reduce the costs incurred by traders.[133] However, while countries continue to integrate, it is necessary to recognise that tax may be a barrier to trade liberalisation efforts either through imposing an unjustified burden on the taxpayer which increases costs for traders; or by acting as a tool to further protectionist and discriminatory principles which contradict trade obligations. The experience at the WTO leads the authors to two main conclusions. One, though countries may challenge the jurisdiction of the WTO to hear tax matters,[134] tax measures directly impact cross-border trade and are therefore subject to trade obligations. By signing trade agreements, states agree to relinquish certain aspects of their sovereignty, including tax sovereignty, for the greater objective of economic integration. Two, non-compliant tax measures can be challenged under trade agreements and though countries may be able to justify certain tax measures under the exceptions, these must meet the conditions set. Therefore, the implementation of trade agreements will have an impact on the domestic tax measures adopted by countries. Within the context of the AfCFTA, which has certain similar provisions to the WTO, African countries cannot overlook the interaction between trade and tax and the long-term impact the trade agreement will have on domestic tax policy. To mitigate potential disputes several recommendations are provided below.

[131] World Bank (2020), pp. 44–55.

[132] World Bank (2020), pp. 44–55.

[133] World Bank (2020), p. IX.

[134] See for instance the United States Trade Representative – Report on the Appellate Body of the World Trade Organisation, February 2020. Available at https://ustr.gov/sites/default/files/Report_on_the_Appellate_Body_of_the_World_Trade_Organization.pdf.

4.1 *Increase Dialogue Between Tax and Trade Policymakers*

Given the interaction between trade and tax, it is necessary that the two communities engage in dialogue to give insight into the obligations set out in the AfCFTA and avoid instances where tax acts as a barrier to trade or where trade obligations unduly limit sovereign taxing rights. The African Union (AU) and ATAF play a significant role in providing a platform for dialogue.

4.2 *Long-Term Harmonization of Tax Policy*

Since both direct and indirect tax measures may act as barriers to trade liberalisation, in the long-term, African states should consider harmonization of policies. The European Union (EU) provides an example for harmonization having made significant progress in harmonization of Value Added Tax across the union. In addition, though harmonization of direct taxes continues to be a challenge, the EU member states are required to ensure that domestic direct tax policies are in line with EU law, which may be seen as indirect harmonization.[135] While this is not an immediate concern for the AfCFTA, continued integration and removal of tariff barriers will require states to address other forms of potential protectionist measures including taxation. Harmonization can begin with indirect taxes, which have a more immediate impact on movement of goods and services, then move to direct taxes. In addition, for the effective implementation of the AfCFTA, states will need to have a regional approach to tax competition. More detailed regional guidance on the use of incentives and subsidies will therefore be necessary to avoid negatively impacting less developed industries.[136]The adoption of a regional minimum tax can also reduce tax competition between states.

4.3 *Time-Bound Carve-Outs for Specific Tax Measures*

States may opt to include specific time-bound carve outs on measures related to tax competition. Given the prevalence of use of tax incentives in African states, increased economic integration may result in tax competition between states which presents opportunities for investors to move funds to low tax jurisdictions and ultimately distorts trade. Carve-outs will allow states to implement domestic measures

[135] Harmonization also plays a role in strengthening the role of the European Court of Justice in setting tax norms. See Cloer (2023), p. 592.

[136] The EU state aid rules are an example of guidance regarding subsidies and incentives. See: EU, State Aid Overview. Available at https://competition-policy.ec.europa.eu/state-aid/state-aid-overview_en.

to mitigate this risk without being subject to the condition on justifiable and arbitrary discrimination. However, to avoid misuse, this carve-out should be time bound until such a time as states have adopted a regional approach to tax competition and/ or a regional minimum tax.

4.4 Strengthening the Dispute Settlement System

Though increased dialogue may reduce instances of cross-border dispute, this will not fully eliminate the potential risk. Therefore, a sound dispute resolution mechanism should be integral to the operationalisation of the AfCFTA. The AfCFTA provides for a quasi-judicial dispute settlement process.[137] It is worth noting that the AfCFTA borrows heavily from the structure at the WTO.[138] For instance, just like the WTO, the AfCFTA establishes the dispute settlement body which comprises of representatives of the member states. In addition, disputes under this mechanism are initiated through consultations, failure of which a panel is established, and an appeal allowed to the appellate body against panel decisions. Alternative dispute resolution mechanisms including good office, conciliation or mediation are also provided for.[139]

A key objection to the jurisdiction of the WTO to hear tax matters was that it lacked sufficient expertise, however, this was mitigated by hiring experts on both tax and trade to sit on panels.[140] A similar challenge may be faced by AfCFTA dispute settlement body and proactively ensuring that members of panels understand both tax and trade will mitigate these concerns. Alternatively, member states may opt to establish a separate institutionalised dispute settlement mechanism that specifically handles cross-border tax disputes. This may be in the form of an institutionalised regional mediation panel made up of tax and trade experts, which considers African states' culture of non-litigation of economic disputes between themselves.[141] Additionally, member states may include provisions empowering tax administrations to review disputes when they first arise as is the case when determining whether a measure constitutes expropriation under the USMCA.[142]

---

[137] Art 20 (1), AfCFTA Agreement.

[138] Kugler and Nyaga (2020).

[139] Parties to a dispute may voluntarily enter alternative dispute resolution mechanisms. Article 8(1) Protocol on Rules and Procedures on the Settlement of Disputes.

[140] Reuven (2005), p. 129.

[141] Akinkugbe (2020), pp. 138–158.

[142] See Annex 14-B 3 (a) to the United States Mexico Canada Agreement on conducting a case-by-case fact-based inquiry to determine whether there has been expropriation.

References

AfCFTA Agreement 2019

Agreement on Subsidies and Countervailing Measures (ASCM) 2001

Akinkugbe OD (2020) Dispute settlement under the African Continental Free Trade Area Agreement: a preliminary assessment. Supp Afr J Int Comp Law 28:138–158

Appellate Body Report: Argentina – Measures Relating to Trade in Goods and Services, WT/DS453/AB/R, April 2016

Appellate Body Report: Report: Japan – Taxes on Alcoholic Beverages, WT/DS8/AB/R; WT/DS10/AB/R; WT/DS11/AB/R, October 1996

Appellate Body Report: United States – Tax Treatment for "Foreign Sales Corporations", WT/DS108/AB/R, February 2000

Appellate Body Report: United States- Tax Treatment for "Foreign Sales Corporations" Recourse to Article 21.5 of the DSU by the European Communities WT/DS108/AB/RW, January 2002

Appellate Body Report: United States- Tax Treatment for "Foreign Sales Corporations" Second Recourse to Article 21.5 of the DSU by the European Communities, WT/DS108/AB/RW2, February 2006

Beyer V (2018) Income tax and non-discrimination in the GATT. J Int Econ Law 21(3):547–566

Cloer A (2023) The role of the ECJ in development of international tax law. In: Haase F, Klofer G (eds) The Oxford handbook of international tax law. OUP, Oxford, p 592

Daly M (2000) Some taxing issues for the World Trade Organization. Can Tax J 48(4):1053–1077

Daly M (2016) Is the WTO a World Tax Organisation? A primer on WTO rules for tax policy-makers. Technical Notes and Manuals 16/03, IMF. Doi: file:///C:/Users/rmaina/Downloads/_tnm1602.pdf

Developing States. National Bureau of Economic Research Working Paper 15261, Cambridge, National Bureau of Economic Research

ElGanainy A (2023) Trade integration in Africa: unleashing the continent's potential in a changing world. International Monetary Fund, Washington DC

Erasums G (2021) What lies ahead for the AfCFTA trade remedies and safeguards regime? TRALAC, 1 November 2021. https://www.tralac.org/blog/article/15407-what-lies-ahead-for-the-afcfta-trade-remedies-and-safeguards-regime.html

EU, State Aid Overview. https://competition-policy.ec.europa.eu/state-aid/state-aid-overview_en

Fact sheet on the European Union, Indirect Taxation. https://www.europarl.europa.eu/factsheets/en/sheet/81/indirect-taxation

Farrell J (2013) "The Tax-Trade Interface." The interface of international trade law and taxation: defining of the role of the WTO (IBFD 2013), Books IBFD

GATT 1994, General Agreement on Trade in Services (GATS) and Trade-Related Aspects of Intellectual Property Rights (TRIPS)

General Agreement on Tariffs and Trade, Council of representatives: Report on Work Since the Thirty-First Session, L/4440, 18 November 1976

General Agreement on Trade in Services (GATS) 1995

Grosso G (2008) Analysis of subsidies for services: the case of export subsidies. OECD Trade Policy

Harrison A, Rodrı́guez-Clare A (2009) Trade, foreign investment, and industrial policy for developing countries. Handb Dev Econ 5:4039–4214

Kugler K, Nyaga K (2020) What lessons can the AfCFTA learn from the WTO's Dispute Settlement Mechanism's Challenges? African International Economic Law Network, 22 December. https://www.afronomicslaw.org/2020/12/22/what-lessons-can-the-afcfta-learn-from-the-wtos-dispute-settlement-mechanisms-challenges/

Launching of Uruguay Round: The most complex and ambitious programme of negotiations ever undertaken by GATT, GATT Newsletter Focus No. 41, October 1986. https://docs.wto.org/gattdocs/q/GG/GATTFOCUS/41.pdf

Lijun Z, Karaivanova A, Zhang P (2021) The complementary role of the WTO in the enhancement of the base erosion and profit shifting project. World 2(2):267–294

McDaniel P (2001) Trade and taxation. Brooklyn J Int Law 26(40):1621–1640
Michalek J (2004) Subsidies in the context of the World Trade Organization. Reflets et perspectives de la vie économique Xliii(1):25–38
Owens J, Zhan J (2018) Trade, investment and taxation: policy linkages. Transnatl Corp 25(2):1–8
Panel Report, United States – Tax Treatment for "Foreign Salles Corporations", WT/DS108R, 1999
Panel report, United States – Tax Treatment for "foreign sales corporations" Recourse to Article 21.5 of the DSU by the European Communities, WT/DS108/RW, 2001, para. 8.142
Panel Report, US – FSC (Article 21.5 – EC), para. 8.143
Panel Report: Argentina – Measures Relating to Trade in Goods and Services, WT/DS453/R, September 2015
Panel Report: Indonesia – Certain Measures Affecting the Automobile Industry, WT/DS54R; WT/DS55R; AT/DS59R; WT/DS64R, July 1998
Panel Report: Indonesia – Certain Measures Affecting the Automobile Industry, supra n 81 at para. 14.80–14.82
Panel Report: Japan – Taxes on Alcoholic Beverages, WT/DS8/R; WT/DS10/R; WT/DS11/R, July 1996
Pitschas C (1995) GATT/WTO Rules for Tax Adjustment and the Proposed European Directive Introducing a Tax on Carbon Dioxide Emissions and Energy 24:478–500
Reuven A (2005) The WTO, export subsidies, and tax competition. In: Lang et al (eds) WTO and direct taxation. Eucotax Series on European Taxation, vol 10. Kluwer Law International, The Hague, pp 115–131
Rubini L (2023) Between sovereignty and complexity: the settlement of tax disputes by the world trade organisation. Asia Pac Law Rev 30(1):204–218
Schott J (1996) Challenges facing the World Trade Organization. In: Schott J (ed) The world trading system: challenges ahead. Institute for International Economics
Shome P (2021) Principles of taxation. In: Taxation history, theory, law and administration. Springer texts in business and economics. Springer, Cham
The GATT years: from Havana to Marrakesh. Available at https://www.wto.org/english/thewto_e/whatis_e/tif_e/fact4_e.htm
The Sovereign Power to Tax (2008) American Society of International Law Proceedings. pp 51–60
The Tariff Revenue Implications of the African Continental Free Trade Area: A Joint Research Initiative of African Tax Administration Forum and the WU Global Tax Policy Center, Institute for Austrian and International Tax Law, WU (Vienna University of Economics and Business) at p 7. Doi: file:///C:/Users/rmaina/Downloads/ATAF_Tariff_Policy_ENG_V2.pdf
Turki A (2010) Dealing with the fragmented international legal environment: WTO, international tax and internal tax regulations. Springer, Berlin
United States - Tax Treatment for "Foreign Sales Corporations" case discussed in section 2.4.1
United States Tax Legislation (DISC) Report of the panel presented to the council of representatives on 12 November 1976 (L/422-23S/98). http://www.sice.oas.org/dispute/gatt/73discec.asp
United States Trade Representative – Report on the Appellate Body of the World Trade Organisation, February 2020. https://ustr.gov/sites/default/files/Report_on_the_Appellate_Body_of_the_World_Trade_Organization.pdf
Van Thiel S (2023) International tax law and international trade law. In: Haase F, Kofler G (eds) The Oxford handbook of international tax law. Oxford Handbooks
World Bank (2020) The African Continental Free Trade Area: economic and distributional effects. World Bank, Washington, DC, pp 44–55
World Trade Organisation (2015) "The Agreements." Chapter 2 in Understanding the WTO, Geneva: WTO. https://www.wto.org/english/thewto_e/whatis_e/tif_e/understanding_e.pdf
WTO, Summary of the key findings of the dispute: Indonesia – Certain Measures Affecting the Automotive Industry. https://www.wto.org/english/tratop_e/dispu_e/cases_e/1pagesum_e/ds55sum_e.pdf

The Growing Potential of Excise Taxation as a Source of Domestic Revenue Mobilisation in the context of the African Continental Free Trade Area

Jérôme Duperrut

Abstract African governments are committed to fund the continent's development and are actively influencing Africa's destiny. The United Nations' Sustainable Development Goals (SDGs) of emphasise the need to strengthen domestic resource mobilisation (SDG Target 17.1) through enhanced domestic capacity for tax and revenue collection in order to increase the financial means of implementing the SDGs. The African Union's Agenda 2063 emphasises that African countries must enhance domestic resource mobilisation by implementing effective, transparent, and uniform tax and revenue collecting processes. One of the main sources of funding, along with government development assistance and private investment flows, is the mobilisation of domestic resources. This chapter demonstrated that, similar to other taxes, excise taxes are the outcome of a combination of appropriate tax policy measures and efficient tax administration procedures. Furthermore, in the African context, the importance and benefits of tax administration methods was emphasised as they are essential to maximising the efficacy of excise taxes. In addressing tax and revenue collection within the framework of the African Continental Free Trade Area, this chapter urged African governments—particularly their finance ministries and revenue authorities—to take the lead in financial resource mobilisation for sustainable development.

1 Introduction

African governments are actively shaping the future of the continent and are determined to take full ownership for financing its development. On a global scale, the United Nations Sustainable Development Goals (SDGs) highlight that the financial

J. Duperrut (✉)
Division for Economic Analysis and International Institutions, SICPA SA, Lausanne, Switzerland
e-mail: Jerome.Duperrut@sicpa.com

T. V. Warikandwa et al. (eds.), *Law and Policy of the African Continental Free Trade Area (AfCFTA)*, European Yearbook of International Economic Law,
https://doi.org/10.1007/978-3-032-01122-0_14

means of implementation of the SDGs need to increase, in particular by strengthening domestic resource mobilisation (SDG Target 17.1) through improved domestic capacity for tax and revenue collection. At a regional level, the African Union (AU) Agenda 2063 emphasises the need for Africa to strengthen domestic resource mobilisation by establishing effective, transparent and harmonised tax and revenue collection systems. Domestic resource mobilisation constitutes one of the key sources of finance, alongside official development assistance and private investment flows. This responsibility lies primarily in the hands of African governments, in particular ministries of finance and revenue authorities.

The African Continental Free Trade Area (AfCFTA) aims at establishing a single market for goods and services, which will have a direct impact on domestic resource mobilisation. The progressive elimination of import duties on intra-African trade is expected to decrease revenue collection in many countries, especially in the short-term. Currently, import duties account for around 1.4 per cent of gross domestic product (GDP) and are the fifth largest source of revenue. In the medium-term, it will take some time for the expected increase in economic activity following the implementation of the AfCFTA to lead to a compensatory increase in revenue collection through higher direct and indirect tax collection.

At the same time, a number of African Regional Economic Communities (RECs) and individual countries have set fiscal convergence criteria or fiscal targets. Africa has numerous RECs, including the Arab Maghreb Union (AMU), the Economic Community of West African States (ECOWAS), the East African Community (EAC), the, the Southern African Development Community (SADC), the Intergovernmental Authority on Development (IGAD), the Community of Sahel-Saharan States (CENSAD), and the Common Market for Eastern and Southern Africa (COMESA), as well as the West African Economic and Monetary Union (WAEMU), the Central African Economic and Monetary Community (CEMAC) and the Southern African Customs Union (SACU). The RECs encompass all African countries. Some RECs, such as the EAC, ECOWAS and CEMAC, provide overall guidance with fiscal convergence criteria, often based on indicators such as the ratio of debt to Gross Domestic Product (GDP) or the size of the public deficit. Many individual African countries have also set their own fiscal targets.

One key way to abide by these fiscal convergence criteria is to set specific objectives for domestic revenue mobilisation. Increasing revenue collection is generally viewed as a more favourable way to consolidate the fiscal position in African countries, as it has a less pronounced impact on economic growth.[1] A minimum revenue threshold might even contribute to accelerating growth and development—it is estimated at around 15 per cent of GDP.[2] These revenue objectives can include specific medium-term targets, such as in Uganda's National Development Plan III, which aims to achieve a domestic revenue mobilisation of 15 per cent of GDP by 2024/25. Similarly, Nigeria's Strategic Revenue Growth Initiative aims at raising its

[1] International Monetary Fund (2017a), p. 28; Mpofu (2022), p. 222.

[2] Gaspar et al. (2016), p. 30.

revenue-to-GDP ratio to 15 per cent by expanding the tax base and countering tax evasion. Kenya has set as the main objective of its revenue strategy to raise its revenue to GDP to 25 percent by 2030. Other countries aim at gradual annual increases in domestic revenue over a defined period.

In this context of the need for revenue mobilisation in Africa, this chapter analyses the potential for additional contribution from excise. This potential can be evaluated through several dimensions. It can be benchmarked against international comparison and African best practices. It can be inferred from data on the size of the informal economy and more specifically on the extent of illicit trade in excisable goods. It can be measured based on well-known fiscal standards, such as the excise gap, the buoyancy and the elasticity of excise, and the mirror trade discrepancy of excisable goods. As for each tax, the contribution of excise comes from a combination of appropriate tax policy measures and efficient tax administration measures. In the African context, the relevance and positive contribution of tax administration measures will be emphasised as they play a crucial role in maximising the effectiveness of excise.

2 Excise Policy

Excise is an indirect tax commonly levied on the manufacture or sale of a list of goods and services. The Organization for Economic Co-operation and Development (OECD) classification of taxes puts excise in the category of taxes on goods and services, under the heading of taxes related to the production, sale, transfer, leasing and delivery of specific goods and services (category 5121). In certain countries, it may also include taxes on specific services (category 5126), as well as other categories such as fuel levy or environmental taxes. In country-specific contexts, the term excise is not always employed. For example, many countries impose a sugar tax or a fuel levy, which essentially fall under the category of excise.

Excise is recognised as an efficient tax, due to its ability to generate relatively large tax collection while causing only minor changes in consumer behaviour. Excise is considered as a more growth-friendly tax compared to most other tax categories. Countries often rely on excise to (i) increase domestic revenue mobilisation, (ii) correct negative externalities, (iii) discourage consumption, and (iv) level the playing field between domestic and imported goods. Excise impacts economic behaviour in the sense that it changes relative prices, unlike the much broader based value-added tax (VAT). While excise rates could be set in a way that maximises fiscal revenue, it may also make sense from a broader policy point of view to go beyond the revenue-maximizing rate especially when the targeted activity is particularly harmful, such as for tobacco and alcohol consumption. In such cases, the revenue-maximizing rate is likely to be below the marginal rate of social cost.[3]

[3] Levell et al. (2016), p. 207; Evans et al. (1999), p. 44; Panggabean et al. (2024), p. 24.

Excise is applied to a growing number of goods and services. Traditionally, the list of excisable products is based on the classification of the Harmonised System (HS) code of the World Customs Organization (WCO) or their domestic equivalent for local production. The current list in the Democratic Republic of the Congo (DRC) contains 79 excisable goods. In Tanzania, the list registers 43 excisable goods (at the HS code level 4). In Ethiopia, there are 19 categories of excisable goods. Within various RECs, the list of excisable products is typically more condensed and may include both mandatory and optional excisable goods. Many countries change the list of excisable goods and services, generally at the time of the budget. In Kenya, the list expanded in July 2023 to introduce excise on imported fish, imported sugar, imported cement, powdered juices, and advertisement related to alcohol and gambling.

The main excisable goods are tobacco products, alcoholic beverages, and fuel. Almost all African countries levy excise on these three product categories, with the exception of countries where the sale of alcohol is prohibited. These three categories amount to the largest share of excise collection in most African countries. Within each product category, there may be specific variations. For tobacco products, many countries have recently expanded the excise base to account for new products, such as heated tobacco products (HTP), shisha, and electronic cigarettes.[4] As for alcoholic beverages, excise on ready-to-drink beverages and alcopops is becoming increasingly popular.

While soft drinks have been subjected to excise for some time, the promotion of "sugar tax" is giving it new impetus.[5] At least 32 African countries levy excise on sugary drinks.[6] Sugar itself is also increasingly becoming the target of excise. While excise rates on soft drinks are generally low, their coverage—several countries started taxing energy drinks—and design vary extensively across countries. Furthermore, bottled water is increasingly subjected to excise, due to its perceived luxury status. Interestingly, bottled water has been found to be more expensive than sugar-sweetened beverages in many countries, including in Africa.[7]

More broadly, excise on luxury products is seen as one approach to address income inequality. Many countries levy excise on cars and other transportation vehicles, with higher rates for new cars. In Ethiopia, the list of excisable goods includes perfumes, cosmetics and beauty products, fireworks, and artificial flowers. In South Africa, luxury excisable goods comprise perfumes, beauty care, fireworks, air conditioning machines, cellular phones, TV/radio, and golf balls. Under the ECOWAS directive, products such as perfumery and cosmetic products, precious stones and metals, caviar, recreational boats, works of art, and marbles are included in the list of excisable products.

---

[4] Tobacco Free Kids (2023).

[5] World Bank (2020a).

[6] World Bank (2023a).

[7] Blecher et al. (2017), p. 14.

The construction sector, particularly the production of cement, is newly subjected to excise. This is likely in response to the under-declaration of taxes by the construction industry.

Telecom services stand out as one of the rare services subjected to excise. This category can include telephone and cellular phone calls, sms, internet data usage, as well as additional mobile services such as money transfer, online gaming and betting, and online advertisement.

Lastly, environmental protection is becoming a new justification for imposing excise. Many African countries have already introduced excise on plastic bags or plastic bottles. With the planned implementation of the European Union (EU) Carbon Border Adjustment Mechanism (CBAM), African countries might consider raising excise on products that are in the scope of the CBAM, such as cement, iron and steel, aluminium, fertilisers, electricity, and hydrogen. This new taxation would generate revenue for African countries, rather than contributing to the EU budget pool. Notably, South Africa introduced a carbon tax on greenhouse gas emissions in 2019.

Various types of tax schedules can be applied on excisable products, primarily based on their volume or their value. The most common excise types are specific, ad-valorem, and mixed systems, each with its own set of advantages and disadvantages.[8] Specific excise applies a fixed monetary amount per determined unit of excisable good (e.g. US$ 1 per litre), while ad-valorem excise consists in a set percentage of the value of the good (e.g. 40 per cent of the price of a cigarette pack). For instance, ad-valorem rates are best applied to the retail sales price of the product to prevent manipulation of the ex-factory price by producers and the import price by importers. However, most African countries charge ad-valorem rates on the ex-factory price of cigarettes, except for Rwanda, Morocco, and Egypt. On the other hand, specific excise rates should be adjusted for inflation to preserve their real value, or ideally, they should follow wage developments to maintain their level of affordability. These tax policies are seldom applied in Africa. In July 2023, Kenya even repealed the provision for annual excise adjustment for inflation.

Best practices concerning the tax burden are promoted by international institutions. The World Health Organisation (WHO) Framework Convention on Tobacco Control (FCTC) recommends a minimum excise share of 70 per cent of the retail sales price of cigarettes[9] and to a total tax share of 75 per cent.[10] The World Bank advises that the total tax share should amount to between two-thirds and four-fifths of the retail sales price of cigarettes.[11] In 2020, the average total tax share for cigarettes in African countries was 42 per cent, which is around 12 per cent below the world average. Only six African countries (Mauritius, Madagascar, Egypt, Morocco,

---

[8] World Health Organization (2010), pp. 40–41; Yurekli (2001), p. 29; U.S. National Cancer Institute and World Health Organization (2016); World Bank (2017a), pp. 18–20.

[9] World Health Organization (2010), p. 103.

[10] World Health Organization (2019), p. 25.

[11] World Bank (1999), p. 83.

Comoros, and Sudan) met the WHO benchmark. The excise share amounted to 29 per cent in Africa, while the world average reached 38 per cent. In Guinea, the excise rate on cigarettes has often been waived.[12]

Closely substitutable excisable products are sometimes subjected to different tax rates, leading to tax expenditure. In Uganda, excise rates for cigarettes differ between hinge-lid and soft-cup packs. In Tanzania, cigarettes are taxed differently based on their length and the presence or absence of a filter tip. These escape clauses create opportunities for taxpayers and consumers to engage in distortionary behaviours, ultimately reducing the efficiency and revenue mobilisation of excise.

Excise policies are meant to treat domestic and imported products equally, but a differentiated treatment can take place *de facto*. It is challenging to argue that a pack of domestic cigarettes generates fewer negative externalities than a pack of imported cigarettes. The principle that excise should not be discriminatory is typically emphasised within RECs. Nevertheless, some countries set different excise rates on excisable products depending on their content or the input used in their production. In Tanzania, fruit juices manufactured from domestic fruits are subjected to lighter taxation than other fruit juices. Similarly, wines with a domestic grape content exceeding 75 per cent are taxed more favourably than other wines. In Uganda, malt beer is taxed at a higher rate than beer produced from barley grown and malted in Uganda.

3 Excise Administration

Excise is sometimes perceived to be easy to administer, but country evidence shows that it is not always the case.[13] As a general principle and to instil confidence in the tax system, every tax should be designed to be simple, transparent, and easy to administer.[14] The ease of administration combines both effectiveness and efficiency. An effective measure ensures that the tax generates adequate revenue in accordance with the legislation, while an efficient measure keeps the administrative cost low compared to the amount of tax collected.[15] The capacity of the tax authority in charge of tax administration is a crucial factor. Capacity includes various elements, such as strategies, governance, structures, and resources in terms of staff and technologies. Claims that excise requires little capacity fail to acknowledge that excise rates are typically much higher than many other tax rates, which provides a strong incentive for non-compliance. In consequence, excise gaps are typically found to be significant. An IMF report about Nigeria excise mentions that 'specific duties

[12] World Bank (2019a), p. 12.

[13] U.S. National Cancer Institute and World Health Organization (2016), p. 182; International Monetary Fund (2011), pp. 37–39; African Tax Administration Forum (2016), p. 36; World Health Organization (2019), pp. 106–110; Bird and Wallace (2010), p. 13.

[14] World Health Organization (2015), p. 35.

[15] World Health Organization (2010), p. 55; Cantens et al. (2013), pp. 4–5.

require only counting or measuring strength or volume',[16] as if this information was straightforward to obtain for the tax authority. Excise taxpayers often under-declare this relevant tax data, leading to numerous instances of inaccurate or incomplete reporting. It is highly unlikely that in a country with low excise collection, increasing excise rates without strengthening excise tax administration will yield the expected fiscal outcome.

In Africa, excise is administered at central level and generally by a single revenue authority. In most African countries, all revenue categories are managed by a unified revenue authority. Some Francophone African countries still have separated revenue authorities responsible for domestic taxes on one side, and taxes on imports on the other side.[17] For example, in Guinea, excise on imported goods is collected by the Direction Générale des Douanes, while excise on domestic goods is collected by the Direction Nationale des Impôts. On the contrary, in the DRC, the Direction Générale des Droits et des Accises (DGDA) is solely responsible for administering excise, although there are three revenue authorities in the country. Within a revenue authority, excise can be handled differently. In some countries, excise is administrated by one vertical entity, an excise department. However, in most cases, excise is administered by various functional departments—in Tanzania, by the Domestic Revenue Department, the Large Taxpayers Department, and the Customs Department for imported excisable goods.

One characteristic of excise is that it becomes due early in the supply and distribution chains. Generally, it is due when an excisable product or service is manufactured and leaves the manufacturing plant (or its warehouse) to be delivered for the first sale and released for consumption. For imported goods, the excisable point often coincides with the point of the customs duty, meaning when the product enters the customs territory. Excise on imported goods is charged based on the customs value of the goods, which is then increased by the import duties. These three components (value of the goods, customs duty, excise) form the tax base of VAT levied on imported goods. For domestic goods, excise is typically charged on the ex-factory price, with VAT levied subsequently. Changing the list of excisable goods and the rate of excise will automatically generate a pass-through fiscal impact on VAT.

The number of registered taxpayers for excise is typically low. Excise is paid for by manufacturers of the domestic excisable goods or importers. In Uganda, there were 250 registered taxpayers for local excise in 2018/19, accounting for 0.02 per cent of the total number of registered taxpayers. Beyond acquiring a tax identification number by the revenue authority, many economic operators of excisable goods (farmers, producers, distillers, wholesalers, retailers, importers) might also need to obtain a license. It is to be noted that a producer or an importer might need to be licensed, but its license is not always directly linked to tax compliance or the tax-paid status of the excisable goods.

[16] International Monetary Fund (2018), p. 13.

[17] Zake (2011), p. 15; Lemgruber et al. (2015), p. 17.

Taxpayers are responsible for the accurate and timely reporting and filing of their excise obligations following the self-declaration principle, and for making the necessary excise payment. This involves submitting an excise return in the prescribed form. In practice, the quantity of excisable sales of the goods determines the taxable basis, to which the applicable excise rate is applied. The excise return is usually submitted in the following month, with the payment of excise typically due on the filing date. This return qualifies as a self-assessment, in which producers self-declare their excisable sales and their related excise payment. In the case of self-reported tax figures, tax evasion tends to be higher in comparison with situations when there is third-party reporting and matching.[18] In Uganda, a number of taxpayers did not report data on excisable sales, the key element to determine the tax base.[19]

The enforcement of excise by the revenue authority focuses on two key aspects: controlling the taxable point and on auditing relevant taxpayers.[20] Enforcement at the taxable point traditionally involves (i) the physical presence of tax inspectors inside production facilities or bonded warehouses, (ii) episodic inspections by tax inspectors, and (iii) field patrols, surveillance of routes, and surprise check points.[21] These control mechanisms are prone to corrupt practices, as excise taxpayers may collude with tax officials to reduce their tax liabilities. Beyond that, the usual enforcement method mechanism involves auditing taxpayers. Audits can differ in scope, coverage of taxes, and elements investigated, but they are generally resource-intensive and time-consuming for a tax authority.

Tax offences and their corresponding sanctions are defined in the legislation. Offences can relate to various forms of misconduct by taxpayers, such as the failure to register, late filing, incomplete payment of taxes, as commonly outlined in the national tax procedures legislation. Specific offences related to excise, such as misdeclaration of goods or the fraudulent declaration of goods for exports, can be explicitly stated in the excise legislation. Sanctions usually include penalties, fines, seizure of goods, destruction of equipment, and even the closure of the business.

4 Excise in the Context of the AfCFTA

The AfCFTA strategic objectives aiming to create a single market for goods and services and establish an African customs union could have implication for excise. The formation of a common market is likely to require some degree of tax harmonisation, including of excise. A harmonised system of excise should improve the efficiency of the single market, reduce cross-border formalities for the movement of

---

[18] World Bank (2017a), p. 18.

[19] World Bank (2017b), p. 69.

[20] International Monetary Fund (2016), p. 7.

[21] World Health Organization (2010), p. 67; East African Revenue Authorities (2017), p. 33; Lemgruber et al. (2015), p. 37.

excisable goods, as well as limit cross-border smuggling and inter-state distortions from excise-induced difference in cost structure. This could build on the current experience by RECs. At the current juncture however, excise harmonisation is not a direct focal point. Harmonisation policies are likely to be driven not only by revenue considerations but also by political economy factors within the AfCFTA.[22]

Several RECs regulate excise and are expected to continue doing so within the framework of the AfCFTA. The AfCFTA allows RECs to maintain their level of integration, especially if it is deeper. The existing RECs might evolve at varying speeds when modifying their excise frameworks. In the ECOWAS, a tax directive requires member countries to harmonise excise standards, in particular the list of excisable products (both compulsory and optional products liable to excise) and the tax rates (with minimum and maximum rates). In the WAEMU, a tax directive similarly aims at harmonising excise, including by setting a list of excisable products and tax bands. Although some countries are members of both ECOWAS and WAEMU, the two tax directives are not entirely coherent. In the CEMAC, a tax harmonisation directive also sets a list of excisable products and determines a minimum tax rate. The most harmonised REC in terms of excise is the Southern African Customs Union (SACU) with a common list of excisable products and excise rates, as well as a common pooling and redistribution of excise collected in the five member countries. The trendsetter in this Union is South Africa, while other countries still have the option to top up excise with additional (excise) levies.

The AfCFTA is bound to have a significant impact on various taxes, both in the short-term and in a dynamic manner. On the tax side, the most immediate impact of the AfCFTA is likely to be a decline in customs duties. There will be a direct impact due to the lowering—and eventual removal—of tariffs on intra-African trade. There may be an additional decline in customs duties due to trade diversion away from imports originating from outside the AfCFTA. Since intra-African tariffs are already low and intra-African trade is moderate, the overall impact should be modest.[23]

To mitigate—and even over-compensate—this decline, excise is a prime tax for African governments to consider. In the short-term especially, the modest decrease in customs duties will be further compounded by the increased necessity to finance much needed infrastructure (roads, ports, airports, trains) to fully realise the benefit of the AfCFTA. Given the situation, there is a pressing need to increase domestic revenue mobilisation, extending beyond the loss of customs duties.

[22] Blecher and Drope (2014), p. 23.

[23] Abrego et al. (2020), p. 8.

4.1 Potential of Excise in the AfCFTA

Excise is one of the main sources of revenue in Africa. Excise collection for African countries is estimated at US$ 32.8 billion in 2020, accounting for 1.57 per cent of GDP. It remained relatively stable as compared to 2019, despite the challenges posed by the COVID-19 pandemic. Indeed, it showed good resilience during the pandemic.[24] Excise ranks as the fourth source of revenue, behind VAT, corporate income tax, and personal income tax, and ahead of taxes such as customs duties, property taxes, and non-tax revenues. It contributes to around 10 percent of total revenue collection. The detailed breakdown for 41 African countries is presented in Fig. 1.

The potential for excise in Africa can be estimated to reach US$ 64.8 billion, if countries adopt best continental practices. The top-5 African performers collect excise amounting to at least 3.1 per cent of GDP. If all African countries were to collect the same share of excise, revenue collection would increase by US$ 32.0 billion, equivalent to an increase of 1.5 per cent of GDP. This means that excise collection would almost double. More modestly, if the performance of African countries was to match the OECD average (2.3 per cent of GDP in 2020), excise would reach US$ 48.1 billion. This would represent an increase of US$ 15.2 billion or 0.7 per cent of GDP. These figures echo the African Union's acknowledgement that excise is an 'underexploited tax'.[25] Similarly, the IMF emphasise the broad untapped potential of excise,[26] indicating that there is room for further exploration of this tax to boost revenue mobilisation on the continent.

There are other ways to assess the potential of excise, such as the size of the informal sector. Estimates about the size of the informal sector are relatively rare, due to the difficulty to measure it. On average, the informal economy was measured at 35 per cent of GDP in Africa in 2015.[27] In Uganda, the size of the informal sector is officially estimated at 43 per cent of GDP.[28] These figures typically encompass the whole economy and do not focus on excisable goods.

A more specific picture can be given by the size of illicit trade in excisable goods. Illicit trade typically includes tax evasion, under-declaration, mis-declaration, illicit manufacturing, smuggling, and all other illegal practices to avoid paying taxes. It is important to distinguish illicit trade from tax avoidance, which relates to duty-free trade and purchase, cross-border trade within the legal limit, and exports (generally

[24] African Tax Administration Forum (2021), p. 49.

[25] African Union Commission (2019), p. 45.

[26] International Monetary Fund (2011), p. 39.

[27] Medina and Schneider (2018).

[28] Republic of Uganda (2015) *Second National Development Plan 2015/16-2019/20* 13.

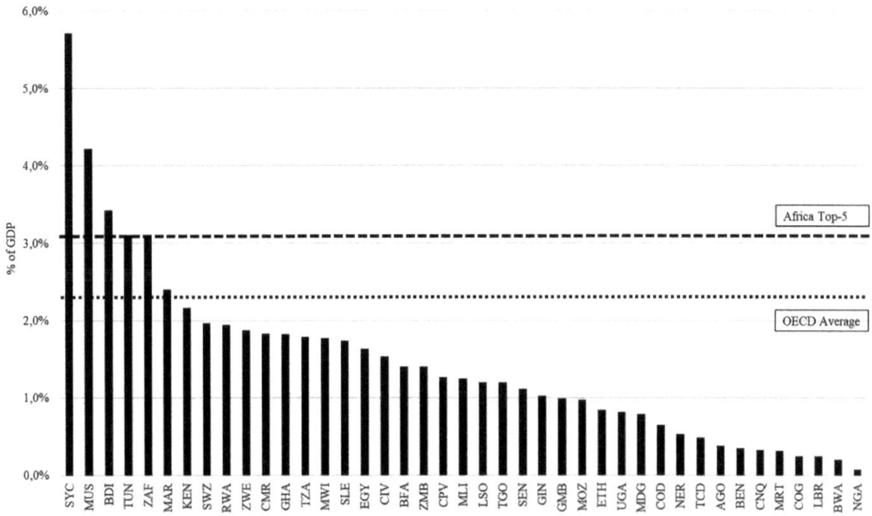

Fig. 1 Excise to GDP ratio in selected African countries in 2020. Author's calculation

exempted from excise).[29] Illicit trade can relate to other issues, beyond taxation.[30] It is very hard to credibly calculate the size of illicit trade, for example, illicit cigarette trade. There is numerous evidence of data manipulation by the tobacco industry itself in the provision of estimates of illicit cigarette trade.[31] In most countries, the only available indicator is the number of seizures of excisable goods.[32] However, this data should not be used as an indicator of illicit trade, due to its many biases.[33] Furthermore, the type of illicit trade activities is likely to evolve over time: illicit products that were previously distributed through informal channels can infiltrate the legitimate supply chain.[34] Illicit trade in many excisable goods endangers the achievement of the Sustainable Development Goals (SDGs).[35] Illicit trade in cigarettes, alcohol and petroleum undermines the achievement of several SDGs, in particular SDG 3 (Good health and well-being), SDG 8 (Decent work and economic growth), SDG 9 (Industry, innovation and infrastructure), SDG 16 (Peace, justice and strong institutions) and SDG 17 (Partnerships for the goals). More specifically, illicit trade affects SDG Target 17.1 (Strengthen domestic resource mobilisation).

[29] U.S. National Cancer Institute and World Health Organization (2016), p. 508; Kieyah et al. (2014), p. 15; Ross and Blecher (2019).

[30] There are also considerations linked to intellectual property rights (e.g. counterfeiting), quality standards (missing or fake certification), and health regulations.

[31] Merriman (2001); Ross (2015); Gallagher et al. (2019); Szklo et al. (2018), p. 265; Ross and Blecher (2019).

[32] Liutkutė-Gumarov et al. (2020), p. 2.

[33] Canada Revenue Agency (2020), p. 14; Zhang and Schwartz 2015 p. 10.

[34] Szklo et al. (2018), p. 267.

[35] Transnational Alliance to Combat Illicit Trade (2019), p. 6.

Lastly, illicit trade in excisable goods has been linked to the funding of other illicit activities and even organised crime.[36]

Another standard measure of excise compliance is the excise gap analysis.[37] The tax gap measures the difference between potential revenue and actual revenue collected by the revenue authority. The concept of potential revenue is that it should account for tax collected on the total consumption of excisable products, which includes both licit and illicit markets. This gap can be disaggregated in two distinctive components. First, the compliance gap measures the difference between potential collection, based on the existing tax laws, and actual collection. It is the result of non-compliance by taxpayers. Secondly, the policy gap compares tax collection under the existing tax laws to tax collection under adapted tax laws, whereby tax rates and exemptions are equalised for similar products. In light of the higher excise burden on excisable goods (cigarettes, alcoholic beverages, fuel), the excise gap—in particular the excise compliance gap—is likely to be greater than the VAT gap.

The excise compliance gap for cigarettes in South Africa provides an illustrative example in a representative African country. Currently, the cigarette excise gap is estimated at 39 per cent of the total market, resulting in a loss in excise revenue of ZAR 9.0 billion for the fiscal year 2022/23, as shown in Fig. 2.[38] Given the size of

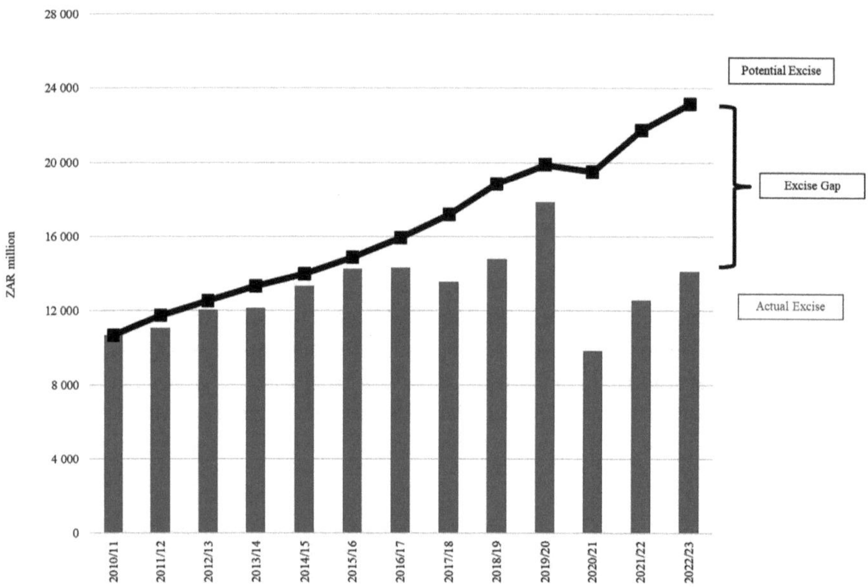

Fig. 2 Cigarette excise gap in South Africa. Author's calculation

[36] Recher (2019), p. 2; Paraje (2019), p. 1079; McLaggan (2020); Mejdini (2020), p. 1; Zhang and Schwartz (2015), p. 3.

[37] HM Revenue & Customs (2023); Stoklosa et al. (2020), pp. 40–57; International Monetary Fund (2013).

[38] Based on the methodology provided in Van Walbeek (2013).

Table 1 Buoyancy of total excise in selected African countries over 2010–2020. Author's calculation

Country	Ghana	South Africa	Nigeria	Sierra Leone	Rwanda	Malawi	DRC	Niger
Buoyancy	3.4	1.4	1.4	0.9	0.9	0.8	0.5	0.4

the gap, it seems improbable that it would be solely attributable to (small) unregistered economic operators and importers. Legitimate actors might have reduced their level of tax compliance, possibly by under-declaring their excise base. The excise gap emerged already in 2017/18 and broadened during the COVID-19 pandemic. The post COVID-19 recovery in excise collection is much more subdued than in most countries, with excise collection still 21 per cent below its peak before COVID-19. This occurred in a context of tax policy decisions to increase the excise rate on cigarettes by 19 per cent. The fact that such a significant increase in the excise rate resulted in such a substantial fall in excise collection highlights the considerable weakness in existing tax administration measures in this country.

A further way to assess the potential of excise is to analyse excise buoyancy and excise elasticity. Tax buoyancy measures the extent to which tax revenue changes with the tax base (typically GDP), indicating the dynamism of taxation. When a tax is said to be dynamic, its revenue increases more than GDP. Estimates of buoyancy are likely more accurate when averaged over a relatively long period, rather than looking at a single year.[39] In the long term, tax buoyancy should be close to one as revenue cannot indefinitely outpace GDP growth. However, for African countries aiming to increase revenue mobilisation, achieving a buoyancy higher than one is a common medium-term objective. Buoyancy can differ from tax to tax, especially if the country seeks to alter the composition of its revenue mobilisation. Buoyancy accounts for any factors influencing tax collection: tax rates, tax base, and tax administration. Tax elasticity also measures the relationship between revenue and the tax base, but stripped of all the discretionary tax policy measures—in that sense, it excludes the impact of changes in the tax rates. Both tax buoyancy and tax elasticity are regularly used as performance indicators by ministries of finance and revenue authorities to assess the responsiveness of the tax system.

Excise buoyancy is relatively low in several African countries, as shown in Table 1. On one hand, this points to a weak performance of excise compared to economic activity and is in line with observations made in OECD countries.[40] This might be attributed to the lack of adjustment of excise rates to inflation, tax relief commonly granted on fuel excise, and inefficiencies in tax administration. In some countries, however, excise buoyancy is elevated, because they added new excisable goods and services over the years, increased the excise rates, and strengthened tax administration.

[39] Naape and Mahonye (2020), p. 835.

[40] Belinga et al. (2014), p. 12.

The mirror analysis of trade is a further tool to assess the potential of excise, when linked to cross-border trade of excisable goods.[41] The primary objective of the mirror analysis of trade is to measure the discrepancy between one country's recorded imports with the mirror recorded exports by the countries of origin of the goods. Logically, these bilateral trade flows ought to match, with a tolerance range of around 10 per cent as the trade value reported by the importing country includes cost, insurance and freight (CIF), while the value reported by the exporting country is typically valued free-on-board (FOB).[42] It is generally acknowledged that reported value data is of higher quality compared to reported volume data.[43] This analysis is relevant for excisable goods that are predominantly imported. Various indicators of the mirror analysis can give insights into the extent of trade discrepancy and the likely type of fraud (undervaluation, smuggling, misclassification of the products).[44] A deeper analysis of the trade discrepancy with neighbouring countries can be informative,[45] also because of the different dynamics taking place at the various types of border posts.[46]

In Africa, trade discrepancies are often observed, in particular for excisable products. In practice, recorded imports and their corresponding recorded mirror exports seldom balance, pointing out a large potential to improve excise collection on imported goods. Figure 3 illustrates the extent of under-reporting of imports compared to the mirror exports declared by partner countries. In the DRC, the gap for imported beer amounted to 72 per cent over the period 2015–2019. In Togo, the gap for tobacco products—this type of excisable products is fully imported in Togo—averaged 44 per cent over the period from 2010 to 2020. This large trade discrepancy raised concerns for the Togolese authorities.

In summary, the potential to increase excise collection in Africa is significant, with additional revenue mobilisation estimated to be in the range of 30 to 100 per cent. Current evidence reveals notable excise gaps, low excise buoyancy and elasticity, large mirror trade discrepancies, and various avenues for illicit trade. In international comparison and considering best practices in Africa, there is considerable room for improvement in excise collection. Concrete excise measures will go a long way to make this potential come true. The additional contribution of excise—if it materialises—should more than compensate for the decline in customs duties. Furthermore, the promising economic prospects of Africa—the AfCFTA might even boost them further—in terms of formalisation of the economy, increased cross-country trade, growing population, urbanisation, enlarging middle-class, and

[41] Merriman (2001), pp. 18–21; Ross (2015), p. 28; Chalendard et al. (2016), p. 7625; Mengistu et al. (2019), p. 48.

[42] Carrère and Grigoriou (2014), p. 2.

[43] Nguyen and Nguyen (2020), p. 29.

[44] Chalendard et al. (2016), p. 7625.

[45] Kalizinje (2018), p. 227.

[46] United Nations Conference on Trade and Development (2021), p. 51.

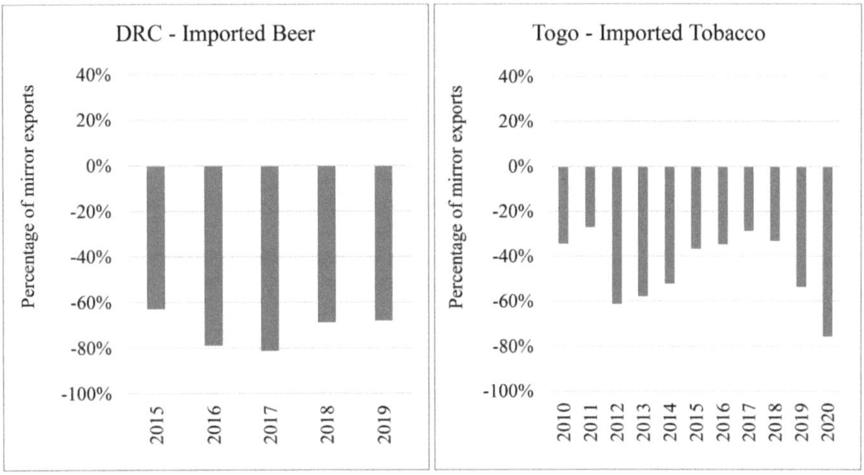

Fig. 3 Mirror trade discrepancy. Author's calculation

evolving consumption trends supports a rising demand for excisable goods and a related increase in domestic revenue mobilisation.

4.2 *Measures to Better Mobilise Excise*

A fully-fledged Medium-Term Revenue Mobilisation Strategy (MTRS) encompasses tax policy and tax administration measures. The MTRS should be comprehensive, provide a medium-term vision, and enjoy high-level political support from the government in order to be effective. The importance of the revenue measures reflects government's priorities as well as society's preferences. In most African countries, indirect taxes (VAT, excise, customs duty) are the main contributors to revenue mobilisation.[47] Direct taxes (corporate income tax, personal income taxes) come second. Other revenue sources include social security contributions, property taxation, and non-tax revenue. Over the recent past, the contribution of domestic taxes has overtaken the contribution of international trade taxes. This trend is expected to accelerate with the implementation of the AfCFTA.

A MTRS commonly addresses a broad range of taxes, including measures covering both excise policy and excise administration. Among the latter measures, Uganda's MTRS planned the full implementation of the digital tax stamps, which has since been completed. Malawi's MTRS includes a review of the list of excisable products (tax policy) and the introduction of excise tax stamps (tax administration). In Liberia and Rwanda, the MTRS targets excise policy measures. The adoption of

[47] African Tax Administration Forum (2021), p. 47.

Table 2 Measures on excise in MTRS and selected national corporate plans

Country	Period	Excise Policy	Excise Administration
Countries with published MTRS			
Malawi	2021–2026	Review the list of excisable products.	Introduce excise tax stamps.
Uganda	2019/20–2023/24	More holistic approach; broaden excise on environment; rationalise multiple rates; inflation-indexation; harmonise excise at EAC level.	Enforce strict regulations; fully implement digital tax stamps.
Liberia	2018–2022	Deepen the use of excise (buoyancy); excise on telecom.	
Rwanda	2021–2024	Reform excise (sugar, cars, milk, water); specific rates with adjustment for inflation.	
Selected corporate plans or strategic plans			
Sierra Leone	2018–2022		Excise tax stamps.
The Gambia	2020–2024	Enact Customs & Excise Act.	Implement excise stamps on excisable goods.
Zambia	2022–2024		Introduce digital stamps for selected excisable goods.

Author's extracts based on mentioned MTRS and strategic plans

MTRS is expected to gain traction in Africa in the near future, with Benin, Cameroon, Côte d'Ivoire, Kenya, Senegal, and Togo currently in the process of adopting one.

At the level of the national tax authorities, several have adopted their own corporate or strategic plans. These plans commonly include initiatives on excise policy and excise administration, as detailed in Table 2. For example, the Gambia Revenue Authority motivates the implementation of excise stamps on excisable goods as a measure to combat tax fraud, in particular the manipulation of tax records by taxpayers, the illegal production of excisable goods, as well as the smuggling across borders. The Zambia Revenue Authority will launch an initiative to introduce digital stamps for selected excisable goods as part of its strategic objective to enhance compliance, ultimately aiming to improve revenue collection.

To increase excise revenue mobilisation in the context of the AfCFTA, measures can be taken on both excise policy and excise administration. The current practice in RECs and well as recent MTRS and national corporate plans can serve as a useful guideline for future developments in these two areas.

A first excise policy measure involves reviewing the list of excisable goods. The implementation of the AfCFTA might at some stage lead to limitations on national authorities' autonomy to decide on the list of excisable goods and services and make changes to it. The current experience of the RECs that legislate on excise indicates that their lists of excisable goods tend to be more compact. As a result, countries such as Ethiopia and the DRC might have to reduce the number of excisable goods. Additionally, the AfCFTA could encourage African countries to treat excisable goods that are produced domestically and those that are imported—in particular from other AfCFTA member countries—equally.

A second tax policy measure is to increase the rates of excise. Many African countries have scope to increase excise rates, in particular on tobacco products and alcoholic beverages. This would align them closer to the world average and follow the recommended best practices from international institutions. The current regulations of several RECs may need to be revised to increase both the minimum and maximum excise rates. This might be carried out in a gradual manner.

A third tax policy measure is to amend the tax base of excise. In this regard, many African countries should similarly consider best international practices. They should use the retail sales price as the excise base, rather than the ex-factory price. They should chiefly consider switching to specific excise rates with an adjustment for inflation—preferably automatic.

Tax administration measures are expected to play an increasing role in strengthening revenue mobilisation, including for excise. The introduction of new technologies by governments is correlated with higher tax collection and reduced corruption, especially since they curb direct interactions between tax officials and taxpayers.[48] In Uganda, the importance of adopting technological innovations as revenue administration measures is considered key to improve tax collection.[49] The adoption of new technologies by the tax authority requires support at the highest levels of government, as well as internal trust in the adopted technology and buy-in by its staff.[50]

For traditional excisable goods, the adoption of a traceability system with secure excise markings represents best practice and is even an international obligation according to the World Health Organization (WHO) Protocol to Eliminate Illicit Trade in Tobacco Products (ITP). The WHO mandates countries to implement secure marking on tobacco packaging and develop a traceability system, in line with the WHO FCTC and the WHO Protocol to Eliminate Illicit Trade in Tobacco Products (ITP). Out of the 67 parties to the WHO ITP, 22 are African countries. The WHO ITP came into force in September 2018. All the parties are required to implement a traceability system by September 2023 to comply with their international obligations. Currently, eighteen African countries—including seven that have ratified the WHO ITP—have implemented a traceability system on one or on a range of excisable goods. Three additional countries have started implementation in 2023. The rationale is that the traceability system should enable the tax authority to ascertain the production and imports of the excisable goods and accurately estimate the tax due by taxpayers, independently of their tax returns. The OECD also recognises that traceability systems to be one of the most effective measures for controlling

[48] International Monetary Fund (2019b), p. 52; SEATINI Uganda (2018), p. 47; United Nations Economic Commission for Africa (2019), p. 105.

[49] Ministry of Finance, Planning and Economic Development (2019), pp. 65–66; Uganda Revenue Authority (2020a), p. 65.

[50] Cantens et al. (2013), p. 127.

excisable goods.[51] The World Bank has provided detailed arguments in favour of the establishment of tobacco traceability systems, including in Kenya,[52] as well as in their practicality in Tanzania and Sierra Leone.[53] The IMF qualifies traceability systems as 'sophisticated marking systems' for excisable goods[54] and has also reported on their contributions, as tax administration measures, to revenue mobilisation in various African countries such as Kenya, Uganda, Sierra Leone, and The Gambia.[55] The case of the DRC is especially interesting, since the implementation of the excise traceability system is a structural benchmark in the IMF Extended Credit Facility Arrangement (2021–2024).[56] It is one of the rare cases where an excise measure—in particular an excise administration measure—is part of the conditionality of an IMF program.

Traceability systems encompass a variety of secure technologies to effectively control excisable goods. A traceability system typically includes (i) unique, secure and non-removable identification markings, such as excise stamps, (ii) equipment inside production facilities for real-time control, (iii) information about the product and its origin enabling track and trace, as it moves in the distribution chain, (iv) tools for field inspection from the taxable point to the retail sales, (v) consumer verification mechanisms, and (vi) data services provided to the tax authorities. In order to access the traceability system and have their excisable goods affixed with the required fiscal markings, manufacturers and importers must be registered in the system by the tax authority. The fiscal markings often contain security features similar to the ones used for banknotes—trust in their features is crucial for the tax authority and for citizens. Forensic security features are useful for potential prosecution, in case of attempts to counterfeit excise markings. These systems have to be anchored in the domestic legislation: in Kenya, the Excise Duty Act, 2015 defines the requirements for the national excisable goods management system, the related secure excise stamps, as well as the excise offences related to the traceability system. Secondary legislation, such as decrees and regulations, specify the characteristics of the system. In most countries, these systems are implemented following a public tender process, where private providers compete on legal, technical, and financial requirements, ensuring a fair and transparent selection process.

Traceability systems have compounding effects on tax compliance and revenue mobilisation. They facilitate the registration of new taxpayers: both the Uganda Revenue Authority (URA) and the Office Togolais des Recettes (OTR) reported a remarkable increase in the number of registered taxpayers for excise of 281 per cent (between 2018/19 and 2021/22) and 1133 per cent (between 2020 and 2023),

[51] Organization for Economic Co-operation and Development (2016), p. 137.

[52] World Bank (2019b); World Bank (2017c).

[53] World Bank (2017c); World Bank (2020b).

[54] International Monetary Fund (2016), p. 8.

[55] International Monetary Fund (2017b), p. 7; International Monetary Fund (2023a), p. 13; International Monetary Fund (2023b), p. 12; International Monetary Fund (2023c), p. 54.

[56] International Monetary Fund (2022), p. 16.

respectively.[57] They strengthen tax compliance with an improvement of 45 per cent recorded in Kenya after the implementation of the Excisable Goods Management System through its contribution to the digitalisation of government systems.[58] Traceability systems chiefly contribute to increased revenue mobilisation. The OTR reported a 40 per cent additional excise for cigarettes and a 30 per cent for beer since the implementation of their national Système Automatisé de Marquage (SAM).[59] In Uganda, URA reported a range of fiscal gains in terms of domestic excise, domestic VAT, imported VAT, and from audits, highlighting the multifaceted contribution of its own Digital Tracking System (DTS) on excisable goods.[60] In Tanzania, the revenue mobilisation from both excise and VAT on a range of excisable goods (cigarettes, beer, spirits, wine, and soft drinks) has seen significant growth of 59 per cent and 26 per cent, respectively, since the introduction of the national Electronic Tax Stamps (ETS) management system. Similarly, excise elasticity has notably improved significantly in Tanzania, as shown in Fig. 4 for soft drinks and beer. Lastly, in Morocco, the authorities report that the prevalence of contraband cigarettes amounted to a very low 1.9 per cent of the market in 2021 compared to 10.3 per cent in 2008, before the introduction of the tobacco excise traceability system.[61] These results align with the potential for excise as presented in Sect. 4.1.

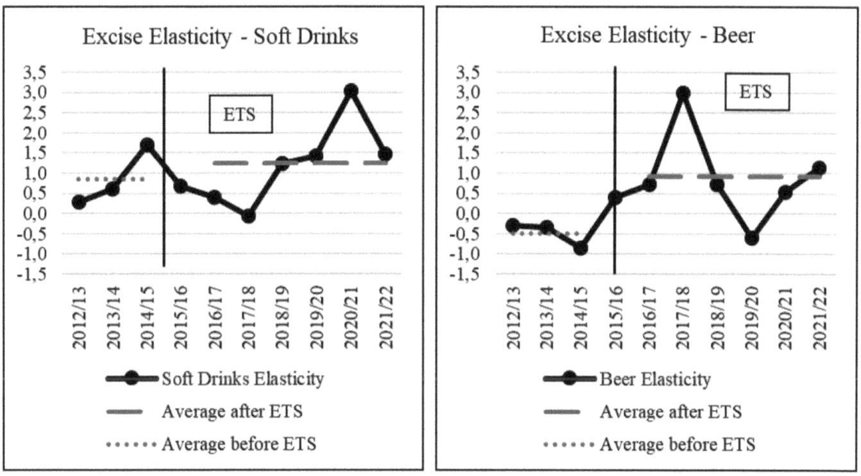

Fig. 4 Excise elasticity in Tanzania. Author's calculation

[57] Office Togolais des Recettes (2023), p. 14.

[58] African Tax Administration Forum (2016), p. 80.

[59] Office Togolais des Recettes (2023), p. 14.

[60] Uganda Revenue Authority (2020b), pp. 7–8.

[61] Administration des Douanes et Impôts Indirects (2008, 2021), p. 29.

For fuel products, molecular fuel marking stands out as a valued tax administration measure. In Africa, 13 countries have deployed or are in the process of deploying fuel marking programs to secure excise on petroleum products, primarily gasoline and diesel. The fuel marking integrates advanced forensic fuel markers, portable laboratories, and digital technologies. Molecular markers are injected at fuel entry points, such as domestic refineries or at the entry into the customs territory. They possess several key attributes: they cannot be laundered, are invisible to the naked eye, and are resistant to extreme weather conditions and temperatures. They cause no harm to the environment and have no effects on vehicles. A fuel analyser mounted in mobile laboratories ensures that fuels can be effectively verified to ensure fiscal compliance at any point along the distribution chain, including petrol stations. All information pertaining to the markers, their injection, and inspection results is recorded in a database hosted by the revenue authority. This tax administration measure enables the tracking, tracing, and monitoring of refined fuel products, ensuring their effective taxation by combating various types of fuel fraud, such as under-declaration, adulteration, dilution, trade diversion, and smuggling, which are still prevalent in many African countries.[62]

For telecom services, tax administration measures for securing excise are entirely digital. These technologies are already operational in 24 African countries. They can be applied to taxes on physical devices (cellphones), telecommunications services (voice, data, sms, and international calls), mobile financial services, online gambling and gaming, and mobile advertisement. The primary goal of this tax administration measure is to enable tax authorities to effectively monitor the high volume of transactions within the telecommunication sector and handle the technical complexity of taxation. As for most taxes, the taxpayers—in this case, telecom operators, which often are subsidiaries of large multinationals—fill out a self-declaration tax return, providing data for assessing the tax base. Due to the inordinate amount of transactions occurring in each period, and the prevalence of pre-paid subscriptions and credit top-ups, tax authorities face the challenge of successfully controlling this information and the accuracy of tax returns. With this digital technology that tracks the logs generated by the operators in real-time, tax authorities gain the necessary digital tools for ensuring proper compliance and accurately computing the revenue of operators and their due taxes. This technology is non-intrusive, meaning that there is neither access to the content of conversations, data, or personal information of users.

Several African countries have either implemented or are in the process of implementing these excise tax administration measures. Morocco was the first African country to implement an excise traceability system in 2010, followed by Kenya in 2013. Most other countries have implemented these systems only more recently, such as Uganda and Togo in 2019, while the DRC began in 2022. Table 3 describes the current adoption status of the three main excise administration measures—traceability system, fuel marking, telecom monitoring—by African countries. Countries where the measures are fully implemented are characterised by **, while countries in the process of implementation are labelled as *. African countries that have

[62] International Monetary Fund (2019a), p. 12.

Table 3 Tax administration measures for excise in selected African countries. Author's investigation

Country	Traceability system	Fuel Marking	Telecom Monitoring
Botswana	**		
Burkina Faso	** (WHO ITP)		
Burundi			**
Cameroon	**	**	**
Central African Republic			**
Chad			**
Democratic Republic of the Congo	**	*	**
Republic of Congo	* (WHO ITP)	**	**
Côte d'Ivoire		**	
Egypt	** (WHO ITP)		
Republic of Equatorial Guinea			**
Gabon			**
The Gambia	* (WHO ITP)	*	*
Ghana	** (WHO ITP)	**	**
Guinea			**
Kenya	** (WHO ITP)	**	
Kingdom of Lesotho			**
Liberia	**		**
Republic of Madagascar			**
Malawi	**		
Mali			**
Mauritius	** (WHO ITP)		
Morocco	**		
Republic of Mozambique	**	**	**
Namibia			**
Rwanda	** (WHO ITP)		**
Senegal		**	**
Sierra Leone	*	*	*
Somalia			**
Sudan	**		
United Republic of Tanzania	**	**	**
Togo	** (WHO ITP)		**
Uganda	**	**	**
Zambia	**	**	**
Zimbabwe			**

Legend: full implementation is characterised by **, while countries in the process of implementation are labelled as*

ratified the WHO ITP are highlighted. Many African countries, despite having ratified the WHO ITP (Benin, Cabo Verde, Chad, Comoros, Côte d'Ivoire, Eswatini, Gabon, Guinea, Madagascar, Mali, Niger, Nigeria, Senegal, and Seychelles) have not yet adopted a traceability system, even though they are under international obligation to do so. In the current context (post COVID-19, Ukrainian war, risk of debt distress, AfCFTA), several African countries initiated the process of adopting excise traceability systems. There is little doubt about the traction of all these tax administration measures, in light of their positive fiscal outcomes. The importance of peer-to-peer learning enables the further sharing of best practices between African tax authorities.

Tax administration measures and the providers of tax technologies should be protected from any vested interest. The guidance from the WHO ITP emphasises that the tobacco industry should not be involved in the discussions and decisions regarding tax policy and tax administration on tobacco. Specifically, the WHO ITP makes it clear that the excise traceability system should not be performed or delegated to the tobacco industry, while the cost of the system should be borne by the industry itself. This requirement could similarly be extended to other excisable goods and other excise tax administration measures. Maintaining strict independence between tax administration measures and the taxpayers involved is crucial for fostering tax compliance and overall performance. The guidance of the WHO ITP is particularly attractive for tax authorities, in the sense that the cost of the traceability system—equipment, technology, database, secure markings and stamps, inspection devices—is to be borne by the excise taxpayers and not by the tax authority.

Still, excise legislation is subjected to political economy considerations, especially when adopting new tax policy and new tax administration measures. Although the universe of excise taxpayers is relatively small, these taxpayers are often well anchored in the economic fabric of the country and well connected with decision-makers. Companies producing and importing excisable goods—especially tobacco products, alcoholic beverages, and fuels—are often part of the large taxpayers and their owners often qualify as high-net worth individuals. They contribute significantly to corporate income tax and personal income tax, beyond their contribution to excise and VAT. In Uganda, the Parliamentary Committee on Finance, Planning and Economic Development typically receives inputs from a range of actors, including from a large number of industry players and associations, in the context of budget discussion around excise.

5 Conclusion

The potential for excise to significantly contribute to revenue mobilisation in Africa and support the well-functioning of the AfCFTA is substantial. Currently, the performance of most African countries in their collection of excise is under-whelming. This is reflected in large excise gaps, significant mirror trade discrepancies, as well as low excise buoyancy and elasticity. It is a manifestation of the large informal sector, pervasive illicit trade, poor compliance, and weak administrative capacity. On the excise policy side, many African countries already apply excise to a relatively large number of goods and services. The AfCFTA might inspire a harmonisation of the list of excisable goods. On the contrary, most African countries have room to increase excise rates to mimic international standards and align with best continental practices. A well-functioning AfCFTA might also require a certain degree of harmonisation of excise rates, which might mean that a convergence to higher rates should be well sequenced. However, the expected gains from tax policy measures—in particular of higher excise rates—will under-perform in the absence of adequate excise administration measures. With technological progress, new measures are being adopted by many African countries, such as the traceability systems for excisable goods, molecular fuel marking, and telecommunications monitoring. In response to administrative capacity constraints, most African tax authorities are keen to leapfrog by adopting tax technologies.

The adoption of these relatively new excise administration measures powered by physical and digital technologies is expected to accelerate in the near future. In most countries, these measures are already interoperable with the main tax management system of the revenue authority. Beyond that, traceability systems and telecommunication monitoring could enable tax authorities to generate pre-populated tax returns, further facilitating compliance and easing filing costs for taxpayers. Excise tax administration measures could be linked with administration measures adopted for other taxes—electronic cash registers, electronic cargo tracking systems, ASYCUDA and customs management systems—to give a broader view of the contribution of individual taxpayers. This approach could be extended to direct taxes, such as corporate income tax and the taxation of high-net worth individuals, by adequately using the data generated by the excise traceability systems or the telecommunications monitoring. The compliance of taxpayers with excise administration measures could be used as a facilitating criterion for granting them the status of an authorised economic operator. The implementation of tax administration measures increases the potential for a win-win with tax policy measures. By providing detailed data, traceability systems for soft drinks could help governments better target their sugar-sweetened beverage taxes. The telecommunications monitoring could support the finetuning of taxation on telecommunications. At a broader government level, the data collected through these tax administration measures could be useful to inform and improve other government functions related to health, trade and industry, transport, energy, statistics, and police. Finally, these excise administration measures enable tax authorities—and more broadly, the government as a whole—to better interact with citizens, strengthening trust. Technologies to deliver mobile government at the service of citizens are increasingly in demand, as seen by the recent push by World Bank to promote GovTech and mobile government solutions.[63]

[63] World Bank (2023b).

References

Abrego L, de Zamaróczy M, Gursoy T, Issoufou S, Nicholls G, Perez-Saiz H, Rosas JN (2020) The African Continental Free Trade Area: Potential Economic Impact and Challenges. IMF Staff Discussion Note SDN/20/04

Administration des Douanes et Impôts Indirects (2008) Rapport d'activité 2008

Administration des Douanes et Impôts Indirects (2021) Rapport d'activité 2021

African Tax Administration Forum (2016) African Tax Outlook 2016

African Tax Administration Forum (2021) African Tax Outlook 2021

African Union Commission (2019) Domestic Resource Mobilization: Fighting against Corruption and Illicit Financial Flows

Belinga V, Benedek D, de Mooij R, Norregaard J (2014) Tax Buoyancy in OECD Countries. IMF Working Paper WP/14/110

Bird R, Wallace S (2010) Taxing Alcohol in Africa: Reflections and Updates. International Studies Program Working Paper 10-31

Blecher E, Drope J (2014) The rewards, risks and challenges of regional tobacco tax harmonisation. Tob Control 23(E1):e7–e11

Blecher E, Liber A, Drope J, Nguyen B, Stoklosa M (2017) Global trends in the affordability of sugar-sweetened beverages, 1990–2016. Prev Chronic Dis 14:160406

Canada Revenue Agency (2020) Tax Gap for Federal Excise Duty on Cigarettes. https://canada.ca/en/revenue-agency/news/2020/12/tax-gap-for-federal-excise-duty-on-cigarettes-and-payment-tax-gap-reports.html

Cantens T, Ireland R, Raballand G (eds) (2013) Reform by numbers: measurement applied to customs and tax administrators in developing countries., 3, directions in development. World Bank, Washington DC, pp 37–58

Carrère C, Grigoriou C (2014) Can Mirror Data Help to Capture Informal International Trade? (2014) UNCTAD Blue Series Papers 65, United Nations Conference on Trade and Development

Chalendard C, Raballand G, Rakotoarisoa A (2016) The use of detailed statistical data in customs reform – the case of Madagascar. World Bank Policy Research Working Paper 7625

East African Revenue Authorities (2017) Comparative Revenue Analysis 2015/16

Evans W, Ringel J, Stech D (1999) Tobacco taxes and public policy to discourage smoking. NBER Chapters. In: Tax Policy and the Economy, National Bureau of Economic Research, Inc, 13:1–56

Gallagher A, Gilmore A, Eads M (2019) Tracking and tracing the tobacco industry: potential tobacco industry influence over the EU'S system for tobacco traceability and security features. Tob Control 29(e1):e56–e62

Gaspar V, Jaramillo L, Wingender P (2016) Tax Capacity and Growth: Is there a Tipping Point?. IMF Working Paper WP/16/234

HM Revenue & Customs (2023) Measuring Tax Gaps 2023 Edition. https://www.gov.uk/government/stattistics/measuring-tax-gaps

International Monetary Fund (2011) Revenue Mobilization in Developing Countries, Prepared by Fiscal Affairs Department, 8 March 2011

International Monetary Fund (2013) United Kingdom: Technical Assistance Report: Assessment of HMRC's Tax Gap Analysis. IMF Country Report No. 13/14

International Monetary Fund (2016) How to design and enforce Tobacco excises? How to notes. IMF, pp 1–17

International Monetary Fund (2017a) Kenya – First Reviews Under the Twenty-Four Month Stand-By Arrangement and the Arrangement Under the Standby Credit Facility. IMF Country Report No. 17/25

International Monetary Fund (2017b) Regional Economic Outlook Sub-Saharan Africa, May 2017

International Monetary Fund (2018) Fiscal Monitor – Capitalizing on Good Times, 6 April 2018

International Monetary Fund (2019a) Fiscal Monitor – Curbing Corruption, 10 April 2019

International Monetary Fund (2019b) Niger – 2019 Article IV Consultation, Fourth Review Under the Extended Credit Facility. IMF Country Report No. 19/239
International Monetary Fund (2022) Democratic Republic of the Congo – First Review under the Extended Credit Facility Arrangement. IMF Country Report No. 22/3
International Monetary Fund (2023a) Sierra Leone – Sixth and Seventh Reviews Under the Extended Credit Facility Arrangement. IMF Country Report No. 23/214
International Monetary Fund (2023b) The Gambia – Sixth Review Under the Extended Credit Facility Arrangement. IMF Country Report No. 23/216
International Monetary Fund (2023c) Uganda – Second and Third Reviews Under the Extended Credit Facility Arrangement. IMF Country Report No. 23/40
Kalizinje F (2018) Combating customs revenue fraud in WCO ESA region: a mirror analysis through the lens of Malawi. Global Trade Cust J 13(5):224–233
Kieyah J, Shibia A, Gitonga A (2014) Situational Analysis of Illicit Trade in Tobacco Products in Kenya. KIPPRA Special Paper 15 of 2014 on Situational Analysis of Illicit Trade in Tobacco Products in Kenya, pp 1–74
Lemgruber A, Masters A, Cleary D (2015) Understanding Revenue Administration: An Initial Data Analysis using the Revenue Administration Fiscal Information Tool. International Monetary Fund Fiscal Affairs Department Paper Series, pp 1–69
Levell P, O'Connell M, Smith K (2016) Excise duties. In: Johnson P, Emmerson C, Joyce R (eds) The IFS green budget: February 2016. Institute for Fiscal Studies, London
Liutkutè-Gumarov V, Glakus L, Petkeviciene J, Stelemekas M, Miscikiene L, Mickeviciene A, Vaitkeviciute J (2020) Illicit tobacco in Lithuania: a cross-sectional survey. Int J Environ Res Public Health 17(19):7291
McLaggan M (2020) When the Smoke Clears. 24 Global Initiative Against Transnational Organized Crime Commodity Report 24:1–50
Medina L, Schneider F (2018) Shadow economies around the world: what did we learn over the last 20 years?. IMF Working Paper WP/18/17
Mejdini F (2020) A Filterless Environment. Global Initiative Against Transnational Organized Crime Policy Report
Mengistu A, Molla K, Mascagni G (2019) Tax Evasion and Missing Imports: Evidence from Transaction-Level Data. ICTD Research in Brief
Merriman D (2001) Understand, measure, and combat tobacco smuggling. In: Yurekli A, de Beyer J (eds) World Bank Economics of Tobacco Toolkit, pp 1–62
Ministry of Finance, Planning and Economic Development (2019) Background to the Budget Fiscal Year 2019/20
Mpofu FY (2022) Sustainable mobilisation of tax revenues to enhance economic growth in Sub-Saharan Africa: challenges, opportunities, and possible areas of reform. Res Bus Soc Sci 11(9):222–233
Naape B, Mahonye N (2020) How Buoyant is the South African tax system? An ARDL Approach. ERSA Working Paper 835
Nguyen A, Nguyen H (2020) Tobacco excise tax increase and illicit cigarette consumption: evidence from Vietnam. Tob Control 29(4):1–6
Office Togolais des Recettes (2023) Expérience dans la Mise en Oeuvre d'un Système de Suivi et de Traçabilité des Produits du Tabac au Togo. Paper presented at the Mission CEDEAO July 18
Organization for Economic Co-operation and Development (2016) Illicit Trade: Converging Criminal Networks
Panggabean L, Hutabarat M, Sitorus FY, Pamungkas F (2024) The contribution of excise tax to government revenue: a case study of developed countries. Int J Commer Manage Res 10(5):24–30
Paraje G (2019) Illicit cigarette trade in five south American countries: a gap analysis for Argentina, Brazil, Chile, Colombia and Peru. Nicotine Tob Res 21(8):1079–1086
Recher V (2019) Tobacco smuggling in the Western Balkan Region: exploring habits, attitudes, and predictors of illegal Tobacco demand. Working Papers 1901, The Institute of Economics, Zagreb
Republic of Uganda (2015) Second National Development Plan 2015/16–2019/20

Ross H (2015) Understanding and measuring the cigarette tax avoidance and evasion. Tobacconomics, Chicago IL
Ross H, Blecher E (2019) Illicit trade in tobacco products need not hinder tobacco tax policy reforms and increases. Tobacconomics White Paper. Tobacconomics, Health Policy Center, Institute for Health Research and Policy, University of Illinois at Chicago, Chicago
SEATINI Uganda (2018) Fair tax monitor study Uganda. SEATINI, Uganda 29 October 2018
Stoklosa M, Paraje G, Blecher E (2020) A toolkit on measuring illicit trade in tobacco products. Tobacconomics, Health Policy Center, Institute for Health Research and Policy, University of Illinois at Chicago, Chicago, pp 1–78
Szklo A, Iglesias R, Carvalho de Sousa M, de Almeida MSL (2018) Trends in illicit cigarette use in Brazil estimated from legal sales 2012–2016. Am J Public Health 108(2):265–269
Tobacco Free Kids (2023) Taxation and Price' 2023. https://www.tobaccofreekids.org/what-we-do/global/taxation-price/tax-burden-htp#all-data. Accessed 18 July 2023
Transnational Alliance to Combat Illicit Trade (2019) Mapping the Impact of Illicit Trade on the Sustainable Development Goals, pp 1–130
U.S. National Cancer Institute and World Health Organization (2016) The economics of Tobacco and Tobacco control. National Cancer Institute Tobacco Control Monograph 21. World Health Organization, Geneva
Uganda Revenue Authority (2020a) Celebrating the taxpayers of Uganda. Uganda Revenue Authority, pp 1–12
Uganda Revenue Authority (2020b) Corporate Plan 2020/21–2025/25
United Nations Conference on Trade and Development (2021) Economic Development in Africa Report 2021. Economic Development Report in Africa, pp 1–224
United Nations Economic Commission for Africa (2019) Fiscal policy for financing sustainable development in Africa. United Nations Commission for Africa, Addis Ababa, pp 1–186
Van Walbeek C (2013) Measuring changes in illicit cigarette market using government revenue data: the example of South Africa. Tob Control 23(1):1–6
World Bank (1999) Curbing the epidemic, World Bank, pp 1–140
World Bank (2017a) Improving Domestic Resource Mobilization in Uganda
World Bank (2017b) Revenue Impact of Proposed Tobacco Excise Tax Increase Scenarios in Sierra Leone
World Bank (2017c) Tobacco Tax Reform – At the Crossroads of Health and Development
World Bank (2019a) Confronting Illicit Tobacco Trade
World Bank (2019b) Guinea – Opportunities for Enhanced Domestic Revenue Mobilization: Value-Added Tax and Excise Taxes
World Bank (2020a) Tanzania Public Expenditure Review FY20
World Bank (2020b) Taxes on sugar-sweetened Beverages: International Evidence and Experiences
World Bank (2023a) Global SSB Tax Database. https://datacatalog.worldbank.org/search/dataset/0063310
World Bank (2023b) Mobile Government How-to Note
World Health Organization (2010) WHO Technical Manual on Tobacco Tax Administration
World Health Organization (2015) WHO Report on the Global Tobacco Epidemic
World Health Organization (2019) WHO Report on the Global Tobacco Epidemic
Yurekli A (2001) Design and administer Tobacco taxes. In: Yurekli A, De Beyer J (eds) World Bank Economics of Tobacco Toolkit
Zake J (2011) Customs Administration Reform and Modernization in Anglophone Africa – Early 1990s to Mid-2010. IMF Working Paper WP/11/184
Zhang B, Schwartz R (2015) What effect does Tobacco taxation have on contraband? Debunking the Taxation – Contraband Tobacco Myth. Ontario Tobacco Research Unit Special Report

Unlocking Africa's Potential Through Customs Reform

Lessons from Nigeria, Liberia, Rwanda, and Mauritius

Chebo Tamajong Nfor and Victor T. Amadi

Abstract A wide range of restrictive practices, like customs and administrative entry procedures, make trade difficult, which can stifle the development agenda. Research shows that most African countries face the challenge of burdensome customs procedures underpinned by complex and poor customs administration and inefficient control of border processes. This chapter conducts a comparative analysis of the legal frameworks and policies enabling customs reforms and facilitating cross-border trade in Nigeria, Liberia, Rwanda, and Mauritius. These countries demonstrate the diverse developmental status of most African countries as either developing (Nigeria and Mauritius) or least developed (Liberia and Rwanda) countries. Further, Rwanda emphasises the landlocked qualities shared by sixteen African countries. As a small island State and developing nation, Mauritius also emphasises the geographical traits shared by five other African countries. This discussion aims to provide recommendations that, if considered or applied in other developing or least developed countries, could result in reforming legal policies and frameworks to facilitate cross-border trade. As a background, the chapter will examine the legal frameworks influencing trade facilitation under the African Continental Free Trade Area (AfCFTA) and selected Regional Economic Communities (RECs), which, if adopted and implemented domestically, would aid domestic reforms and bring about a positive role in facilitating trade in Africa.

C. Tamajong Nfor (✉) · V. T. Amadi
Centre for Comparative Law in Africa, Faculty of Law, University of Cape Town, Cape Town, South Africa
e-mail: tmjche001@myuct.ac.za; victor.amadi@uct.ac.za

T. V. Warikandwa et al. (eds.), *Law and Policy of the African Continental Free Trade Area (AfCFTA)*, European Yearbook of International Economic Law,
https://doi.org/10.1007/978-3-032-01122-0_15

1 Introduction

No matter how wealthy a country is and what it possesses, it has to relate and interact with other countries, as no country can exist independently. The phrase "he who controls the trade controls the world economy" has forever remained true.[1] International trade has played a significant role in determining countries' economic and political strength. Ensuring and sustaining such economic gains requires adopting policies and measures which are progressive to allow for the ease of trade. In Africa, intra-Africa trade remains low[2] and a compelling factor to this low level of trade is the conditions under which goods move across borders. Cumbersome and complex procedures, poor infrastructure, lack of transparency and awareness of trade formalities are cited as challenges stifling cross border trade.[3] Tackling such challenges requires trade enabling policies and measures making trade facilitation essential to any trade process. Post establishing the World Trade Organisation (WTO) in 1995, to sustain its overriding objective to ensure free trade, a Trade Facilitation Agreement (TFA) was adopted in 2013 to speed up goods' movement, release, and clearance across borders. In Africa, with the adoption and phased implementation of the African Continental Free Trade Area (AfCFTA), there is a potential for increased cross-border trade.[4] The AfCFTA Agreement strongly emphasises cooperating on customs matters and implementing trade facilitation measures to actualise this potential and its objectives.[5]

Keying in on the imperative of trade facilitation to particularly further the objectives of the AfCFTA, the discussion proceeds as follows: First, the chapter briefly explains trade facilitation and the fundamental approach that underlines its relevance in Africa. Secondly, the paper proceeds to study the legal environment that enables trade facilitation. This discussion will briefly explore the WTO TFA, and the AfCFTA Annex on Customs Cooperation and Trade Facilitation. Further, this section will examine four African countries in 3 different regions operating at varying degrees in facilitating trade. These countries are Rwanda, Mauritius, Liberia and Nigeria. These countries demonstrate the diverse developmental status of most African countries as either developing (Nigeria and Mauritius) or least developed (Liberia and Rwanda) countries. Rwanda emphasises the landlocked qualities shared by sixteen African countries.[6] As a small island State and developing nation, Mauritius also emphasises the geographical traits shared by five other African

[1] Buhari (2013), pp. 13–47.

[2] Chidede and Sandrey (2018).

[3] Amadi and Lenaghan (2020), p. 312.

[4] Tsowa and Girmaa (2022), pp. 54–68.

[5] Art 4 of the AfCFTA Agreement, 2018.

[6] The 16 Landlocked countries in Africa are Botswana, Burkina Faso, Burundi, Central African Republic, Chad, Ethiopia, Eswatini, Lesotho, Malawi, Mali, Niger, Rwanda, South Sudan, Uganda, Zambia and Zimbabwe.

countries.[7] Thirdly, given that the European Union (EU) is one of the most successful forms of regional integration, the chapter also looks into the legal policies and frameworks applicable in Europe that inform custom practices and trade facilitation within its member states. Finally, considering the progressive legal frameworks and policies applicable in Rwanda and Mauritius, the chapter provides recommendations for Nigeria, Liberia and other African nations with low trade facilitation to facilitate cross-border trade in Africa.

The fundamental premise of this research is that trade facilitation needs to be practised at both the national and regional levels. Facilitating the customs and trade procedures at the national borders and within regional economic communities can increase trade and lower production costs, thus boosting development levels. Also, the research argues that continental implementation of trade facilitation reforms can significantly benefit all nations. Adopting similar frameworks or implementing similar policies can ensure that traders are not burdened by different cross-border requirements, which could slow down cross-border trade.

2 Trade Facilitation

One benefit of international trade is its ability to provide more economic opportunities for people. It is argued that reducing tariffs and institutional trade barriers has resulted in better trade performance for countries more open to trade than countries less open to trade. This liberal approach not only affects the economy but also impacts areas such as poverty alleviation, reduction in unemployment and inflation levels.[8] However, such benefits cannot accrue due to the excessive bureaucracy, and inefficiencies involved in the cross-border movement of goods. The United Nations Conference on Trade and Development (UNCTAD) estimated that an average of 30 different parties, 40 documents, and 200 data elements are involved during customs transactions, usually due to a lack of adequate infrastructure and poor national governance structures.[9] According to the World Bank's Logistics Performance Index,[10] Africa is lagging in customs, infrastructure, competence in trade-related logistics and timeliness of exports and imports. The cumbersome processes involved in cross-border trade often make it challenging for businesses to take advantage of the economic opportunities that international trade offers. To address these challenges, trade facilitation measures are crucial for promoting efficient and effective cross-border trade.

[7] The 6 Island nations in Africa are: Cape Verde, Sao Tome and Principe, Madagascar, Comoros, Seychelles and Mauritius.

[8] Tsotang (2020).

[9] Buyonge and Kireeva (2008), pp. 41–54.

[10] The World Bank (2023).

There is no universally accepted definition of trade facilitation, however, a generally accepted definition stems from the WTO which defines trade facilitation as

> the simplification and harmonisation of international trade procedures' where trade procedures are the 'activities, practices and formalities involved in collecting, presenting and communicating and processing data required for the movement of goods in international trade.[11]

Further, several international organisations and trade institutions have sought to define the concept. According to the OECD, when policymakers speak of trade facilitation, they refer to a 'set of measures that streamline and simplify the technical and legal procedures for products entering or leaving a country to be traded internationally.'[12] The World Customs Organisation (WCO) defines trade facilitation as the 'avoidance of unnecessary trade restrictiveness which can be achieved by applying modern techniques and technologies while improving the quality of controls in an internationally harmonised manner.'[13] In other words, trade facilitation simplifies, harmonises, and modernises trade procedures. The scope of this definition can be defined to narrowly focus on easing the administrative processes involved in cross-border trade in goods.[14]

However, trade facilitation is a concept that goes beyond the dimension of simplifying and harmonising customs administrative procedures. Holistically, it is a concept that considers, measures that reduce the time and costs in the supply and logistics process in importing and exporting goods from one country to another. In essence, it embodies improving soft infrastructures like improving policies, simplifying customs procedures and documentation to enhancing hard infrastructures like roads, ports, railways and utilising information technology.[15]

In Africa, to ensure economic development, there is a strong emphasis on an approach of development regionalism which underscores the relevance of trade facilitation. The UNCTAD, posits developmental regionalism as a 'development-based integration agenda aimed at securing the traditional benefits of regional integration, ensuring that such benefits flow to all member countries and seeking to enhance the integration of member countries into the world market as a means of fostering sustainable development.'[16] Further, within Ismail's rubric of developmental regionalism, he emphasises 'cooperation on investment in cross-border infrastructure and trade facilitation among other pillars to increase connectivity and facilitate inclusion of less developed countries.'[17] As noted by Scholvin, developmental regionalism is about 'proactive economic policies advanced and coordinated by states of the region in question as opposed to a politically passive approach of

[11] World Trade Organization (2022).

[12] OECD (n.d.).

[13] World Customs Organization (2022).

[14] Portugal-Perez and Wilson (2012), p. 1295.

[15] Zaninovic et al. (2023), p. 1. See also, Amadi and Lenaghan (2020), p. 312.

[16] UNCTAD (2013), pp. 96–97.

[17] Ismail (2018).

mere liberalisation'.[18] Highlighting South Africa's perspective of this approach, Scholvin highlights rehabilitation of infrastructure as a core pillar.[19]

Africa's economic development partly depends on the reduction of trade transaction costs which are unacceptably high.[20] If a holistic approach to trade facilitation is to be applied, proactive legal and regulatory systems and improved hard infrastructures are imperative in creating developmental economy. African countries have become parties to numerous agreements and sought to take reformative steps towards enabling trade. One such agreement is the TFA, and as of 5 July 2022, out of 44 African countries that are members of the WTO, 41 African nations have ratified the TFA. Similarly, 48 African countries have ratified the AfCFTA Agreement, and as mentioned earlier, the Agreement strongly emphasises cooperating on customs matters and implementing trade facilitation measures. Therefore, the subsequent section discusses both Agreements to highlight the measures they propose.

3 Trade Facilitation Measures Under Law

The TFA outlines steps to improve customs operations, focusing on streamlined border procedures and transparency. The first five articles of the agreement require the publication of import/export information online.[21] Further, the TFA has a set of guidelines aimed at simplifying customs procedures and promoting trade liberalisation. Articles 6–12 cover the necessary procedural formalities that Member States must follow. Specifically, Article 7 outlines the formalities that must be carried out to ensure efficient customs procedures, such as pre-arrival processing, electronic documentation,[22] electronic payment,[23] and a risk management approach that enables low-risk goods to clear customs quickly.[24] Furthermore, post-clearance audits are mandatory.[25] Article 10 encourages members to review their current formalities and documentation requirements to minimise complexity and reduce the requirements for import, export, and transit formalities.[26] The article also highlights the importance of using international standards, accepting copies, implementing a single-window concept, avoiding pre-shipment inspections for tariff classification and customs valuation, using customs brokers, and having uniform documentation. There are provisions for rejected goods, temporary admission of goods, and inward

[18] Scholvin (2019), p. 118.

[19] Scholvin (2019), p. 118.

[20] Buyonge and Kireeva (2008), pp. 41–54.

[21] See Arts 1–5 of the Agreement on Trade Facilitation (TFA).

[22] Art 7.3 of the TFA.

[23] Art 7.3 of the TFA.

[24] Art 7.4 of the TFA.

[25] Art 7.7 of the TFA.

[26] Art 10.1 of the TFA.

and outward processing. These regulations pave the way for an efficient and transparent customs system that benefits all parties involved in international trade.[27] Article 12 further highlights the need for customs coordination by providing that customs officials should cooperate by way of information sharing.[28]

The TFA allows for the implementation of the above provisions within three different categories, namely Category A, Category B and Category C.[29] For example, a country can give notice that it will apply certain provisions based on Category A[30] and other provisions under Category B.[31] This approach to implementation enables governments to evaluate their preparedness to implement trade facilitation measures and seek assistance to build their capacity to adopt their intended trade reforms. Further, the TFA encourages members to develop a board or a "permanent committee" that will address and deal with trade facilitation issues.[32]

Like the TFA, the AfCFTA recognises the importance of trade facilitation, particularly in customs matters, and aims to foster cooperation among Member States to implement measures to achieve this objective. The Agreement, together with the Protocol on Trade in Goods, contains comprehensive annexes on "customs cooperation," "trade facilitation," and "transit" that should be read with the Protocol.[33]

Annex 3 on customs cooperation prioritises compliance with internationally accepted instruments, standards, practices, and guidelines applicable to customs and trade. Article 5 emphasises the importance of customs laws and procedures based on these instruments, including the TFA.[34] Article 6 highlights the need for cooperation through data exchange, while Article 9 promotes transparency in the customs process.[35] Annex 4 on trade facilitation aims to simplify and harmonise international trade procedures and logistics to expedite goods' movement, clearance, and release.[36] State parties must adopt and maintain procedures for pre-arrival processing,[37] electronic payments of taxes, duties, and charges,[38] and risk

[27] Art 10 of the TFA.

[28] Art 12 of the TFA of 2017.

[29] Art 13 and 14 of the TFA.

[30] Category A suggests that a developing country Member or a least-developed country Member designates for implementation upon entry into force of this Agreement, or in the case of a least-developed country Member within one year after entry.

[31] Category B contains provisions that a developing country Member or a least-developed country Member designates for implementation on a date after a transitional period of time following the entry into force of this Agreement, as provided in Art 16.

[32] Art 23 of the TFA.

[33] Arts 14, 15 and 16 of the AfCFTA Protocol on Trade in Goods refers to adopting appropriate measures regarding customs co-operation, trade facilitation, and transit respectively. This is to be done in accordance with specific annexes.

[34] Annex 3, Art 5(1)(a) of the Protocol on Trade in Goods.

[35] Annex 3, Art 6(2) and Art 9(1) of the Protocol on Trade in Goods.

[36] Annex 4, Art 2 of the Protocol on Trade in Goods.

[37] Annex 4, Art 7 of the Protocol on Trade in Goods.

[38] Annex 4, Art 8 of the Protocol on Trade in Goods.

management systems for customs controls.[39] Additionally, State parties must conduct post-clearance audits to ensure compliance with customs and other related laws,[40] and the average release time of goods must be published to promote transparency.[41] The Annex also provides for the publication of information on the Internet, in line with Article 1 of the TFA.

With these expansive provisions, which afford participating States to be proactive, exploring the domestic frameworks of African countries becomes imperative to highlight trends and approaches. The subsequent section of this chapter comparatively analyses the policies and practices of selected African countries, namely Rwanda, Mauritius, Nigeria and Liberia, which have variedly taken significant steps to facilitate cross-border trade.

3.1 Rwanda

Rwanda is a landlocked republic in the East-central part of Africa and has one of the highest population densities in sub-Saharan Africa.[42] In 2020, its population stood at 12,671,00 people, with GDP growth of 2.0% and USD 823 per capita.[43] The socio-economic development in Rwanda can be attributed to its implementation of reforms and the prolonged period of peace and political stability that has reigned in Rwanda post the genocide.[44]

According to the Constitution of Rwanda, 'international treaties and agreements which have been duly ratified or approved have the force of law as national legislation.'[45] This is important because it shows how treaties and bilateral agreements can be applied in Rwanda. To that effect, Rwanda ratified the WTO TFA in 2017 and ratified the AfCFTA in May 2018.[46] Further, Rwanda is part of the East African Community (EAC). As a party to the EAC, under Article 75(m) of the Treaty for the Establishment of the East African Community, member states agreed to create a Customs Union to ensure the simplification and harmonisation of trade procedures.[47] This core goal is further enabled through the Protocol on the Establishment of the East African Community Customs Union. To administer and manage the EAC Customs Union, the East African Community Customs

[39] Annex 4, Art 10 of the Protocol on Trade in Goods.

[40] Annex 4, Art 11 of the Protocol on Trade in Goods.

[41] Annex 4, Art 12 of the Protocol on Trade in Goods.

[42] 'Rwanda' *Britannica* accessed May 16, 2021. https://www.britannica.com/place/Rwanda/Rwanda-under-German-and-Belgian-control.

[43] Congressional Research Service (2021), p. 2.

[44] Congressional Research Service (2021), p. 2.

[45] Art 168 of Rwanda's Constitution of 2003 with Amendments through 2015.

[46] Tralac (February 13, 2023) https://www.tralac.org/resources/infographic/13795-status-of-afcfta-ratification.html.

[47] Art 75(m) of the Treaty Establishing the East African Community.

Management Act (EACCM) was assented to by Heads of EAC Partner States in 2004. To implement the Act, an EACCM Regulation was adopted in 2010.[48] These instruments operate as national legislations in Rwanda.

The EACCM Act and Regulation emphasise various measures to facilitate trade across the border and it informs most of the measures adopted by Rwanda. For instance, it authorises the electronic declaration of goods carried aboard an aircraft or vessel.[49] Also, it allows for payment of duties by electronic transfer per the prescribed manner in a said nation.[50] Further, the EAC adopted the One-Stop Border Posts (OSBP) Act and Regulations which ensures cooperation between two partner states at a single location to address unnecessary duplication of processes.

Rwanda has invested significantly in modernising it customs by integrating technology into its customs operations. Practically, to ensure transparency and predictability in trade processes, as suggested under Articles 1 to 5 of the WTO TFA, trade procedures and documentation are integrated into Rwanda's Trade Information Portal.[51] Since 2012, the Rwandan Revenue Authority has adopted an electronic single-window system for filing, issuing and modifying import and export declarations. This has helped reduce declaration procedures and automation of clearances.[52] To further improve the trading environment, Rwanda is in the process of implementing a 'digitalising global trade initiative'.[53] This initiative will ensure Rwanda complies with aspects of expediting the release and clearance of goods and improving formalities related to import, export and transit as provided for under Articles 7 and 10 of the WTO TFA. Similarly, this measure will contribute towards implementing certain provisions of the AfCFTA referred to above such as Article 7 on pre-arrival processing. These trade facilitation measures are implemented through the National Trade Facilitation Committee (NTFC), an institution encouraged to be established under Article 23 of the TFA and Article 27 of the AfCFTA Annex on Trade Facilitation.

With its landlocked location, Rwanda relies on good infrastructure for domestic transportation. Rwanda has been able to achieve this mainly through cooperation in the EAC. As party to the EAC, many regional highways have been built, other projects such as the standard gauge railway from Dar es Salaam, Tanzania to Kigali, Rwanda, are underway, and various OSBP have been established.[54] As noted by Nugent and others, such hard infrastructures improve domestic transport making border compliance more time and cost-efficient.[55] Also, in a 2021 a study on OSBP

[48] East African Community Customs Management Regulations, 2010.

[49] East African Community Customs Management Regulations, 108(3).

[50] East African Community Customs Management Regulations, 131(3).

[51] *Rwandan Trade Portal.* Accessed August 14, 2023. https://rwandatrade.rw/.

[52] Nizeyimana and De Wulf (2015), pp. 78–81.

[53] "Digitalizing Global Trade – Rwanda: Introduction of Pre-Arrival and Pre-Departure Processing and Export Facilitation for Postal and Express Shipments" accessed August 14, 2023.https://tradefacilitation.de/wp-content/uploads/DGT-Factsheet-Rwanda_EN.pdf.

[54] African Union Commission (2019), p. 23.

[55] Nugent and Soi (2020), p. 433.

in Rwanda, it was noted that the OSBPs trade facilitation initiative has immensely contributed to the improvements trade facilitation by reducing the factors that make the movement of goods complex and unpredictable along the Rwandan customs posts.[56]

3.2 *Mauritius*

Unlike Rwanda, Mauritius is an island State situated in the Indian Ocean in Eastern Southern Africa. It is commonly known for its sublime and beautiful natural and touristic sites. It has a population of about 1.4 million people with a USD 14.4 Billion GDP.[57] Mauritius has moved from a low-income agricultural economy to a middle-income economy with a growing industrial, financial, and tourism sector over the years. And the vision of Mauritius is to be 'a high-income country based on growth that is sustainably generated and equitably distributed by 2025.'[58]

Mauritius has taken several steps to facilitate cross-border trade. These steps are underpinned by multilateral and regional commitments. Mauritius is a longstanding member of the WTO and was the first country to ratify and adopt the WTO TFA in Africa. It is a member of two sub-regional blocs, the Common Market for East and Southern Africa (COMESA), which it joined in 1981, and the Southern African Development Community (SADC), which it joined in 1995. Furthermore, it participates in the COMESA-EAC-SADC Tripartite Free Trade Area based on its membership in the SADC and COMESA. Also, Mauritius is a state party to the AfCFTA, as it ratified the AfCFTA agreement in October 2019.[59]

Some key instruments that inform its domestic policies and measures on trade facilitation aside from the TFA and AfCFTA referred to earlier are the 1996 SADC Protocol on Trade, as amended in 2010. This agreement illustrates the member state's desire to reduce customs duties and other barriers to trade on imported products among the SADC Member States.[60] It is mentioned in Annex II of the SADC Treaty that customs cooperation shall be ensured through simplification,

[56] Nkundabaramye and Njong (2021), pp. 22–23.

[57] African Development Bank Group (2021).

[58] African Development Bank. "Mauritius: Country Strategy Paper 2014 – 2018." https://www.afdb.org/fileadmin/uploads/afdb/Documents/Project-and-Operations/2014-2018_-_Mauritius_Country_Strategy_Paper.pdf.

[59] Mauritius Trade Easy. "Trade under the AfCFTA starts on 01 January 2021." http://www.mauritiustrade.mu/en/trade-agreements/afcfta.

[60] Southern African Development Community (SADC). https://www.sadc.int/themes/economic-development/trade/#:~:text=The%20Southern%20African%20Development%20Community,products%20amongst%20SADC%20Member%20States.

harmonisation and cooperation of customs laws, procedures, systems, and documents, and additionally through training of customs officials.[61]

In Mauritius, the Customs Act[62] is the primary document that informs customs cooperation and procedures. To facilitate trade across borders and ensure that less time is being used during transactions, the Act permits the Director-General to allow the submission of documents and additional information regarding imports and exports to be done electronically.[63] The Act also permits electronic payment of tariffs and duties through an electronic system provided for and approved by the Director-General.[64]

In line with Article 9A (3)(b) of the Customs Act of Mauritius, the Mauritius Revenue Authority was established with the objective of, amongst others creating trade facilitation measures for legitimate trade across the border to increase imports and exports and encouraging foreign direct investment by reducing costs and time, resulting in a fluid and secure customs clearance process for the business community.[65] The Authority is to achieve this by setting up a legal structure[66]through which all the simplifications for the trader are possible. This trade facilitation role is supplemented by the National Committee on Trade Facilitation, established in 2014. As a pioneer in Africa, Mauritius launched the first single-window portal called Mauritius TradeNet in 1994, enabling the country to facilitate cross-border trade.[67] This single window system has been revised and operates as Mauritius TradeLink since 2016. In addition, the Mauritius Network Services, on behalf of the MRA, has launched 13 projects[68] over the last 25 years that have successfully simplified trade processes.[69]

Mauritius implemented and made trading across borders easier by "introducing electronic submissions for customs declarations and lading bills with no physical copies requirements.'[70] This played a crucial role in reducing the time taken to facilitate data collection while assessing the amount of risk and taking the necessary

---

[61] Southern African Development Community (SADC), Declaration and Treaty of the Southern African Development Community, 1992.

[62] Customs Act 47 of 1988 – 1 January 1989. (Mauritius).

[63] Customs Act 47 of 1988 Section 16A.

[64] Customs Act 47 of 1988 9A (2)(b).

[65] Mauritius Revenue Authority. "Introduction to Customs." https://www.mra.mu/index.php/customs1/more-topics?highlight=WyJ0cmFkZSIsImZhY2lsaXRhdGlvbiIsInRyYWRlIGZhY2lsaXRhdGlvbiJd.

[66] Examples for such regulations are: Customs (Movement Certificate EUR 1) Regulations 2005; Customs (Cargo Community System) Regulations 2008; Customs (Export to the African Continental Free Trade Area) Regulations 2021 etc.

[67] Mauritius Network Service. https://mns.mu/our-solutions/trade-facilitation-solutions/#1464209820722-31383ead-13f4.

[68] Customs Management System (1997); e-permits and e-payment of customs duties and taxes (2000-2001); Freeport Online Cargo Tracking (2010); e-freight (2018) etc.

[69] Mauritius Network Service. https://mns.mu/about-mns/.

[70] World Bank Group (2021).

action in line with the risk assessment. Mauritius introduced a risk-based management system to ease the exporting process. These systems helped in facilitating the customs inspection procedure.

In Mauritius, when exporting goods, it takes 24 hours to carry out border compliance and 9 hrs to do documentary compliance. At the same time, it costs USD $303 to carry out border compliance and USD $128 to carry out documentary compliance. It takes 41 hours to carry out border compliance and 9 hrs to do documentary compliance when importing goods. At the same time, it costs USD $371 to carry out border compliance and USD $166 to carry out documentary compliance.[71]

In 2017, Mauritius adopted the Business Facilitation (Miscellaneous Provisions) Act, 2017 to enable a more conducive business environment. The Act amended several legislations in view of easing doing business in Mauritius. Some of the amendments involve the mandatory application of permits through TradeNet; the introduction of a statutory timeframe for the issue of permits; the introduction of the concept of authorised officers and the delegation of powers of Permanent Secretaries/ Ministers; Section 25B Customs Act was amended to ensure the Director General may release goods from Customs Control pending clearance from a Government Agency (import and export).

3.3 Nigeria and Liberia

Nigeria and Liberia are member states of the Economic Community of West African States (ECOWAS), a REC comprising twelve-member states.[72] A key objective of ECOWAS is to promote development within Africa with a specific interest in the fifteen West African countries that are member States of ECOWAS. ECOWAS seeks to, among other things, promote regional integration and economic development in the sub-region.[73] As of 2019, ECOWAS countries produced more than US $650 billion, or around 40% of Sub-Saharan Africa's total GDP. Members of the ECOWAS community produce around 25% of the Sub-Saharan Africa's merchandise import volume and 32% of its merchandise export volume in terms of international commerce. These statistics highlight the significance of ECOWAS in Sub-Saharan Africa and the critical role that international trade plays in the economies of ECOWAS member states.[74]

One of the earliest trade facilitation enabling agreements developed by ECOWAS is the Trade Liberalization Scheme (ETLS) which began operating in 1979.[75] The

---

[71] World Bank Group (2021), p. 46.

[72] ECOWAS "Member States." https://ecowas.int/member-states/.

[73] Oloruntoba (2016), p. 295.

[74] Safaeimanesh and Jenkins (2021), p. 164.

[75] ECOWAS "ECOWAS Trade Liberalization Scheme ETLS." https://ecotis.ecowas.int/policy-development/common-market-and-custom-union/.

primary purpose of the ETLS is to facilitate trade in the ECOWAS area by creating a free trade area by eliminating customs fees for goods originating from ECOWAS member States.[76] The result of this is that the goods can move freely across borders. Furthermore, the framework of ETLS facilitates the adoption of a uniform competition and industrial policy and investment code to enable the free travel of goods within the ECOWAS region. The ETLS specifies a customs code, supplementary Acts, and training support to facilitate the free movement of goods.[77]

The ECOWAS Customs Code (ECC) prescribes rules and procedures determining common tariffs the member states must apply to goods exchanged within the ECOWAS region.[78] The ECC was drafted considering international conventions outside the ECOWAS region, including the European Union Customs Code, which will be discussed subsequently.[79] The ECC seeks to harmonise customs codes in the ECOWAS region by adopting a common external tariff and, among other things, guidelines for customs authorities to facilitate common customs procedures and taxes. The ECC prescribes that customs processes are done electronically,[80] and data is exchanged electronically through an electronic system that countries are compelled to adopt and maintain to facilitate these processes.[81] The clearance processes adopted, and processing procedures should be done electronically, thus making Nigeria, Liberia, and other ECOWAS States modernise customs systems.

3.3.1 Nigeria

Focusing on Nigeria, it is one of the largest countries in West Africa, with an estimated population of 213 million.[82] Nigeria's vast oil reserves and large population make a central continental and regional trade pillar.[83] Nigeria is a party to the WTO and has ratified the TFA. Further, it has signed and ratified the AfCFTA.

With the comprehensive legal framework adopted at an international and regional level, these measures can only be effective if domesticated by Nigeria. The domestic legal framework that pertains to the facilitation of customs and processing procedures will be examined and the extent to which they incorporate international and regional guidelines and policies. Firstly, the criteria outlined in international law, such as having a platform to ensure transparency of trade processes have been

[76] *Ibid.*

[77] ECOWAS. "From an ECOWAS of States to an ECOWAS of People." https://etls.ecowas.int/.

[78] ECOWAS. "Customs Code." https://ecotis.projects.ecowas.int/policy-development/custom-union/#:~:text=The%20ECOWAS%20Community%20Customs%20Code,well%20as%20among%20Member%20States.

[79] Ibid.

[80] Art 33 of ECOWAS Customs Code.

[81] Art 35 of ECOWAS Customs Code.

[82] World Bank (2023). "Nigeria Population." https://data.worldbank.org/indicator/SP.POP.TOTL?locations=NG.

[83] Saredau (2021), p. 573.

adopted in Nigeria through the Nigeria Trade Portal, which also serves as a single window system for submitting electronic documents. Further, the processes and procedures applied in administering the movement of goods across Nigerian ports are mainly regulated through the Customs and Excise Management Act (CEMA).[84]

The CEMA primarily regulates the collection of customs and excise duties in Nigeria.[85] To that effect, the CEMA provides for the establishment of the National Customs Board, which is responsible for *among other things*, the collection of customs, which is critical for facilitating legitimate trade and preventing smuggling.[86] The CEMA creates clear guidelines for the processes and clearing procedures for the clearance of goods and payment of duties.[87] CEMA prescribes guidelines on the responsibilities that can be imposed and the circumstances in which goods will be exempt from duty.[88] To facilitate the payment of customs in Nigeria, persons can give security for the payment of customs through bonds.[89]

The CEMA, had largely been silent on adopting electronic systems to facilitate trade and clearance of goods. However, in 2023, the CEMA was amended through the Business Facilitation (Miscellaneous Provisions) Act, 2023[90] to provide for a single window under Section 25. This provision introduced the principle of a single window by inserting section 18A and 18B into CEMA.[91] The Act defines a single window to mean 'a platform that allows parties involved in trade and transport to lodge trade-import, export or transit-data required by government departments, authorities, or agencies through a single-entry point interface to fulfil all import, export, transit related and other regulatory requirements.'[92] Further, the Business Facilitation Act under Section 18(a) mandated the Board of Customs and Excise to establish and maintain a single window that allows traders to submit all necessary documentation and information relation to the import, export or transit of goods through a single-entry point. Relevant agencies may make use of the data in the window.[93]

The 2023 Act also made changes to goods that are uncleared or missing from vessels, aircraft, ships and other vehicles. The 2023 Act now requires that a list of goods uncleared should be reported on the fifth day after clearing of such vessels.[94] This is contrary to the former provision of Section 31 which allows for fifteen days.

---

[84] Cap. 84 Laws of the Federation of Nigeria 1990.

[85] Ibid.

[86] Sec 3 of CEMA.

[87] Secs 46–57 of CEMA.

[88] Secs 37–40 of CEMA; Sections 41 and 42 of CEMA.

[89] Sec 144(1) of CEMA.

[90] The objective of the Act is to promote the ease of doing business in Nigeria, eliminate bottlenecks, amend relevant legislation to promote the ease of doing business in Nigeria and to institutionalize all the reforms to ease implementation.

[91] Sec 25 of the Business Facilitation (Miscellaneous Provisions) Act, 2023.

[92] Sec 26, Part III, Schedule of the Act.

[93] Sec 18(a) of the Business Facilitation (Miscellaneous Provisions) Act, 2023.

[94] Sec 27 (a) Business Facilitation (Miscellaneous Provisions) Act, 2023.

Additionally, the 2023 Act provides for four days instead of fourteen days after unloading, for which a customs officer is to transfer uncleared goods to a government warehouse.[95] Also, the inspection of goods under the Act or any other law shall be scheduled to ensure that the inspections by any officer and other relevant authorities are co-ordinated and if possible carried out at the same time.[96]

3.3.2 Liberia

Liberia like the previous countries of focus is a member of the WTO and has ratified the TFA. Further, it signed the AfCFTA in May 2018 and ratified the AfCFTA Agreement in July 2024.[97] Domestically, the law regulating trade across borders in Liberia is the Revenue Code—Modernised Customs Code of 2019.[98] Liberia's involvement in international and regional trade initiatives would also help it enhance and facilitate trade.[99] The tariffs prescribed in the Customs Revenue Code follow international best practices. The terminology used in the Customs Revenue Code and the procedures are aligned with international regulations.[100]

According to the amended law, the Customs Department of the Liberia Revenue Authority is responsible for setting and assessing customs duties or other taxes.[101] Like Rwanda and Mauritius, Liberia adopted provisions that allow for online submission of customs forms and enhanced risk-based inspection at the borders.[102] However, the legislation does not say anything regarding the payment of money electronically. Despite the developmental challenges in Liberia, the Customs Revenue Code embraces an electronic approach to trade processes. Traders can file electronic documents, and a record of these is stored electronically.[103] Electronic signatures are recognised and can be used in trade transactions.[104] The law recognises electronic records and signatures that can be notarised for verification purposes and serve as evidence where necessary.[105]

---

[95] Sec 27 (b) Business Facilitation (Miscellaneous Provisions) Act, 2023.

[96] Sec 18 (b) Business Facilitation (Miscellaneous Provisions) Act, 2023.

[97] TRALAC. "Status of AfCFTA Ratification." https://www.tralac.org/resources/infographic/13795-status-of-afcfta-ratification.html

[98] Revenue Code – Modernised Customs Code of 2019.

[99] Revenue Code – Modernised Customs Code of 2019.

[100] Revenue Code – Modernised Customs Code of 2019.

[101] Section 3(7) of the Revenue Code – Modernised Customs Code of 2019.

[102] Secs 102 to 105 of the Amendment of Part 1 of the Revenue Code on the Act amending the revenue code of Liberia, Phase One of the Reform tax Code of Liberia, A.D 200 to Adopt a Modernized customs Code (2018), Accessed on July 31, 2023. https://revenue.lra.gov.lr/08/REVENUE-CODE-MODERNIZED-CUSTOMS-CODE-2019-CUSTOMS.pdf.

[103] Secs 102 and 104 Customs Revenue Code.

[104] Sec 103 Customs Revenue Code.

[105] Sec 105 Customs Revenue Code.

Compared to Nigeria, Liberia has taken strides to adopt electronic processes to enhance the processes and procedures that pertain to customs and tariffs. However, these developments are impeded by among other things poverty and the need for infrastructure. These challenges exist across the African continent. Despite the extensive international, regional, and domestic legal framework, these factors must be considered in recommending and adopting measures to implement these trade facilitation regulations.

4 The European Union

The EU recognises that trade facilitation is vital for making international trade possible. Though a core driver of trade facilitation has been the WTO with the adoption of the TFA, several commitments in the TFA were part of the EU customs regulatory framework under the Community Customs Code of 1992, which was further developed under the Unions Customs Code of 2013. This code will be examined briefly.

4.1 European Union Customs Code

In 2013 the EU launched and adopted the new Union Customs Code,[106] revoking the old Community Customs Code. However, most of its substantive provisions only became applicable from the 1st of May 2016. It sets out new rules for applying common customs tariffs and calculating customs duties in all the EU member states.[107]

The Union Customs Code applies to the now 27 EU member states, Monaco and British Territories.[108] They oversee a solitary system for handling the import, export, and transit of goods. All members work together to establish the same import tariffs from other nations.[109] Some of the critical functions of the EU Customs Union are to 'protect the citizens and the environment against many different hazardous goods; combat counterfeiting and piracy; support the fight against fraud, crime, drugs and terrorism; encourage legitimate trade and enhance competitiveness; ensure the

[106] Regulation (EU) No 952/2013. Note however, that although it was adopted on the 9th of October 2013 and entered into force on the 30th of October 2013, most of its substantive provisions only became applicable from the 1st of May 2016.

[107] Valentiejus (2017), pp. 58–78.

[108] WTO Committee on Trade Facilitation (2018) "European Union Customs Transit including arrangements with neighbouring countries under the Common Transit Convention." May 2, 2018. https://www.wto.org/english/tratop_e/tradfa_e/comm_e/meet26june_eu_nonpaper_2_e.pdf.

[109] European Commission. "Taxation and Customs Union: 50 years of the EU Customs Union." accessed July 10, 2023. https://taxation-customs.ec.europa.eu/50-years-eu-customs-union_en.

correct payment of duties and taxes due on imports into the EU; and implement trade policy measures.'[110]

A significant advancement within the EU is its electronic approach to customs processes. This was underpinned by a 2003 European Commission decision communicated to the EU Council and Parliament to create a simple environment for customs and trade.[111] Following this decision, in 2008, the European Parliament passed Decision No 70/2008/EC which prescribes member states to 'set up secure, integrated, interoperable and accessible electronic customs systems for the exchange of data contained in customs declarations, documents accompanying customs declarations and certificates.'[112] This system as stated in Article 2 of the Decision, aims to: facilitate import and export processes; lower compliance and administrative costs and speed up clearance times; coordinate a common approach to the control of goods; help ensure the proper collection of all customs duties and other charges; ensure the prompt provision and receipt of relevant information with regard to the global supply chain; and enable the seamless flow of data.[113] Given that the law directly applies to member states in the EU regardless of whether there has been ratification of the law, this means that the decision and the aims of the Union Customs code can easily be implemented within the member states.

The EU Single Window Environment for Customs, which aims to enable 'interoperability between the customs and non-customs domains to streamline the electronic exchange of documents and information' necessary for the goods clearance process, was created by the EU to make this process simple and seamless. The framework formally provides a centralised system to link the import, export, and transit networks of the Member States with the non-customs networks of the Union that control non-customs formalities. The EU Customs Single Window Certificates Exchange System (EU CSW-CERTEX), which has been operational in pilot mode since 2017, is the name of the system. By guaranteeing that these agencies obtain the original data in its native format, this approach is intended to improve the sharing and processing of data supplied to customs and non-customs authorities by economic operators.[114]

According to the Regulation laying down the Union Customs Code[115] which repealed the Regulation laying down the Community Customs Code (Modernised

---

[110] Ibid.

[111] EUR-Lex "Communication from the Commission to the Council, the European Parliament and the European Economic and Social Committee - A simple and paperless environment for Customs and Trade." https://eur-lex.europa.eu/legal-content/EN/TXT/?uri=celex%3A52003DC0452%2801%29.

[112] Art 1 of Decision No 70/2008/EC of the European Parliament and of the Council on a paperless environment for customs and trade.

[113] Art. 2 of Decision No 70/2008/EC of the European Parliament and of the Council.

[114] European Commission. "Taxation and Customs Union: the EU Single Window Environment for Customs." https://taxation-customs.ec.europa.eu/eu-single-window-environment-customs_en.

[115] Regulation (Eu) No 952/2013 of the European Parliament and of the Council of 9 October 2013 laying down the Union Customs Code.

Customs Code),[116] the preservation of information as required by the customs legislation, and any exchanges of information, such as declarations, applications, or decisions, between customs authorities and between economic operators, shall be made using electronic data-processing techniques.[117]

In addition, regarding goods in transit in the EU, Article 127(3) specifically allows traders to lodge entry summary declaration at the customs office of first entry within a specific time limit before the goods are brought into the customs territory of the Union. Furthermore, it also makes provision for cases where such summary declaration is lodged at another customs office. It does this by permitting Customs authorities to allow at their discretion entry summary declarations lodged at another customs office, provided that the latter immediately communicates or makes available electronically the necessary particulars to the customs office of first entry.[118] The time taken at customs offices with regard to goods in transit usually stands out as one of the barriers to trade. The approach thus adopted by the EU here makes trade facilitation very easy and quick, thus allowing for development and greater economies of scale.

5 Recommendations for African Countries

While countries have adopted various approaches to facilitating trade, it must be acknowledged that some have moved faster than the others. However, there are some common traits which can be picked up from the countries discussed. To begin, all the African nations discussed have signed the TFA as well as signed the AfCFTA (though Liberia only recently ratified the AfCFTA in 2024). In addition, the pattern of continuous amendments to domestic laws and policies regulating trade and customs is evidence that steps are being taken towards making trade and customs practices very seamless. For instance, while Rwanda and Mauritius adopted domestic laws and policies with provisions directed at facilitating the electronic declaration of goods and the electronic payment of customs duties, Liberia amended its Revenue Code in 2019 in a manner that permits the acknowledgement of electronic declaration of goods. Nigeria also, through the 2023 Business Facilitation Act has mandated creating and utilising a single window system. These patterns are demonstrative of the political will to engage in domestic reforms and match up with international best practices.

Further, there is evidence that regional agreements are also fundamental towards promoting development and that where regional frameworks and policies are in place to promote and facilitate trade and customs across borders, the member states

[116] Regulation (EC) No 450/2008 of the European Parliament and of the Council of 23 April 2008 laying down the Community Customs Code (Modernised Customs Code).

[117] Art 6(1) of the Regulation (Eu) No 952/2013 of the European Parliament and of the Council.

[118] Art 127(3) of the Regulation (Eu) No 952/2013 of the European Parliament and of the Council.

that ratify and implement these agreements tend to rip the benefits. Within the African context, the EAC has been instructive in influencing Rwanda, similarly, the ECOWAS has been influential to Nigeria and Liberia. Also, the EU through its extant Decisions and Regulations which are directly applicable to member states and do not require the EU member nations to adopt legislation have also enabled reforms. Based on this, the AfCFTA will be instructive in enabling and coordinating further regulatory reforms and building the capacity of countries to implement trade-facilitating measures. Considering the diverse development status of countries in the continent, principles enshrined in the AfCFTA Agreement such as variable geometry will be fundamental in implementing trade facilitation measures. With this, countries that are at a certain level of development will not be expected to implement the laws or policies immediately. However, the AfCFTA will be instructive in capacity building to ensure such measures are implemented.

6 Conclusion

It is evident that most regional economic communities have taken some steps and their member states to facilitate cross-border trade within the continent. However, while some nations have benefited from this initiative, others have yet to benefit from it or see the bright side of it, primarily due to their undesiring nature and unwillingness to implement the treaty properly. One of the hurdles highlighted is the need for more infrastructure and the failure to properly enforce the treaty in the domestic laws. The research has thus suggested that these be considered and that the countries experiencing low cross-border trade take the necessary measures to ensure that they benefit from trade facilitation. In addition, it suggests that a single customs check be done within regional economic communities as is the case in the EU, where traders are only required to show documentation at the point of entry, and this is sufficient for the trader to use until such trader reaches its final destination within the EU. This means adopting a generally acceptable payment and required document to facilitate regional trade. Finally, with trade just beginning under the AfCFTA and the Secretariat finding ways to ensure that it is appropriately implemented, the African nations must participate in this agreement to be included in the benefits it is said to bring.

References

AfCFTA Agreement 2019

AfCFTA Protocol on Trade in Goods 2019

African Development Bank. Mauritius: Country Strategy Paper 2014 – 2018. https://www.afdb.org/fileadmin/uploads/afdb/Documents/Project-and-Operations/2014-2018_-_Mauritius_Country_Strategy_Paper.pdf

African Development Bank Group. Mauritius. https://www.afdb.org/en/countries/southern-africa/mauritius
African Union. List of countries which have signed, ratifies /acceded to the Agreement Establishing the African Continental Free Trade Area. https://au.int/sites/default/files/treaties/36437-sl-AGREEMENT_ESTABLISHING_THE_AFRICAN_CONTINENTAL_FREE_TRADE_AREA.pdf
African Union Commission (2019) 2019 African Regional Integration Report: Towards an integrated and prosperous and peaceful Africa: Voices of the RECs. Addis Ababa: African Union
Agreement on Trade Facilitation (TFA) 2017
Amadi V, Lenaghan P (2020) Facilitating trade and strengthening market access in the Southern African customs union: a focus on South Africa's customs reform. South Afr Mercantile Law J 32(3):309–333
Amendment of Part 1 of the Revenue Code on the Act amending the revenue code of Liberia, Phase One of the Reform tax Code of Liberia, A.D 200 to Adopt a Modernized customs Code (2018). https://revenue.lra.gov.lr/08/REVENUE-CODE-MODERNIZED-CUSTOMS-CODE-2019-CUSTOMS.pdf
Britannica. Rwanda. https://www.britannica.com/place/Rwanda/Rwanda-under-German-and-Belgian-control
Buhari CM (2013) An analysis of Nigerian Seaborne Trade (dry Bulk) and the demand for transport. Int Aff Glob Strategy 15:13–47
Business Facilitation (Miscellaneous Provisions) Act, 2023
Buyonge C, Kireeva I (2008) Trade facilitation in Africa: challenges and possible solutions. World Cust J 2(1):41–54
Cap. 84 Laws of the Federation of Nigeria 1990
Chidede T, Sandrey R (2018). Intra-African trade-Focusing on trade within Regional Economic Communities. Tralac Trade Brief. https://www.tralac.org/publications/article/13567-intra-african-trade-focusing-on-trade-within-regional-economic-communities.html
Congressional Research Service. Rwanda: In Brief. 16 May 2021 https://fas.org/sgp/crs/row/R44402.pdf
Customs (Cargo Community System) Regulations 2008
Customs (Export to the African Continental Free Trade Area) Regulations 2021
Customs (Movement Certificate EUR 1) Regulations 2005
Customs Act 47 of 1988 – 1 January 1989
Customs Management System 1997
Decision No 70/2008/EC of the European Parliament and of the Council
East African Community Customs Management Regulations, 2010
ECOWAS. ECOWAS Trade Liberalization Scheme ETLS. https://ecotis.ecowas.int/policy-development/common-market-and-custom-union/
ECOWAS. From an ECOWAS of States to an ECOWAS of People. https://etls.ecowas.int/
ECOWAS. Member States. https://ecowas.int/member-states/
ECOWAS. Customs Code. https://ecotis.projects.ecowas.int/policy-development/custom-union/#:~:text=The%20ECOWAS%20Community%20Customs%20Code,well%20as%20among%20Member%20States
EUR-Lex. Communication from the Commission to the Council, the European Parliament and the European Economic and Social Committee - A simple and paperless environment for Customs and Trade. https://eur-lex.europa.eu/legal-content/EN/TXT/?uri=celex%3A52003DC0452%2801%29
European Commission. Taxation and Customs Union: 50 years of the EU Customs Union. https://taxation-customs.ec.europa.eu/50-years-eu-customs-union_en
European Commission. Taxation and Customs Union: the EU Single Window Environment for Customs. https://taxation-customs.ec.europa.eu/eu-single-window-environment-customs_en

Ismail F (2018) A developmental Regionalism Approach to the African Continental Free Trade Area (AfCFTA). Working paper presented at the OluAkinkugbe Business Law in Africa Fellowship Conference, Lagos, 28 November 2018
Mauritius Network Service. https://mns.mu/about-mns/
Mauritius Network Service. https://mns.mu/our-solutions/trade-facilitation-solutions/#1464209820722-31383ead-13f4
Mauritius Revenue Authority. Introduction to Customs. https://www.mra.mu/index.php/customs1/more-topics?highlight=WyJ0cmFkZSIsImZhY2lsaXRhdGlvbiIsInRyYWRlIGZhY2lsaXRhdGlvbiJd
Mauritius Trade Easy. Trade under the AfCFTA starts on 01 January 2021. http://www.mauritius-trade.mu/en/trade-agreements/afcfta
Nizeyimana C, De Wulf L (2015) Rwanda electronic single window supports trade facilitation. World Cust J 9(2):78–81
Nkundabaramye V, Njong MA (2021) Effects of one stop border posts (OSBPs) trade facilitation initiatives on the movement of goods along the Rwandan Custom's Post. Open Access Libr J 8:22–23
Nugent P, Soi I (2020) One-stop border posts in East Africa: state encounters of the fourth kind. J East Afr Stud 14(3):433–454
OECD. Trade Facilitation explained in 90 seconds. https://www.oecd.org/trade/topics/trade-facilitation/
Oloruntoba SO (2016) ECOWAS and regional integration in West Africa: from state to emerging private authority. Hist Compass 14(7):295–303
Partners in Transformation. Digitalizing Global Trade – Rwanda: Introduction of Pre-Arrival and Pre-Departure Processing and Export Facilitation for Postal and Express Shipments. https://tradefacilitation.de/wp-content/uploads/DGT-Factsheet-Rwanda_EN.pdf
Portugal-Perez A, Wilson JS (2012) Export performance and trade facilitation reform: hard and soft infrastructure. World Dev 40(7):1295–1307
Regulation (EC) No 450/2008 of the European Parliament and of the Council of 23 April 2008 laying down the Community Customs Code (Modernised Customs Code)
Regulation (EU) No 952/2013
Regulation (Eu) No 952/2013 of the European Parliament and of the Council
Regulation (Eu) No 952/2013 of the European Parliament and of the Council of 9 October 2013 laying down the Union Customs Code
Revenue Code – Modernised Customs Code of 2019. https://revenue.lra.gov.lr/08/REVENUE-CODE-MODERNIZED-CUSTOMS-CODE-2019-CUSTOMS.pdf
Rwanda's Constitution of 2003 with Amendments through 2015
Rwandan Trade Portal. https://rwandatrade.rw/
Safaeimanesh S, Jenkins GP (2021) Trade facilitation and its impacts on economic welfare and sustainable development of the ECOWAS region. Sustainability 13(1):164
Saredau DP (2021) Law and Nigeria's development: how to strengthen the efficacy of law for development in Nigeria. Afr J Int Comp Law 29(4):551–573
Scholvin S (2019) Developmental regionalism and regional value chains: Pitfallls to South Africa's vision for the tripartitie Free Trade Area. Afr Spectrum 53(3):115–129
Southern African Development Community (SADC). https://www.sadc.int/themes/economic-development/trade/#:~:text=The%20Southern%20African%20Development%20Community,products%20amongst%20SADC%20Member%20States
Southern African Development Community (SADC), Declaration and Treaty of the Southern African Development Community, 1992
The World Bank (2023) Connecting to Compete 2023 – Trade Logistics in an Uncertain Global Economy: The Logistics Performance Index and its Indicators. https://lpi.worldbank.org/sites/default/files/2023-04/LPI_2023_report_with_layout.pdf
Tralac. Status of AfCFTA Ratification. February 13, 2023 https://www.tralac.org/resources/infographic/13795-status-of-afcfta-ratification.html

Treaty Establishing the East African Community 1999
Tsotang T (2020) Trade facilitation in the Southern African development community: the potential contribution of the World Trade Organization's trade facilitation agreement. PhD dissertation, University of Cape Town
Tsowa K, Girmaa M (2022) From ratification to implementation of the African Continental Free Trade Area: what we have learned in the state parties. In: Mangeni F, Att-Mensah (eds) Existential Priorities of the AfCFTA. UNECA, Addis Ababa, pp 54–68
UNCTAD (2013) Boosting Intra-African trade in the context of developmental regionalism. Chap 4 in Economic Development in Africa Report 2013 - Intra-African Trade: Unlocking Private Sector Dynamism Geneva: United Nations 96–97
Valentiejus G (2017) Are the EU Member States ready for the new union customs code: emerging legal issues on the national level. Econ Cult 14(1):58–78
World Bank (2023) Nigeria Population. https://data.worldbank.org/indicator/SP.POP.TOTL?locations=NG
World Bank Group (2021) Doing Business: Measuring Business Regulation (Mauritius). https://www.doingbusiness.org/en/data/exploretopics/trading-across-borders/reforms#:~:text=DB2010%3A%20Mauritius%20reduced%20the%20time,no%20requirement%20for%20physical%20copies
World Customs Organization (2022) What is Securing and Facilitating Legitimate Global Trade. http://www.wcoomd.org/en/topics/facilitation/overview/customs-procedures-and-facilitation.aspx
World Trade Organization (2022) Trade Facilitation. https://www.wto.org/english/tratop_e/tradfa_e/tradfa_e.htm#:~:text=Trade%20facilitation%E2%80%94the%20simplification%2C%20modernization,for%20the%20world%20trading%20system
WTO Committee on Trade Facilitation (2018) European Union customs transit including arrangements with neighbouring countries under the common transit convention. https://www.wto.org/english/tratop_e/tradfa_e/comm_e/meet26june_eu_nonpaper_2_e.pdf
Zaninovic PA, Kejzar KZ, Skender HP (2023) Assessing the effects of hard and soft infrastructure on traditional vs supply-chain trade: the case of Central and Eastern EU Member States. Appl Econ 56(3):249–264

MIX
Papier aus verantwortungsvollen Quellen
Paper from responsible sources
FSC® C105338
FSC
www.fsc.org

If you have any concerns about our products,
you can contact us on
ProductSafety@springernature.com

In case Publisher is established outside the EU,
the EU authorized representative is:
Springer Nature Customer Service Center GmbH
Europaplatz 3, 69115 Heidelberg, Germany

Printed by Libri Plureos GmbH
in Hamburg, Germany